THE LIFE AND DEATH
OF LORD ERROLL

Errol Trzebinski is the author of *The Kenya Pioneers*, *The Lives of Beryl Markham* and *Silence Will Speak*, the biography of Denys Finch Hatton which was used as the source for the love story in the Oscar-winning film *Out of Africa*. She lives in Mombasa.

Also by Errol Trzebinski

SILENCE WILL SPEAK
THE KENYA PIONEERS
THE LIVES OF BERYL MARKHAM

THE LIFE AND DEATH
OF LORD ERROLL

THE TRUTH BEHIND THE
HAPPY VALLEY MURDER

Errol Trzebinski

WITH EMMA PERY

FOURTH ESTATE • *London*

This paperback edition first published in 2001
First published in Great Britain in 2000 by
Fourth Estate Limited
6 Salem Road
London W2 4BU
www.4thestate.co.uk

Copyright © Errol Trzebinski 2000

1 3 5 7 9 10 8 6 4 2

The right of Errol Trzebinski to be identified as the author of this
work has been asserted by her in accordance with the Copyright,
Designs and Patents Act 1988.

A catalogue record for this book is available from the
British Library.

ISBN 1-85702-894-5

Typeset by Rowland Phototypesetting Limited,
Bury St Edmunds, Suffolk.
Printed in Great Britain by
Clays Ltd, St Ives plc

*For the grandchildren and their children
especially the Hon. Harry, Amelia, Laline and Richard Hay*

'There's something the dead are keeping back'

Robert Frost

Contents

Illustrations

Prologue

On 24 January 1941 Captain the Hon. Josslyn Victor Hay, 22nd Earl of Erroll, Hereditary Lord High Constable of Scotland, was shot in the head. His body was discovered in a hired Buick at a crossroads on the Ngong–Nairobi road, a few miles from Nairobi. The murderer has never been found. The prime suspect was Sir Delves Broughton, 11th Baronet, whose wife Diana was having an affair with Erroll at the time. Broughton was tried for the murder, but acquitted. There the matter rested – though not exactly in peace. The shooting of Lord Erroll set off a volley of speculation that resonates to this day.

In the early 1980s James Fox's *White Mischief* was published. An intriguing search for the culprit, it had all the ingredients of a classic detective story, enlivened by a cast of glamorous characters determined to be the sources of their own ruin, whether by excesses of drink, drugs or sex or general fecklessness. The main players in *White Mischief* were all members of Nairobi's notorious Muthaiga Club – so snobbish that even Kenya's governors were vetted for membership. Posterity found it convenient to regard Muthaiga almost as a stage upon which these colourful characters paraded their vices in all their glorious decadence. Broughton, the jealous old cuckold robbed of his luscious young bride, wreaked murderous revenge upon his rival. The implication was that he escaped justice thanks to his privileged position in a society that closed ranks and protected its own. Fox drew a dazzling portrait of this clique of 1930s settlers of the Wanjohi Valley – known as Happy Valley – in the Aberdare mountain range about a hundred miles north of Nairobi. His version of events was an indictment of this exclusive society, a perfect story for a post-colonial age when there was no room for sympathy for any European settlers – past or present – on the African continent. During the final years of the apartheid regime in South Africa, the prevailing impression was that white settlers in Africa were simply no good.

White Mischief was rapturously received in Britain and the States. The Wanjohi Valley settlers were not best pleased with the light in which the book portrayed their forebears, however. Its publication caused a furore there – some members of this community begged the Kenya-raised writer Elspeth Huxley to go into print to defend their reputations.[1] The pioneers' lives had contained almost intolerable hardships and, for the majority of settlers, the struggle to survive the African climate *and* make a living continued into the generation that included Lord Erroll. Yet they all seemed to have been condemned by *White Mischief* for the sins of a few. Whenever the book came up in conversation among Wanjohi Valley's European inhabitants, hackles were raised.

The 1988 film version of *White Mischief* – with Charles Dance, Greta Scacchi and Joss Ackland playing out the ill-fated love-triangle – reinforced the muck-raking, cinematic treatment necessitating further distillation of plot and characters at the expense of factual accuracy. The release of the film spawned an astonishing amount of hype and resentment. Letters were published afresh, reviews proliferated all over again. Cannibalised articles fomented all the inaccuracies and misrepresentations, again inflaming the second-generation settlers who had known the original characters. There was a variety of reactions from speculation on who the murderer really was to outrage at the kind of coverage the case has received ever since, in which Lord Erroll's reputation certainly seems to have been exaggerated. He was no angel, but there is not a shred of evidence that he drank heavily; or that he indulged in orgies – accusations that have since his death been levelled at him by gossip-mongers. The only record of an orgy comes from a couple who turned up at Lord Erroll's first wife Idina's home Clouds in the early thirties – after she and Joss divorced. They came into the drawing-room that moonlit night to find the room 'full of writhing bodies'.[2] Joss had not even been present.

Joss's affairs were not as numerous as the public have been led to believe since his death, and he had never impregnated women carelessly. Also, he had had the realism not to marry anybody whose feelings would be hurt by infidelity. Far from corrupting the young – another frequent allegation against him – he had only one love affair with a woman younger than himself – she was twenty-seven. He did not smoke or take drugs; in fact, as far as these habits were concerned, he was abstemious in the extreme.

Sir Iain Moncreiffe of that Ilk, who married Lord Erroll's daughter, fumed about the 'unprovable scandal about the defenceless dead' whose only purpose was to 'sell a gossip column masquerading as history'. Moncreiffe's loyalty to his father-in-law's memory made him less impartial than most. Yet there are inaccuracies in *White Mischief*. Lord Erroll did not move with Idina to a house called Clouds in 1925, as described by Fox. She moved there alone after she and Lord Erroll separated. Nor had Lord Erroll ever found it necessary to close down Oserian, his second home on Lake Naivasha, after the death of his second wife Mary, owing to lack of money. 'To hell with husbands!' was Idina's saying, not his, and at no time did he pose a threat to the marriage of his friends the de Janzés. Such basic inaccuracies show that there is room for other interpretations of Lord Erroll's life and death.

It is of course by no means unusual for books to contain errors, often at the fault of the publisher. Yet all hitherto published accounts of Lord Erroll's murder have provoked dissatisfied responses from readers, a reaction that suggests the whole story has not been told before now. As Attorney-General Walter Harragin, who prosecuted for the Crown at Broughton's trial, observed after his acquittal: 'Whoever murdered Lord Erroll, Broughton was innocent by law – having been found "not guilty" by the jury after a fair trial.'[3] Despite the reams of material about Lord Erroll's murder, the elementary question still begs to be answered: whodunnit?

I

Quest for the Truth

'The great sensation locally has been the murder of poor Joss Erroll. It is indeed ironic that the Ngong road should have proved more dangerous than Tobruk.'
Nellie Grant to her daughter Elspeth Huxley, 30 January 1941

I had been living in Kenya for nine years before the Erroll murder meant anything to me. Then, in 1962, my husband and I bought a house in Miotoni Lane in Karen, today a suburb of Nairobi, near where Lord Erroll's corpse was discovered. One of our neighbours, a rather self-important character called Colonel Clarence Fentum, implied to us that he had been in charge of the investigation of the Erroll case, Kenya's most notorious murder. As we now lived so close to where the body had been found, my curiosity began to be aroused.

Fentum was mentioned in Rupert Furneaux's *The Murder of Lord Erroll*, based on the trial evidence, published in 1961. In fact Fentum had been newly seconded into the Kenya Police as an inspector at the time of the murder and had been in charge of the station responsible for the Karen area, not in charge of the investigation itself. I discovered later that he had been the third European officer to arrive at the scene of the crime.[1]

For six years, my family and I lived where the scandal still thrived in people's memories. We would frequently drive along that stretch of the Ngong road, with its wide grass verge, where Erroll's hired Buick had come to a halt. Little had changed in that landscape except that a forest of blue gum trees had been planted along the road and St Francis's Church stood on a hummock above the murder site. At the now infamous crossroads (more of a left-hand fork and T junction), we often took the Karen road, a red murram track, as it had been in Erroll's day, which we locals referred to as the *vlei*★ road.

While researching biographies of the former colony's leading figures, I inevitably came across Lord Erroll's circle. My unusual Christian name frequently prompted questions as to whether Erroll and I were related. We are not, but throughout my writing career those settlers I have interviewed have pressed upon me snippets of information about Erroll – in fact, the ritual continues to this day. Wary of giving away anything that might further tarnish their reputations, which had suffered so badly since Lord Erroll's death, this somewhat esoteric group were cautious in confiding what they knew about the murder. But gradually, having lived in Kenya for so long and in some ways sharing their predicament as part of a censured society, I gained their trust and confidence. Like all biographers, not wishing to lose those final links with a fading world, I filed away their disclosures.

I met Juanita Carberry in the 1970s. She was the daughter of one of the colony's aviation pioneers, J. C. Carberry, and her stepmother had been a close friend of Erroll's. Swearing me to secrecy, Juanita explained how, as an adolescent in January 1941, a couple of days after Erroll's murder she had been at her parents' home, Seremai, alone but for the servants, when Sir Delves Broughton turned up. I kept to myself what she told me about her conversation with him, as she had requested. After all, it was one of many stories about the murder that I encountered over the years – they were as conflicting as they were numerous. One even had it that Juanita's father, J. C., had been involved and had 'arranged' for Erroll to be shot while he was in South Africa, having discovered that his wife June had been unfaithful to him with Erroll. A Somali had been paid to do the shooting, apparently.[2]

Genesta Hamilton, a close friend of Joss's in Naivasha, linked Erroll's death to Germany: 'Jock's [Broughton's] South African

★ *Vlei*: in South Africa, a shallow piece of low-lying ground covered with water in the rainy season.

lawyer brought a ballistics expert to examine the cartridges. He said it was impossible to say for certain that these bullets had come from Jock's gun. Jock was acquitted ... My theory is different. There was a German gunsmith's shop in Nairobi. Joss spoke good German. He never joined up. I think he was asked to watch these Germans. I think they got him murdered.'[3]

Elspeth Huxley was always convinced that Joss had been regarded as untrustworthy and killed by one of Britain's Security Services. She assumed his death had somehow been linked to the top-secret Abyssinian campaign.[4]

Of the stories I heard about Lord Erroll many, like these, were based on supposition and theory. Some were rooted in first-hand experience, however. Sir Derek Erskine, a contemporary and great friend of Erroll's, wrote an unpublished memoir which his daughter, a friend of mine, allowed me to read. It sheds a fascinating new light on Broughton. Erskine describes three intriguing episodes between himself and Broughton, two during the week running up to the murder, one after Erroll had been shot.

Beatrice MacWatt had lived in the Wanjohi Valley and kept diaries since 1932. She had been the object of amorous advances from Lord Erroll (which she had rejected). Her daughter Alison Jauss told me about Beatrice's diaries in 1987. Alison claimed that everyone had been 'barking up the wrong tree' as to how and why Lord Erroll had been murdered, and that the truth was contained in her mother's diaries, but not until her mother, June Carberry and Diana Lady Delamere (as Diana Broughton became) were dead could the contents be disclosed. Only then would everyone realise that the end to Erroll's life was different from what people had been led to believe.[5] By 1993 Beatrice MacWatt and the other two women had all died, but her diaries never materialised. At the end of 1994 I gave up the waiting game. But the frustration and delay had given me time to delve. Early in the New Year of 1995 I went to consult my old friend Edward Rodwell – known as Roddy – who lives half a mile away from my Mombasa home as the fish-eagle flies, across Mtwapa Creek.

Roddy has published a weekly column, 'Coast Causerie', in the

East African Standard since the late 1940s. He had been editor of the *Mombasa Times* during the war when he had met Erroll briefly and liked him. Over the years he wrote many articles on the subject of Lord Erroll's death, the last two of which were published in unusually quick succession. Following Diana Lady Delamere's death in London in 1987 the BBC released a documentary called 'The Happy Valley'. After the programme aired, the *Standard* (Nairobi) published a small piece by Sandra Maler, 'Murder Secret Goes with Lady Delamere'. Roddy maintained that it was not only Diana who had a secret that might have altered the whole of the Erroll story. Lord Erroll's first wife, Idina, had told him shortly before she died: 'I know who killed Joss Erroll and before I die I will tell you who was responsible.' However, days later Idina had slipped into a coma without revealing her secret. 'I feel I should record my recollections of Lady Idina's remark made so many years after the trial. It would seem that Lady Idina did not believe in Broughton's guilt and that someone else was the culprit. Perhaps the story is not told in full,' Roddy wrote in the *East African Standard*.

The usual flurry of letters had arrived in response to Roddy's article, but this time there was a new element. Very late one Sunday night, he was woken by an anonymous long-distance phone call. Roddy told the story in a follow-up article:

> A man's voice from a far distance said that my article, the film and the book had the whole business wrong as to who the killer was ... it had been well known in England that Erroll had been a member of the British Fascist party and continued to be a member after he arrived in Kenya. When it appeared that war between Germany and Britain was a possibility, he had stated that he had withdrawn his support for the Fascist Nazis. But that was incorrect. Erroll was a full-blown Nazi. The British Secret Service had noted that Erroll was involved in Kenya politics ...

Here, for the first time in print, someone was pointing the finger at the British Government.

Roddy mentioned another source who blamed the same body:

the Mercedes-Benz agent in Nairobi in the thirties had told him that the Chief of Police was ordered to have Erroll shot, on account of his Nazi sympathies.

After publication of his second article Roddy had received another anonymous phone call, informing him that Broughton did not kill Erroll, but this tale had a new twist: the real killer had left the country.[6]

Roddy looked out a file of information for me on the Erroll case – material that had come in to him over the years. One of the letters in his file had come from Mervyn Morgan – the coroner who held the inquest into Erroll's death in 1941. Morgan had underlined certain words for emphasis and methodically numbered each point he wanted to make:

(1) Firstly, I myself had the last word. That is because I held the inquest on Broughton [sic]. The inquest of necessity had to be adjourned <u>when</u> Broughton was prosecuted. It was resumed after his <u>acquittal</u> and the only possible verdict I could bring in was murder by a person or persons unknown.

(2) The late much married Diana, Lady Delamere, was a wonderful and kind person and let no one dare to suggest otherwise. She loved all animals as her fellow human beings and <u>she</u> had nothing to do with Erroll's murder. I can make that last observation with confidence since I was one of the first to see the . . . Buick in the ditch on my early way to work from Karen (my house was next door to the Broughton house). I am <u>fairly confident</u> that I know <u>exactly</u> how it was done, by whom, and at whose instigation, but as no one has been sufficiently interested to ask me I have never given any explanation (which I <u>did not know at the time of</u> holding the Inquest) to anybody and never will.

(3) Broughton after being rightly acquitted by a jury left a note for the Coroner in Liverpool at the inquest of his death.* NB The Liverpool Coroner declined to make public

*Broughton was to commit suicide in Liverpool.

Broughton's letter and wouldn't disclose the contents to anyone
– he was rightly or wrongly much criticised for his acts and
omissions but a Coroner does have almost <u>omnipotent powers</u>.

That fact seems quite unknown to you. If you had contacted
me I could have told you at least most of what I know but
you didn't think of it and may not even have known the part
my humble self played – a very minor part it is true even though
I did have the last word![7]

Intriguing though this letter was, by the time I read it Morgan
was no longer alive. Another letter in Roddy's file proved more
fruitful. Marked 'Confidential and not for publication', it was from
an English settler called Kate Challis:

When *White Mischief* was being filmed in Kenya, a neighbour
who worked for MI5 [*sic*] during and before the war told me
that, as it was now over forty years ago, she felt able to say that
Errol [*sic*] was a severe security risk and he was shot, because
unlike the Oswald Mosley Nazis who could be interned, Erroll's
case was much more complex.[8]

Further research revealed that the 'MI5' agent/neighbour of Kate
Challis's was a woman called Joan Hodgson.[9] Three separate sources,
two of whom worked or had formerly worked in Intelligence, confirmed that she was a bona fide Secret Service agent: 'She was
nondescript as are so many MI5 and MI6 personnel,' one of the
sources said.[10] Another went so far as to hazard that Joan Hodgson
was probably working for Section 5 – counter-espionage.[11] So, with
Joan Hodgson's testimony, I had it on excellent authority that Lord
Erroll had been eradicated by the British Government – but *not*
because he was a Nazi . . .

I determined to scrutinise Erroll's life as a whole, to analyse what
motives there might have been to get rid of him. Two cuttings from
an acquaintance, who'd sent them to me purely because they were
connected with Kenya, were to prove surprisingly useful. One, 'Tarporley Man Puts the Finger on Alice', led me to Captain Gordon

Fergusson, secretary of the Tarporley Hunt Club in Cheshire, whose enthusiasm for collecting data on the subject of Erroll's murder was indefatigable.[12] The second cutting was from the author J. N. P. Watson, a cousin of Dickie Pembroke, a friend of Erroll's who had been infatuated with Diana. Pembroke had fired the young Watson's imagination about the Erroll murder and, as a result, Watson had tracked down and befriended a former superintendent in the Kenya Police, Colin Imray, by then living in the south of England, who shared his keen interest in the subject. Imray had discussed the case at length with Arthur Poppy, the officer in charge of the investigation into Lord Erroll's murder.

Imray regarded the Erroll murder as the 'crime of the century'. He had joined the force as a 'rookie' in 1932, gone to West Africa as a cadet, rising steadily through the force to be awarded the King's Medal in 1953 for his conduct during the riots in Accra in 1948.[13] Imray's obsession with the Erroll case had begun even before his posting to Nairobi, thanks to meeting Attorney-General Walter Harragin on the Gold Coast in 1948. They had often discussed the case and Harragin had revealed to Imray that he had from the outset been so convinced of Broughton's innocence that he had considered a *nolle prosequi* – not proceeding with the case against him.[14]

In the 1950s during his stint in Kenya, Imray conducted an experiment to time how long it would have taken Broughton to cover the ground he would have needed to had he shot Erroll. Imray started to follow the route he might have taken from his house in Marula Lane to the crossroads where the Buick was found, but had been forced to abort his experiment on account of lions on the prowl – one reason why he always held that Broughton would have felt too threatened to have contemplated that solo foray.

Imray's talk of Arthur Poppy as an extremely able officer was thought-provoking, as the investigation of Erroll's murder had been incredibly inept. Imray pointed out that each new article on the case blamed Poppy for the oversights. Imray had never understood how Poppy – such a thorough investigator – came to give the kind of evidence that was so easily overturned by Henry Morris KC, counsel for the defence. I had sight of Arthur Poppy's papers, passed to me by his widow, in which there were notes on Lord Erroll's background dating back to 1927. Poppy had been obsessed with the case, and had never recovered from the damage it inflicted on his career.

Imray mentioned another officer assigned to the murder investigation, Assistant Superintendent Desmond Swayne, who had spoken of 'a perversion of justice'. Swayne had been convinced that 'only a very limited inner cabal knew the truth'.[15] Imray could not bring himself to believe Swayne's suggestion that 'their guns had been spiked by a higher authority'.[16] Inspector Fentum, the detective in charge of Karen police station, and Imray eventually became colleagues. By the time they met, Fentum had, according to Imray, 'crawled to his position of Assistant Superintendent'. Like Swayne he had believed that an 'inner cabal' had been involved.

At one point Imray broached a subject that appeared to make him nervous. He warned: 'this information is very near the knuckle' and should 'remain in the shadowlands just in case there [is] any reprisal'.[17] Imray also told me about an ex-policeman who had known Diana for years, whom I might be able to persuade to meet me. But Imray cautioned me that he had encountered again and again a 'certain disinclination' in police colleagues in Nairobi to discuss this long-past event. At first Imray had put this reluctance down to the fact that the case had not brought credit to the force, but later, despite his own high position in the force, his own fear had prevented him from attempting to gain access to the police files or the court proceedings: 'to do so would be inviting trouble. There would have been all sorts of complications.'[18]

Imray also informed me that after his departure from service in Kenya the possibility of recruitment to MI6 had cropped up. Following his interview, he had decided against the job, but confessed to me that at this point he too had come across the theory that Erroll had been 'rubbed out' by British Intelligence in Kenya.

The Erroll family have always been dissatisfied with the many salacious accounts of Lord Erroll's life and death. Dinan, his only child, suffered greatly to see her father so misrepresented. There was even a rumour spread some time after his death that she was not Lord

Erroll's daughter – as if not satisfied with blackening his name, gossip-mongers wished to taint the lives of his progeny also. The physical likeness of her son Merlin, the 24th Earl, to his grandfather Lord Erroll put paid to that rumour.[19]

The Erroll family had made attempts to find out the truth about their forebear. When I visited the Earl and Countess of Erroll in August 1995 I was handed a file to scrutinise. It contained correspondence from Merlin Erroll's father, Sir Iain Moncreiffe, going back to 1953. His fruitless search through official archives on Erroll had led him to conclude that something ominous was lurking.[20] Merlin Erroll had drawn similar blanks in 1983 when he had turned to the head of the Search Department in the War Office Records for information on his grandfather. In fact, there had even been an apology from the Ministry of Defence 'for such a negative report', and the hope had been expressed that further information 'might be forthcoming'.[21] It was not. It was general knowledge in the family that Erroll had received a posthumous Mention in Dispatches for 'doing something on the Eritrean border', but when Merlin entered into correspondence with a Major A. J. Parsons to find out more about it, he did not get far. Parsons pointed out, 'The major campaign did not start until after he was dead', and he could confirm only the Earl's 'suspicion that Mention in Dispatches can be awarded for both meritorious and gallant service'.[22] He had enclosed photocopies of the supplement to the *London Gazette* which published 'the award to your grandfather', and, he pointed out, 'you will note that the preamble clearly states that awards were made to members of the Staff', but there was no more detailed indication of how Lord Erroll had earned the Mention. Parsons had requested that the Army Records Centre trace Erroll's personal service file. Having studied the file carefully, Parsons sent Merlin a copy of Erroll's Army Form B199A recording his 'intimate knowledge of France, Belgium, Scandinavia, Kenya Colony and Germany (four years)' and stating that his French was fluent and his German was 'fair'.[23] His covering letter said, 'Unfortunately, it is sparse in content and gives very little detail of his military career, other than those shown ... It is regrettable that the file does seem to have been "weeded" quite severely.'[24]

The weeding of sensitive information is well known to researchers. Material in files closed under the thirty- or fifty-year rule is sometimes burnt or shredded before the files are released.[25] I had been advised by one of the former secret agents I interviewed to watch out for any evidence of arson, missing documents, and papers scattered among alien files, since these could have been acts of sabotage perpetrated by agents in time of war.[26] One example of this was the Public Record Office file at Kew on Sir Henry Moore, Governor of Kenya at the time of Erroll's murder. Marked 'secret', its contents had obviously been shuffled as there was no discernible order to the documents inside.[27] The only month for which the file contained no information was January 1941, the month of the shooting.

Among Merlin Erroll's papers there was a 1988 article in the *Glasgow Herald* by Murray Ritchie: 'Hundred-year Shroud on Happy Valley Mystery'.[28] While researching his article at the Public Record Office at Kew, Ritchie had come across a file listed under the general files for Kenya, marked with an asterisk denoting 'Closed for a hundred years'. He was informed such closures were highly unusual – normally involving security, the royal family or personal records whose disclosure would cause distress to living persons. Ritchie had taken the number of this mysterious file. In his article he describes how the file had been brought towards him at the counter, but the bearer, pausing briefly to have a word with a colleague, had then carried it away.

Following the release in the 1990s of certain colonial files, I came to see the file that had eluded Murray Ritchie. While there were matters to do with Kenya in it, there was no mention of Lord Erroll. Instead there were some two dozen folios – each stamped 'secret', pertaining to Prince Paul and Princess Olga of Yugoslavia. They and their children had been kept under house arrest on Lake Naivasha in 1941.[29]

I then discovered evidence of another file: it was listed in the Kenya Registers of Correspondence – under 'Legislative Council. Death of Lord Erroll (103/3)' – but marked 'Destroyed Under Statute'. Fortuitously I stumbled across a document in yet another file that must have been transferred from this destroyed file – an instance of 'papers scattered among alien files' perhaps. It was a minute from Joss's brother Gilbert, '[w]ho would be glad of any information in connection with the death of his brother' – dated 27 January 1941.[30]

By August 1996, I felt that my search for governmental documents on Lord Erroll was a wild-goose chase. The Metropolitan Police Archives had redirected me to the Public Record Office at Kew. They had warned me that there were no records about the policing of Kenya, suggesting I contact the Foreign and Colonial Office, which I did in July 1996 only to discover that my request had already been automatically referred there from the Met. The Foreign and Colonial Office simply referred me back to Kew again, to what transpired to be the Prince Paul file.

I began to realise that I had as much chance of finding any official papers on Erroll, as he had of leaping from his grave in Kiambu to tell me himself what had really happened to him. Even Robert Foran's *History of the Kenya Police*★ is silent on the subject of the Erroll murder.[31] It contains not even the names, let alone any other details, of the team investigating it. References in Foran's book to relevant issues of *The Kenya Police Review* led me to believe that I would be able to locate these at least. Yet not a single copy was in the possession of any library in England. I was able to trace only one issue, through a private source. And I could not find any copies of *The British Lion*, a fascist publication in which, I had been assured, Erroll's name had appeared. When I applied at Colindale Newspaper Library, I was informed that all three volumes of it that they possessed appeared to have been stolen the year before.

In 1988, Merlin Erroll had invited anyone to come forward who could throw light on his grandfather's military or political career, observing, 'Some say that the affair with Diana was a red herring.'[32] One response came from a retired Lieutenant-Colonel John Gouldbourn, who had been with the Kenya Regiment in 1940. Gouldbourn's view was forthright: 'I do not doubt that there was a

---

★In 1903, W. Robert Foran had been in charge of Nairobi police station with the help of only three other European police officers ('The Rise of Nairobi: from Campsite to City', *The Crown Colonist*, March 1950, p. 163)

"cover-up" of the murder by the judiciary, the police and the military in that order. There were sufficient persons with an interest for there to be an "inner cabal" . . . You will appreciate the East African Colonial Forces (the KAR)* and the South African Division were poised to attack Somaliland. The dates would have been known to Joss Erroll. How discreet Erroll was is anybody's guess.'[33]

When I first met John Gouldbourn in October 1995 he had whipped out his army identification papers and handed them to me – 'so that you know that I am who I say that I am'. In all my years meeting interviewees, this procedure was a first. But for Gouldbourn, accustomed to the etiquette of the Intelligence world, proving one's identity had become a matter of common courtesy. He provided me with names, but no addresses, of people who he thought would be helpful to my research.[34]

I managed to track down some of those who were still alive. I located Neil Tyfield in 1996. He had been in Military Intelligence at Force HQ in Nairobi and had had a 'team of young ladies' working for him there. Tyfield told me that a number of officers had been posted out of Nairobi after Erroll's death so that they would not be able to testify at Broughton's trial. But the most valuable contact name that Gouldbourn gave me was, ironically, that of someone who insists on anonymity but has allowed me to use his 'official' cover name, S. P. J. O'Mara, because 'those few who may be interested in the identity behind it will recognise it'.[35] Gouldbourn was insistent that O'Mara had had something to do with the 'cover-up' surrounding Lord Erroll's death.

O'Mara had been an extremely young officer in the King's African Rifles in 1940. Ian Henderson, the son of a Kenya settler family and he too an officer in the KAR during the war, was his commanding officer in Nanyuki in 1940. Roddy Rodwell had told me how this same man had tried unsuccessfully to recruit him for MI6 after the Second World War. O'Mara knew all about Ian Henderson's career both during and after the war, including specific dates, corroborating what Roddy had told me. O'Mara threw light on many of the twists

*KAR = King's African Rifles.

and turns that had set Erroll's fate. When I told him that I had encountered fear among several interviewees he responded, 'Fear of whom?
[Fifty] years later? Only an SIS operation carries such a long shadow.'[36]

Stymied by the lack of access to official government papers on
Lord Erroll's career, I published a request for information in the
Overseas Pensioner and *Jambo*, the English organ of the East African
Women's League, from anyone with anecdotes or photographs of
Erroll. Through *Jambo* I received a letter in autumn 1996 from
Anthea Venning, whose father had been a Provincial Commissioner
in Kenya and had worked with Erroll on the Manpower Committee
when war loomed. Anthea Venning was a rich source of information.
In particular she led me to an old friend of hers called Tony Trafford,
whose testimony is at the heart of the account of Lord Erroll's death
propounded in this book.[37]

Tony's father H. H. Trafford had been taken out of retirement
on account of the war to undertake certain Intelligence duties. A
former District Commissioner, he had confided to Tony that records
existed in the Commonwealth Office, East Africa Section, indicating
that it had been a woman that had shot Erroll. The theory that a
woman pulled the trigger was well worn in Kenya. In the early
1980s H. H. Trafford had been approached by the maker of the film
White Mischief and by someone at the BBC for any light he could
shed on the murder. He told the latter bluntly that 'though he had
left the service there were certain matters he was not allowed to
make comment on. Erroll being a case in point.' He was similarly
reticent with the *White Mischief* crew. Trafford had in fact been
required to take the oath of the Official Secrets Act twice, once at
the outset of his career and then again when he came out of retirement during the war.[38] His Intelligence duties involved among other
things a top-secret interrogation of Broughton in 1941 entirely separate from the police and the court proceedings.[39]

Tony Trafford, Kenya-born, was seconded to British Intelligence
in 1940.* He had worked all over Kenya and lived in Naivasha until

---

*Major Hamilton O'Hara, chairman of the Kenya Regiment Association, UK,
confirmed this for me after Trafford died.

1963, leaving at Independence. He now lived on the Isle of Wight. Our initial exchanges revealed a character very sure and knowledgeable. Out-of-the-way places in Nairobi, road names most of which had been changed at Independence, the layout of the Maia Carberry Nursing Home were details that only someone who had worked there would know. His knowledge of Kenya's topography, of the idiosyncrasies of its tribes and elderly settlers – contemporaries of his father with whom I was so familiar from my own research – convinced me that he had a brilliant memory and eye for detail. I checked the details of what he told me about the battalions moved into Kenya for the preparation of the Abyssinian campaign and found these were accurate. Tony was even able to provide me with the reason why during the war the RAF had been stationed at Wilson Airfield rather than Eastleigh, the newly built aerodrome. He also knew that Joss had been up for promotion shortly before his death. This is not general knowledge; I discovered the fact only through private correspondence between the 24th Earl of Erroll and the MOD.

Throughout my dealings with Tony Trafford, he was nervous about discussing Lord Erroll's murder on the telephone. In order to protect his identity he chose his own cover name, Mzee Kobe (which means 'Old Tortoise' in Swahili). He wrote a twenty-five-thousand-word document for me detailing exactly how and by whom Erroll had been shot. This document, which I shall call the Sallyport papers, took him months of effort to compile and its contents reveal an extraordinary story of intrigue. Trafford died on 25 August 1998 shortly after completing his account. Interestingly, both the Sallyport papers and O'Mara's correspondence uphold the same theory as to why Lord Erroll was killed.

The resounding implication of my research was that a new portrait of the 22nd Earl of Erroll needed to be made, not only to redress the calumnies, errors and exaggerations which have so tarnished his reputation in the past half-century, but to make clear that there were far more compelling motives for killing Erroll than sexual jealousy.

2

Gnarled Roots

'A HAY, A HAY, A HAY!'
Clan slogan: armorial bearing of the Earldom of Erroll

Josslyn Victor Hay was born in London on 11 May 1901, eleven days before the first wedding anniversary of his parents, Lord and Lady Kilmarnock. Their son and heir was fair; his skin would easily turn golden under tropical sun and his blue eyes were mesmerisingly pale. Shortly after his Protestant christening, his proud parents took him to Scotland where, before he could even focus, he was introduced to Slains, the Erroll family seat, near Cruden Bay, about twenty miles north up the coast from Aberdeen. This was where his father Lord Kilmarnock, a diplomat working in Europe since 1900, had been born in 1876. Joss's mother Lucy would regard the visit to Slains as an important initiation rite for her children, following the same procedure later with Joss's younger brother and sister.[1]

Joss's brother, Gilbert Allan Rowland Hay, was born in January 1903 at the British Legation in Brussels. Lady Kilmarnock produced her next child, a daughter, soon afterwards: Rosemary Constance Ferelith was born in Vienna on 15 May, in 1904.

The coronation of Edward VII took place when Joss was just over a year old, in August 1902. His parents were over in England for the occasion, prior to their annual holiday north of the border – they were always in Scotland in time for the start of the shooting season on the Glorious Twelfth. It could easily have struck Lady Kilmarnock that one day her son would take his ceremonial place in Westminster Abbey for a coronation, as indeed her father-in-law Charles Gore Hay, the 20th Earl, was doing in 1902: first as Master of Erroll, Page to the Lord Lyon, King of Arms, and next – directly behind the monarch – as Hereditary Lord High Constable of Scotland.★

From the twelfth century, when reliable records of its activities began, the Erroll family history had been tumultuous, a curious mixture of glorious heroism and despicable double-crossing. Like Joss, a number of Erroll ancestors had their lives prematurely curtailed, though many fell courageously in battle, defending their faith and their King. Joss was descended from a steadfast line of military men and diplomats whose traceable origins go back to the Norman conquest, though family lore has it that the Hays were already performing acts of heroism in Scotland in AD 980. William de Haya of Erroll, the first Chief of the Hay Clan, who came to Scotland in about 1166 as butler to the Scots king William the Lion, was sent to the newly crowned King John of England in 1199 to negotiate a truce between the battling factions, and the return of Northumberland to Scotland.

William de Haya provides the earliest example of the Hay men's tendency to marry with a view to increasing the family fortune. He married Eva of the Tay Estuary, who brought him Pitmilly in Fife and probably the Angus lands as well as the falcon-lands of Erroll.† However, as the Hay estates seldom generated enough income to cover the costs of upkeep and family lifestyle, debts built up that were passed down the generations. Thus the Erroll family fortune gradually dwindled over the centuries and, when Joss's turn came, 'there would be little for the 22nd Earl to inherit'.[2]

Sir Gilbert Hay of Erroll, 5th Chief, was created Hereditary Lord High Constable of Scotland, an office combining the functions of

---

★The Earl of Erroll takes precedence in Scotland before dukes and every other hereditary honour, after the Blood Royal. Joss's grandson, Merlin, 24th Earl of Erroll, still holds the hereditary titles of Lord Hay, Baron of Slains, the Mac Garadh Mor and 33rd Chief of the Clan Hay. He also holds the office of 28th Lord High Constable of Scotland.

†Apocryphal though the legend may be, it is said that after a falcon had encompassed a circuit seven or eight miles long by four or five miles broad over a tract of land called Errol (sic), the Hay family became lords of that barony.

Secretary of State with that of Commander-in-Chief,* by King Robert the Bruce in 1314 for helping to defeat the English at Bannockburn, leading a thousand horses to the battlefield to do so. Sir Gilbert's service to Robert the Bruce established a tradition of loyalty to the Scots Crown which earned the family many privileges and granted them much local power. They could levy taxes on their tenants, raise an army and dispense justice on wrongdoers. Gilbert was also given Slains Castle, which stood on the coast of Aberdeenshire about fifteen miles south of Peterhead, in recognition of the part he had played in the war against Edward II. The name 'Slains' evokes but mildly the slaughter which befell this family. For the Hays were nothing if not courageous. Eighty-seven of them fell with James IV at the battle of Flodden in Northumberland in 1513.

However, the corrupting influence of power was fully in evidence too. Plenty of scandals – beheadings, imprisonment, treason, suicide – occurred in the Erroll dynasty, but there has been only one murder.

Three strong family characteristics would surface in the Errolls over the centuries: an inclination for politics, a natural penchant for subversion and a tendency to hedge their bets, the latter a useful survival mechanism. These qualities abounded in Francis, the 9th Earl. He collaborated in the Catholic rebellion of 1594 with George Gordon, Earl of Huntly. The 9th Earl had always been a Catholic, and his father and grandfather had both been staunch supporters of Mary Queen of Scots and the Catholic party. James VI was lenient towards Francis for his part in the rebellion, the quid pro quo being that Francis's son, the 10th Earl, be educated at court as a Protestant. But that was not the end of the story. In 1594 James marched north to supervise in person the burning of Slains Castle, reducing it to a ruin and giving rise to the differentiation between 'Old Slains' and 'New Slains' used by the Erroll family ever since. After the destruction of Old Slains, the Errolls moved seven miles away, north-east of Cruden Bay, where Francis initiated the mammoth construction project that was to be their next castle.

The 10th Earl was dismissed – possibly unfairly – as extravagant.

*In the absence of a male heir, this title descends through the female.

It had cost him so much to attend the coronation of Charles I that he was compelled to dispose of his ancestral estates. Attending a coronation was a costly business for families as grand as the Errolls. They would be expected to provide an impressive train of retainers, which on one occasion included 'eight mounted esquires, four pages, ten grooms, twenty-five marshalmen . . . and a large body of high-landers'.[3] In addition the 10th Earl was continuing the construction of 'New Slains', which would take a hundred years.[4] It is clear that by now the precariousness of the family fortune was a feature – and a thorny issue for its scions – of the Errolls' history.

New Slains was the Scottish seat where Joss would get to know his great-grandmother Eliza Gore and his grandparents. It had left so deep an impression on him as a boy that he would name his first home in Africa after it. Joss and his siblings would occupy Slains Castle for only a few weeks at a time, but the place was ever-present in family conversation and had obviously captured the imagination of this intelligent child. What lad could resist stories of the wagers made in times gone by within the Erroll household on the chances of walking all the way round the castle's outer wall without falling off. It was built so close to the cliff edge that one of its walls virtually overhung the ocean. The most famous victim of this dare-devil exercise was one of the Hay butlers, who fell to his death two hundred feet below the castle.

The assumption was that Joss would inherit Slains. Therefore, like the heirs before him, he learned by anecdote of its romantic history: how Slains came to be the principal landing-place for undercover Jacobites, as well as the centre of subversive activity at the start of the eighteenth century when Scotland and England were attempting to negotiate what became the 1707 Act of Union between the two countries. The wife of the 12th Earl, née Lady Anne Drummond, was responsible for 'victualling the French ships' that carried Jacobite agents to Scotland – notably Captain Nathaniel Hooke.[5] The 13th Earl spent time in France, scheming among intelligence gatherers and spies at court.

Machiavellian tactics, the playing-off of one side against the other while pretending to serve both, had become second nature to the

Hays of Erroll. The conclusion drawn by one government spy about the 14th Countess, who inherited the title on the death of her brother, the unmarried 13th Earl, was that she was a 'very intriguing and wily lady as is any in Britain'. Being an ardent supporter of the Jacobite cause in the lead-up to their last rebellion, in 1745, whenever circumstances called for secrecy she 'had written for concealment in milk'. Obviously, the 14th Countess's diplomatic skills were also considerable, for she managed to keep her titles and estates, whereas many of her Hay relatives' reputations suffered for their involvement in the Forty-five. She was also greatly admired for her physical courage: 'that magnificent old lady ... only with considerable difficulty' was dissuaded from leading the Clan in person to fight for Bonnie Prince Charlie, whose army set off for England under the command of her chamberlain.

In 1758, when he succeeded his childless aunt, James Boyd, the 15th Earl of Erroll, took the surname of Hay. Having officiated as Lord High Constable at the coronation of George III, and while under suspicion of being both Catholic and Jacobite, he was entrusted with conducting the King's fiancée, Charlotte of Mecklenburg-Strelitz, to London – which inevitably involved him in huge expense, in addition to that incurred by attending the coronation. According to the Hay family, the escort mission was deliberately and needlessly drawn out in order to ruin James financially, so much was he mistrusted.[6]

Nor did the 16th Earl, George, manage to inspire confidence in those who held the reins of power. Apparently, while drunk, he had blabbed about an official secret entrusted to him by Mr Pitt, the Prime Minister. Having leaked this 'confidence ill-advisedly to a so-called friend, who promptly published it together with the source ... he determined to destroy himself' and committed suicide soon after his *faux pas*.[7] To the Errolls who came after, George Hay's legendary remorse was a stark warning against intoxication. Indeed, George's descendants seem to have learned from somewhere – perhaps their forebear's indiscretion had been but a momentary lapse in an otherwise dutiful career, or maybe his suicide had galvanised the next generation into facing responsibilities at a young age – that it was high time to clean up the Erroll family record.

The 17th Earl's son and heir died honourably – in the typical fashion of his ancestors, defending king and country – at the battle of Quatre-Bras in 1815 at the age of only seventeen. Also contributing to the reversal of the Erroll fortunes, Joss's great-great-grandfather, the 18th Earl of Erroll, William George Hay, agreed to marry one of the future King William IV's illegitimate daughters. In 1820, through this match at the age of nineteen, the Earl re-established favour with the English monarchy. Joss's great-great-grandmother, Eliza Fitzclarence, was the illegitimate daughter of the Duke of Clarence and his mistress Mrs Jordan. Eliza was one of ten children, all given the surname Fitzclarence, but popularly known as the 'Great Illegitimates'. Several beguiling aspects of Mrs Jordan's character would turn up in Joss; besides his gift for the theatrical, he would possess her ability to charm for ever those who fell in love with him. Friends and lovers alike would remark that he was the most entertaining of companions, as much for his joie de vivre as for his bawdiness.[8]

The Duke of Clarence acceded to the throne in 1830 as William IV and thereupon improved the status of the 'Great Illegitimates'. His eldest son was given the title Earl of Munster; the rest were awarded the style and precedence of children of a marquess. In the hand-out of honours, as Eliza's husband, Joss's great-great-grandfather was made a peer of the United Kingdom, styling himself Baron Kilmarnock, and was appointed Master of the Horse to Queen Adelaide. The Errolls stayed at court until the King's death in 1837.[9]

Joss's great-grandfather, the 19th Earl, married another Eliza, whom he met in Montreal. This Eliza, the daughter of General the Hon. Sir Charles Gore, was a person of enormous spirit. She accompanied her husband to the Crimea, and throughout the campaign they slept rough, forgoing even the simple comfort of a camp-bed. Battle-weary, they both returned to Slains to face the daunting task of keeping the estate from bankruptcy. Eventually, in 1872, Eliza became Lady of the Bedchamber to Queen Victoria. When her husband died at Slains in 1891, she buried him at Cruden, outliving him by twenty-five years. Joss got to know her on his intermittent visits to Scotland and also while he was at Eton. Towards the end of her life Eliza occupied a grace-and-favour dwelling at Kew, where she died in 1916.[10]

A portrait of the 19th Earl which hung over the chimney-piece at Slains inspired a character in a Bram Stoker novel. Bram Stoker visited Slains at least twice and, having hiked along the two-hundred-foot cliffs to visit Joss's great-grandfather, found at Slains 'the furious contentment he wanted'.[11] Inspired by meeting the Hay family, Stoker chose the original castle Slains, then in ruins, as the setting for his Dracula book.[12] With so vivid a past on which to draw, small wonder that the Hays bobbed up in literature. Joss, too, would appear en passant – posthumously – in works of fiction. In *Justine*, the first volume in the *Alexandria Quartet* set in Egypt just before the Second World War, Lawrence Durrell features 'Erroll' as a member of a dawn duck-shooting expedition, during which a political assassination occurs.

Over the centuries the Errolls played host to many distinguished visitors at Slains, just as Joss would do one day in Africa. The great English lexicographer Samuel Johnson visited Slains with Boswell during their tour of the Highlands. Johnson concluded that 'the situation was the noblest he had ever seen'.[13]

By the time Joss was born, Slains, whose 4,249 acres produced in 1903 an annual income of £9,599, was still the principal residence of his grandfather the 20th Earl. The Erroll family also owned Walls, at Ravenglass in Cumbria, a home with a landholding of its own – which, in the long-held Erroll tradition of wealth-increasing marriages, had originally come into the Erroll family through Joss's grandmother – and an estate in Northumberland known as Etal.[14] Joss's grandfather was Lord-in-Waiting to King Edward VII, and during his reign lived at Carlton Terrace in London.

The picture that emerges of Joss's father shows a responsible and pensive young man. Married at twenty-four, he set out on his career as a diplomat. His first posting was to the British Legation in Brussels, as an attaché. He also harboured literary ambitions and had quietly taken up writing fiction in his last year at Eton. Inspiration seems to have followed Bram Stoker's first visit to Slains. After the novelist left, Victor began 'sloping off' to work in his father's library, writing away, drawing on images of his own ancestral pile for his fictional 'Glamrie Castle'. During his time at Cambridge, when the Diplomatic Corps already beckoned, he never gave up his dream of becoming a writer. His first novel, *Ferelith*, was published in 1903 and was warmly received.[15]

Many family characteristics showed up in the 22nd Earl. His genetic inheritance, at least, was rich, even if in material terms he was heir to little. His creativity and the easy handling of power that had been bred into him would serve him well when he assumed political responsibilities in Kenya, even if his atavistic defiance of authority did not. Indeed his life was to be yet another colourful and dramatic chapter in the family history – but with important departures from family tradition. Like his ancestors he would enjoy political intrigue, but unlike them he had no taste for bloodthirsty solutions. By an ironic twist of fate, he would die in military uniform as did his ancestors, though not in the front line nor by public execution.

3

Boyhood and Eton

'My men, like satyrs grazing on the lawns,
Shall with their goat feet dance an antic hay.'

Edward II, Marlowe

Joss's first word was 'Josh', which he liked to say over and over
again. His parents, humouring him, made a pet name of it: 'Josh
Posh'. The child enjoyed the rhyming sounds, and would wander
about chuffing 'Josh Posh, Josh Posh' like a confident, well stoked
steam engine.[1] Not much is known about his early schooldays. Fortunately, some of Lady Kilmarnock's albums and scrapbooks – a doting
pictorial record – have survived. Through these we catch glimpses
of Joss's development from birth until the age of eight along with
the progress of his brother and sister, Gilbert and Rosemary. Inter-
spersed with snapshots, Lady Kilmarnock pasted in miscellaneous
scraps – raffle tickets, billets for the Ostend–Dover mail boat in which
the family sailed regularly to and from Europe; picture postcards from
all manner of places; the sheet of order for the 'Blessing of the Sea',
a ceremony at the beach, La Digue at Middelkerke; old theatre
programmes; invitations; press cuttings and menus. These provide
an overview of her own activities with her husband, as well as those
of the formative years of their offspring. Resonating through Joss's
boyhood were not only the sounds of the bagpipes and the clatter
of hooves on cobbles, but the sighing of string quartets; and temper-
ing the salty air of Scotland's east coast was the smell of newly baked
apfelstrudel – although there was never any suggestion that strudel
was better than oatcakes or shortbread. The first eight years of
his life are laid out in the albums – sometimes chronologically,

sometimes not – as if from time to time Lady Kilmarnock has been called away suddenly, her peaceful contemplation of past events disrupted, perhaps, by the children themselves.

The Kilmarnocks did not enjoy the stability of a permanent home during Joss's childhood. Perhaps their peripatetic existence brought the family all the closer emotionally as they followed Lord Kilmarnock's career across Europe, having to get to know new places and make new friends at every stage. It certainly made for diversity, and Joss must have acquired a precocious polish and sophistication from such a varied exposure to life abroad. He would never settle in Britain, thanks to the wanderlust acquired in childhood.

Joss's first home was in Belgium, from 1901 until 1904, at 8 rue du Taciturne in Brussels, where his father was 3rd Secretary at the British Legation.[2] In May 1904 Lord Kilmarnock was posted to the British Legation in Vienna and promoted to 2nd Secretary two years later. From October 1907 he worked for some months at the Foreign Office in London and then in Stockholm until his posting to Tokyo, which came through in early 1913. He was promoted to First Secretary in July of that year, while in Japan. After his return, in 1915, he was sent back to the British Legation in Belgium, then based in Le Havre because of the war. Joss's parents spent three years in Le Havre, then in July 1918 they were off to Copenhagen. From January 1920 until mid-1921, Lord Kilmarnock was Chargé d'Affaires in Berlin. His final posting was as British High Commissioner on the Inter-Allied Rhineland High Commission, in Coblenz.

The Kilmarnocks' life at the British Legations was very grand – celebrating the King's birthday, dining with the Empress Eugénie de Winterhalter or the Habsburgs at the Vienna Hofburg, meeting the Duke of Teck or Lord Boothby on some diplomatic errand. Regular callers at the rue du Taciturne during Joss's infancy were Prince and Princess Albert of Belgium, with their sons Princes Leopold and Charles. (Crown Prince Leopold would be in the same year as Joss at Eton and accede to the Belgian throne in 1934 when his father's reign was cut short in a mountaineering accident.)[3] Early exposure to the faubourg life ensured that Joss would not grow up to be a conventional Englishman. His ability to master foreign

tongues came naturally, his acute ear helped along by the chatter
from his mother's maids be they Austrian, Flemish, French or Scandinavian. His sense of tone, pitch and modulation was almost faultless.
He was a gifted mimic, a talent which he enjoyed showing off. If
he went too far, the Kilmarnocks would remonstrate, somewhat
indulgently, at his high spirits, ascribing them to 'the Mrs Jordan
coming out'.[4] Joss was fluent in English, French and German even
before going to school.

In Brussels, one of the earliest snapshots of Joss was taken while
he was being wheeled in his pram along the Bois de la Cambre at
the end of Avenue Louise, as Princess Clémentine *en promenade*
dashes by in her carriage and pair. A swansdown and satin bonnet
is tied firmly under his chin; Joss's fine blond locks were otherwise
kept off his face with a ribbon. In a photograph of him taken when
he was three, dressed in white flounces and mounted on a donkey,
posing for the camera, one could be forgiven for mistaking him for
a little girl. Sailor suits came later. Lady Kilmarnock's boys wore
frocks of white lawn, pin-tucked, embroidered or frilled, and with
puffed sleeves.[5] A stark change in Joss's appearance occurred when he
was four when Lady Kilmarnock decided his hair could be barbered.
Almost unrecognisable, he suddenly looked like a real little boy,
dressed in shorts, a warm, dark double-breasted coat with silver
buttons, boots and a cap.

Throughout Joss's boyhood Lord Kilmarnock perpetually had
ideas in development, from light sketches to full-length plays. In
March 1903 he had staged the *Dîners de Têtes* at the Café Riche in
Brussels, and had been working on a tragedy set in a classroom, for
six men and three women, *The Anonymous Letter*, which would be
published the following year.[6] Few realised that Joss's father was a
published dramatist. He had always written under his nom de plume
'Joshua Jordan' – a tribute to his actress forebear – but now, with
new-found confidence, he would publish under the name Victor
Hay, Baron Kilmarnock. Two more of his titles were staged in the
suburbs of London during Joss's twenties – *The Chalk Line* and *The
Dream Kiss*.[7]

In April 1904, Lady Kilmarnock warned her two little boys that the bulge in her stomach was a baby, so that their sister's arrival would come as no shock. Rosemary Constance Ferelith Hay's christening caught the imagination of the press when the entire family descended from Scotland upon Vienna. The newspapers announced that Princess Charles Fürstenberg and Lady Muncaster were her godmothers; her godfathers were her uncles, Victor Mackenzie of the Scots Guards (Lady Kilmarnock's brother) and Lieutenant the Hon. Sereld Hay RN. 'Ferelith, it may be remembered, is the title of the book published last year by Lord Kilmarnock,' one columnist observed. Princess Charles Fürstenberg was the daughter of a lady-in-waiting to Emperor Franz Joseph's wife, Elisabeth. The Kilmarnocks and their children went to Hungary many times to stay with the Fürstenberg family. In due course, the Fürstenbergs' daughter Antonia married the Duke of Schwarzenberg, whose palace in the heart of Vienna stood just round the corner from the British Legation.[8]

In Vienna the family occupied an apartment in an enormous house which dwarfed the tiny church next to it, standing in the quiet, tree-lined Metternichgasse. Life was more sophisticated among the Viennese than among the Belgians.[9] Sunday mornings in Vienna would see the Kilmarnocks among the congregation at the Stefanskirche at the same service as the ageing Emperor Franz Joseph, and they would dine at the Belvedere with him too.[10] One of the earliest pictures of Joss in Austria shows in the background Château Neuville, where the family stayed at Huy twice a year. Joss became accustomed to café society, the cobbled streets, the Spanish Riding School and the shop windows displaying *Sachertorte*, a favourite Viennese delicacy. He would have walked across one of the city's most beautiful squares, the historic Judenplatz, where the composer Mozart had once lived, with its plaque – 'Angry flames raged through the city and atoned for the dreadful sins of the Hebrew dogs' – marking the spot where in 1421 eight hundred Jews killed themselves following the accusation that they had used the blood of babies in religious ceremonies. Joss came to know the buildings of the Ringstrasse, returning there later as a budding diplomat, when he was saddened by the changes in its inhabitants wrought by the Great War.

Like other Edwardian children, the Hay offspring travelled with an entourage, although Lady Kilmarnock seems rarely to have left them for long periods in the sole charge of nannies. Photographs of annual gatherings at Slains display, in fading sepia, images of themselves, their friends, their maids, their cooks, their grooms, their clothes, their pets – including Bonci their father's Jack Russell terrier.

One of Lady Kilmarnock's own sketches of Joss stands out particularly from the pages of her albums, apparently inspired by an incident in the garden of Walls, the house in Cumbria that belonged to Joss's grandmother, where the Kilmarnocks fetched up each year. Named after the remains of Roman ruins in the grounds of Muncaster Castle,[11] Walls was a typically gloomy Victorian pile, all the more so for being 'tucked away in a wood'. The sketch captures much of Joss's impulsive nature; one of his chief characteristics was his unpredictability. Lady Kilmarnock portrays him as a cavalier in miniature, complete with sash and double lace collar.[12] For all her adoration of him – Joss was her favourite child – she seemed to sense that his spontaneity might prove to be his undoing. In front of his outstretched toe lies a huge carved stone head, severed from its body. It looks as if Joss has just toppled this massive object, twice his own size. Her caption 'Josh Posh on the warpath' reinforces the idea. With uncanny maternal insight, her portrait of Joss unwittingly foreshadowed trouble ahead.

Joss's childhood, however, was very secure. Whether at Huy or touring in Italy, where Castello di Tersatto, Monte Maggiore, was their watering hole, the company that Lord and Lady Kilmarnock kept was wealthy, aristocratic and powerful. Inevitably, their hosts and hostesses held influential positions in Europe or in Britain, and conversation with old money oiled the wheels of diplomacy. From an early age Joss learned the importance of communication, and at his father's elbow absorbed the workings of the Foreign Office, which endowed him with every advantage when he eventually followed in Lord Kilmarnock's footsteps. The 'right' castles, the 'right' schools, the 'right' reputations, the 'right' clubs, the 'right' expectations – all these influences bolstered Joss's confidence such that he never felt bound by convention. His independence led him later to break with social constraints, taking him into other worlds far beyond the confines of his noble roots. In Joss's book, the rules of the aristocracy were there to be broken.

A formal photograph of Lord Kilmarnock, taken in the year of Joss's birth, shows a severe man whose preoccupations were often melancholy and who took his responsibilities seriously.[13] But he was not as forbidding a husband and father as he looked. His writing shows that he lacked neither humour nor perception. Thanks to his love of literature and his imagination, his children learned all the family traditions and legends before they could read. Indeed, encouraging them to learn about the historic struggles of the Hays for themselves would probably have been a good way of introducing them to reading. One wonders whether Joss felt any need to live up to his heroic ancestors. His initiation into Latin and Greek was undertaken early by his father, and it was from him that he inherited his lively sense of beauty – although perhaps at first he would be too readily inclined to see beauty in mere decoration. His sense of the theatrical was an appetite whetted and nurtured by both his parents.

Joss's mother was handsome and big-boned, given to flirtation, prone to flattery, and of the sort who improved in looks as she grew older. She tended to keep press cuttings about herself, as if requiring proof of her own persona; often such entries were restricted to remarks about her jewels '. . . a superb tiara and necklace of diamonds and pearls'. It was she who taught Joss that pearls must be worn next to the skin, for otherwise they lose their lustre, a statement he repeated often as an adult.[14] Lady Kilmarnock's coiffure, her gowns and her hats were intended to catch the eye. As a small boy, Joss would stand in her dressing room while the maid brushed her long dark hair, piling it elaborately on to her head, before she dressed and departed for dinner with his father by horse-drawn carriage.[15] Watching his mother's toilette, handing the hairpins to the maid as she worked, mesmerised Joss as a small boy and sparked a lifelong fascination with this private ritual. Before going to bed, the well scrubbed little Joss would arrive in her rooms to kiss Lady Kilmarnock goodnight. She would playfully check that his face, neck, hands and teeth were clean. Extracting a promise that he had done his ablutions properly, before dispatching him to the nursery to say his prayers she would occasionally insist, out of principle, that he wash his face again. Joss loved the smell of his mother's soap on the sponge or flannel hanging over her wash-basin, and would breathe in the scent.[16] His mother's maxim, 'Cleanliness is next to godliness', had a lasting effect on him. He was to become fastidious to a degree and like a Continental male, would pay particular attention to his hands and feet, undergoing regular professional manicures and pedicures.[17]

For the first eight years of their marriage Joss's mother doted on her husband and her children, with whom they both believed in sharing everything. Even in Europe, Slains would never be far from the conversation. All three children visited their Scottish home regularly, and Lady Kilmarnock kept their memories of it alive through postcards. Like all children, Joss and his siblings loved to be terrified as long as they knew that they were perfectly safe, and while in Scotland they enjoyed their introduction to the turbulent family history, with its legends of ghosts and mistletoe, brought to life during walks to local beauty spots made famous by Johnson and Boswell. They would stand on former battle sites and on the lofty cliff at Port Erroll, four miles north of the earlier Slains stronghold. Earthy smells permeated the grasses and flowers through which wild rabbits scampered among the dunes as the sun rose over the icy North Sea. They would go to look at a local curiosity, a strange rock near the shore, where sea-fowls congregated, or peer into 'Bullers o'Buchan', 'a huge rocky cavern open to the sky, into which the sea rushes through a natural archway'. Or they would clamber along the bed of a small stream called the Cruden that fell into the sea at Slains, giving its name to the neighbouring bay – Cruden Bay means 'Blood of the Danes', an epithet through which the children learned of the slaughter said to have taken place in the days of Malcolm and Macbeth. As Bram Stoker had discovered, the history of the Errolls was as 'full of dark rituals, rumours of fertility cults and blood sacrifice as anything that he might have dreamed up for Dracula'.[18]

Victor Kilmarnock's dramatic inclinations would have helped him to convey to his children the family's mistletoe legend – mistletoe was the Hays' 'plant badge'.* According to Thomas the Rhymer's prophecy, recorded in Frazer's *The Golden Bough*, it had grown upon an ancient oak that stood on the Erroll land in Perthshire, and the fate of the family was held to be bound up with the mistletoe that grew on this great oak. For centuries the Hay family had danced around the tree at Hallowe'en. Soon after the 10th Earl's death in 1636, his Perthshire lands had to be sold off to pay his debts, and somewhat symbolically the oak collapsed.

Lady Kilmarnock's hoard of cuttings from *The Times* and other newspapers constitutes more than milestones in the professional life of Joss's father: they are indications of her pride and affection, her steadfast interest in everything undertaken by 'Vic', be it the landing of a fine salmon, speaking well in public, shooting the largest stag of the season or receiving a good book review. Their annual interludes in Scotland contrasted sharply with life on the Continent. Once the royals had departed for Balmoral and Parliament was in recess, just before the Glorious Twelfth, Joss's family partook of gentlemanly pursuits, taking to the glorious tracts of heather to stalk, to shoot and to fish – luxuries that drained the Hay purses like those of other old Scottish lairds.[19] Joss's father went deerstalking at Braichie Ballater, a village on Deeside near Balmoral. His wife faithfully recorded Vic's prowess and annual bag: 'Spittal Beat 1 stag 13 stone 13 pounds = 6 points' or 'Horne Beat 1 stag 15 stone = 7 points'.[20]

Blood sports would leave Joss cold – one cannot help but wonder whether his repulsion for killing began in Scotland with the display of these huge dead beasts. He was never squeamish, but unlike his father or his contemporaries he would never kill for the sake of killing.

In the sincere belief that he was preparing his son for the wilder excesses of the Scottish calendar – 'Burns' Night, the St Andrew's Ball at Grosvenor House, the Caledonian Ball, and of course Hogmanay – Lord Kilmarnock introduced him to whisky before he was six. 'Have a sip,' he would say whenever the decanter was lifted while Joss was in the room. But Joss did not want a sip.

'No, thank you.'

*Plant badges were symbols used to distinguish clans.

'Come on, just a little sip,' cajoled his father. 'Try.'

'No, thank you, sir.'

'Just try.'

His father's 'lessons', while well intentioned, constituted an early conflict, and since often the first exercise of power is in denying someone something, it is not difficult to imagine Joss's private satisfaction when he discovered that one could reject a request, even from one's father. However, since the boy was well mannered, he would eventually give in and take a sip, just to have done with the matter. That scene was to be re-enacted many times. Joss's acute sensitivity to smell meant that he was never able to stomach the odour, let alone the taste, of whisky. His adult drinking habits would be confined to the occasional sip of wine, and even then, more as a courtesy to others who were drinking than for his own pleasure.[21]

For all his delicacy in the matter of hunting and drinking, no one ever called Joss faint-hearted. He would become an excellent shot, riding well and hard on the polo field; and by the age of seven, when in England, he rode to hounds with his parents, going out with packs such as the Marquess of Exeter's – accompanying them at Guthrie, Lumley Castle, Burghley House and Clifton Hall. Once the choice was his alone, he preferred going out on foot with draghounds or playing ball games – polo, football, squash racquets, tennis and cricket – and he would excel at each.[22]

As time went by, Joss's brother and sister could not help noticing that Joss was the apple of his mother's eye. No doubt she loved all three deeply, but her partiality eroded any chance there might have been of Joss and Gilbert being close. Their aloofness towards one another affected Rosemary too. Joss was unshaken by their baby sister's arrival. Nearly four years old when she was born, he was already certain of his place, tending to feel more loved, more sure and more deserving of his mother's attention than either of his siblings. Not surprisingly, Gilbert and Rosemary grew closer, regarding themselves as a pair. Enjoined against Joss, they may actually have had an easier ride as youngsters, and they would remain close as adults, although by then Joss had disappeared to Africa. Gilbert would become a quiet, reliable family man – to an almost plodding degree – never quite managing to live down the differences between himself and the more flamboyant Joss.

Joss's interest in clothes and dressing up was due in part to his father's interest in things Thespian – dancing, literature, music, costume and even lighting. Naturally, all productions by the Kilmarnocks were put on for charity. Joss was the audience to everything in rehearsal at home and thus became au fait with the underpinnings of stage production. In plays such as 'Le Cours de Danse de Monsieur Pantalon' his parents performed the Highland schottische in kilts for 'the assembled distinguished company of Viennese society'. Joss's father adapted this entertainment from the classic *Harlequin* and it would become integral to Joss's Christmas activities. Lady Kilmarnock's fund-raising in Brussels was undertaken with a Monseigneur and Madame Le Comte de Flandre, with whom, heading the Committee for the Scotch Kirk, she instigated fêtes, 'fancy fairs', dinners, balls and masquerades. Joss developed his astonishing eye for detail as a child through watching his parents as they debated issues such as: should Harlequin dress in the 'torn' or in the 'patched', or in the stylised Victorian pantomime costume?[23]

Joss would soon slip into playing, posing and speaking in the style of whichever country he and his family happened to be living in. At home he was encouraged to cast inhibitions away; because he was funny his parents enlisted him to mimic or join in as the adults went through their lines, singing songs and doing dance routines. The importance of make-up, lighting and – most vital of all for an actor – timing Joss learned from his father, as well as how to draw upon the classics, recasting men in drag, setting an ancient piece in modern costume, giving a fresh twist to an old theme. One day Joss would give several hundred weatherbeaten colonials the impression that they had stepped into the Opera House in Vienna.[24]

The effects of these theatrics learned from his parents would be revealed in many ways later on. His interest in costume would border on fetishism. His mother's fine clothes and sophistication triggered an acute awareness of female attire and scent in Joss – always the first attributes he noticed in a woman.

Lady Kilmarnock was hardly ever far away from him during his childhood, and when she was he must have felt her absence acutely. He was seven years old when she suffered something akin to a nervous breakdown, following the miscarriage of her fourth child, a son who had been born prematurely. Lady Kilmarnock needed privacy during this period of misfortune – the family had been staying with Count Hugo and Countess Ilona Kinsky in Bohemia at the time of the tragedy. Determined never to forget the loss of her third son, she marked the infant's passing in a sketch in purple ink – mourning the tiny 'Sacha Louis' suspended in a shawl from the beak of a miniature stork, and recording his name in mirror writing. Her children were quite unaware of the disaster. Their mother was confined to bed, while they were taken up with the world of the gymkhana and polo matches at the Kinskys' at Chlumetz, Bohemia. The Kinsky family were passionate equestrians: 'The great challenge of every year . . . was the steeplechase of Pardubitz.' In Europe this competition was recognised as the world's most difficult course and so it was an occasion when 'they could show off their prowess on horseback to the full – in other words – the Kinskys could win outright'.[25]

Lord Kilmarnock played a good deal of polo himself, and on his eighth birthday Joss was among the spectators at the Parc Club in Budapest, where his father was competing. He would develop a good eye for the ball, though his reflexes were to be more mercurial. Joss would later help to improve standards of polo in Kenya, establishing and encouraging new young teams.

The event that inspired Joss's lifelong passion for beautiful cars also occurred in Hungary, on an earlier visit to Budapest when his parents took him to the Magyar Automobile Club, an event 'with floats and fancy dress'. Joss experienced first-hand the dramatic changeover from horse-drawn traffic to automobiles. His mother's hats now had to be clamped on with netting and veils as they charged through Bohemia, faster and faster, a journey that was repeated the following spring when Joss found himself again sitting in the back of an open tourer en route for Lauschin Castle to stay with his parents' friend, Princess Marie von Thurn und Taxis, whose later love affair with Rainer Maria Rilke in Italy at Duino inspired his

Duino Elegies.[26] Before going on to Pardubitz they stayed at Csazany Streczhof, attending 'a peasant wedding' at Ivanc where Joss's parents are pictured with a stuffed bear.[27] His father was already in the habit of buying expensive automobiles of the latest design. During the next decade motor-cars would epitomise the tremendous romantic appeal of speed, power and status. Once Joss was allowed to get behind the wheel himself, he would be as discriminating as his father – his favourite model of all was to be the 1937 black Straight Eight Buick.[28]

Every jaunt made by the Kilmarnocks tended now to be interpreted in mileage and horsepower. Their digressions took them on trips to Paris, Grasse, Gorges de Loup, Nice, Cannes and Monte Carlo. Whenever in Monaco, they stayed at the Hermitage Hotel so as to have a flutter at the opulent Casino Salle. Perhaps thanks to the example set by his parents' busy lives, as an adult Joss was always highly organised, sticking punctually to a packed routine.

Whether the loss of Sacha Louis was so mentally dislocating that Lady Kilmarnock afterwards lost all motivation for keeping records we can only surmise, but the pages in her album dwindled to emptiness at this time. The last photograph shows Joss and Gilbert with Gustav Adolph, a grandson of Gustav V of Sweden, sharing a sledge and dressed in Fair Isle caps and pullovers against the icy blast, while staying with the King's family.[29] Lady Kilmarnock seems to have been at a watershed in her life with Vic, too. The following March, 1909, he packed her off to Bournemouth for complete rest by the sea. Once she had recuperated, the pattern of Joss's pre-bedtime audience with her resumed seamlessly. Kissing his mother goodnight would remain important to him, and their closeness may have seemed to border on the incestuous when Joss kept up these childhood routines into his twenties.[30] The obsession with his mother may provide a clue as to why he was drawn towards older women. Joss was always on excellent terms with his darling mother and Lady Kilmarnock never became disillusioned with him, through all vicissitudes.

Mother and son were to be parted again in 1914, when Lord Kilmarnock was posted to Tokyo as First Secretary. If her absences were difficult for Joss to adjust to at the time, they also seem to have taught him valuable lessons. He gained more independence, and learned that love can endure absences; even after a long bleak year of separation, their mutual affection was as strong as ever. Indeed, Joss's close relationships would tend not to be affected by distance or time, enduring for life despite long absences.

Between 1909 and 1911, Joss and Gilbert were taught by a private tutor in Stockholm. Harder parents than the Kilmarnocks could have dispatched their sons off to English boarding school at a far earlier age. However, Joss was ten and Gilbert eight by the time they were sent to A. M. Wilkinson's School, Warren Hill, in Eastbourne, to prepare them for entry into Eton.[31]

In 1911, the summer before the boys started boarding, the Kilmarnocks were in London for the coronation of George V on 22 June, where Joss acted as page to his grandfather, the 20th Earl. As a doting mother, Lady Kilmarnock must have been miserable at the thought of her sons' impending departure to Eastbourne, where rules and conditions could have come only as a rude shock to two little chaps who had never before been exposed to the bleakness of boarding school. A cousin of Lord Kilmarnock's, part of the Foley branch of the family, who lived at Westbrook Meads near the boys' prep school, ensured steady communication about their progress and welfare.[32]

In 1910 the 20th Earl took out a five-year lease on Barwell Court, a manorhouse in Surrey. He had finally admitted financial defeat: the upkeep of Slains was too much. Plans for selling it were now mooted and a drift southwards must have seemed logical. Possibly, the Earl wanted to be closer to the family, with his grandsons at boarding school in the south and his elderly mother Eliza living in her grace-and-favour apartment at Kew. At any rate the house became a base for Joss and Gilbert and was given as their home address on their school records.[33]

Barwell Court's colourful history appealed to the boys. In the early sixteenth century it had belonged to Merton Priory. Then during the Reformation the manor had been surrendered to the Crown, with the rest of the Catholic priory's possessions. Henry VIII had allegedly kept a mistress here. The cellar housed a four-foot-deep pond, or 'underground fish larder', where the monks had kept fish for their Friday meals. Barwell Court's park was made for exploration by boys of Joss's and Gilbert's age, with its noble trees, a 'nut walk' and a 'pond teeming with carp . . . where once upon a time, it had teemed with dace and tench'.[34] While Joss was living there he became fascinated by the Foley family history. Richard Foley was a famous seventeenth-century industrial spy. Originally a village minstrel, he earned his nickname 'Fiddler Foley' by carrying stolen papers into England from Europe in his violin case.[35] Posing as an iron-worker, he wandered through Belgium, Germany, Italy and Spain, working in various foundries where he collected technical information on 'splitting', an iron-forging process that was a carefully guarded secret. Eventually after years of cribbing information, Foley smuggled enough technical data back home to be able to construct a 'splitting machine', an 'invention' on which the fortunes of the Foley family were founded. After his death in 1657, Fiddler Foley's ingenuity earned him a place in the annals of British spying, as well as hoisting the Foley family into the landed gentry of Worcestershire.[36] Coincidentally, a Francis Foley was the MI6 resident at Berlin in 1939. In fact he would be there with Joss in 1919, and it was Francis Foley who learned that the German Army were experimenting with a cipher machine called Enigma.[37]

Gerald Hemzy Foley, 7th Lord Foley, another distant cousin of Joss's, had already been at Eton since 1909 and would be expected to guide him through some of the nastier rites when he joined the college.[38]

Meanwhile, Rosemary's compensation for having had her brothers wrenched away from her was the gift from her parents of Cherry, a King Charles spaniel puppy. With them and her nanny, Rosemary boarded the SS *Lutzgow*, embarking in February 1913 for Tokyo and life as an only child, clutching a bevy of dolls. Perhaps the withdrawn nature she manifested in later years was formed during her separation from Joss and Gilbert; she was to become a solitary young woman.[39] Lady Kilmarnock is pictured on deck of this German ship – 'writing letters . . . on our way to Japan'. Much of her correspondence will have been addressed to her sons. None has survived the years. All signs of depression seem to have been banished: carrying a stylish muff of cheetah skin, she looks rejuvenated at the prospect of Tokyo. There she played tennis every afternoon, often partnered by a Captain Butt whose name features more and more frequently until, in due course, he accompanied Joss's parents on all excursions, which tended to be dominated by temples, cherry trees in bloom, lacquered bridges and parasols. As she revelled in the company of young officers, Lady Kilmarnock was showing signs of not wanting to accept her age.[40]

She and her husband returned from Japan to England in the summer of 1914 just before the outbreak of the First World War to see Joss into Eton for the 'Michaelmas half' – Eton jargon for the autumn term starting in September – for which the preparation was elaborate. The correct top-hats, black coats, white ties and shoes could be obtained only from monopolist establishments in Eton High Street. Windsor Castle stood sentinel above the town.

Joss would spend his free time wandering around Windsor's streets with friends, buying ices in the summer half, looking for books. One of the highlights of that Michaelmas half was when he and Sacheverell Sitwell spotted some 'Bohemians leading a bear around on a chain' about Windsor. The boys were witnessing part of the great gypsy coppersmith invasion of those years in England.[41]

Eton's aim was to prepare its pupils for the service of the British Empire abroad as administrators, soldiers or diplomats – hardly necessary in Joss's case. Boys boarded in houses known by the initials of their housemasters – Joss's housemaster was Raymond Herney de Montmorency.[42] Activities of the house were organised by the house captain, who was assisted by a group of boys known as 'the library'.

Joss's own bedsitting room, in which he was supposed to do three hours of prep each day, like every other boy's was furnished with a 'burry' – a desk with drawers – and one easy chair. Fagging did not begin at once, but usually by October most newcomers would have had their share of the horrors associated with bullying.[43] Ablutions were bitterly cold, leaving hands and feet clean but more freezing than ever. A can of water would be delivered – the allowance was half an inch per bath – which was already cold and made icier as it hit the porcelain. Joss was left with a lifelong appreciation of luxurious bathrooms. He would select the most modern fittings for his own, insisting upon scalding-hot water in abundance.[44]

While no precise record of his academic achievements survives, Joss's ability to quote liberally from the classics in later life suggests that he was an able pupil. He studied modern languages as well as Greek and Latin.[45] He was astute at mathematics. He shared classes – known in Eton parlance as 'divisions', invariably abbreviated to divs – with children destined for a life of wealth, position and privilege: Prince George of Teck was one of his contemporaries, along with Ian Douglas Campbell, 11th Duke of Argyll, Alan Colman of Reckitt & Colman, Wilfred Thesiger and Gubby Allen, 'a great athlete and cricketer'.[46]

A high percentage of Old Etonians would be reunited later in Kenya, among which were Derek Erskine, Fabian Wallis and Ferdinand Cavendish-Bentinck.* Other Old Etonians would find themselves in Joss's company again when he was Kenya's Assistant Military Secretary on account of postings to Nairobi, such as Viscount Gerald Portman and Dickie Pembroke, 'a nice P. G. Wodehouse guardsman'.[47] The Highlands of Kenya had a reputation for attracting rarefied members of English society.

Eton's claim of making boys into men would resound and backfire when Joss turned fifteen. Already good-looking and tallish for his age, he was causing comment. He had suddenly shot up in height, developing into an almost Aryan-looking youth with well defined bones, a handsome high-bridged aristocratic nose, blond hair beginning to darken, blue eyes and a strong jaw. The pellucid eyes compensated for his rather too small mouth and would always be his most distinguishing feature. His hair was brushed back from his temples, with his parting low in the fashion of the day; his hair was so fine that he could keep it tidy only by slicking it down with brilliantine, darkening it further.

Joss's strongest asset was his gaiety. His smile and the light of

*Later the Duke of Portland.

enjoyment would not be kept out of his hypnotically pale gaze – nor would they fade in the memories of those who loved him. Many would remark on his playfulness. He learned early and quickly to hide his inner, vulnerable feelings and concealed them behind a knowing, adult expression which gave the impression of hauteur. This sophistication would have been seductive to boys with less self-confidence, and may well have been another factor in Joss's popularity.

Only months into the Great War, Eton began to notice the drain on its older pupils as they enlisted. Twenty new boys, led by Joss's friend Prince Leopold, arrived from Brussels in November 1914 to 'fill some of the empty rooms'. His greatest friend at Eton was Hubert Buxton, who would for ever remain loyal to Joss's memory. Hubert became head of the Eton Society, better known as 'Pop' – the self-electing oligarchy of senior boys who were the admiration and envy of the entire school. But Joss would not be there to benefit from Hubert's position. In their first year, Joss and Hubert began their joint hero-worship of Pop's former head, the Hon. Denys Finch Hatton, whose reputation for 'athletic and intellectual prowess' sprang from his days at Eton.[48]

For the duration of the war Eton's gaudy summer rituals were to change. Plans were amended for 4 June – 'Eton mess', strawberries and cream mashed together, was now a thing of the past – and a quiet lunch took place instead; a game of cricket followed, but fireworks were cancelled and so was the Henley Regatta.[49] St Andrew's Day and the Harrow match became too poignant reminders of happier times. Rather than providing such gaiety as they would have done in peacetime, they cast long shadows over tradition. As the obituaries of Old Etonians increased as the war progressed, rationing tightened and it became a point of patriotic honour and discipline that the boys should eat all their food, without comment or complaint, however unpalatable it sometimes seemed. This may be why Joss never questioned the meal put in front of him. He enjoyed haute cuisine but he could live without such luxuries; he always entertained well, but without ostentation. Since food was greatly restricted, when the growing boys were ravenous their

supplies were now mostly supplemented by tinned sardines and cara-
mels from Fortnum and Mason's.[50] The shortage of fuel meant that
fires were few and far between in the cold months, so that the
normal rigours of school life were accentuated. In addition, a pall
of gloom was evident on every page of the *Eton Chronicle* – hardly
surprising – with a grim, industrialised war raging as the world had
never before known it. By the second issue of the Michaelmas half,
a list of forty fallen was published under the heading 'Etona Non
Immemor':* when the challenge had come, Etonians, like so many
young men all over England, had responded and enlisted. The life of
the college was profoundly affected by so many unexpected leavers,
including nine masters. Some masters were even recalled from service
to step into the breach. None could forget that Eton was in the grip
of the war. Every home was saddened by losses among the generation
of boys above Joss. Poetic epitaphs appeared in Latin or Greek, as
well as in English.[51]

The effect on Joss was to be lasting. He would never be able to
fathom the eagerness of the young men to reach the front line –
over the first five days of the war 10,626 men had enlisted. All Joss
could see, at barely thirteen years old, was the meaningless waste of
young and healthy lives. In the *Chronicle* it was not uncommon for
a letter from a friend to appear, or a brief obituary by a tutor,
speaking of the 'cheerfulness' with which some young officer had
died.

During the summer half of 1915 Hubert and Joss began a lifelong
passion for bridge when they started playing Pelmanism, a card game
demanding, as does bridge, an excellent memory and great concentration. The deck would be scattered face down on the lawn. At
each turn, the player turns over two cards, but to score a trick the
upturned cards must match. Joss's success in pairing cards off was
almost impossible for Hubert to beat,[52] his perfect recall on the lawns
of Eton is early confirmation of his 'photographic' memory. The
two boys also shared an interest in drama. Joss's forte was reciting
from *Don Quixote* and Thackeray's *Esmond* at 'speeches'. His ability

*Eton does not forget.

to take in everything at a glance gave his parodies an accuracy that could be quite cutting. His performances for friends were spontaneous, broken up with snatches of German, gesturing, accenting, mimicking hysterical Italians or one of the pompous 'Danish Schleswig-Holstein Sonderberburg Glucksburgs', or fussing about in farcical parody of one of his mother's Austrian maids.[53] Joss took a delight in playing the buffoon. Making capital out of his surname, he would imitate a yokel, with bits of straw in his hair, using such phrases as 'Neither Hay nor grass', 'Making Hay while the sun shines' and 'Hey nonny-no'. If his repartee was sometimes too quick for the slow-witted, puns such as 'a roll in the Hay' and 'Haycock' never missed the mark and could be relied upon to raise a lot of sniggering.[54] Victor Perowne, editor of the *Eton Chronicle*, allegedly composed several poems and pieces of prose about 'Haystacks' for the *Chronicle*, although none can be found today so possibly these jottings were private. Perowne eventually became Ambassador to the Holy See. At Eton, according to Sacheverell Sitwell, Perowne had fallen for Joss 'hook, line and sinker'. Sitwell was never able to see Joss's appeal yet he spoke of his magnetism, witnessing him 'more than once, followed down Keate's Lane by a whole mob of boys'.[55]

Joss's academic progress is impossible to assess, as copies of school reports were not made at Eton in those days.[56] Other sources show that in 1916 he was a 'dry bob' (he played cricket rather than rowed in the summer term) and was 'very keen on football, being one of the first to play the Association game at the school'.[57] He also participated in the Lower Boy House Cup, 'Ante Finals', 'J. V. Hay playing in De Havilland's team for the Field Game when he was in the 28th Division' (Hubert Buxton was in the twenty-seventh).[58] However, cricket and cards were but minor pastimes that summer of 1916 compared to Joss's discovery of sex.

There was a lot of talk about Joss being 'very much AC/DC' while at Eton.[59] These rumours were strongly denied by his brother Gilbert and his son-in-law Sir Iain Moncreiffe. By 1916 Joss had already been a member of the Eton College Officer Training Corps for a year, where apparently there were always 'a lot of tents heaving on the job. One young and popular boy charged £3.00 per go.' At school he was great friends with Fabian Wallis, who was then openly homosexual, a friendship that resumed in Kenya.[60] Flirting with the boys down Keate's Lane does demonstrate his tendency at least outwardly to defy sexual conventions. He was of course attractive to women, but even those who had slept with him described him as 'a pretty-looking man', accepting that he might have been bisexual. As one admirer put it, 'Etonians had a certain reputation. There was something feminine about Joss, which one could not ignore.'[61]

Joss's initiation into heterosexual sex began at fifteen: in the Michaelmas half of 1916 he was caught *in flagrante delicto* with a maid, a woman old enough to be his mother. He had obviously confided in his great friend Hubert Buxton, but naturally the latter never elaborated beyond the fact that 'Joss had been sent down for being a very naughty boy indeed'; he added wistfully that Joss had been 'so attractive and so smart', implying that he only wished that he too had had the guts and ingenuity to get himself into bed with a woman at so tender an age.[62]

If his peers admired his seduction skills, the authorities at Eton did not. Usual punishment procedure was followed while the decision to 'sack' (expel) Joss was being made. While routine offences were dealt with in the headmaster's and lower master's 'bill', and floggings were recorded in a book open only to masters, more serious matters such as stealing or sexual misdemeanours were noted in separate confidential books. Because Joss's offence was sexual and therefore considered to be serious, the beating was to be carried out in private. A praepostor (a senior boy) extracted Joss from class. Ritual prevailed.

'Is there a Mr Hay in the Division?'

'There is.'

'He is to report to the head master in lower school after 12.'

Did Joss blanch? Probably not. It was not in his nature. Nor was it in his nature to blush. Just after Lupton's Tower chimed midday, two praepostors accompanied 'Mr Hay' from the twenty-eighth division to the headmaster Dr Edward Lyttleton's schoolroom; Lyttleton had found homosexuality so prevalent in 1915 that he had denounced the practice openly. (He left Eton soon after Joss.)[63] Dressed in a clergyman's cassock and accompanied by the head porter, carrying a birch rod in solemn procession, Lyttleton now ordered Joss to take down his trousers and underwear and to bend over the flogging block. After reciting his offence and outlining his punishment, six strokes of the birch rod, complete with twigs and leaves, were administered. It was bad form to cry. After Joss rose from the flogging block, Lyttleton presented him with the object that had given him his painfully wealed skin.[64]

We do not know if Joss's parents hastened back from Le Havre to England on account of his dismissal. As a result of his fall from grace, however, poor Gilbert's name was withdrawn from Eton. He was educated at Cheltenham College and Cambridge instead.

Quite apart from the thorough disgrace Joss would have been made to feel over his dismissal from Eton, he had already endured a rotten few months before being caught with the maid. Worsening an already insecure situation for Joss and his siblings, Slains, along with Longhaven House which belonged to its estate – Joss's rightful inheritance – had been sold off to Sir John Reeves Ellerman, who would dispose of these dwellings without even occupying them, a callous blow to the Erroll family.[65] Eliza Gore, their great-grandmother, also died that year in the Royal Cottage at Kew, leaving only Sir Francis Grant's painting as a reminder of her spirit and of the adventures that her descendants had heard from her own lips. Grant's portrait has her standing by her grey Arab pony, a gift from the Sultan of Turkey, ever reminding them that on this steed Eliza Gore had followed her husband without complaint throughout the Crimean campaign.[66]

With Eliza Gore's passing and the loss of Slains, all in one swoop Joss's childhood had disappeared. The ruins of both Old and New Slains still stand today, there to be looked upon by his great-grandchildren even though fierce winds have torn away the last traces of plaster. They can hear the same cries from sea-birds, the echoes of gulls and puffins, swooping and screaming through the castles' once proud corridors.

4

To Hell with Husbands

'Come, come,' said Tom's father, 'at your time of life,
There's no longer excuse for thus playing the rake –
It is time you should think, boy, of taking a wife' –
'Why, so it is, father – whose wife shall I take?'

Thomas Moore

Whereas a weaker young man might have been unable to recover from the shame of having been removed from one of England's finest schools, Joss's disgrace appears to have had no effect on his confidence.[1] If his parents were livid with him, they did not let it show publicly. They allowed his education to continue at home in Le Havre, the British Legation to Brussels' wartime base. Lord Kilmarnock found a tutor for him, a man who before the war had worked at the University of Leipzig. Through him Joss brushed up his German, and according to fluent German-speakers he spoke the language extremely well, some even claimed 'beautifully'.[2] (In later life, without daily practice, his command of German weakened somewhat.) His French also benefited from his return to a francophone country.

In a press interview in the 1930s Joss said of his time in Le Havre, vaguely, that he had been 'performing liaison work with the Belgians'. Perhaps his father had pulled strings to get him some practical experience of Foreign Office work and to broaden the narrow horizons of his studies at home. When Lord Kilmarnock moved on after the war Joss too was transferred to the British Legation in Copenhagen as an honorary attaché. Lord Kilmarnock acted as Chargé d'Affaires there until August 1919.[3] Joss was eighteen by this time and, help from his father or no, he was beginning to gain some very valuable Foreign Office experience.

Meanwhile, Lord Kilmarnock was made a CMG in June 1919 and a Counsellor of Embassy in the diplomatic service three months later. His father's impressive career was starting to awaken ambitions in Joss, for that same year he applied to sit the Foreign Office exam in London. Candidates were told to bring a protractor with them.* The result of this strange instruction was that on the morning of the exam, outside Burlington House, 'a multitude of officers converged with protractors in their hands'.[4]

Since Joss had 'one of the best brains of his time' he sailed through his Foreign Office examination – no mean achievement. At the time the Foreign Office exam was considered to be 'the top examination of all'. The Kilmarnocks must have been very relieved that their son appeared to be looking to his laurels at last. On the strength of his exam results Joss was given a posting, on 18 January 1920, as Private Secretary to HM Ambassador to Berlin for three years – 'a critical post at a critical time'.[5]

Two days later he reported for duty at 70–71 Wilhelmstrasse, Berlin.

For a few months it transpired that Joss was working in the same embassy as his father: a week earlier, on 10 January, Lord Kilmarnock had been appointed to Berlin as Chargé d'Affaires, to prepare for the arrival of Britain's new ambassador now that diplomatic relations with Germany were resuming. He was the first diplomat to be sent to Berlin after the Armistice. Having got his posting on the strength of his Foreign Office exam result Joss was probably somewhat non-plussed to appear still to be working under his father's wing. However, Lord Kilmarnock was soon appointed Counsellor to the Inter-Allied Rhineland High Commission in Coblenz and in 1921 was made British High Commissioner. Lord and Lady Kilmarnock were to remain in Coblenz until his death.[6]

Joss stayed on in Berlin for the time being. He obviously enjoyed

---

*In those days, applicants also had to prove they received a private income of at least £400 per annum.

Teutonic company. He would later socialise with the German and Austrian settlers in Kenya, and he returned to Germany on a couple of visits to Europe in the 1920s and 1930s.

The British Ambassador in Berlin, Sir Edgar Vincent, 16th Baronet D'Abernon, was an Old Etonian; his wife, Lady Helen, was the daughter of the 1st Earl of Faversham. They were a charming couple of whom Joss was very fond. Under their auspices he would come into contact with a wide range of influential and up-and-coming personalities – figures such as Stresemann, Ribbentrop and Pétain, just three whose names would be familiar to everyone in Europe by the outbreak of the Second World War.[7] The British Embassy stood only doors away from Field Marshal Paul von Hindenburg's Presidential Palace, which had once been occupied by 'the Iron Chancellor' Prince Otto von Bismarck and, in 1938, became Ribbentrop's official residence as Foreign Minister to Adolf Hitler. Prior to that appointment, Ribbentrop was to be German Ambassador to London from 1936.

When Joss met him in 1920 Ribbentrop, six years his senior, had just recently been demobilised. He was a tall, fair-haired man who 'held his head very high', was very arrogant and 'inaccessible'.[8] He looked like a caricature of an English gentleman in a humorous magazine and 'wore a bowler hat and carried an umbrella in spite of a cloudless sky'. At this time, Ribbentrop was ADC to the German peace delegation.[9] Joachim von Ribbentrop and his wife Annlies worked extremely hard at penetrating the circle of Gustav Stresemann, a statesman of first rank who was briefly German Chancellor in 1923. D'Abernon and Stresemann were close and, after Joss left Germany, together instigated the Anglo-American Treaty and the Pact of Mutual Guarantee embodied in the Treaty of Locarno in 1924. Stresemann's son, Wolfgang, recognised the social pushiness of the Ribbentrops and how they 'even got into the British Ambassador's functions'. The Ribbentrop networking technique was so effective that some of their hosts, 'Lord D'Abernon included, were surprised to find themselves entertaining their brandy merchant' – Annlies's father. [10]

By contrast, Joss, who had no need to elevate himself socially, was an ideal candidate for D'Abernon's needs at a sensitive time in Germany when constant communication between different countries was vital. D'Abernon was a fine diplomat with a wealth of experience. In him Joss found a man to emulate and, while he appeared to take a delight in outraging his father, he knuckled down under D'Abernon and never stepped out of line, respecting the Ambassador's opinions on many governance matters. He also sought his views on historic battles, modern warfare, thoroughbred horses and champion tennis – subjects which were to be of continuing interest to Joss. D'Abernon's informality endeared him to Joss and, in his friendship with the older man, he found his attention drawn to more serious aspects of life. D'Abernon had taken risks – successfully – with his own career, and Joss admired him for this adventurousness, a quality he shared. D'Abernon had at one stage been Chairman of the Royal Commission on Imperial Trade: this was to be the field that most impressed itself on Joss, whose understanding of it became almost as profound as his mentor's. The conclusions that Joss reached at this time would enable him to argue, off the cuff, about reforms to the Congo Basin Treaties in Kenya a decade or so later. His liaison work in his capacity of Private Secretary to the Ambassador was honing his skill in retaining detail – he was becoming proficient at storing away information to use later, a habit which would pay off time after time.

In 1920 Joss accompanied his parents twice to the American Cemetery in Coblenz, in the Allied Rhineland; on 20 May they went to the Decoration Day service, then in November attended the Remembrance service. Standing on the dais, looking sombre, Joss was the youngest among dignitaries such as Monsieur Fournier, the Belgian Ambassador, Herr Delbrucke, the Austrian Ambassador, Monsieur Tirade, the French Ambassador, and Marshal Pétain. On each occasion he gazed down from the stand at the huge garden, and all that he could see stretching into the distance was row upon row of white military crosses. He would never forget this display of tragic waste.

Joss's work involved a lot of travel from one European capital to another. Being based in the country of the vanquished provided him with a view of the war from both sides. He had witnessed the decimation of Eton's sixth form, and Le Havre too had shown him a facet of war. Then there was the neutrality of Scandinavia: he discovered that there was also something to be learned from those who had stood back. The next three years were to provide ample time to listen to the experiences of the former enemy.

Joss's dislike of bloodshed showed too in his reluctance to take part in blood sports. Some regarded his detachment with suspicion. According to Bettine Rundle, who knew Joss in those days, he was quite unpopular with Lord Kilmarnock's staff on account of not joining in their hunting pursuits. However, he did play football regularly against teams formed by the various different Allied armies based in the area. Association football was particularly popular in the British Army, and on one occasion Joss captained the side that beat the American Army team.[11] He was also a very experienced polo player by this stage.

Equally, his unpopularity with his father's staff could have been due to jealousy; they probably resented his plum job at the Embassy and wrongly assumed he had got the post purely through his father's influence.

Whatever feelings he inspired among embassy employees, Joss enjoyed great popularity in his social life and on his travels around the capitals of Europe. The temptations in the cities were plentiful, affording men opportunities for unrestrained pleasure – in this respect Joss was very much a player. In the society in which he had been raised, sexual mores for men were liberal. It was expected of Continental grand dukes and archdukes that they should seek to indulge their sexual fantasies with mistresses rather than their wives. During the late summer, the fashionable German spas turned into the hunting grounds of the most famous courtesans of Europe. By the standards of the day Joss did nothing that others did not do, and many indulged in far more excessive behaviour.

From 1919 onwards Joss paid regular visits to Paris, where he got to know a wealthy American socialite, Alice Silverthorne, with whom he enjoyed an intermittent affair. His girlfriends were usually blondes but Alice was dark and, also unlike the majority of his lovers, close to him in age. In 1923 she married a young French aristocrat, Frédéric de Janzé. Alice was bewitchingly beautiful, rich, self-willed and neurotic. 'Wide eyes so calm, short slick hair, full red lips, a body to desire . . . her cruelty and lascivious thoughts clutch the thick lips on close white teeth . . . No man will touch her exclusive soul, shadowy with memories, unstable, suicidal' – this was her husband's adoring and, ultimately, prophetic verdict.[12] Alice was to become notorious as the Countess de Janzé, when she was tried for attempted murder in Paris in 1927. She had shot her lover Raymund de Trafford in the groin at the Gare du Nord. She married him five years later and they separated about three months after that. Alice and another beauty Kiki Preston – a Whitney by birth – were part of the American colony in Paris who welcomed Joss into their social circle.

The early twenties saw the Paris of Hemingway, Molyneux and Cecil Beaton.[13] Joss thrived in this glamorous climate. Beaton's photography drew the fashionable world's attention to the beauties of the day. Joss would get to know most of them well. One of Beaton's 'finds' was Paula Gellibrand, a 'corn-coloured English girl' who became one of his muses. When Paula and Joss first met, she was untitled and the daughter of a major who lived in Wales. Joss's relationship with her would surface haphazardly at distant points on the globe since she would become the wife of no less than three of his friends and, being an inveterate traveller, would appear wherever the glamorous foregathered be it Paris, Venice, New York, London or Antibes. She was tall and languid, and according to Beaton, her 'eyelids were like shiny tulip petals . . . [she was] the first living Modigliani I ever saw'.[14] Ultimately Paula would happen up on Joss's doorstep in the Rift Valley, married to Boy Long (whose real first name was Caswell), a rancher and another neighbour of Joss's – by then Joss and Paula had been friends for fourteen years.

Once Joss disappeared into the wilds of Africa with his first wife Idina, another eccentric socialite in Paris – she and Alice fell for Joss, separately, at roughly the same time – Kiki Preston, Frédéric and Alice, among other friends, would flock after them. The clique which became infamous as the Happy Valley set was formed in France before any of them left for Africa.

History does not relate where Joss and Idina first met. It could have been in Paris, for Idina was there in 1919, mixing with a Bohemian set that would have appealed to Joss. It is possible that they had met in more conventional society even earlier, in Helsinki, when Joss was still living in Denmark, because Idina's younger sister Avice was then living in Helsinki with her husband Major Sir Stewart Menzies, and Idina would have visited her there. Menzies was a military man but he usually established ambassadorial contact wherever he worked. When Joss was in his thirties, he would become head of the Secret Services.*

It is likely that Joss and Idina had been circling one another for at least eighteen months before their affair started. Idina was another of the beauties who caught Beaton's imagination – he noticed the way she 'dazzled' people.[15] Her red-gold hair was styled like a boy's and, her bosom being too ample for the dictates of fashion, she flattened it so as to look perfect in the gowns created for her by Captain Molyneux – or 'Molynukes', as she called him.[16] She had been a devotee of his since he opened his house in 1918; his designs made her look taller. It was Molyneux who dressed her when Joss first met her and he would continue to adapt fashion to suit her style for nearly forty years: she had 'a rounded slenderness . . . tubular, flexible, like a section of a boa constrictor . . . [she] dressed in clothes

---

*Menzies had served with distinction in the First World War. There was a widespread belief in the services that he was the illegitimate son of Edward VII. He was certainly closely connected with court circles through his mother, Lady Holford, who was lady-in-waiting to Queen Mary. He also had considerable influence in important government circles, and 'as a ruthless intriguer' used it shamelessly. In personal relationships Menzies was polite but never warm, 'hard as granite under a smooth exterior', as the wife of one of his Security Service colleagues observed. He drank heavily, loved horses and racing and was a club man (Philip Knightley, *The Second Oldest Profession*, p. 112). When he took over the SIS after Admiral Sinclair's death in 1939 he was forty-nine. His successor, Sir Dick White, noticed that the file on Menzies was missing from the registry. The wartime chief had deliberately avoided any records 'to preserve the fiction that he was the illegitimate son of Edward VII. "I paid ten shillings," laughed White, "and got the name of his real father from Somerset House."' (Tom Bower, *The Perfect English Spy: Sir Dick White and the Secret War 1935–90*, p. 209).

that emphasised a serpentine slimness'. Joss, fashion aficionado, thought that the way she looked and dressed was wonderful. [17]

Twice married by the time Joss knew her, Idina was eight years older than him. She was the elder of two daughters born to the 8th Earl De La Warr (pronounced Delaware). Their brother, the heir, was Herbrand Edward Dundonald Brassey Sackville and, by the time Joss made his maiden speech in the Upper House, had become 9th Earl De La Warr, Under-secretary of State for the Colonies and Lord Privy Seal in the House of Lords.[18] Idina was a legendary seductress. Joss, only nineteen years old, impressionable and driven by lust, had not resisted her wiles.[19] He pursued her from 1920 although not exclusively.

Joss called virginity a 'state of disgrace, rather than of grace' and was not interested in seducing virgins. Lady Kilmarnock's view was that young men should have affairs only with married women. Joss, whom she had so bewitched as a young boy with the mysteries of her toilette, seems to have paid a lot of attention to her on this issue as well, as Daphne Fielding can testify. Daphne's memoir, *Mercury Presides*, contains a forgiving description of Joss's flirtation with her (a virgin when Joss knew her): 'It was inevitable that he should be conscious of such wonderful good looks as he possessed, and with these he had an arrogant manner and great sartorial elegance.' When her father learned that Daphne had sat out on the back stairs with Joss during a dance, a furore ensued. After she told Joss about the row, he sent her an 'enormous bunch of red roses'. She had been terrified that the sight of the flowers would incur her father's wrath all over again, and had hidden them from him – 'in my bedroom basin until they died – the first present of flowers that I had ever received'. Her fascination with Joss grew as her father's disapproval intensified: Joss's scornful way of looking at people, 'an oblique, blue glance under half-closed lids', was impudence personified.[20] Joss, however, did not return her interest. He would without exception make a beeline for married women.[21]

The easygoing lifestyle – in which people exercised sexual freedom without anyone suffering – that Joss now adopted would always be attractive to him. Idina, herself an advocate of promiscuity, found

Joss irresistible – and one can see why in a picture taken of him as whipper-in to the American Army drag-hounds. As the best-looking in a bunch of four young bloods, he was as usual with the prettiest girl in the group. For his part, Joss relished the element of danger in his relationship with Idina. Her reputation was to him deliciously *louche*. Her first husband, Captain the Hon. Euan Wallace, MC, MP, had been in the Life Guards Reserve; she produced two sons by him, but after six years the marriage was dissolved. The two boys remained with their father and Idina virtually abandoned them. The society she kept in Paris was decidedly disreputable. Only her pedigree redeemed her. But her family life had not been happy; Idina was only nine years old when her parents separated, and, like Joss, she had grown up precociously and was easily bored. Even at school, classmates had been wary. She was smarter than them. One of her school contemporaries, coming across her years later in Kenya, admitted how terrified she had been of her. On this occasion Idina was as withering as ever: 'Oh, yes,' she murmured on meeting her old classmate, 'I remember you – you never powdered.'[22]

Joss, madly in love with Idina, was longing to share his life with her. They made secret plans to marry and Joss played the eligible bachelor as Idina waited for her divorce from her second husband, Captain the Hon. Charles Gordon of Park Hill, Aberdeen. Charles had fallen for one of her younger unmarried friends and had wanted the divorce too. There was no uproar and terms were mutually agreed. In fact, Charles and Honor Gordon would be neighbours to Idina and Joss in Kenya. Charles Gordon had benefited from Kenya's Soldier Settlement Scheme in 1919, and he found himself with 2,500 acres in the Wanjohi Valley above Gilgil. Idina received just over half the land as part of her divorce settlement.[23]

Joss, meanwhile, was 'causing tremendous consternation in the hearts of the ripe young things' in the marriage market-places. He was much in demand where débutantes flourished. He was scanned by dukes and dowagers, among bespoke kilts and bejewelled bosoms, upon which rested heirlooms.[24] In 1922 he played the season – Ascot, Cowes, Henley, Cowdray Park and the Royal Caledonian Ball (the biggest of the London season) – having resigned his job at the

Embassy in Berlin in March that year, nine months before the posting was due to end. His father must have been aghast at such fecklessness. But though his patience must have been wearing rather thin by this stage, he seems to have done his best to get his son back on to his career path. Perhaps Lady Kilmarnock put in some persuasive words for her favourite child, for in 1923 Joss became secretary at the Inter-Allied Rhineland High Commission.[25] Nepotistic though the appointment may have been, he would undoubtedly have been able to make a useful contribution to the work of the High Commission. By now, he had acquired extensive experience in the Foreign Office and could switch to another language without a moment's hesitation.

Adding to the tension in the British residence household at the time was the recent resale of Slains. Ellerman had arranged for the estate agents Frank Knight & Rubenstein, W. D. Rutley to auction it off.[26] In the spring of 1922 Slains was sold for scrap – a considerable humiliation for the Erroll family.[27]

Idina was not long in following Joss out to Coblenz for a visit during the interlude between her decrees nisi and absolute. Joss wanted his parents to meet her, but he never let on to them his intention to marry her. He obviously realised that his parents were unlikely to share his enthusiasm for Idina, and even if he believed that she 'could have walked off the bas-relief of dancing nymphs in the Louvre' Lord and Lady Kilmarnock would take a lot of persuading.[28] None the less, they would welcome her as his girlfriend.

Coblenz was a picturesque town at the mouth of the Mosel River, and had long been established as the trading hub for wine-growing countries and furniture factories. It was a sociable place: racing was popular, and since there was a good theatre, everyone went to the opera at least once, if not twice, a week.[29]

The British residence was surrounded by tall trees; in summer the building was entirely draped in Virginia creeper but during the winter its fish-scale tiled roof was exposed. It stood in the best spot of all among the French, Dutch, Belgian and American embassies, on the edge of the Rhinelagon, directly opposite the 'bridge of boats' which parted to allow barges through as they sailed up and down the river.[30] Lord Kilmarnock's position as High Commissioner entitled him to a guard and a sentry-box outside the gates of the residence; a Cameron Highlander did duty, marching up and down in a kilt. One of his more ceremonial roles was to pipe out distinguished guests down the drive as they left the house. Visits by dignitaries to the residence were photographed by the firm Lindstedt & Zimmermann, who specialised in turning photographs of the more important guests into postcards.[31]

Idina spent a lot of her time in Coblenz shopping for furniture for the new home in Africa that she would receive through her divorce settlement, choosing table linens and 'ordering crêpe de chine sheets and exotic bathroom equipment' including 'a splendid green bath which in Kenya achieved a reputation all of its own ultimately, when it was believed to have been made from onyx'.[32] Joss would accompany her, not letting on to his parents that he planned to share this future home of hers.

Joss's general behaviour towards Idina and his family in Coblenz during Idina's stay was observed by one of his contemporaries, Bettine Rundle from Australia, who had been sent to stay with her guardian's daughter Marryat Dobie, one of Lord Kilmarnock's aides. Bettine found herself at the British residence for eighteen months, party to the sensation created by Idina and to the interactions between Joss's family and the staff attached to the residence. Thanks to Joss's and Gilbert's kindness, Bettine was included in the young people's social life, attending the many parties and witnessing the childish pranks perpetrated by Joss and Idina. The staff were shocked at the spectacle of Idina with her Eton crop, and at how old she was. 'Her figure resembled that of a boy, too; very, very slim', her breasts flattened, 'which seemed to make Joss complement her physically . . . . They seemed like brother and sister; there was something alike in them.'[33]

These partners in crime masterminded a 'little surprise' to mark a visit from Monsieur Tirade, the French High Commissioner. While everyone else was bathing and changing for dinner they 'sneaked downstairs and tied numerous pairs of knickers and brassières from the top to the bottom of the banisters of the grand staircase into the hall below, where functions were always held. They had gone to the trouble of dying the underwear like the Tricolour, stringing the garments up like bunting in a totally inappropriate manner.'[34] Lord and Lady Kilmarnock descended and – *Voila!* Joss's father was acutely embarrassed before his guest of honour; Joss looked on in glee. Apparently his elders were always fearful of what he might do next. 'He was generally regarded as something of a loose cannon,' Bettine said. Today Joss's and Idina's prank might be regarded as harmless fun, but in the old school to which Lord Kilmarnock belonged one simply did not do that sort of thing.

Idina used lingerie for maximum arousal in the bedroom and taught Joss many tricks involving its removal. His favourite was to touch the strategic four points on a skirt undoing the suspenders underneath so deftly that the wearer would notice nothing until her stockings collapsed about her ankles.[35] Underwear would continue to be a sensitive subject during Idina's stay. She never fell short of taking 'delight in Joss's near-the-knuckle jokes'. 'Covered in hay' did the rounds in Coblenz.[36]

Such mockery of decorum outraged the Kilmarnocks. Joss's father remarked that since Idina was so much older she should have known better.[37] If Joss involved himself with such a woman, how could he expect to move expertly as a diplomat? Lord Kilmarnock feared for him and told him so, but his warnings fell on ears tuned only to amusement. If Joss had been smarting from the telling-off, his doting mother would soon have soothed his wounded vanity.

A portrait of Lady Kilmarnock painted that year shows a stunning woman. She exuded confidence and, like Idina, 'was very stylish, usually surrounded by a good many subalterns from Cologne – and officers of the Guard . . . seeming not to want to grow old'. Joss 'seemed to cultivate a peculiarly intimate relationship with Lady Kilmarnock', and Bettine Rundle noticed that, even while Idina was staying, he continued to appear in his mother's dressing room before dinner for a private chat. One evening, sauntering in, Joss had picked up the flannel dangling over the side of her wash-basin and gestured as if to wipe his face, when his mother snatched it away with a shriek, 'That's my douche cloth!' 'A lot of tittering between mother and son had gone on over his mother's washcloth.' According to

Bettine, when Joss exercised his sense of humour he 'always had to score a point – usually it had a smutty side'.[38]

Joss's smuttiness could be hurtfully embarrassing. On his father's staff was a stenographer, a Miss Sampson, with whom Joss had flirted. Sammy, as she was known, was dark, plain and middle-class but Joss made a point of never overlooking plain girls. Sammy had been invited to attend Gilbert's birthday party, along with fifty others. She would be returning to London on leave the next day. A risqué innuendo in Joss's impromptu speech during dinner had horrified everyone – 'now that Gilbert had *come* . . . of age,' he remarked at one point.[39] His brother had never taken his jokes easily. Worse was to follow. Strolling across to Sammy, Joss wished her a good holiday; then, in falsetto, mimicking her Essex accent and loud enough to be overheard, he said, 'Don't forget to take your sanitary towels, will you?' There was a hush. His father was very upset and there had been murmurs about the 'Mrs Jordan coming out'. Sammy, having admired Joss, took a long time to get over the indignity. On the whole, though, his own generation tended to regard him as 'killingly funny'.

Joss may have been in love with Idina but he was too bright not to realise that she would never be a model diplomat's wife. She would earn a reputation as a superb hostess, she would never give a damn about what other people thought. 'To Hell with husbands' may have been *her* dictum, but they both lived by it.[40] Even before his father had had his say, Joss must have known that the Foreign Office would never have kept him on as Idina's husband. Divorced persons were not accepted at Ascot nor at court. Lord Kilmarnock had made it his business to discover all that he could about Idina and he gathered a considerable ballast against her. Both his parents remonstrated with him, cajoled him, reminded him of what his future could entail. 'Lord Kilmarnock begged Joss not to marry Idina. Even making him promise.' Joss had agreed, and Lord Kilmarnock was convinced that he would comply.[41]

However, unbeknown to the Kilmarnocks, arrangements for their register office wedding were put in hand for 22 September 1923. Idina, Alice de Janzé and Avie Menzies were in and out of London that spring and summer. If either of the 'Sackville sisters' was spotted, they made news: at the Chases or the Guards point-to-point, 'over a line at Lordland's Farm, Hawthorn Hill'.[42] Joss joined Idina in England that summer and they simply enjoyed one another's company, participating in the dance craze which was already in full swing. George Gershwin, currently billed as 'the songwriter who composes dignified jazz', arrived in London for the broadcast of 'Rhapsody in Blue' by Carroll Gibbons and the Savoy Orpheans. The Savoy was one of Joss's favourite spots – the Orpheans and the Savoy Havana Band played simultaneously there on different floors; sometimes he and Idina would move off the dance floor to watch 'speciality dancers' in cabaret. They lapped up the city's night life, going to Ciro's to dine and dance after the theatre, to the Criterion, to the Café de Paris, to Oddenino's and to the Piccadilly Hotel, where Jack Hylton's band was also playing Gershwin in the ballroom. The Vincent Lopez Orchestra from the USA at the new Kit-Kat Club in the Haymarket was another hit, and since everything was within walking distance they could stay out all night, sometimes until dawn rose over the Thames. Avie was in London too, sharing Idina's excitement while she had the chance.[43]

Idina's engagement to Joss was announced in the *Tatler* on 19 September: 'Lady Idina Gordon . . . is taking as her third husband, Mr Josslyn Hay, who will one day be the Earl of Erroll.' The couple were on holiday at the Palazzo Barizizza on the Grand Canal in Venice when the announcement came out. Their hostess was Miss Olga Lynn, an opera singer manquée. Joss and Idina knew her as Oggie. She was not popular with everyone but had a loyal following, giving amusing and glamorous dinner parties for twenty at a time. Witty epigrams would be exchanged and 'stunts' performed for everybody's entertainment. Oggie's exotic set included Cecil Beaton, Tallulah Bankhead, Lady Diana Cooper, and Sir Oswald Mosley and his wife Cynthia – known in that circle as Tom and Cimmie. They would dine out at the Restaurant Cappello, much favoured by the Prince of Wales.[44] Everyone knew one another. Whether swimming naked by moonlight in Venice, or attending Goodwood or Henley, their individual appearances and frolics were almost religiously recorded in the *Tatler* and the *Sketch*. This holiday in Venice cemented Joss's friendship with Tom Mosley and ensured Joss and Idina a place in Oggie's circle.

The Mosleys and Joss and Idina epitomised the postwar exuberance – they were highly optimistic about their own futures as well as the world's, and they went about their lives on billows of hedonism. As Tom Mosley wrote, 'We rushed towards life with arms outstretched to embrace the sunshine, and even the darkness . . . [we experienced the] ever varied enchantment of a glittering and wonderful world: a life rush to be consummated.'[45] They were rich and they believed they could do anything. As far as they were concerned, war was over for ever.

In one photo, Joss and Idina parade on the Lido, Idina in a pleated white dress by Molyneux, as always, happy to show off her size-three feet by going barefoot. Hand in hand with his future wife, Joss follows the trend for 'wonderful pyjamas in dazzling hues'.[46] Tom Mosley, having been invalided out of the war, was forced to wear a surgical boot to redress an injury from an aeroplane crash. But his charisma more than compensated for his handicap, which was no impediment to attracting the likes of Idina and other beauties of the day with whom Joss had also dallied.

Mosley was the youngest Tory MP in 1919 but, within a year of meeting Joss, would leave the party in protest against the repressive regime in Ireland, switching allegiances to join Labour. Mosley would also give Neville Chamberlain 'a terrible fright' at Ladywood, Birmingham, contesting his seat and losing by only seventy-seven votes. Joss would emulate Tom's style. They both fell for the same type of woman, and politically Joss's ideas tallied with his at that time. They both believed that they could turn the world into a better place, providing they were given the power to act.

The Mosleys attended Joss's and Idina's wedding on 23 September. In their wedding picture, all arrogance is missing from Joss's demeanour, replaced by a seldom seen expression of shyness or self-consciousness. Idina's cloche hat is pulled firmly down. Wearing a brocade dust-coat trimmed with fur and her corsage of orchids, the bride looks, at best, motherly; she was thirty. Joss's best man, the

Hon. Philip Carey, and Idina's brother Lord De La Warr were the witnesses. After the ceremony, Idina's brother, Prince George of Russia, Tom and Cimmie Mosley and Lady Dufferin celebrated with them at the Savoy Grill.[47] Joss's family is conspicuous by its absence. The couple cannot have been inundated with wedding presents, given the circumstances, but Tom and Cimmie gave Idina 'a crystal-and-gilt dressing table set, personally designed by Louis Cartier, and engraved with her initials and a coronet'.[48]

Lord Kilmarnock went berserk when he heard the news from London that Joss and Idina were married. According to Bettine Rundle, the rumpus had to be seen to be believed. For all Joss's defiance of his parents' wishes, he must have had a twinge of conscience because he returned to Coblenz with Idina to make his peace early in the New Year of 1924.[49] Despite their rage and disappointment over Joss's squandered abilities Lord and Lady Kilmarnock appear to have forgiven the couple for when their stay at the residence ended they were piped out by Lord Kilmarnock's sentry, Captain Alistair Forbes Anderson. This was an honour they would not have received unless they were back in Lord Kilmarnock's favour.[50]

Having ruined a promising career with the Foreign Office, possessing no money, and limited by the social restrictions that marriage to a divorcee imposed, Joss must have looked on Africa as an ideal escape. It was being said that he had 'married . . . because he was very young and very headstrong and because Lady Idina had considerable income from De La Warr'. If this criticism was fair, Joss was following in the tradition of his ancestors. However, the Hays inspired jealousy in those who weren't so witty or as attractive, and these allegations of marrying for money could have been thus inspired.[51] Idina would always have her detractors; she was too successful with men not to attract criticism. Being well read and knowing absolutely 'everybody' – from Diana Cooper to Florence Desmond – she did summon a certain envy. And her legendary sexual appetite did not endear her to people. Even her future son-in-law Moncreiffe, not prone to exaggeration, pointed out, 'My mother-in-law was a great lady, though highly sexed.'[52]

Some time after their visit to Coblenz to make peace with the Kilmarnocks, Joss and Idina Hay sailed off with all their chattels, ready for their first home together. Joss was embarking on his first voyage to the Dark Continent with the recklessness of a schoolboy gambler. Their fellow passengers would have consisted of government officials, business entrepreneurs, missionaries and big-game hunters. During the voyage attempts were made by most of those expecting to stay in Kenya to study a slim volume called *Up Country Swahili*. However, Idina and Joss were up to their usual pranks, courting scandal in a manner for which they were soon to become infamous. After a week or more cooped up on board Joss found himself shoved into a lavatory in one of the state rooms with the key turned on him by his female companion, 'in order to escape an outraged husband'.[53] Joss had narrowly missed being caught in the act of fellatio when the woman's husband had arrived at their state-room door wondering why on earth she was taking so long to dress for dinner. She apologised coolly and promised to join him after she had completed her toilette. Meanwhile, as the sun went down, Idina had been sipping 'little ginnies' in the ship's cocktail bar. She recounted the incident with evident relish and amusement to someone who, on a visit to the British residence in Coblenz, relayed the anecdote to Bettine Rundle. According to Bettine's informant, Idina had blamed herself for Joss's behaviour; he had learned from her how to be such a rake.[54]

5

Slains

'Africa – the last continent with a soul of its own'
Carl Jung

Joss decided to call his first home in Africa after his ancestral castle. This new Slains was backed by a dramatic forested ridge and watered by it streams, reminiscent of a Scottish landscape; the setting seemed to pay implicit homage to Joss's past. Dinan, his heir, would begin her life here in the Wanjohi Valley, whose occupants were not so far removed in temperament from his ancestors: here too settlers had laboured, suffered, loved and lost. Instead of the fog that curled up from the North Sea to engulf icy ramparts, in Africa soft morning mists rose and rolled towards a rambling farmhouse to dissolve under the hot mid-morning sun.

When their ship dropped anchor off Mombasa's old town, Joss and Idina were rowed ashore with their steamer trunks and all their heavy luggage. Two flags fluttered over the old Fort Jesus, built by the Portuguese: the Union Jack and the scarlet *bandera* of the Sultan of Zanzibar.

Joss was an experienced traveller in Europe, but nothing would have prepared him for the scenes in Mombasa's old town. Its narrow streets were peopled with many different races. Women veiled in black purdah strolled among near-naked non-Muslim women, moving nonchalantly along in the heat with their unevenly shaped loads – such as bunches of green bananas or even a bottle – balanced perfectly on their heads. Commerce was noisy, shouted in many tongues as locals haggled for business; government officials, turbaned

Sikhs and Indian *dukawallahs*★ seemed oblivious to the stench of fish and shark oil hanging on the air. In MacKinnon Square, another Union Jack hung limply from its flagpole above the District Commissioner's office with its rusting corrugated-iron roof. Feathery coconut palms, blue sea and sky gave a feeling of infinite peace, yet Fort Jesus and the cannon standing resolutely beneath its low walls spoke of a history of bloodshed and strife.

The Hays spent one night at Mombasa Club, dining under the moon on its terrace, sleeping under nets as protection against mosquitoes; translucent geckos about the length of a finger darted about the walls, consuming the insects. One train per day left for Nairobi at noon, and the three-hundred-odd mile crawl on the single narrow-gauge track up country began, taking about twenty-four hours.[1] 'Penniless, dashing, titled and an accomplished sportsman', as he was described in a newspaper profile a decade after his arrival in the colony, Joss would now make Kenya his home.[2]

Kenya would suit him because he was not afraid of the unexpected. Africa is nature's Pandora's box and the gambler in Joss would respond to its uncertainties. Idina loved everything about the colony too; she 'could muster wholesome fury against those who she thought were trying to damage the land of her adoption'.[3] Her instinct that Joss would share her enthusiasm and strong feelings had been right. Life in the colony demanded hard work, rough living and life-threatening risks, but for an adventurer like Joss, who had all the right contacts and, thanks to Idina, plenty of money, Kenya offered the promise of the Imperial dream fulfilled. In addition, Joss had an open, inquiring mind and a willingness to seek advice from those more experienced than he was.

The Uganda Railway, by which the couple travelled to their new marital home, had been completed in 1901. The Maasai called it the 'iron snake' and those who opposed it the 'lunatic line'. It ended at Port Florence (later called Kisumu) on Lake Victoria, and was a formidable achievement that took five years to complete, traversed wilderness and cost a staggering £5,500,000 without a jot of evidence

★Shopkeepers.

to justify the expense. The Foreign Office, adept at muddling through, had then enticed out white settlers with cheap land flanking the railway-line.

Joss and Idina journeyed on the train from Mombasa in square compartments, nicknamed 'loose-boxes' – there were no corridors – and the train jolted ceaselessly while on the move, stopping, only for meals, at a series of Indian dak-bungalows. These breaks were refreshing on a long journey, which could be drawn out further if elephant or rhino blocked the line. Choking red dust coated every passenger. Any attempt while the train was at a standstill to remove the wire screens at the windows to get more air was met by a scolding from the invariably Goan stationmaster: 'Bwana! Mosquito bad, Bwana. Malaria bad.' The first stop at Samburu for tea was accompanied by toast and rhubarb jam. Menus were always the same.

Dinner was taken at Voi, where large hanging lamps like those suspended over billiard tables were bombarded by insects, *dudus*, which bounced off to lodge themselves in the butter or the lentil soup. The fish was smothered in tomato sauce to disguise its lack of freshness, and followed by beef or mutton, always curried, for the same reason. Lukewarm fruit salad or blancmange rounded off the meal, with coffee.[4] Stewards made up bunks for the night with starched sheets, pillows and blankets, and in the dark, as the train rattled onward and upward, occasionally a cry would intrude in the night: 'All out for Tsavo!' Joss could mimic the sing-song Goan accent perfectly.[5] At dawn everyone clambered on to the line to stretch their legs. Hot shaving water would materialise in jugs, produced from the steam by the engine driver and delivered with the morning tea by waiters in white uniform and red fezzes. Breakfast was taken further up the line at Makindu.[6]

As the journey progressed, Joss shared the excitement felt by every pioneer: at the spectacle of Kilimanjaro under its mantle of snow at sunset; at the endless scrub and the trickles of water optimistically called rivers; then disbelief, on the final approach to Nairobi, at the sheer dimensions of the Athi Plains, where mile upon mile of grassland teemed with gazelle, rhino and ostrich, and herds of giraffe, zebra and wildebeest roamed wild against the deep-blue frieze of the Ngong Hills. Seeing creatures in their natural habitat instead of behind bars was like rediscovering the Garden of Eden. And finally, beyond Nairobi, awed silence at the spectacle of the Great Rift Valley.

When Joss first laid eyes on Nairobi in 1924 it had become something akin to a Wild West frontier town patched together with corrugated iron. Windswept and treeless a quarter-century earlier, it had been unsafe after dark 'on account of the game pits dug by natives'. Her Majesty's Commissioner for British East Africa, Sir Charles Eliot, had embarked on a policy of attracting white settlers. When the European population amounted to 550 it was decided to build a town hall. All around was evidence of plague, malaria and typhoid as the shanty-town grew. These same diseases were still a life-threatening problem in Nairobi's bazaar in Joss's and Idina's day.

By 1924, Nairobi had become a melting-pot, with settlers from all over the world bringing their different ways to the colony – their languages, their recipes, their religions, morals and social customs. Joss was no stranger to foreign languages, and before long Swahili would encroach too on his conversation: *shaurie* for 'problem'; *chai* for 'tea'; *dudu* for any form of insect life from a safari ant to a black widow spider; and *barua* for 'note' – important when there were no telephones by which to communicate. Sometimes English words with no Swahili equivalents were adopted into the language by the addition of an 'i' – *bisikili*, *petroli*. Indian words seasoned the mélange: *syce* for 'groom', *gharrie* for 'motor-car', *dhersie* for 'tailor'. Settlers developed a local pidgin Swahili of their own, known by natives as Kisettla. When the settlers began conversing in Kisettla, notice was being given that all convention was henceforth left 'at home'.

Beyond Nairobi the Uganda Railway traversed escarpment and volcanic ridges along the Rift Valley, with its lakes scattered like pearls; and further north, at Timboroa, the line rose to almost 8,000 feet in a stupendous feat of engineering, scaling ravines and descending again until it halted abruptly above the next large expanse of water, Lake Victoria, in Nyanza. At the railhead at Kisumu, the main crops were bananas and millet. There was still talk at the local bridge tables, of missionaries in the area who had disappeared, thanks to cannibals.[7]

Joss and Idina got off the train at Gilgil, about three-quarters of the way along the Uganda railway-line. A tiny dot, hardly on the map, Gilgil was so small that it boasted only a railway-siding, but it provided a vital link with Nairobi as travel by car was barely feasible because of the appalling state of the roads. The Wanjohi Valley was tucked away in the hills behind Gilgil. This broad and undulating virgin territory, where yellow-flowering hypericum bushes grew in profusion, was watered by two rivers. The Wanjohi and the Ketai, flanked by beautiful podocarpus, ran more or less parallel and fed many icy, turbulent, gravel-filled streams, crisscrossing the valley. Ewart Scott Grogan, a pioneer settler who played an important role in the development of Kenya, had stocked these with fingerlings in 1906 – brown as well as rainbow trout. As one left the valley going uphill to 'Bloody Corner', so called because so many vehicles got stuck in the mud there, the Wanjohi changed its name to the Melewa. Fed by the Ketai, it flowed down towards Gilgil, 'through the plains and past an abandoned factory and former flax lands, through dust and mud, over rocks and stones, to Naivasha, the lake thirty miles away'.[8]

Joss's and Idina's new home, Slains, was situated just eighteen miles north-east of Gilgil. On arriving at the railway-siding they were met by their farm manager, Mr Pidcock, who drove them the forty-five-minute journey to the farmhouse. Slains nestled at one end of a private two-mile murram track leading in the opposite direction from Sir John 'Chops' Ramsden's seventy-thousand-acre Kipipiri Estate and his home, Kipipiri House. Slains was a rambling, charming farmhouse, low-lying and beamed, with a corrugated-iron roof, open ceilings, verandas and long bedroom wings. The kitchen, as usual in Kenya, was housed separately. The rooms were vast with partitioned walls which allowed sound to travel freely, affording little privacy.

In Kenya, this style of housing, reminiscent of Provençal dwellings, was the inspiration of Chops Ramsden and unique to the district. The houses were constructed by a builder from Norfolk whom

Ramsden, a hugely wealthy landowner, had initially brought to Kenya to construct Kipipiri House. This had pleased him so much that the builder stayed on and was employed to build every additional manager's house and the neighbours' homes as well. Before leaving for Kenya, Idina had asked Chops Ramsden to supervise the construction of Slains ready for her and Joss's arrival. The uniformity of the Wanjohi Valley settlers' houses reinforced the club-like atmosphere of the area.

Slains' setting was as dramatic as its namesake in Scotland. The early-morning mists that swamped this moorland wilderness were damp enough to warrant the wearing of wellington boots. At sundown, a chill would come into the air, making night fires a necessity. Yet by day its climate was that of a perfect English summer. The equatorial sun at an altitude of 8,500 feet produced an exuberance of growth. Looking out from the front of Slains towards Ol Bolossat, which was more often a swamp than a lake, except when it was fed during the rains by the Narok River, occasionally one could see the gleaming water flowing over a two-hundred-foot shelf at Thomson's Falls. In the distance up the valley behind the house rose the mountain Kipipiri, which joined the Aberdare range. The cedar-clad forest ridge which ran along the valley, dubbed by Frédéric de Janzé 'the vertical land', dwarfed everything below, and this haunt of elephant and buffalo lent grandeur to the simplicity of daily existence.

For life in Kenya in 1924 was far from an unbroken idyll. Joss was joining a community of pioneers who were still trying to redress the effects of their absence from their farms during the First World War. These early settlers might have picked up land at bargain prices but there had been a catch: every decision affecting their livelihood was made in London. Land for farms had in the early years of the twentieth century been parcelled out under ninety-nine-year leases 'with periodic revision of rent and reversion to the Crown with compensation for improvements', which meant that the settlers would forfeit everything unless they developed the property to pre-fixed standards.[9]

Only a few months before Joss first arrived at Slains, the Duke of

Devonshire, then Colonial Secretary, had put the wind up European settlers in Kenya by declaring that 'primarily Kenya is African territory', and reminding them that His Majesty's Government would pursue the 'paramountcy of native interests'; furthermore, 'if the interests of the immigrant races should conflict, the former should prevail'.[10] While this meant little to Joss in 1924, he would become a champion of the European settlers' interests in due course.

In 1920 Sir Edward Northey, the Governor, had made seven major innovations. Firstly, in that year the Protectorate graduated to Crown Colony. Secondly, a new Legislative Council was set up to represent the settler and commercial interests, and European settlers were granted the vote. The colony's affairs could now be debated in the local parliament, 'though it was stressed that the colony was still to be ruled from Whitehall'.[11] In due course Joss became a member of 'Legco', as it was known. Thirdly, the railway was reorganised; its finances were separated from those of the Protectorate and the railway system was placed on a business footing. Four, under the control of an intercolonial council, the first big loan was raised for a new branch railway. Joss would see its construction, as well as the harbour works, begun and completed. Five, the Civil Service was reshaped. The rates of pay were raised to put them on a level with other colonial services. Six, the budget was balanced and inflated expenditure was cut drastically 'so as to bring the country's coat within measure of its cloth'.[12] These innovations formed the framework of the political structure within which Joss would move and be affected as a settler.

Finally, it was under Northey that the Soldier Settlement Scheme was launched. In spite of setbacks, this was acknowledged to be the most successful postwar settlement project in the Empire. And – through Idina's ex-husband, Charles Gordon – Joss benefited from the Government's second attempt since the building of the Uganda Railway to fill the empty land with potential taxpayers and producers of wealth. These ex-soldiers got their land on easy terms, and Charles Gordon had been one of many applicants. Sir Delves Broughton, too, had drawn soldier settlement land, coming out initially in 1919 to inspect it. Allocation tickets could be bought in Nairobi and at the

Colonial Office in London. 'By June 1919 more than two thousand applications had flooded into Nairobi to take their chance at a grand draw held on the stage of the Theatre Royal.' Like a lottery, the tickets were placed in barrels to decide who was to get what. 'It took two revolving drums all day to distribute the empty acres by lottery to an audience of nail-biting would-be farmers.'[13]

One of the first settlers in Kenya, Hugh Cholmondeley, 3rd Baron Delamere, had trekked on foot into Kenya in 1897 with camels from Somalia, arriving with a doctor, a photographer and a taxidermist. Africa infected him with its potential. In 1903, Delamere applied for land in British East Africa on the ninety-nine-year-lease scheme and was granted a total of a hundred thousand acres at Elmenteita near Gilgil and at Njoro beyond Nakuru; he called his first home Equator Ranch. Njoro was already regarded as the cradle of European settlement by the time Joss and Idina arrived in Kenya. While D, as everyone called him, was not the first to take up land, he became the most influential of all the settlers. He was to have a powerful influence on Joss – they were virtually neighbours – and gradually Joss would find himself drawn into local politics. D'Abernon had taught Joss about the Scramble for Africa, and so he knew more than most neophyte settlers about the political machinations with foreign Imperial powers that had gone before. Joss and D, both Old Etonians, were utterly different types who stood for quite different things, but they were united in their love of Kenya and a willingness to use all possible means for their cause.

D was the leading light among the settler community. When not working his farms, he headed deputations to Government House, even taking a delegation to London in early 1923 to fight the settlers' cause with a Government now much less in favour of colonialist expansion. He also found time to sit beside his own hearth with several Maasai who had walked for miles to chat with him at Soysambu★ wearing only a *shuka* and beads. Gilbert Colvile and Boy Long, D's former manager – the other two in the colony's great trio of cattle barons – would also often consort with the Maasai, who

★D's second farm, overlooking Lake Elmenteita, to which he moved in 1910.

were greatly respected for their knowledge of cattle-breeding.

Gilbert Colvile was a highly eccentric character, almost a recluse. His mother Lady Colvile ran the Gilgil Hotel with her maid.[14] The hotel was something of a focal point for European settlers, who would regularly call upon Lady Colvile. Her son would later get to know Joss when Joss moved to Naivasha. Colvile became one of the most successful cattle barons in Kenya, doing a great deal to improve Boran cattle by selective breeding. He had been at Eton with Delves Broughton and Lord Francis Scott. The latter, like Broughton, whose commanding officer he had been during the Great War, had drawn land from the 1919 Soldier Settlement Scheme. Scott was chosen to replace Delamere as Leader of the Elected Members of Legislative Council and as their representative to London after D's death in 1931.[15]

Once Joss and Idina had settled in, the rhythm of life at Slains was orderly and as balmy as the daytime temperature. Their prelude to each day was a glorious early-morning ride. Their horses would be groomed and saddled, waiting for them to mount. Before the dew was burnt off the grass by the sun, they would ride out for miles over the soft, turf-like vegetation that rose up as if to meet the sky. The muffled thud of hooves would send warthog scurrying and the needle-horned dik-dik bounding away in pairs. Ant-bear holes were a hazard for their sure-footed Somali ponies, as the scent of bruised wild herbs rose from warm, unbroken soil under their unshod hooves in their jog home afterwards. Joss would change into a kilt and then breakfast on porridge and cream.

Labour was cheap after the war, but not readily forthcoming. District Commissioners had applied to the local chiefs to exert 'every possible persuasion to young men to work on the farms'.[16] Every servant needed training from scratch – most candidates had never set foot in a European household before. Appointing a major-domo was a complete lottery. The Hays had two Europeans on their staff, one of whom was Marie, a French maid who would become integral to Idina's households. At times of crisis, Marie could be heard throughout the house 'wringing her fat little hands, her voice rising higher and higher, "*Cette affreuse Afrique! Cette affreuse Afrique!*", her high heels tapping out her progress on the parquet floors as she sought out Lady Hay with the latest disaster'.[17] Then there was Mr Pidcock, their farm manager, who also ran the Slains dairy.

Butter-making was done early in the morning or late in the evening; the butter was washed in the clear river water, which gave it its wonderful texture. Every other day it would make its way to Gilgil by ox-cart, wrapped in a sheet torn from the *Tatler*.[18] The Slains cuisine would never want for supplies of farm produce and, thanks to a good kitchen garden, the table there was superb. Idina's menus were sophisticated, and Marie taught the African cook how to make soufflés and coq au vin on a blackened Dover stove fuelled by *kuni*.* The ring of the axe was a familiar sound since wood heated the water for baths.

Waweru, Joss's Kikuyu servant, came to work for him in 1925 as a 'personal boy' and may well have started life as a kitchen toto, when Joss spotted his potential. He was only a little younger than Joss – the Africans kept no precise record of the year they were born – and had never been to school. He would work for Bwana Hay until Joss's death, and was utterly dependable. By the time he was called as a witness during the murder trial in 1941 as 'Lord Erroll's native valet' this Kikuyu man had been privy to many intimacies in Joss's life. Eventually promoted to major-domo at Joss's next home, Waweru ran the household very capably, performing his duties with all the expertise and dignity of a seasoned English butler, making callers welcome in Joss's absence, arranging flowers and overseeing junior staff.[19] Waweru's opinion of Joss as a 'good man' made an impression in court during the trial, and certainly debunks the rumour spread after Joss's death that he mistreated his staff.[20] At Slains, the African servants were given presents on Boxing Day, amid much celebration. As Joss once explained, one had to 'budget on the basis of two to three wives, and half a dozen children per wife per family'. Nevertheless, everyone received presents.[21]

Another inaccurate assessment of Joss was the assumption that,

*Firewood.

because he was rich and titled, he was nothing but a 'veranda farmer'. He certainly enjoyed life and drove around the area dangerously fast in Idina's Hispano-Suiza with its silver stork flying over the crest of its great bonnet. His hair-raising driving earned him his Swahili name, Bwana Vumbi Mingi Sana, meaning 'a lot of dust'. For all his high-spirited behaviour, though, Joss was serious about farming. The Hays were the first settlers to breed high-grade Guernsey cattle in Kenya, for example. And thanks to advisers such as Boy Long and Delamere, they were able to avoid the most common blunders made by newcomers, such as putting very large bulls to native heifers, which would result in calving difficulties. The pioneers had learned the hard way. Once the conformation problem was recognised, half-bred bulls were used instead and heifers fared better.[22]

Joss knew a lot about horses from all his polo experience, and entrusted only Captain George Marcus Lawrence, a soldier settler who had ridden for the British Olympic team, with the schooling of his polo ponies and the training of his modest string of racehorses. Marc Lawrence would oversee the estate and the staff during Joss's absences in Europe.[23]

Livestock auctions were held in the Rift Valley at Gilgil, Naivasha and Nakuru, through which the only road to Nairobi passed. Each boasted a post office, a DC's office flying the Union Jack and a police post with the usual sprinkling of Indian *dukas*;* the only petrol to be found between Nakuru and Nairobi was at the garage Fernside and Reliance Motors Ltd in Naivasha.[24] At the auctions Boy and Joss always stood out amongst the crowd, chatting together. Boy Long, like Joss, was good-looking and popular with women. According to Elspeth Huxley, Boy dressed 'like an English country squire with a dash of the cowboy, accentuated by a broad-brimmed Stetson hat and a bright Somali shawl'. Joss too was establishing something of a reputation for his eccentric dress, but behind the libertine appearance of these two men were fine brains attuned to the business in hand.

On sales days just before 9 a.m., sumptuous cars would park behind

*A small shop.

the auction stand. A fine red dust with a peculiarly harsh smell would be lifted by the wind, spiralling into the sky. As the dust settled behind Joss's Hispano-Suiza when he stepped out, it would rise again around the hooves of the Abyssinian ponies as they were trotted out for inspection, 'thin, footsore and weary', having been driven down by Somali herders. Joss's polo ponies as well as his hacks were taken from Abyssinian stock, because they were exceptionally sure-footed and coped well in the rough terrain.

Wives 'looking radiant and glamorous, smoking Egyptian ciga-rettes', would gaze down at pens full of pawing, butting cattle as the bidding went on.[25] Idina never seemed to suffer in the dust and heat – one of her least tolerable offences in the eyes of her detractors. Joss and she both seemed to tolerate African conditions effortlessly.

Joss often met up with D and Boy, whether at Soysambu or Nderit, where Boy lived, or Slains, and the three of them would discuss farming problems. Emergencies were forever cropping up: everyday *shauries* – crises among the African staff, thefts, sicknesses, snake bites and the sudden need for a vet.[26] Within eighteen months of arriving in Kenya Joss, who was not a vain man, felt that he had learned enough through practical experience to describe himself as a cattle farmer.

To diversify their produce, Joss and Idina tried planting pyrethrum – in those days nobody knew for sure what would or would not grow at any altitude – a flower used in the production of crop insecticides. For this the land had to be tilled; teams of doe-eyed oxen, sixteen at a time, would drag the heavy tiller through the earth. If the wooden harness broke, it took Pidcock more than an hour to drill each hole through the hard olive-wood using a brace and bit, to make a new one. Slowly and painfully, several hundred of the Slains acres were transformed into furrow upon furrow of lacy white pyrethrum. What Joss learned here formed the basis of arguments he would later use as a member of Legislative Council, defending the high-quality production of pyrethrum for export.

Elspeth Huxley praised the Hays' farming activities: 'They enhanced rather than damaged the natural charms of their valley, by leaving native trees alone and . . . by paddocking green pastures for

butter-yellow Guernseys, stocking streams.' Idina taught her *shamba**
boys how to lay and look after lawns, to prune, and to cultivate
English spring bulbs. Her legacy survives today on Mombasa's north
coast, where a garden of exotic shrubs and trees enhances the house
where she died. At Slains they grew pansies, Albertine roses and
petunias with success and around the cedar trees they planted daffodil
bulbs. When these bloomed the effect was that of an English country
estate. Elspeth Huxley's parents, Joss and Nellie Grant, would drive
over from Gikammeh to swap yarns and exotic cuttings.

Joss's and Idina's neighbours ran into one another in Gilgil –
everyone used the railway-siding there. The dusty main road sported
one signpost, which pointed north to Nakuru and south to Nairobi.[27]
Vitalbhai's in Gilgil was the largest in a string of iron-roofed *dukas*.
Just outside its entrance, a *dhersie*† toiled away on his treadle Singer
sewing machine. Here, Joss and Idina bought basic provisions as well
as yards and yards of corduroy in different colours on the chit system.
The *dhersie* would stitch *kanzus* – long, white cotton robes rather
like night-shirts – which were worn with a red cummerbund by
houseboys. He also made Idina's and Joss's slacks in the corduroy –
a fashion set by Idina, so practical that everyone followed it.

The 'cow-town' of Nakuru was the farming heart of the Rift
Valley, and was Lord Francis Scott's nearest shopping centre. The
Scotts were never invited to Slains, though Joss and Francis Scott
would become friends later. The Scotts, having met Idina first as
Charles Gordon's wife, never stopped condemning her. Eileen Scott
wrote in her diary: 'She has done a lot of harm to this country and
behaved like a barmaid.'[28] Elspeth Huxley's description of Eileen
suggests that the disapproval would have been mutual: 'Eileen Scott
lingers in my memory draped in chiffon scarves, clasping a French
novel and possibly a small yappy dog, and uttering at intervals bird-
like cries of "Oh François! François!".'[29]

Notwithstanding her low opinion of Idina, Lady Eileen was
among the first to recognise potential in Joss: once he joined the

---

*A garden, smallholding or estate.
†An Indian tailor.

Naivasha Farmers' Association she found him 'much improved'. Joss's success there came as a surprise to some, Lady Eileen continued: 'Contrary to the expectations of most people, Joss Erroll was voted to the chair . . . It is a pity Joss hasn't had a year's more practice and experience; he has a brain like lightning and it is difficult for him to listen patiently to this slow-minded, if sound, community. However it is a very great step in the right direction, he is very able and a gentleman.'

While the Scotts were never guests at Slains, Joss and Idina did not want for extra companionship. With an eclectic flow of friends and visitors, local or from overseas, at Slains the mood of each gathering was dependent on kindred spirits – playful, debauched, sophisticated or civilised. Idina would preside, perpetually reloading her long amber cigarette-holder. The more often her glass was recharged – 'Another little ginnies, dahling,' she would drawl – the more amorous she became, a signal that things were about to liven up.[30] Joss, however, 'never smoked, seldom drank, sipping wine in small quantities at dinner; he never touched spirits'.[31] He would act as barman to his guests, topping up their glasses for hours on end without any sign of irritation. Whenever alcohol was served at parties, whether in the role of host or guest, Joss kept his glass full to avoid seeming to be a killjoy when others were knocking it back. He would decline courteously if anyone pressed him to drink more and, with a knowing twinkle, would murmur, 'I'm not going to impair my performance.'[32]

Joss and Idina had their own polo ground at Slains and played at weekends, generally attracting a crowd of spectators.[33] The polo crowd loved Joss: 'He was a first-class player . . . Clever, always had a brain . . . and was always ready to take advice.'[34] A typical gathering would include some of Joss's Old Etonian friends, neighbouring settlers and a sprinkling of titled guests from abroad.

Reclining in leather-covered armchairs, with those relics of life in England, a fox's mask and crossed whips on the wall, they would talk of 'light things – horses and the latest gossip from Government House'. Inevitably their exchanges would include chat about any new divorcees. Since the arrival of the new Governor Sir Edward

Grigg, divorcees were blacklisted. 'Queen Mary had issued her own writ to Lady Grigg: no divorcee was to be received at Government House.'[35] Idina could not have cared less, though the exclusion was humiliating to some.

It soon became custom in the Wanjohi Valley for each household to throw one huge annual party. Guests converged, bringing with them a bevy of servants and tents, to be erected in the gardens as accommodation. Having come from afar, they expected to spend at least three days there − longer if the rains were making the roads impassable. A visiting *mpishi** would usefully pick up tips for new dishes, and this practice caught on rapidly, further enhancing Slains' excellent culinary reputation.

Visitors from abroad would be especially enchanted, after a dusty journey along a remote unpromising track, to reach such civilised surroundings. Slains was filled with comfortable old furniture, Persian carpets, family portraits, silver ornaments, and studded Zanzibar chests gleaming from applications of lime juice and salt. Unlike most homes in Kenya, however, there was not a stuffed animal trophy to be seen. There were baronial arrangements of flowers, spacious bedrooms with private bathrooms and a library − 'huge and varied . . . full of biographies . . . No one knew more about contemporary literature than Idina.' This room was dominated by Joss's desk.[36]

According to its owner in the fifties, Slains' principal bathroom was 'superb . . . vast, and in the centre stood a bath of green onyx . . . Idina would bathe in champagne occasionally. She was a darling but very naughty.' Idina's excesses were conspicuous to all, and her reputation for outrageousness did nothing to improve opinion of Joss among serious-minded settlers. Idina had a walk-in cupboard, leading off their morning-tea room, which housed her shoes, shelf upon shelf and pair by pair − which was a puzzle to her African staff since she went about barefoot, even when riding, just as they did. Idina often suffered from chafed feet. One young woman friend, while applying a bandage to one foot which 'was very swollen and obviously painful', failed to see how Idina could bear her touch.

*A cook.

Noticing that she did not flinch, the friend asked her if she was not afraid of anything: '"Yes," Idina had replied, "old age."'[37]

In every bedroom a bottle of whisky and tumblers stood on a tray, and on each pillow was a pair of folded silk pyjamas.[38] This courtesy was extended to guests from overseas because they were unlikely to be accustomed to changing into glamorous dressing-gowns and pyjamas for dinner. Joss had decided to use those boldly patterned beach pyjamas from Venice where they had been all the rage as daytime wear. Since they were comfortable, attractive and practical the fashion became de rigueur as evening wear. Boy Long concluded that 'the quality and colour of one's pyjamas and dressing-gown worn for dinner revealed one's social standing'.[39] This fashion did not meet with everyone's approval – King George V was not impressed when he heard about the habit after the Duke and Duchess of York's visit to Kenya in 1925.

When Idina saw her guests off with her husky 'Goodbye, my dears!', they were always sad to leave. Often they could not expect to return for a whole year. Their only meeting, meanwhile, might be by chance at Muthaiga Club. Being separated by such great and hazardous distances, the settlers were inclined to make the most of their get-togethers, an exuberance that unfairly contributed to their reputation for debauchery.

In May 1925 Idina discovered she was pregnant – her baby was due the following January. But her condition evidently did not get in the way of her social life. Shortly after finding out about her pregnancy, the Hays invited Frédéric and Alice de Janzé to Slains – in the autumn, when the weather made Paris less appealing. They agreed to come out to Kenya for two months including Christmas. Leaving Paris in late November, the de Janzés treated this holiday as a delayed honeymoon as, in the two years since they had married, Alice had produced their two daughters, Nolwen and Paola. The girls stayed behind in France.

Frédéric and Alice were seduced by the glorious Wanjohi Valley, and no doubt by the thought of becoming neighbours with such close friends. Wanjohi Farm, about five miles from Slains, came up for sale while they were staying there, and Alice bought it. She and Frédéric did not move in until the end of 1926, however.

Idina seemed to be fully aware of, but indifferent to, Joss's affair with Alice. She knew they had been close since Paris days and their flirtation carried on intermittently during their stay as well as when the de Janzés came to live in Kenya. Some say that Alice turned up in Kenya because she could not bear to be parted from Joss, but this theory exaggerates hers and Joss's feelings for one another. They enjoyed hopping into bed together occasionally, but Alice had far stronger feelings for other men, such as Raymund de Trafford, and Joss found the temperamental Alice far too much trouble to become seriously committed to her. Frédéric was also unaffected by Joss's and Alice's sporadic affair. He would nonchalantly refer to Joss as 'the Boyfriend'.

The de Janzés accompanied Joss and Idina to Muthaiga, an exclusive residential area about three miles from Nairobi's centre, where they spent Christmas of 1925, so that Idina could be in Nairobi for the birth of the baby. Their daughter was born on 5 January 1926 and they called her Diana Denyse Hay. As a toddler Diana took to calling herself Dinan, a nickname she soon came to be known by.

The first ten months of 1926 would see an epidemic of the plague in Nairobi's Indian bazaar. There were to be no fewer than sixteen deaths by November, when Dinan was ten months old. Worries over raising children were not confined to the plague. Malaria was another life-threatening disease, and at the time there was a widespread conviction that the altitude and the sun would have an adverse effect on growing European children. For this reason, there were few living in the Wanjohi in the twenties. Even as a toddler, Dinan was made to wear a double *terai* and a spine pad★ between the hours of eight and four. Joss, pictured in a snapshot holding his baby daughter, looks incredibly happy – even astonished by the tiny

★The *terai* was a felt hat, usually double-brimmed, recommended for young and old alike to be worn between 7 a.m. and sundown as essential protection against the sun. The spine pad was a device lined with red flannel designed to be worn by children to protect the spine from the sun, whose rays were thought to have a damaging effect on it.

doll-like creature in the crook of his right arm. Whatever his paternal instincts, however, Dinan would be raised by a nanny, as was customary amongst the aristocracy in those days.

While Idina was still in Nairobi recovering from Dinan's birth, Joss had stopped on his journey home to Slains at the water-splash in the Kedong Valley, where everyone took on extra water before attempting to climb the two-thousand-foot escarpment. At this bubbling stream the glade was inhabited by a pride of lions – quite uninterested in the presence of humans – whose footprints could be seen in the mud; handsome black and white Colobus monkeys leapt about among the branches above. From the splash, the more cautious would reverse their cars up the hairpin bends, to lessen the strain on the engines. Joss had Waweru with him: no European ever travelled alone in Africa then, a wisdom that has never changed. Not long afterwards, Cyril Ramsay-Hill fetched up with his gun-bearer.[40] He too was on his way home, but from safari to a newly completed house on Lake Naivasha into which he and his wife Molly had just moved. Ramsay-Hill, dying to show off its splendour, invited Joss back for the night to save him driving on up to the Wanjohi.

Though they had not met before Joss had heard of Ramsay-Hill: it was rumoured that he had made his money out of hairdressing. In fact he had been attached to the 11th Hussars. Apparently the natives, who could not pronounce the word, much less understand what a 'Hussar' might be, had concluded that Bwana Ramsay-Hill was a hairdresser. Frédéric de Janzé had already come across him that Christmas – a flamboyant fellow, he said, resembling Salvador Dali, replete with moustache and monocle. During conversation Frédéric discovered that he and Ramsay-Hill shared an interest in the cinema and in literature. It then transpired that Ramsay-Hill's 'interest' involved a collection of classic French pornography, paintings and books, many of which were eighteenth-century originals.[41] Next to the library in his new house was a small locked room where he housed his 'secret library', 'a very special collection of books and highly erotic pictures by Boucher, Lancret, Fragonard and Watteau from the collection of the Duc de Richelieu'.[42]

Ramsay-Hill would live to regret his impulsive invitation by the

1. Josslyn Victor Hay aged two in August 1903.

2. A much more boyish-looking Joss aged four with the severe walls of Slains Castle, the Erroll family seat, behind him. After a daughter was born to her in 1904, his mother Lady Kilmarnock had allowed his hair to be barbered.

3. Joss's mother Lucy Mackenzie, the new Countess of Erroll, shortly after his grandfather the 20th Earl's death in 1927.

4. A sketch of Joss by his mother. She understood his defiant spirit and would always forgive him for spurning authority.

5. Joss and his brother Gilbert in Stockholm. They learned to skate and toboggan with the children of the king of Sweden.

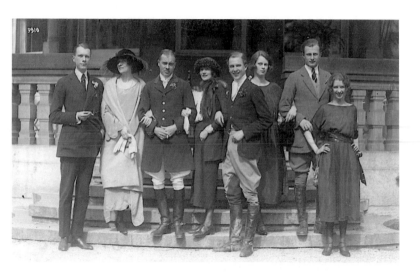

6. Joss, whipper-in, among friends and other members of the American Army Drag Hunt on the steps of the British Residence, Coblenz. His sister Rosemary is on the far right.

7. Joss's parents and sister at the British Residence, Coblenz, in the 1920s. A contemporary observed, 'Lady Kilmarnock had a penchant for young officers.'

LADY IDINA GORDON AND THE HON. JOSSLYN HAY

A snapshot recently taken at a well-known Italian resort. Lady Idina Gordon is the Earl of De la Warr's sister, and the Hon. Josslyn Hay is a son of Lord Kilmarnock and a grandson of the Earl of Erroll. The engagement of Lady Idina Gordon and Mr. Josslyn Hay was announced a short time ago.

8. On the dais at the American Cemetery in Coblenz, Remembrance Day 1920. Joss (left), Private Secretary to HM Ambassador to Berlin, was the youngest among the diplomats and dignitaries present who included Marshal Pétain.

9. Joss's and Idina's flamboyant love affair makes the cover story of the *Tatler*, September 1923. Joss's marriage to this notorious divorcee enraged Lord Kilmarnock.

10. Despite his initial fury over their marriage, Lord Kilmarnock granted Joss and Idina the honour of being piped out of the British Residence by his sentry, shortly before the couple's departure for Africa in 1924.

11. Slains, Joss's first home in the Wanjohi Valley, named after the Erroll family seat in Scotland. This style of farmhouse was unique to the district. The cedar–clad ridge behind the farm was dubbed the Vertical Land by Frédéric de Janzé.

12. Lady Idina and Joss at Slains, 1925. Joss was not put off by the basic living standards in the colony at the time. He picked up farming know-how from some of Kenya's best-known pioneers, Lord Delamere and Ewart Grogan.

13. Making a deep hole for the goal posts for the polo ground at Slains. Joss was highly popular with the polo crowd, who rated him 'a first-class player'.

14. One of Ali Khan's mule teams on Government Road, Nairobi, 1920s. Seizing Ali Khan's rhino-hide whip, a cuckolded Major Ramsay-Hill lashed Joss in full public view at Nairobi Station in 1928. The incident was never forgotten by Joss's enemies.

15. Kiki Preston with Lord Delamere at Loresho, his Nairobi home. Kiki became close friends with Joss's second wife Mary and introduced her to drugs.

16. Joss at Gilgil with Gerry and Kiki Preston on his right and Michael Lafone on his left. According to one settler, 'The quality and colour of one's pyjamas and dressing-gown worn for dinner revealed one's social standing.'

17. Raymund de Trafford, Frédéric de Janzé, Alice de Janzé and Lord Delamere at Loresho, 1926. The de Janzés were Joss's and Idina's closest friends in the Wanjohi Valley, and the foursome formed the core of what became known as the Happy Valley set.

water-splash, for it was thus that Molly Ramsay-Hill was introduced to Joss, the man who would 'remake her world'. Their affair, which began some time later, was managed very discreetly and, just as Joss had kept his parents in ignorance about his intentions towards Idina, so here no one guessed at the outset that there was anything other than Joss's habitual flirtation and charm in his conduct with Molly, who was nine years older than he was, the same height as Idina and 'petite and quite a beauty, Titian-haired with green eyes and a flaw-lessly pale skin'.[43] In contrast to many women of her age in the colony, whose faces were devoid of any artifice and weatherbeaten, Molly's face was 'deadly white as if it had been dipped into a flour bag; she wore dark red lipstick and dark red nail lacquer to match. Everyone thought her terribly exotic.'[44]

Kiki Preston, who had been part of the American glamour set in Paris, came back to her splendid house Mundui at Naivasha some time in 1926, having been persuaded to stay by a friend who had given her land on the lake. Frédéric called Kiki and Gerry Preston 'Black Laughter'. The Paris clique was beginning to re-form around the shores of Lake Naivasha and along the Wanjohi Valley.

When Frédéric and Alice came to live in Kenya at the end of 1926, as before, their daughters were left behind in France. At this time the Wanjohi Valley was inhabited by less than a dozen Euro-peans, including the Hays and the de Janzés. Since their arrival the Hays had held court here and, with Frédéric and Alice, they would form the core of an exclusive set. As with all groups of intimate friends they developed certain rituals and habits which marked them out from others. Idina frequently held hands with Alice in the garden at Slains, illustrating how relaxed they were in their shared passion for Joss, which seemed only to bring them closer together. Alice would often sing for her three friends, accompanying herself on the mandolin.

They would go on safari together. The fact that Joss chose not to hunt, fish or shoot did not prevent Idina from doing so. Joss seemed content to be out in the field. Every evening on safari they would gather by the fire between seven and eight, before bathing and changing for dinner, to devote an hour to composing limericks and storytelling. Each took it in turn to recite to the others. This was Frédéric's idea. He had moved in literary circles in Paris, keeping company with people like Maurice Barrès, Proust and Anna de Noailles; his standards were high. Frédéric's creations were the cleverest, Joss's the funniest, Idina occasionally cheated, and Alice always tried to outwit the men. A typical contribution from Joss ran:

> There was a young lady from Nyeri
> Whose lusts were considered quite eerie,
> On the night that she came,
> And we both did the same,
> It was fun, until I said, *Kwaheri*.'[45]★

Rules were strict when it came to the stories. First, a round of 'cold hands' at poker was played, to determine who should start. Whoever won must begin with 'Once upon a time, Kenya was not Kenya but British East Africa . . .' and follow with any subject except shooting.[46] Sometimes Idina, in her low throaty voice, would declare Kenya taboo: 'Let's be jolly and think of Paris tonight.' They would all shut out Africa and everyone in it until the Swahili servant interrupted their reveries – '*Chakula tyari*' – and they would go into the camp tent for dinner.

The foursome also enjoyed jaunts to Nairobi, usually confined to race week four times a year when they would make merry like everyone else, staying at Muthaiga Club. The visits involved a drive of a hundred miles, taking six hours. The de Janzés had a Buick and they would race the Hays to Muthaiga Club, testing the qualities of the Hays' Hispano-Suiza against the Buick.[47] The de Janzés frequently won, which is perhaps why Joss favoured Buicks later himself.

Fernside and Reliance Motors Ltd, the garage in the 'tiny dorp' of Naivasha, looked after the Hay vehicles for Joss all his life. Its European mechanics would lay bets with him on whether he would break his own record time to Nairobi. 'Bwana Hay was no remittance

★*Kwaheri* is Swahili for 'farewell'.

man, cheerful when he lost, and bills were always paid eventually, if spasmodically.' Robert Creighton serviced all the Hay engines, including the Hispano-Suiza. Joss was the only man Creighton had ever met to leave a Rolls-Royce in a ditch after it had skidded off the road in the rains and turned over. Joss's ignorance of car engines left Creighton baffled. 'How could so intelligent a man learn nothing about motor-car maintenance?'[48]

The murram road from Naivasha to Nairobi formed easily into corrugations, shaking vehicles mercilessly and making travel for farmers with heavy loads very laborious; the Hay–de Janzé races cannot have been comfortable. It was always a relief to arrive in Nairobi. Alice, 'in grey slacks and green jumper, and wide-spaced grey eyes', would calmly defy all the club rules, gliding into Muthaiga Club and daring anyone to stop her bringing in her animals – 'a tiny monkey, an Airedale and a lion cub'.[49] Even when she was persuaded to leave them in the car, each was brought indoors to her for regular inspection.

By now Nairobi had street lights, so fewer citizens were likely to fall into the open drains at night. Rickshaws plied their trade along Government Road between graceful blue gum trees, lining both sides of the wide thoroughfare between Nairobi Station and the Norfolk Hotel. In the mid-twenties Government House was rebuilt on the orders of Sir Edward Grigg, who was Kenya's Governor until 1930.* Joss, who had barely set foot in the old black and white 'Tudor' residence, would frequent this stately new building often in the 1930s. The cost, an astronomical £80,000, would be made much of by taxpayers, who 'squealed indignantly and spoke of *folies de grandeur*'.[50]

Idina, coolly defying the harsh African climate itself, would appear at the Nairobi races in one of Molyneux's latest innovations, on one occasion a brown hat covered in oiled ostrich feathers.[51] Because

---

*Sir Edward Grigg arrived as the prophet of federation, believing that Kenya, Uganda, Tanganyika and Zanzibar would soon be united. On the assumption that he was likely to be Governor-General, Grigg invited Britain's greatest Imperial architect, Sir Hubert Baker, to design a grander Government House.

Joss liked black and white, he had hit on the idea of Idina wearing unmatching earrings as a pair – one white pearl and one black pearl – a fashion she made her own.[52]

Joss always paid one visit to his barber Theo Schouten's whenever up in Nairobi – men tended to visit their barber every three weeks then. His only alternative, meanwhile, was to get Idina to trim his hair. Theo Schouten was a 'cheerful little man' who, having been in Nairobi since 1911, was already looked upon as one of the town's characters, running his Government Road establishment with 'West End staff'.[53] Schouten's catered for both sexes in a humble wood and iron building with a corrugated roof and, like the best barbers everywhere, knew everyone and everything that was going on. Joss and Schouten came to know and like one another, and the barber's was conveniently near to Joss's and Idina's lawyer, Walter Shapley of Shapley, Schwartze & Barratt. In London Joss had always used Truefitt & Hill in Bond Street, including their range of lotions known as CAR, and eventually he would persuade Schouten to stock this exclusive range. Joss's dance partners were always aware of the pleasant scent. Men noticed it too – the distinctive aroma would pervade a changing room shared with Joss before a game of cricket or polo.[54] Later, when Schouten moved to grander premises in the New Stanley Hotel on Delamere Avenue, and Joss was living in Nairobi, the one appointment he never missed was his massage and manicure, so as to garner information, useful gossip, about town.[55]

The Hays and the de Janzés took their rituals to Muthaiga Club: 'the squash court ladder was sacrosanct'. They all began at the bottom, playing their betters, climbing rung by rung until each found his place, either to be 'ousted by or ousting the rung just ahead'.[56] Joss would always reach the top of the ladder, the champion for two seasons. He usually won at poker too, notwithstanding the fancy footwork that was going on with Alice under the table. He went along with that old poker adage – if you can't spot the mug at your table in half an hour, it's you! He relished that moment when the atmosphere became taut to breaking point and the game was played out in silence but for the orchestra of insects outside.[57] Joss was of course an excellent bridge player, remembering easily which cards had gone into each trick.

The parties at Muthaiga during race week were notoriously wild. Evenings began with sundowners in the peristyle before dinner, and the celebrations lasted well into the night. According to one who saw it all for himself:

> The gayest and most light-hearted community in Africa was to be found amongst the British settlers in Kenya, possibly because the Highlands, where most lived, were 7,000 feet above sea-level and this seemed to stimulate gaiety and exuberance. Many lived and worked on the farms that had developed from a country previously uncultivated and uninhabited bush. This was a community mainly of young people who worked hard and played hard and enjoyed life. The leading Muthaiga Country Club was the scene of many of the evening festivities. These would start very correctly with men and women in full evening dress gravely sipping glasses of sherry before dinner. By the end of the evening the company would probably be playing some riotous game or if an occasion such as New Year's Eve, dancing round a bonfire in the garden. [On one occasion] six people were placed at the same table in the luncheon tent at the race meeting in Nairobi, who had by chance all been married (to one or the other) before . . . An air of restraint dominated until one of the men broke the ice, observing that it was quite like an old comrades' dinner.[58]

After race week, back to the Wanjohi Valley the Hays and the de Janzés would go, for another month or so of isolation.

While out riding one morning, Frédéric and Alice discovered a lioness with three cubs hiding under some rocks and went regularly to the lair to observe them. Soon afterwards two young Indian princes with an older ADC called at Wanjohi Farm to invite the Hays and the de Janzés to come for dinner at their camp. They accepted gladly and discovered the camp was supplied with every luxury. The hunters displayed their trophies, 'a greater kudu and two lion skins'. When Frédéric found out where these had been shot, he realised the princes had found their family of lions. 'But didn't you see any cubs?' he asked. No, they had only seen the male and female, who had charged so they shot them both. Next morning Frédéric and Joss rode out to look for the cubs. 'The poor little brutes had starved for three days, one was already dead, another died that night.' Frédéric and Joss were angry with the hunters, for they believed that the killing of a female 'of any of the species' was a crime.[59] Samson, the surviving cub, remained with the de Janzés, and gradually the dogs, ponies and even Valentino the baboon accepted him. Samson and Frédéric established a deep rapport. When Frederic fell ill with malaria, Samson would sit by his bed like a dog, waiting for his master to regain health.

They all had adventures with wild animals. One insistent elephant wandered up the valley from Laikipia on to Slains, trampling the Hay *shamba*. Joss would not allow anyone to shoot the animal but, needing a gunshot to scare it off, sent over to a neighbour for help. The neighbour appeared with a large rifle and some servants, and this shooting party succeeded in driving the elephant away, getting within a hundred yards of it, into thick forest. Then it came swiftly down wind, having heard the men, ambushing and knocking the helpful neighbour down with a side slash of its tusk. The man squirmed between the elephant's front feet as it dug around with its trunk. He then claimed he stuck his fingers in its nostrils and was finally saved by being kicked backwards into a clump of thorns. Dr Henderson of Nakuru treated him for three broken ribs and a dis- located shoulder, 'all in return for the kindness of loaning his gun'. He was black and blue all over.[60]

Samson disgraced himself at the first party that the de Janzés gave at Wanjohi Farm. The place was 'hectic with twenty people staying, in and about the tents in front of their big veranda, and the courtyard at the back . . . was cluttered with cars'. The African staff loved entertaining and parties, notwithstanding all the additional work. Guests often brought their own cooks with them, who were 'bringers of news from afar' for the household staff. Africans are born chefs. The local staple diet is *posho* – maize meal – hardly varying over the years, and yet they astonished their employers with their diverse repertoire. Idina's chef whipped up omelettes as light as air, or produced paupiettes of sole or truite meunière for as many guests as was wished, often at short notice. At Wanjohi Farm, every bench, easy chair, camp chair and dining chair had been brought into commission, and, 'for once the table looked magnificent with a tablecloth and all necessary "adjuncts" in their place'. Samson, 'much petted and spoiled', soon got into the party spirit. Frédéric, changing indoors, heard the first crash: 'I was in my bath ... a towel, a leap and I was rescuing the table fittings where Samson tugged determinedly – a sparkle of fun in his eyes. A broken plate, sundry glasses on the floor – he was thoroughly enjoying himself.'

Everyone contributed to their 'Dutch treat party', where Joss and Frédéric, 'mere abstainers', handed out cocktails. Joss would mix the fashionable drinks of the day expertly, shaking up Manhattans and Martinis. Cocktails and jazz were expressions of modern life which Idina and Alice had brought from Paris. From Naivasha, the two newcomers Major and Mrs Ramsay-Hill had brought along stout and champagne because Molly's favourite cocktail was Black Velvet, a mixture of champagne and Guinness.[61] Idina's tipple was gin and orange bitters. During the main course at dinner Molly Ramsay-Hill suddenly leapt to her feet and let out a wild shriek as a servant dropped a bowl of mayonnaise down her back, having tripped over Samson. Now, as Molly retreated to clean herself up, she too almost tripped over Samson's outstretched paw. Someone leapt forward in time to prevent a heavy fall. 'The good lady took a lot of pacifying ... dinner came to an end without interruption.'

The de Janzés' party went on until just before dawn, as parties so often did in the Wanjohi Valley. No one would appear before 10.30 next day, giving the servants a chance to clean up before 'brunch' when jollities would get going all over again. That particular morning the hosts found themselves summoned 'pretty bedraggled from our chambers by a frantic shout'. Frédéric draped himself in a towel and went to investigate: 'The eldest souse of us was sitting up in bed and gesticulating', claiming that there was a lion in bed with him. After upsetting, almost literally, Molly Ramsay-Hill the night before, Samson had wandered off and quietly gone to sleep in a bed in one of the tents. Being too inebriated to notice, the tent's owner had clambered into bed and slept soundly until Samson decided that it was time to get up and crawled out, waking the 'old fellow who naturally thought he had DTs'. It took all of an hour 'to fortify the jittering guest'.[62]

The harmony between the Hays and the de Janzés was broken not long after the de Janzés came to live in Kenya by what Frédéric would call the 'infernal triangle' – not that between Joss, Idina and Frédéric, but one formed by the sudden appearance in their midst of Raymund de Trafford. Raymund, a bachelor, was a very heavy drinker and a notorious womaniser, who suffered from chronic asthma. He fell heavily for Alice and decided soon afterwards to buy a maize farm, Kishobo, at Njoro, on the far side of Nakuru from Wanjohi Farm. Raymund's intensity and violent moods imposed on the serene, live-and-let-live friendship between the two couples. He had a ferocious temper when drunk and would argue viciously with Frédéric about literature. Both the Hays and Frédéric were surprised by his persistence, having expected him to disappear and their happy foursome to resume its previous calm intimacy. However, Raymund continued to come and go, mostly at Alice's whim, following her about until they eventually married in 1932.

Already by the late 1920s the days of unbroken bonhomie were over: Idina grumbled to her friend Nina Drury about the upsetting of the Wanjohi applecart.

6

Oserian

'Love in a palace is perhaps at last
More grievous torment than a hermit's fast.'

Keats, from 'Lauria'

The Wanjohi applecart was upset in more ways than one, Raymund
de Trafford being not the only interloper into the intimate circle of
friends. Although Idina had not realised at first that Joss was conducting a serious affair on the other side of Lake Naivasha with
Molly Ramsay-Hill, Frédéric had soon guessed what was going on.
'They had been lovers for six months,' he wrote in his memoir;
'under some excuse or other, Joss managed to be with her as often
as he could.'[1] Joss's ability to confine his activities to discrete pockets
of secrecy was already firmly entrenched. He was a superb compart-
mentaliser, keeping various relationships and potentially explosive
situations ticking over, so that everyone concerned remained more
or less content.

At the time Joss first met Molly Ramsay-Hill in 1926, she was
thirty-four and 'incredibly pretty still', even if her ankles were thick
and her legs were best ignored. If Joss's looks and charm dazzled
her, his title dazzled her even more. Molly was a sexually experienced
woman with a powerful intuition, recognising at once that women
were Joss's weakness, and with enough common sense and experience of men's sexual appetites not to believe that he would remain
faithful to her.[2]

From the age of sixteen, Molly seems to have made up her background as she went along. All that was known for certain was that
her fortune was hers independently. Joss seemed not to care about

her origins. He seems never to have questioned her claim to be an heiress to Boots the chemists' fortune and Molly successfully convinced everyone else of it in Kenya as well.

When Molly was born on 3 November 1893, her father Richard Watson Maude worked as a clerk at Crystal Palace in London and, by the time Molly was three, had been discharged from his job for embezzling funds on season-ticket sales and had gone bankrupt. Twelve years later, creating a second scandal in the family, Molly fell pregnant. Older men had begun to make sexual advances to the petite and beautiful Molly Maude by the time she was fifteen. She had been ripe and curious about sex and had responded with alacrity. Guy Hughes, her twenty-eight-year-old boyfriend, married her when both sets of parents had insisted on legitimising the child. On 21 July 1910, Molly Maude became Mrs Guy Hughes and their son, Kendrick, was born five months later. Guy Hughes departed for France in uniform soon after the outbreak of the First World War. When the war ended the couple were legally separated. Hughes agreed to pay Molly £424 per annum on condition that Kendrick Hughes remained with him.[3] Molly was only twenty-one. Desperate somehow to make a fresh start, she moved to Cairo in 1922 possibly as the mistress of an army officer, guessing that Cairo would offer far more opportunities to meet well-to-do cavalry officers – and better still a new husband – than back home in England where her reputation was so tarnished. She was right. Enter Major Cyril Seys Ramsay-Hill, who was three years older than Molly and already married. Major Ramsay-Hill was smitten enough with young Molly to pay for the legal unravelling of both their earlier ties so as to make her his wife.[4] In Kenya it was generally believed that Molly Ramsay-Hill was worth £30,000, from which she derived an annual income of about £8,000.[5] Where she acquired her wealth remains a mystery to this day, though perhaps her manipulation of Ramsay-Hill prior to their divorce gives us one or two pointers.

Molly handled men with the skill of a courtesan. Ramsay-Hill's collection of pornography can only have diversified her range of sexual techniques. She would always somehow bring up the subject of sex with young bachelors, knowing it would make them feel awkward and well aware of the power that could wield.[6] She had no qualms about using her charms and money to secure a title for herself, which she had determined to do from the moment she met Joss. By the age of thirty-four, she was practised enough to bag an aristocrat.

Joss must have been impressed by this beautiful creature, who was even more experienced in the boudoir than Idina. Her immense wealth cannot have escaped him either. He admitted to a friend that in his experience lovemaking was reduced to duty after three years with the same partner. By now Idina was 'only a drain on his vitality'.[7] After Dinan's birth, Joss and Idina had drifted apart, casually indifferent to one another's infidelities. Idina was having a 'blistering affair' with Boy Long at the time that Joss and Molly were starting to come out into the open about their own affair. In the future, Genessee Long would always be jealous if Boy so much as glanced in Idina's direction.[8]

When his grandfather died in July 1927, on the eve of the royal visit to Edinburgh – which lasted upwards of a fortnight – Joss went to London where he met his parents and Gilbert and his first wife Rosemary to attend the funeral. It was held at South Ascot Church on 13 July, and the casket containing the 20th Earl's remains was escorted from the station by a detachment of the Royal Horse Guards (the Blues). The King and Queen sent a message of sympathy to the Dowager Lady Erroll and the Princess Royal sent a wreath. The death of his grandfather meant that at least Joss could count on a small income of his own, about £300 per year, whereas his father, the 21st Earl of Erroll, was saddled with heavy death duties.[9]

Since Molly Ramsay-Hill had followed Joss to London their affair must have been steady and serious by now, though it is highly unlikely that he introduced her to his parents. It would seem from arrangements that followed upon their return to Kenya, however, that Joss and Molly were plotting to get married. Molly returned to Oserian in November 1927, and on 17 December she took Ramsay-Hill to see Walter Shapley of the solicitors Shapley, Schwartze & Barratt, having persuaded her husband to sign over to her 'an undivided half share and interest' in their palatial house.[10] Prior to this the deeds to Oserian were in Ramsay-Hill's name only and Molly must have realised that were she to separate from him she stood to lose her wonderful home. Joss, no doubt, did not discourage her – she had after all used his lawyer for drafting the new deed to Oserian – and Ramsay-Hill seemed, incredibly, to be oblivious to her motives.

Idina's and Joss's marriage came unstuck in 1928 when Joss declared that he wanted to marry Molly. That January the couple appeared together on probably the first, and definitely the last, occasion as Lord and Lady Kilmarnock, when Michaél Lafone married Lady Elizabeth Byng, the Earl of Stafford's daughter, at what was described as Kenya's largest society wedding.[11] Ramsay-Hill offered them Oserian for their honeymoon.

Less than a month after the Lafone wedding Joss's father also died, very suddenly, aged only fifty-two, on 20 February in Coblenz.[12] As British High Commissioner at the Inter-Allied Rhineland High Commission, he was given a state funeral, held on 23 February. This untimely event came as a great shock to his mother and Joss decided he must return to Europe immediately, even though he could not be in time to attend the memorial service at St Margaret's, Westminster. His mother had not the strength, after the state funeral in Coblenz, to go through another service in public and she did not attend 'due to illness'.[13]

Ramsay-Hill and Idina were now to be the victims of Joss's impulsiveness. Joss had capitalised on one of Ramsay-Hill's absences on safari to persuade Molly to throw up everything for him and come with him to London to see his mother. She was the one who paid for the tickets. The major returned from the bush with his gun-bearer Zubeiri only to find that his wife had gone. Molly's house-servant Sabweru had told him that Memsahib had packed a suitcase only a short while earlier and had gone with Bwana Hay to the station at Naivasha. Ramsay-Hill was furious. His reaction was to grab a pistol and, with Zubeiri and another servant, set out for the station, only to find that the train had left already. Ramsay-Hill now drove in a rage to Nairobi, knowing that he could beat the train to its destination while it was slowly chugging up the escarpment. He passed it near Kabete and raced on into Nairobi, but had obviously by then thought better of shooting Joss and hit on the idea of thrashing him instead. Ali Khan's transport company met every train and he himself would be at the station with one of his horse-and-carriages, carrying a traditional rhino-hide whip. Ramsay-Hill seized Ali Khan's whip as he ran on to the platform to wait for Joss to alight from the carriage, then 'in full view of the other passengers' he set about him with the whip.[14] Years later, after Joss's murder, this incident was made much of, driving home in the public mind the connection between Joss and the blind, vengeful outrage of a cuckold. However, the real sting in the scandal at the time was not so much the adultery as the fact that Joss, a white man, had received his redressal publicly in front of a mixed audience of Europeans, Indians and Africans.[15] Somehow some of the story managed to filter through, in exaggerated and distorted form, to the mourning party in Coblenz, which must have come as a blow upon a bruise to poor Lucy Erroll. Bettine Rundle had heard that Joss had been set about with a riding whip by a husband who had caught his wife with him *in flagrante delicto*.[16]

Joss and Molly spent several months in London and Europe in 1928, Joss having succeeded to the earldom. Dinan was now his heiress. According to friends, there had been no acrimony between Joss and Idina over getting a divorce. 'She always adored Joss, and the divorce seemed not to matter.' The Ramsay-Hills did not part amicably. Molly somehow managed to get the major's half of Oserian in her settlement. It is doubtful he would have given up his share in this sumptuous residence without a struggle, but then Molly was well aware of the contents of the locked room at Oserian which had been specifically designed to safeguard his pornography, ownership of which was illegal. Her knowledge would have been a useful lever in negotiations. The loss of Oserian had not been one of her fears during her difficult and much publicised divorce.[17]

In June of that year, the *Daily Express* covered the divorce proceedings initiated by Ramsay-Hill. Mr Justice Hill's summing-up was a scalding indictment of the guilty parties, calling Joss a blackguard and Molly a woman of low character, though 'that may be largely due to the influence of the co-respondent'. In fact, for all the vilification he received then, as well as after his death, this was the only occasion on which Joss was cited as a co-respondent in a divorce suit.[18]

As much to escape the opprobrium as to broaden their horizons, Joss and Molly went travelling. It made sense to avoid society while they waited for their divorces to become absolute.[19] They decided to take a look at America, Brazil and the Argentine, visiting Buenos Aires among other places. Molly loved to travel and took her house-servant Sabweru with them.[20] Sabweru had been employed by her since she first settled in Kenya and he accompanied her when-ever she stayed with friends overnight locally, as well as on trips abroad.

Joss and Molly lived openly together on their travels. As a sop to convention they had booked into hotels as 'Mr and Mrs Hay'. While on the Continent, Molly had given Joss a dog, called Boris, a languid white and tan borzoi hound. In return he gave Molly a black schip-perke, a tiny, tailless creature with very mobile, erect, triangular ears. They will have laughed over the difference in the heights of these two much favoured pets – reflected in themselves. In January 1930 they acquired a pied-à-terre, 46 Ashley Gardens, just off Victoria Street, which was to be their London base until they died. The flat was contained in an Edwardian brick building with its entrance directly opposite the iron gates leading to the Westminster Cathedral Choir School, along one side of the Cathedral itself.[21] During the week before their wedding, Joss stayed at St James's Place Hotel in Bury Street while Molly occupied a flat in Pall Mall.

Joss's divorce from Idina became absolute on 5 February. During the course of the next three days he drew up a new will, leaving Molly all his worldly goods – another victim of her manipulative skills. They married on 8 February 1930, at St Martin's Register Office.[22] Winifred Moreton and Clemment C. Dennis were the witnesses and, for all that is known about them, they could have been hailed off the street. On their marriage certificate Molly is described as being of 'independent means'.[23]

Once she became Countess of Erroll, she abandoned usage of the name Molly. 'Nobody in Joss's circle called her anything but Mary.'[24] Behind her back, though, for the rest of her days she would be referred to as either 'Molly Countess' or 'Miss Boots'.

On 15 February Joss and Mary boarded the SS *Modasa* at Beira on the east coast of Africa, bound for Mombasa. They had flown to Beira in the Furnesses' private plane, and there Viscount Furness also joined the ship. His wife Thelma had been part of the bohemian Anglo-American set Joss mixed with in Paris. The Furnesses would often drop in on Oserian by plane when visiting the colony to go on safari. Thelma was then the mistress of Edward, Prince of Wales, who was on board already. Joss and Mary were in a hurry to reach Mombasa to catch Prince Eugène de Ligne of the Belgian royal family with whom Joss had stayed as a small boy. Prince Eugène was on his way home to Europe from safari in Kenya. Joss and Mary appeared on the ship's list as Mr and Mrs Hay, possibly erroneously, or as a joke recalling their travels as an unmarried couple; or perhaps, now that they really were the Earl and Countess, calling themselves plain Mr and Mrs Hay would have appealed to Joss's sense of the ridiculous.[25] Edward Prince of Wales and his entourage, consisting of Joey Legh, Brigadier General G. F. Trotter and Major J. R. Aird, were heading for Mombasa too.[26] 'Edward P' was returning to Kenya for a second safari, following his earlier hunting trip in 1928.

Joss and the Prince of Wales had views in common and would have had plenty to talk about. The Prince's reaction to the sacrifice of thousands of young lives in the Great War was similar to Joss's and they both blamed the Old Order for the slaughter. Joss was already forming opinions on governance, following his travels in South America to countries which coincidentally the Prince had also toured a little earlier. Naturally there would have been discussions about women. They shared a preference for older women. The Prince of Wales and Joss already enjoyed mutual friends in Kenya and elsewhere. Denys Finch Hatton was known to both as an excellent friend and hunter. The Prince had backed Denys's recent campaign for getting the Serengeti protected, which insisted that game should be shot with a camera rather than a gun. Once at Oserian Joss would take up the hobby, taking pictures of the wild animals on his own estate. Sadly, none of the photographs he took survived the police raid on Oserian after his murder.[27]

The two would very likely have discussed white settlement of Kenya, on account of the series of engagements that the Prince was called upon to attend, a duty he called 'princing'. Like Joss, the Prince took the part of the settlers, questioning the wisdom of handing over land into which a lifetime of effort had been invested in meeting every challenge, including drought, locust invasions and slumps in world prices, among other disasters. The Prince argued, 'Why should they who have been pioneers in Kenya for thirty years, who have taught the natives everything they know, and who know them far better than any official ever could, why should they submit to a policy of equal rights with natives and Indians which would change their position of "bwana", or master, out here to that merely of the white section of the population?'[28]

A few days after leaving Beira, the *Modasa* docked at Mombasa. Joss and Mary arrived back in Kenya to find the colony staggering under the first blows of the world Depression. As the author of *Happy Valley*, Nicholas Best, observed:

> In a sense the Depression helped to sort out the wheat from the chaff among Kenya farmers, for it enforced with a vengeance the Darwinian principle of survival of the fittest. Only those who really knew their jobs were able to weather the storm . . . Two other factors worked to Kenya's advantage during the Depression . . . The gold fields at Kakamega came into production . . . And it was discovered that good-quality pyrethrum flourished at an altitude of 8,000 feet or more, producing a high yield that enabled Kenya to break the world monopoly of the crop shared previously between Yugoslavia and Japan.[29]

After two years' absence Joss was happy to be home, but the world and Kenya had been affected economically as commodity prices had begun to drop. Delamere's campaign to promote 'the solidification of the white ideal' in Kenya, Tanganyika and other Central African countries had ended with the economic crisis. Although D had been appointed KCMG for his public services in 1929, by now the British

Government had veered from the belief prevalent in Northey's day – 'that our main policy and legislation should be to found a white colony' – to the Duke of Devonshire's view that primarily Kenya 'is an African territory, and . . . the interests of the African natives must be paramount'. D could never bow to this arrangement. The year 1930 would see his last deputation to London to put forward the colonists' point of view to the Labour Government.

In Joss's absence D had married again, in May 1928. His new wife Glady Markham was a glamorous woman, who masked her face under the fashionable heavy white make-up and drifted about in a cloud of Chanel No. 5. Her other trademark was the gardenia she always wore on her lapel. Glady's energy was as abundant as Joss's; they became close friends in their joint concerns about the running of the colony following D's death in 1931, but they were never lovers.

Idina had sold Slains even before her divorce from Joss was made absolute. Now she had built a similar property on the far side of Kipipiri adjoining the Kinangop, called Clouds, to which Dinan would come and go like a migrating swallow. To his lasting regret Joss could never count on when he might see Dinan. He was 'deprived of all that lovely childhood and youth', he confided to a friend.[30] Joss was anxious that Dinan should be part of his family. When in England in 1937 for the coronation, he arranged for her to meet her cousins Alastair and Laura, his brother Gilbert's children. Joss was good with children and was particularly kind to friends' daughters who were of the same age as Dinan. His friends interpreted this as his way of compensating for her absence. For all that, he managed to see Dinan now and then, as she was always shuttling to and fro between Kenya and England with Idina. One day when Joss was sitting on the Norfolk Hotel veranda a small girl had come trotting along. 'Come to daddy,' he had called out to her. Pat Fisher, one of Chops Ramsden's managers, not recognising Dinan, mistakenly believed that Joss had been making a joke in poor taste. Forty years later, when Mrs Fisher's version was quoted in *White Mischief*, Diana Broughton, by then Lady Delamere, was so incensed by the light in which her remarks painted Joss that she cut her dead for the rest of her life.[31]

Friends were quite frank in their opinion of Joss's second wife: 'Joss would never have married Mary, had it not been for her money.' No one could ignore the discrepancy in their ages: 'They were a most ill-suited couple.'[32] After all, she was thirty-seven years of age when she became Countess of Erroll and Joss was only twenty-nine. However, her well groomed looks and 'animated personality' were definite assets. Even though Joss was not a snob, he would never have considered taking her as his wife, given her precarious start as Richard Maude's daughter, unless she could appear well bred enough not to irritate his sensibilities.[33] Joss recognised that their backgrounds were not the same and helped her to redefine herself, taking a hand in choosing her clothes, insisting that she wear black and white rather than gaudy prints. After marrying Joss Mary seldom wore anything more ostentatious than beige. She never attempted to hide her curves; in contrast to Idina's svelte style, she favoured tulle and furs. Joss took her to Norman Hartnell to create the best of these fluffy concoctions. Mary's trademark became two silver fox furs.

In November 1931, not entirely unexpectedly, Lord Delamere died at Loresho, a terrible loss for the European settlers. His health had been in decline for some time and Joss, who had known D far longer as a widower than as a married man, had been concerned over his worsening condition. Glady buried him at Soysambu, on the land he had loved, in accordance with his wishes. Joss and Mary, Boy Long and his wife Genessee, among others, attended the funeral. Genessee's diary entry shows the respect accorded to D: 'The Maasai have always revered Delamere ... a great many of them came ... carrying spears and shining from head to toe with red mud. The elders wore karosses [hyrax-skin cloaks] and carried sticks, to show their age and dignity.'[34] Joss was determined that D's contribution to the colony should not be forgotten. Four years after his death he came up with the idea of perpetuating his memory by renaming 6th Avenue after him. Indeed, this main thoroughfare did officially become Delamere Avenue after the war.

For all the criticism levelled at Joss's second marriage, according to Derek Erskine who knew them both well, 'Mary proved to be quite an inspiration [to Joss]'. 'After the odium of the divorce' Joss began to settle down and to play an increasingly important role in developing the area's recreational facilities, and this was much appreciated by all with whom he came into contact.[35] In July 1932 he and other yacht owners around Lake Naivasha inaugurated the Naivasha Yacht Club. At the inaugural meeting, held at the Anglers' Rest, Joss was elected on to the club's committee as rear-commodore. The new club's aims were to encourage yacht-building and sailing by amateurs, and to promote racing and regattas, though it realised that it would take a while to get going because of the 'present depressed economical times'. Members were to be proposed, seconded and elected and membership was open to both men and women from all over the colony. It was hoped that a regatta would be held during the Christmas season.[36] Joss never lost his enthusiasm for introducing new sports into the colony. Even when heavily involved in local politics in the late 1930s he found time to put together a proposal for dog racing in Nairobi. As the entrepreneur Joss himself sent out circulars bearing his signature, intending, if sufficient support was forthcoming, to form a company with a capital of £10,000 for a greyhound racing club. He envisaged that Saturday night greyhound racing would become a regular fixture. All the details, from opening times to budgets, had been meticulously worked out.

Pat Donnelly, a teenager at the time who spent his school holidays at Sparks Hotel on the shores of Lake Naivasha near the Anglers' Rest, recalls that the Naivasha Yacht Club was eventually housed on what became known as Yacht Club Island, across the waters opposite the Anglers' Rest. To reach Yacht Club Island one needed to use a boat when the lake level was high. However, thanks to the drastic variation in the levels there were, and still are, years when the waters of Naivasha recede far enough to lay bare a path to Yacht Club Island. In 1932, Joss owned an ex-RAF launch which, compared to the other craft, was extremely powerful. Its engine was so fast that he was always the first to come to the rescue of anyone who got into trouble on the lake. Whenever he left his mooring at Yacht Club Island to return to Oserian he created huge waves, departing at great speed, curiously heedless of the danger of capsizing smaller craft at anchor near the same moorings. Pat Donnelly remembers Joss coming in and out of Sparks Hotel, and particularly his popularity: he made everything happen at the Yacht Club. 'Erroll was *the* social event on Lake Naivasha.'[37]

Joss's first public project was the laying-out of a proper polo ground for the newly opened Naivasha Sports Club, near the tiny trading centre. He laid it out and supervised its completion, setting new standards: 'It was the best polo ground in the country by the time Joss had finished with it.' He would inaugurate the first polo tournament, too, in 1934 – the gate for which would soon reach the substantial sum of £175. The project seems to have given Joss a taste for undertaking work for the local community. Gradually he turned his attention to other schemes, providing yet more facilities for Naivasha Sports Club, including a golf course, though he did not play the game himself, and a lending library. Yusuf Khan remembers being taken on by him as librarian and barman.[38] It was Joss who showed him the ropes at Naivasha Sports Club in 1933; after he had explained his duties to him, Joss had joked, 'Now you know everything, but just don't go trying to sign Club cheques.'[39] Later Yusuf Khan would observe Joss's entry into politics at close hand, in this very spot. He liked him as a man and would defend him against those who called him a womaniser, saying, 'It wasn't his fault that women liked him.'[40]

Whenever Joss appeared at the Naivasha Club house, women would greet him eagerly, running up to give him a kiss, as inexorably attracted as moths to a kerosene lamp on safari. 'They were mad about him.' Among the settlers' wives and daughters around Lake Naivasha 'Joss got away with metaphorical murder socially'. Married females permitted extraordinary liberties, such as allowing him to lift the hem of their skirt with the tip of his shoe – flirting outrageously. None made the slightest protest. Yusuf Khan recalls, 'Joss paid for everything for everyone at the Club. He was incredibly generous.'[41] By 1933 Joss was Naivasha Club president.

Joss kept himself busy at Oserian, which was as different from Slains as it is possible to imagine. Indeed, it was unique among colonial dwellings. A place of great architectural beauty, its Saracen castellations and two arabesque domes could be picked out in silhouette for miles across 'the little lake', as their section of Lake Naivasha was known. There was a gazebo, where one could read undisturbed and gaze over towards Crescent Island. The domes were obviously a source of great pride to Mary; later on she got Joss to persuade their friend from Rongai, Ginger Birkbeck, to paint one interior with a night sky representing the Milky Way.[42] The house sat upon smooth lawns which sloped down to the lake, edged by sun-stippled trunks of yellow-barked fever trees. Within the walled courtyard laid with Spanish tiles warm breezes coiled themselves pleasantly around a fountain, on whose rectangular walls perched six colourful ceramic frogs. Across the courtyard there were small rooms for the 'under-servants' and a 'dungeon-like feature' which contained the kitchens and probably quelled both noise and culinary odours. But however convenient in design, it was an arrangement that was to play havoc with the service of meals at Oserian.[43] Accommodation was lavish – there were five bedrooms, each with a dressing room and bathroom attached. For the master bathroom Mary had chosen a sunken black-marble bath, surrounded by black and gold mosaics.[44] The huge sofas and deeply cushioned armchairs, furnishing the many terraces as well as the rooms, spelled a home of even greater comfort than Slains had been.

Downstairs, delicate marble columns supported the arches. The library was 'pure Spanish' with its high coloured ceilings and heavy beams. Ramsay-Hill had furnished it with fifteenth- and sixteenth-century paintings, Spanish chairs with black leather seats, a painted Cordoban screen, and a long refectory table with a centre tablecloth of faded red velvet from the altar of the cathedral of Seville.

The drawing-room was huge with an inglenook fireplace, painted beams and a 'ceiling of brilliant colours'.[45] After she married Joss, Mary had brought back from London white polar-bear skins which were scattered in the drawing-room 'in a bizarre fashion'. Each of Oserian's rooms gave on to the inner courtyard.[46] Sweet-smelling plants and shrubs had been established in the six-foot-deep flowerbed where tuberoses, jasmine and night-scented tobacco plants gave off their perfume. Rainwater which fell in the courtyard was channelled through a conduit to a storage tank beside the house. Down by the lake there was 'a powerful pump' which sent water up to a large reservoir in the hills, and provided the house with great pressure for the bathrooms and the fountain.'[47]

The birdlife was superb. Wading birds picked their way delicately through water-plants in the shallows of Lake Naivasha; purple galinule, lily-trotters and Goliath heron fished, and pelicans lazily skimmed the water among tiny pied kingfishers and black-faced duck. Hyrax lived here as well, and their sounds mingled in the evening with the chorus of the frogs. The glassy mirror of the water could become churned up with surface currents in the afternoons; as the light altered dramatically, mean-looking white-capped waves would disturb the calm of minutes before. The bird-haunted shoreline of Lake Naivasha was to become the setting for Babar sur l'Île aux Oiseaux, thanks to Joss's friends and neighbours Captain Mario Rocco and his wife Giselle, whose yarns about Congolese elephants had been the inspiration for her cousin Jean de Brunhoff's Babar books.[48]

Oserian's new master began – subject to Mary's approval – to improve the existing facilities. Before long he added a squash court and extended the inadequate jetty.[49] This became the centre of activity at weekends. Fabian Wallis was a regular visitor, as he had been at Slains. Sailing had always been a favourite pastime of his and, through him, Joss would renew the pleasures of sailing experienced fleetingly with Bobbie Casa Maury, at one time the husband of Paula Gellibrand, Joss's friend from Paris days.[50]

Joss employed Jani Khan, a young Indian who was doing his apprenticeship at Fernside & Reliance Motors Ltd in Naivasha, on a part-time basis to look after the motorised appliances and cars at Oserian. The systems there were complex and modern: garaging for four cars, an inspection pit, a repair shop, motor generators and batteries for electric light needed a lot of expert maintenance. There was also the tuning and mending of the cars, a Ford V-Eight and the Oserian lorry – which Joss occasionally liked to drive himself – and the care of the boats. Joss nicknamed Jani 'Roman' – his second name was Rehman. This became a standing joke between them.[51] Jani adored Joss, acting as his and Mary's part-time handyman the whole time that they occupied Oserian, and only leaving to go into the Army in 1939.

Tennis, squash, riding, polo and yachting were all part of daily life at Oserian, plus the endless bridge parties in the evenings. Oserian had its own polo ground. When Jack Bunyan, a neighbouring dairy farmer, asked Joss whether he played squash racquets often, since he had his own court, he grumbled good-humouredly that he did not often get the chance – 'because I can never find anyone good enough to give me a game'.[52] A friend of Jack's who was a Cambridge blue in squash confirmed that Joss was hard to beat. Guests could choose between swimming in the lake or in the brand-new pool. As the day wore on Joss would hand out sundowners, adhering to his customary few sips himself, and offer cigarettes from the gold case he carried in the pocket of his shorts.

Joss and Mary gave annual Christmas parties for the children in the district, which were always anticipated eagerly. Joss had a pet chimpanzee, Jules, who was a great attraction with the lakeside children. Joss had known Jules since the chimp was a baby and had forged a strong relationship with him, referring to him as '*mon ami*'. Jules endlessly amused guests of all ages with his antics. The children believed that he only spoke French. They listened amazed as Joss talked to his pet in this foreign language.[53] The chimpanzee was treated quite simply as another member of the Oserian household. Jules reacted intelligently when spoken to and really did seem to understand precisely what was being said. Margaret McCrae* remembered him stealing the limelight at parties. 'Jules would grasp us around the ankles; our parents were terrified that he might bite us.'[54]

While Jules showed no signs of viciousness, as he grew up Joss had to keep him on a tether. He became boisterous, and much more of a handful. His performances lacked all inhibition and he took to hurling his water container, an old enamel chamber-pot that had lost its handle, with great effect so as to attract attention. One of his

---

*A relation of Kenya's famous cabinet-maker, Andrew McCrae, founder of the furniture shop in Nairobi.

favourite games was to wait for vehicles coming up the drive; as soon as he heard the engine, he would prepare his missile for launching. 'He was a very good shot. If the driver braked, the potty usually hit the windscreen, but if, in anticipation of this missile, the driver had accelerated, Jules hit the car in the back.'[55] Occasionally he threw stones too, though Joss always reassured people, 'Don't worry. He's a pretty rotten shot.'[56]

Jules' most engaging trick was smoking. When Joss offered his pet a Balkan Sobranie from his gold cigarette-case, Jules would carefully select the elegant black cigarette with its golden filter tip, and Joss would light it for him. The chimpanzee would then smoke this down to the tiniest stub, and stamp it out afterwards with one foot. As a luncheon party came to an end Joss would unleash him from his tether and allow him to wander through the dining-room, whereupon Jules would walk round the table inspecting all the wine glasses, emptying the dregs from each and handling the stemmed glasses delicately, without dropping or breaking any. Joss would then suggest that someone offer Jules an open packet of cigarettes. The chimp would enchant his audience, selecting and then tearing the cigarette in half; he would place one half unlit behind his ear, holding out the remainder to be lit, then puff away with deep satisfaction, placing the burning end in his mouth.[57]

Bathing costumes were taken along to the children's Christmas party at Oserian. Swarms of boys and girls would arrive, all dolled up in party frocks and smart outfits, changing to swim, then drying off and getting back into their party clothes before sitting down to a sumptuous tea. The highlight was trooping indoors afterwards with Joss and Mary to look at the Christmas tree, under which was a gift for each one of them. The Errolls 'were wonderful hosts, and always so generous and if Joss was always a tease, he was marvellous fun. We all adored him.' Margaret McCrae and her siblings and cousins remembered his car because each of its four doors was embellished with a small coronet.[58]

Kiki Preston's daughter 'Sister' sometimes came to the Christmas party. She taught the McCrae children 'a naughty rhyme':

Ask your mother for sixpence,
To see the new giraffe,
With pimples on his whiskers,
And whiskers on his arse.[59]

Joss thought this was hilarious and would chant it with the children. Toby Hemsted, the son of one of Joss's sailing companions, admired the shape of Joss's legs and 'longed to have the same type of legs himself, when he grew up!'[60] As adults, these children who had known and liked Joss all their lives had difficulty accepting the exaggerated stories that circulated about him after his death. In general the lakeside dwellers regarded the Errolls and their contemporaries as 'just ordinary people, including Lord Erroll. They merely enjoyed terrific parties and showed [us] every kindness.'[61]

Mary became a confident hostess, drawing from an eclectic list. Guests were recruited from overseas as much as within the colony. Joss, of course, had his experience in the Foreign Office on which to draw, as well as his cosmopolitan childhood with his parents entertaining royalty. Oserian welcomed distinguished visitors of state and royalty from all over the world. The Duke and Duchess of Gloucester were to stay there in the late 1930s just after the Munich Agreement; following their sojourn with the Errolls, the Gloucesters went on to visit the Duke and Duchess of Windsor in Paris. The Aga Khan and his French Begum enjoyed the Errolls' hospitality – Joss helped organise the Aga Khan's Silver Jubilee celebrations in Naivasha in the mid-1930s – as did every member of Nairobi's diplomatic corps. The German consul Baron von Plessen was a frequent visitor too.[62]

Excellent conversation and erudite political discussions on the problems of running the colony went on around Mary's dining table. Invitations from the Earl and Countess of Erroll were much sought after, and locally Mary and Joss became renowned for their hospitality and generosity. During the following eight years, for cosmopolitan society, Oserian offered an important balcony from which to wave. Joss was a consummate host. He 'was quick-witted, with an uncluttered mind . . . he took pains to know everybody and never forgot

a name or face. He treated his servants well. His memory was photographic.'[63] Others who had stayed at Oserian reiterated the view that
he was 'wonderful to his servants'.[64] His flattering knack of never
forgetting a name worked unfailingly in his favour with men and
women of all ages, colours and creeds.

Joss's sense of humour was often playful. Alluding to its Saracen
architecture, he famously called Oserian the 'Djinn Palace', but the
more obvious interpretation of the epithet – 'Gin Palace' – was the
one that stuck. (In fact, gin was rarely consumed at Oserian. Mary's
favourite Black Velvet prevailed.) Joss nicknamed Mr Curry, Pat
Fisher's manager, 'Damned Hot'.[65] He could mimic all the various
accents to be found in Kenya, each to perfection and much to the
amusement of his guests. At charity functions, he became more and
more in demand to make speeches or to compère, as he was reliably
entertaining in public too.

Over at Nanyuki lived a couple called Major and Mrs Baynes,
who in the thirties held private race meetings and gymkhanas on
their estate, Oltarakwai. Afterwards the Byneses would hold a dinner
for all the competitors at the Silverbeck Hotel, followed by dancing
to Appleby's band.[66] Mrs Baynes was 'a bit of a snob and . . . prim
and starchy'. On one occasion Joss agreed to compère the event –
which she considered quite a social coup. She was delighted when
her own pony, Tite, came first in two of the day's events, but when
she heard Joss's straight-faced announcement booming over the
loudspeaker, 'Mrs Baynes' Tite again', her sense of humour was
somewhat stretched. The spectators thought him hilarious. A couple
of years later at a Christmas gymkhana, Mrs Baynes' entry was called
Bustier (pronounced the French way). It is not difficult to imagine
the sniggers and guffaws when Joss announced the winner, 'Mrs
Baynes' Bustier' (pronounced the English way).[67]

Oserian was a natural watering-hole for the new Governor, Sir
Joseph Byrne, an Irishman, once the disapproving Grigg moved on
at the end of 1930. Byrne's appointment was significant for Joss
because he was the first Governor to recognise the younger man's
political potential.

In early 1932 his respect for Joss was reflected in an announcement

in the *East African Standard*: 'The Earl of Erroll . . . has been nominated by the Governor to fill the vacancy [for councillor] for the
lake ward on the Naivasha District Council.' For by the early thirties
Joss had begun to take a serious interest and an active role in politics.
Less than two years after his nomination by Byrne he was chairman
of the Naivasha District Council. In March 1933 he spoke at 'one
of the largest public meetings ever held in the Nanyuki' – 125
people attended. The aim of the meeting, held under the auspices
of Nanyuki Farmers' and Breeders' Association, was to register determined opposition to the proposed introduction of income tax into
Kenya. Joss's voice united with that of Major Ferdinand Cavendish-
Bentinck – they both expressed their convictions that the prospect
of income tax was driving capital out of the colony. 'There must
be cuts in Government's overhead expenses,' Joss urged.[68] A week
later, as Naivasha's delegate, he was off to the Kenya Convention
of Associations at Memorial Hall in Nairobi. Glady Delamere and
Major Cavendish-Bentinck attended too. The Convention of
Associations was a sort of settlers' parliament whose members gathered annually to debate on matters of policy, often at loggerheads
with decisions made by the Colonial Office in London. Joss soon
joined the Convention's executive.[69]

    As well as involving himself increasingly in local matters, Joss
busied himself from sun-up to sundown in the running of Oserian.
Down near the lake he grew lucerne as fodder, farmed a little, ran
a fine kitchen garden, and kept some cattle, a few good racehorses
and a string of polo ponies. In Joss's and Mary's absence – for
they travelled everywhere together – Marc Lawrence, whom Joss
continued to retain since leaving Slains, would take up temporary
residence at Oserian to pay out wages, oversee staff and keep the
polo ponies up to scratch. His children Joan and John would exercise
the polo ponies for Joss during their school holidays, riding into the
hills behind the house, getting close to big herds of zebra, kongoni,
Grant's and Thomson's gazelle, which they reported paid no attention to them.[70] The Lawrence children would fish for black bass in
Joss's little rowing boat, which was tied up to the jetty. Oserian
became a second home to them.[71]

Waweru, Joss's personal Kikuyu servant, also followed him from Slains to Oserian, where he became major-domo. Musa, his second houseboy, was taught to do floral arrangements for dinner parties by Mary.[72] Zubeiri Musyoke wa Ndunda, a devout Muslim, became one of Joss's permanent staff as *neapara* – in charge of the exterior staff and answerable, in his master's absence, to Marc Lawrence.[73] Joss liked to employ Muslims because he considered them disciplined and abstemious. When Zubeiri accompanied him to England on one of his visits, he allowed him to dress in European shirt and trousers, with the standard wine-coloured tarboosh which he would have worn with his usual *kanzu*.[74]

Joss's Abyssinian syce was a splendid horseman called Gabrab Marram. He was responsible for the gleaming tack and turnout of Joss's polo ponies, riding them over from Oserian to Gilgil, Rongai, or as far as Molo, about twenty-five miles away, and hacking them home the next day. By 1933 polo matches were played every Saturday.

Among the assortment of splendid residences built at intervals around the lake was a cluster of thatched rondavels occupied by Captain Mario Rocco, his wife Giselle and their burgeoning family. Mario was Italian, and Giselle was French and had already had two husbands; the fact that she knew Paris appealed to Joss, who knew the city so well; indeed, the Roccos had much in common with himself, being wealthy, well travelled and unconventional. The two couples were drawn to one another instantly. Giselle had studied painting and sculpture under Auguste Rodin, and following an extended safari she and Mario had entered Kenya from the Congo in 1929 while Joss and Mary were touring the Americas. Giselle had lost their first baby girl in New York, but now had one infant son, Dorian. Mary, who was hankering after a son of her own, was particularly kind and sympathetic towards Giselle.[75] Joss and Mary were both fond of Dorian; on his sixth birthday Mary gave him Moose, his first pony, a dun-coloured Somali.[76] Joss and Mario shared a love of the turf and of gambling.[77]

So keen on gambling was Joss that on impulse he decided to import by air at huge expense a pair of old-fashioned fighting cocks and a hen so as to breed from them himself. One evening, approaching the sideboard in the dining-room to carve the joint for his guests, he asked Waweru what manner of fowl the cook had prepared, since they had not been out bird-shooting. Waweru went to ask the *mpishi* and came back with the message that he had roasted the *kuku kidogo sana* – the 'very small chickens'. Joss was outraged. The air went blue. This was the only time, Mary claimed, that Joss ever showed his displeasure towards her – she should have checked the menu, he castigated furiously – rage being quite out of character for him.[78]

However, if Mary had slipped up over checking her menus, she was ever vigilant over matters concerning her land. The 'riparian question' concerned the imposing of boundaries on newly exposed land which, formerly covered by the lake water, was suddenly laid bare. It affected everyone living on the shores of Lake Naivasha. As early as 1928 lakeside owners realised that water levels altered cyclically. The Lake Naivasha Riparian Owners' Association was formed, and forged an agreement with the British Crown. Lines were drawn from the lakeshore boundaries of each property to a point at the centre of the large sheet of water. The agreement was that all land within such extended boundaries would become available to lakeside owners; Mary signed the riparian document in 1932, thereby 'adding gratuitous acres to her holding'.[79]

Joss's driving habits were as reckless as ever. By now he had a bright-red Buick – a coupé – a make of car he stuck to faithfully from then on. One day, he was driving along the Nyeri road with Mary beside him and Kamau, one of their Kikuyu staff, in the dicky seat at the back. Unlike Sabweru, Kamau was unused to sitting in a motor-car, so when the Buick hit a bump the poor man bounced out of the back, unnoticed by Joss. Mary tried to alert his attention but the noise when travelling at speed in an open-top car did not ease communication. Eventually, glancing in the rear-view mirror, Joss saw no sign of Kamau's head. He drew to a halt, and Mary told him that she thought they had 'lost Kamau about half a mile back', so Joss raced back down the road to where the unfortunate servant lay, groaning still from the impact of the fall. He did his best to reassure Kamau, as he complained that he could not move. They somehow lifted him into the car, and drove him to the nearest hospital for treatment. Kamau did recover but he would suffer pain ever after. He had damaged his back permanently.[80]

Joss's road manners were not always so dangerous, however. His neighbour Jack Bunyan remembers breaking down on the main road near Gilgil, and along came Joss at great speed en route for Rongai to lunch with Lord Francis Scott. Since Joss had divorced Idina and was showing signs of becoming a political colleague of some weight, his friendship with Scott had grown. 'Suddenly,' Jack recalled, 'Joss swept past me in a cloud of dust but, recognising me, kindly stopped and reversed back to the scene. "Are you in trouble?" he said, a little impatiently, "only I'm late for lunch at Deloraine."' Since the trouble was only a puncture, and having assured himself that his neighbour was all right, Joss 'looked quite relieved. I just had time to say, "Thank you for stopping" before he shot forward covering me in another cloud of dust!'[81]

Joss's hard driving took its toll on his cars. He was a frequent client of the garage mechanics at Fernside & Reliance. The easy fraternity he developed with the Asians who worked there enabled him to glean all that was going on in the close-knit small-town community.[82]

The aristocratic farmers, Comte and Comtesse Périgny, were neighbours of Joss and Mary along the shores of Lake Naivasha. Their estate, Kongoni, was vast. Whenever there was a party in full swing, they would hoist a red light to their flagpoles to let their lakeside neighbours know. At Comte Périgny's bridge tables Joss played 'high-powered bridge', often until the early hours of the morning.[83] Pépé Périgny and friends Gabriel Prudhomme and Lorna Swinburne-Ward, who came from afar by plane and car respectively, were all avid bridge players – as avid as Joss – and these three played frequently at Oserian too. Occasionally Kiki Preston made up the four. Joss quickly became close to Lorna, a generation older than him. When he was first introduced to her at Muthaiga Club, he took her on to the dance floor. She had lately arrived from India and was especially conscious of Joss's 'beautiful manners'. As they glided round the floor, making polite conversation, it suddenly dawned on her that she was in the arms of one of the seducers of

'Happy Valley', as the Wanjohi was already being referred to. Renowned for her directness, she exclaimed, 'I know who you are! You're a member of the huntin', shootin', fishin' and fuckin' set!' Joss was delighted by such forthrightness and declared himself 'enchanted'.[84]

In the other direction from the Pérignys lived Kiki and Gerry Preston. Kiki and Mary became close friends – not altogether a healthy influence on Mary. Kiki had a dubious reputation for introducing her friends to drugs, one victim being George, Duke of Kent, with whom she was involved for some years. Kiki would take out her silver syringe to inject herself, oblivious to onlookers. She had so much money that, as soon as her supplies were in danger of running low, she used to send her own pilot from Mundui to Frank Greswolde-Williams★ at Knightwyck in the Kedong to fetch a fresh batch of drugs. When Greswolde-Williams died in 1932, new suppliers had to be sought out by Kiki and other drug users. As a result, certain pilots became adept at smuggling, concealing their illicit but lucrative cargo by punching a small hole in their plane's wing fabric and hiding the packet of heroin or cocaine inside. A patch was then slapped over the hole with glue, and away they went.[85]

It was Kiki who initiated the drug habit in Mary, offering her doses from her own supplies. Mary was beginning to feel rather vulnerable, as she seemed unable to produce a son and heir for Joss. Signs of strain were apparent in her and her behaviour was becoming extreme. In 1933 Jack Bunyan, then twenty-two and still a bachelor, was delighted to receive an invitation from her to one of Oserian's renowned house parties. The young man was shocked however, when, encouraged by Mary Erroll, the conversation turned to European women settlers who were sleeping with their servants – a subject which in those days would have been deeply taboo.[86] Also at this house party were the District Commissioner for Naivasha, Mr J. W. E. Wightman, and his 'charming and beautiful wife'. Mary and Joss always invited a member from the administration to their

★A long-time settler in Kenya who became notorious as a drug supplier to the Happy Valley set.

house parties, which was quite unusual in an ultra-snobbish atmos-phere in which boundaries between settlers and officials were observed from the club house to the cricket pitch. On this occasion the house-party guests foregathered for sundowners around the Oser-ian art deco bar on the veranda, among them the author Sir Edward Buck who wrote *Simla, Past and Present*. Joss was interested in Edward 'Pass the Buck', as he called him, because by 1935 Buck was chairman of Amalgamated Press and Associated Hotels and of the Government of India's Audit Department.[87] Joss would fire his enthusiasm for Kenya, persuading him to visit the colony and having him to stay a number of times, specifically so that Buck could gain 'more shrewd impressions' for his articles.[88] In the late thirties Buck would be part of Joss's public relations exercise to promote tourism in Kenya.

The advent of the aeroplane in Africa in the thirties opened up travel to Joss's circle. Four newly introduced Hannibals, owned by Imperial Airways reduced the journey to London from Wilson Airfield in Kenya by nine days.[89] A number of wealthy settlers, such as J. C. Carberry, owned more than one aeroplane. Airmail was also introduced, speeding up written communication consider-ably.

J. C.'s third wife, June Carberry, was a 'bottle blonde' with a 'voice like a corncrake', her vowels accentuating her loud conversations.[90] Despite being considered not *comme il faut* by some of Joss's circle, she was accepted on account of her generous nature. She was com-patible with J. C. because she stood up to his bullying, taking on whatever unkind challenge he might present. He used to boast, 'Junie baby, my Junie baby would never be unfaithful to me', drawling out the words in his pseudo-American accent. However, J. C. had been overconfident. A mutual friend, Patsy Chilton, claims: 'But of course she was unfaithful. And she was unfaithful with Joss.' J. C. had not noticed the new collection of gramophone records that June had acquired, and which she played with greater and greater frequency as she relived her moments in bed with Joss, dancing on the makeshift dance floor at Seremai, the Carberry estate. Having thought that her extramarital relationship had gone undetected, June almost gave the game away when Diana Broughton entered Joss's life. In 1940 after a party at her home, having observed him and Diana together, in a jealous tantrum she smashed each gramophone record that Joss had given her.[91]

Another friend who was important to Joss in those days was Jack Soames, an Old Etonian settler and friend of Sir Jock Delves Broughton, who had come out to Kenya in 1920. Joss would drive the sixty-odd miles over the Aberdares to Soames' estate, Burgaret, at Mweiga in the Nanyuki area. The white hunter Bunny Allen would frequently help out his brother Dennis, who was Soames' manager. (When Bunny was not taking out hunting parties for Jack's guests, he would pick up such casual farm labour.) Bunny recalls an 'unmistakable whiff' about Joss's person whenever they played cricket or polo against one another, or happened to be in the changing rooms together. He could not identify the smell precisely. He was a ladies' man himself; to him the smell conjured images of Joss 'having just come from the bed of some beautiful woman', and he imagined that the scent Joss used must have 'turned him on sexually' because it almost smelled like a woman's perfume.[92]

In August 1933 the Erroll Cup race was held for the first time, with Joss as commodore of the increasingly popular Yacht Club. Joss envisaged the Erroll Cup as an annual event at which he and Mary would present the handsome engraved trophy, which they had brought back from London. The club was still 'very young', but there were more members every month and sailing was becoming one of the leading attractions of Naivasha. The maiden race for the Erroll Cup was a huge success. Joss had intended to lay out a course round a group of islands, but the presence of a herd of hippos near the north end of Crescent Island forced him to change his plans. He overcame the problem of the seasonal low water levels by having temporary landing-stages erected for the event, so that visitors 'walked up a long easy slope along the backbone of the island to Mr Wills' house', continuing to climb another half-mile to the highest point of Crescent Island. Ten yachts faced the starting gun, to sail a triangle of nine miles. The eccentric cattle baron Gilbert Colvile won in *Quest*.[93]

Single-minded in his devotion to cattle and sheep, Gilbert Colvile lived the life of a recluse, eschewing women entirely. He was virtually monosyllabic but Joss found him fascinating on the subject of the Maasai. He admired the way Colvile had learned to speak their language, cocked a snook at the establishment and adopted Maasai culture, chewing their snuff and forgoing all creature comforts as their Spartan lifestyle demanded. Where before he and Joss had been merely nodding acquaintances on the rare occasions when they had seen one another in Naivasha, they now became good friends, although by the end of the thirties Gilbert was such a recluse that he would send his ox-wagon to Naivasha with a servant to pay his bills, fetch his post and bring back supplies to his farm.[94]

That year, political events were taking place in Europe that cast a shadow over settler interests. The new German Chancellor, Adolf Hitler, was determined to claw back former colonies lost under the 1919 Versailles peace treaty, vowing to strengthen the Reich by doing so. Doubtless on account of Tanganyika's potential mineral wealth, that territory was one of the first under consideration. From 1933 onwards the German settler community in Tanganyika began to swell its ranks, a cause of unease in neighbouring Kenya.

Discontent was now rife in the colony. Lord Francis Scott, thoroughly exasperated with the Colonial Office over its income tax proposals, its views on Asian settlers' rights and the European settlers' lack of political muscle, among other things, arranged and chaired in secret a six-day meeting of the Convention of Associations at Naivasha Sports Club – a rather different activity from the club's standard offerings of golf or polo tournaments. Young Yusuf Khan, Joss's protégé, behind the bar as usual, witnessed the first meeting. The gathering appeared to be 'debating a proposal to kidnap Kenya's Governor so as to enforce their will'.[95] Possibly inspired by an earlier aborted plan in the twenties to capture the then governor Sir Robert Coryndon, someone had hit upon the bright idea of holding Byrne on Crescent Island. The owner of the island, R. B. Wills, offered it for this purpose. In a coup d'état, the Kenya Defence

Force* would take over. Before drawing the meeting to a close that Monday, someone recommended that 'Erroll be gathered into the fold'. Presumably Joss's and Byrne's friendship had barred the way initially to his inclusion. That these men imagined they could hold clandestine meetings over several days on Joss's stamping ground without his finding out seems unlikely. Perhaps the practicalities of keeping the meetings secret from him forced them to overcome their reservations.

Joss was duly summoned to the second meeting on the Tuesday morning. He drove up in his crimson Buick, dressed as usual in an open-necked Aertex shirt, shorts and tennis shoes. Francis Scott greeted him with Lord Egerton, and Wilfrid Havelock's father and other 'diehard generals'. They now outlined the crackpot notion of holding Byrne under house arrest in return for their 'own consti-tution': the Convention of Associations was proposing unilateral independence, wresting control of the colony away from Whitehall and into the hands of the European settlers. Yusuf Khan noted that Bwana Hay gave his standard response to any matter that required consideration: he formally sought permission to think about the proposal and promised to come back to them in two days.

On the Thursday morning a quite different Bwana Hay presented himself. For once Joss was in no laughing mood. 'I knew Bwana Hay well, but I had never seen him attired so formally' – in a pinstriped suit and tie. Yusuf Khan thought that Joss was so dressed to underline the seriousness of what he was about to say. He had never before seen him draw attention to who he was. The Earl of Erroll brought along with him half a dozen tomes from which to quote, but addressed the gathering with barely a glance at them. He was blunt about their proposal: 'Gentlemen, you are really over-estimating yourselves ... playing with the British Empire ... this will be the signal for the British Fleet to come to Mombasa. It will

*The Italian conquest of Ethiopia by early 1936 highlighted the fact that in Kenya the military forces were unable to provide adequate defence. The decision was taken to disband the KDF and to replace it with a battalion-strong volunteer force called the Kenya Regiment (territorial force) which was formed on 1 June 1937 (Malcolm Page, *KAR*, Leo Cooper, 1998, pp. 240, 294).

be the shortest-lived insurrection ever known and you will all be imprisoned. What about the Indian contingent in this country?' he asked, reminding them that they were, after all, Imperial subjects who belonged in Kenya because the British had brought them here. 'The Viceroy of India will become involved and the drums will roll.' The recriminations would be more severe than even they had supposed, he warned, and then brought his speech to a conclusion – 'if they thought that he, Erroll, would become a traitor to his country, then they were wrong'. Dismissing the power of the Convention of Associations, he warned them that they would also be 'no match – even for a day – for a Kenya Defence Force'. (In fact the KDF was already woefully inadequate. Ironically it was to be Joseph Byrne who set up the committee to review the local defence force.) The enthusiasm of the gathering cooled, and after Yusuf Khan had served drinks they disbanded, feeling somewhat stunned by Joss's admonishments.[96]

The following year Joss's political activities began to raise eyebrows among the establishment too.

7

Blackshirts in Kenya?

'Britain first, Dominions second, Foreigners nowhere'
Blackshirt slogan, 1934

On 21 April 1934 Joss and Mary took the Imperial Airways service from Nairobi, night-stopping at Khartoum, to spend the summer in London, basing themselves at 46 Ashley Gardens. The visit would mark Joss's entry into controversial politics.[1]

A week before his thirty-third birthday, on 3 May 1934, Joss paid his first visit to the Black House, on the King's Road in Chelsea, to sign up as a member of the British Union of Fascists. Three days later he and Mary were 'flash-shotted' at Quaglino's. Prince Otto von Bismarck, the grandson of the 'Iron Chancellor' and First Secretary at the German Embassy, was at their table, as were Lady Warrender, wife of the member for Grantham, and Lord Gage, a captain in the Coldstream Guards who was lord-in-waiting to the King. 'All the intelligentsia' had been to a private view of Duncan Grant's pictures and had supper together afterwards at Quaglino's.[2]

Tom Mosley* was the dominant influence in Joss's decision to join the British Union of Fascists. Since Joss and he had become friends in Venice in the early twenties, Mosley's political profile had risen considerably. In October 1932, following a visit to Mussolini in Rome in January that year, he had established the British Union of Fascists and set about, with some success, in converting Britain to the tenets of fascism. After the General Strike and the Wall Street Crash of 1929, popular sentiment supported the cause, which

*Oswald Mosley's friends called him Tom.

through protectionism seemed to reassert the primacy of Britain and its empire. Many believed at the time that Mussolini was sorting out disorder and, indeed, Musso was fêted in many English newspapers including Kenya's *East African Standard*. He was also on good terms with George V. In the late thirties there were rumours (inaccurate ones) among the higher echelons of Kenya's Civil Service that Mario Rocco was being groomed to take over as Governor in the event of Mussolini's successful invasion of Kenya.

When Joss and Mary arrived in London Mosley had just concluded plans to spread the fascist gospel in the colonies too. He aimed to impose the fascist system of government on the whole Empire, in fact. Through his increasing involvement in local politics in Kenya and his deepening commitment to developing his land, Joss was aware of just how profoundly disillusioned the settlers had become with government by Westminster. Somehow Kenya had survived devaluation of the rupee during the First World War, and the repeated devastation of its agricultural economy through drought and plagues of locusts, not to mention the Depression. But Joss and other prominent settlers believed that if Kenya's economy was fully to recover, the men on the spot must be allowed to make decisions without the endless delay they suffered through colonial adminis-tration.

Joss looked upon Mosley's brand of fascism as a solution to Kenya's problems. He added his voice to Mosley's rallying cry on behalf of the colonies: 'We must begin to organise our own Empire to take the place of foreign markets as they close against us. Empire trade must be developed in a long-term plan to make the Empire a great self-contained economic unit and to build within its border the highest standard of civilisation in the world.'[3] Joss, so keen to see Kenya's economy developed, and continually frustrated in his efforts by trade restrictions imposed by the mandate system and the Congo Basin Treaties, leapt at these ideas. He and Mosley both thought that Britain's Government was obsolete and tradition-ridden.[4] Mos-ley's plans for a new integrated market based on the development of resources in the British Empire especially appealed to Joss, who saw in it wealth creation and a constructive role for the colonial settler.

That summer of 1934 Joss trailed around after Mosley in London. Encouraged by Mosley, he steeped himself in fascist ideology, attending every rally, urging other like-minded friends to join him. He and Mary attended the January Club★ dinner at the Savoy Hotel in late May, where Tom Mosley was to speak. Other sympathisers to Mosley's cause were Sir Charles Petrie, Lady Ravensdale, Fruity Metcalfe, a close friend of the Prince of Wales, the Count and Countess of Munster and Mr William Joyce – who would later gain infamy as Lord Haw Haw and would be hanged as a traitor in 1946.[5]

A new fascist badge was produced with a small enamelled Union Jack and a miniature gold *fasces* mounted down the centre. Its purpose was to distinguish the nationality of the wearer, and so that 'British Blackshirts' would be made welcome while travelling in Germany. Joss liked the new badge well enough to have it copied in silver for the sporran badge he wore at the Blackshirt Cabaret Ball at the Prince's Galleries in Piccadilly on 27 June where Tom's mother Maud, Lady Mosley, spoke, as did Tom.[6] Lady Ravensdale was host-ess. The Blackshirt Dance Band and the Blackshirt Salon Orchestra provided entertainment.[7] In his speech that evening Tom Mosley urged that 'a great quickening up must occur', emphasising that 'having built a Blackshirt organisation throughout the length and breadth of the land, now we must create an electoral machine . . . which can mobilise the voting strength of this country behind the Blackshirts.' 'We know enormous strength lies behind us throughout the country,' he concluded.

Joss was impressed by the BUF leader, who saw himself as one of the great 'fact men of history leading his followers to a higher destiny'. His mood dazzled Joss, instilling in him a sense of the power that he might similarly achieve. The possibilities of himself becoming a leader in the colony occurred to him for the first time.

Far from being clandestine, Joss's and Mosley's relationship was

★The January Club was Mosley's front organisation, aimed at attracting respectable support for the BUF. Even Lord Lloyd of Dolobran lectured to members – with the proviso that he was never cited by the press. Lord Lloyd became Secretary of State for the Colonies in 1940. He died eleven days after Joss. The reason given for his death was cancer.

public at a time when it was not disreputable to be a fascist.[8] Witness Lord Rothermere's early support of the BUF which amounted to a campaign, beginning in January 1934 in his newspaper the *Sunday Dispatch* (later absorbed into the *Daily Mail*), in the form of weekly articles that sang fascism's and the Blackshirts' praises. Later, when Mosley's anti-Semitism became apparent, Rothermere would withdraw his support, but initially his commitment to Mosley had been strong.

However, less publicly known at the time was that the BUF movement was financed by Mussolini. To keep an eye on its activities, the Secret Intelligence Service employed W. E. D. Allen to infiltrate the BUF, posing as a paid-up member. Bill Allen was a friend of the de Janzés as well as of Joss. His friendship with Joss can only have helped him to report back to SIS on Joss's part in the BUF's activities – the British Government was somewhat disquieted to learn that the Hereditary Lord High Constable for Scotland had ambitions to act as Mosley's delegate in Kenya, and started to watch him closely. Joss and Molly were present at the most infamous of all Mosley's rallies, on 16 June 1934 at Olympia, where fifteen thousand Blackshirts congregated. The fascists and communists had come to blows and the police had charged the crowds. This 'Blackshirt style' of clashing with the police would culminate in 1936 in the battle of Cable Street, where six thousand police were in position in order to keep the fascists and anti-fascists apart. It is easy to understand the alarm signals that Joss's decision to act as Mosley's delegate in Kenya aroused.

The 22nd Earl of Erroll was nothing but an asset to Mosley. His title and the fact that he lived in Kenya attracted all the more publicity to the fascist cause in London and the colony. *The Times* covered his decision to represent Mosley in Kenya and, once this news was syndicated to the *East African Standard*, every move that Mosley made was covered extensively by Kenya's respected broadsheet. Joss had social standing. He was charming and witty. And not to be overlooked were his highly placed contacts – several uncrowned heads of Europe as well as the likes of Ribbentrop and Pétain. His fluency in German and French and his intimate knowledge of East Africa were bonuses. Indeed, it is likely that Joss was the reason why Mosley made Kenya his first target for converting the Empire to fascism.

In early July, Kenya learned that Lord Erroll had joined Sir Oswald Mosley's radical movement and that the 'Blackshirts were preparing for Kenya elections'. A week later – it took that long for such news to filter through – settlers were startled by the headline in the weekend issue of the *East African Standard*, 'BLACKSHIRTS IN KENYA? SPECIAL DELEGATE APPOINTED'. The article read: 'The Earl of Erroll, who is at present in England, has been appointed delegate of the British Union of Fascists for Kenya Colony. The Earl is reported to be returning . . . with a constructive and energetic plan to convert the Colony to the Blackshirt policy.'[9]

Unfortunately, also covered in that particular issue were the revolt of the Nazi stormtroopers and the 'bloodbath' in Germany, following the earlier arrest of General von Schleicher, when Dollfuss was shot dead. This news broke at a time when relations between Italy and Abyssinia were at breaking point. Kenya felt threatened. In addition there had been page upon page of coverage of Mosley's campaign, quite apart from Joss's new role. Everywhere, the initial reaction was of disbelief that numerous meetings had taken place between Erroll and Mosley.[10] But the announcement that followed a week later made clear Joss's commitment when he claimed, echoing Mosley's turn of phrase, that 'already much has been done by way of creating a Blackshirt electoral machine with which to fight the general election'. Every report, every interview and every syndicated release drew attention to the fact that Joss was 25th Hereditary Lord High Constable for Scotland and to his growing stature in Kenya, 'where he plays a prominent part in local affairs'.

Settlers were disconcerted by Joss's plans. Some wrote straight away after the first report of his intentions:

Another disturbing element is to be introduced into this restless Colony of ours . . . I refer to the Fascist movement otherwise known in Britain as Mosley's Blackshirts. The Earl of Erroll, it is reported, has been commissioned to convert this Colony to the Blackshirt policy. This policy, the slogan of which is 'Britain first, Dominions second, Foreigners nowhere', is gaining ground among a certain section of young people at home and is already responsible for some bloodshed in Great Britain . . . will Government permit this apple of discord to be planted in this territory?[11]

The Blackshirt – Mosley's official organ in Britain – undertook an interview with Joss, highlighting him yet again as 'Lord High Constable . . . and after the Royal family, the first subject in Scotland'. Joss underwent a series of interrogations by journalists. He appeared confident when the *East African Standard* representative asked why he had joined the Blackshirt movement: 'Chiefly because it believes in action, rather than talk. It is obvious that the present system tends to prevent, rather than expedite, action being taken to put right the affairs of the nation.'

When asked for his opinion of the House of Lords as a legislative body Joss was dismissive: 'I never go there. The House of Lords has no financial details to deal with and has very little constructive power at all. Indeed, it shows the obsolescence of the present form of Government.' Joss explained that he had 'plenty of ideas for converting the Colony to the new creed'. 'On arrival,' he went on, 'I shall get in touch with various people in the capital . . . who I know are favourably inclined towards the Blackshirt movement, and will so form a nucleus with which to work. Then I intend to hold a public meeting to expound the policy of the movement and point out how this policy, when applied, will be of enormous value to the future development of the British Empire generally and in Kenya in particular. I am certain that it will prove popular in Nairobi.'[12]

'What do you propose to do about the outlying districts?' the journalist asked.

'I will probably circularise with pamphlets the various farming districts . . . laying stress on the agricultural policy of the movement and also addressing meetings in these areas. Periodically, for example, at the time of the Agricultural Show or the Race-Meeting, when Nairobi is flooded with settlers from farming districts, I shall have a public meeting in the capital.' His headquarters would be in Nairobi.

In a press profile which was also syndicated to the *East African Standard* during the course of these weeks, but in which fascism is unmentioned, Joss emerges as a man brimming with leadership qualities. The journalist wrote of him: 'Among the representatives of one of our longest-established Scottish families . . . he became a landowner, concentrating as a farmer principally on cattle and cattle breeding . . . and it is well for us, who remain in England, to know how they are progressing.' Joss's contribution to the success of polo and sailing in the colony was acknowledged, as well as the fact that 'he has one interesting hobby, taking photographs of animals'.[13] Joss told London journalists about the thrust of his plans for the colony's future. He intended to develop the assets of Lake Naivasha, giving every encouragement to sailing 'in the delightful surroundings at 6,000 feet above sea level on the lake of an area of 84 square miles'. He predicted that Kenya Colony would become the holiday resort, the 'ruling paradise for fashionable England'.

By late July 1934, letters to the *East African Standard* editor in Nairobi had reached fever pitch on the matter of Joss's appointment: 'Sir – I hope and trust that our Government will, in timely fashion, put a stop to the establishment of any "Blackshirt" brigade in Kenya . . . No one can deny that the world is in need of greater intelligence to solve its problems today than appears to be at the moment available, but no one can make me believe that the Earl of Erroll, Hitler, Mussolini and Sir Oswald Mosley . . . can in any way assist by their united intelligences the destinies of the English nation.'[14]

The fiery third Indian member of Legislative Council, the Hon. Isher Dass, initiated questions about Joss's fascist intentions during a Legco debate, referring to the movement as 'the direct negation of all civil rights of liberty' and asking whether it 'meets with His Majesty's approval? If the answer is negative what action [does] it [intend] to take?' When in August the Secretary of State for the Colonies Sir Philip Cunliffe-Lister returned an answer to Isher Dass, he confounded everyone in Kenya with the following statement: 'This Government has no information regarding any introduction of fascism into the Colony. The second part of [Dass's] question therefore doesn't arise.'[15]

Isher Dass was a Punjabi who had overcome the contemporary barriers of racial prejudice and taken an English wife. He was a couple of years older than Joss, and their friendship had been forged despite the differences in religion and background; neither was hidebound by convention. Dass also became the first to support the African cause with revolutionary zeal. Joss respected his moral courage and found no fault with his flamboyance and passion for the opposite sex (a trait found in so many politicians), although this irritated other white settlers. Isher Dass's concern for the masses was unquestionable: in the eyes of the Indian contingent he was 'the people's man', and in 1939 Joss and he worked on the Manpower Committee for their respective communities. Both would end up with bullets in their heads – Isher Dass was shot about eighteen months after Joss. His murder, too, remains unsolved.

At the end of August 1934, Joss and Mary flew back to Kenya. Joss had brought back with him a substantial amount of literature on the BUF.

They found Kenya in poor shape on their return. Debates about taxation were raging. The colony had had no rain in February, keeping the land in ceaseless punishment, so that by now the heat and dust dominated and stretched the livelihoods of the farmers to breaking point. Water tanks had been empty for two months, and consequently 'everybody is in a hot-weather frame of mind, snappy and strung up'. Everyone agreed that Kenya's financial position was disastrous. Business had never been so bad and, in Nairobi, there had been 'one long drain of capital out of the country and they say they can't last more than six months. There has been no rain and the promise of bumper crops – whatever they are worth – has vanished'.[16]

Joss did not immediately campaign for the BUF on his return to Kenya, meeting other commitments first after the best part of four months' absence. For now, he threw his weight behind the Kenya Association, a project intended to promote new settlement in the colony. Founded in 1932 by James Mostyn Silvester, the Kenya Association saw an opportunity in transforming mismanaged land that was going cheap, turning derelict properties into viable concerns again. When Joss became involved with the Association, Silvester, or J. M. as Joss called him, was working in an office on the outskirts of Nairobi on the site of the old Nairobi saw mills. Silvester was 'a great man for the Kamba', and fluent in their language. He had a gift for vernacular languages, mastering Kikuyu, Kikamba and Kiswahili.[17] Joss admired his practical approach and keenly supported it. He helped J. M. acquire better offices within Memorial Hall, which housed Legislative Council. This new location, situated in the heart of Nairobi, saw the Kenya Association besieged with requests for land both by settlers who were potential farmers and by newcomers inquiring about prospective farms. Silvester's young daughter, Patricia, remembers just how much her father had valued Joss's opinion. Patricia met Joss in her father's office when she turned up during one of their lunch-hour meetings. 'I found them having a picnic meal together – fruit cake, peaches and strong tea – all from my mother's farm at Limuru.' Joss got up courteously, shook Patricia's hand and proceeded to ask her about her training as an art teacher. 'He was so nice looking . . . had so much warmth and charm for a tall and tongue-tied girl!'[18]

Another programme of the Kenya Association was to encourage settlers to raise their children in Kenya rather than send them to boarding school in England. It promoted the good local schools such as Loreto Convent, Limuru Girls' School and St Andrew's School at Turi. Joss went along wholeheartedly with the notion of keeping children in Kenya, having never forgotten the closeness of his own family during his childhood. His enthusiasm was an asset to the Kenya Association, and his persuasive manner encouraged better education facilities locally. Joss talked a good deal to J. M. about Dinan, expressing his deep regret and his feeling of deprivation at not watching her grow up.[19]

In mid-November 1934, on the evening following a triumph on the polo field, Joss, as Chieftain of Nakuru's Caledonian Society, made his first public speech since declaring his alliance to Mosley's party. Joss, the gifted performer, was on form. He would emerge from both events that day as a figure of success – a brilliant tactician on the polo field and a speaker of persuasion, capable of forthrightness as well as of subtle nuance.

The turnout that night at Nakuru's Rift Valley Sports Club was large – many had come a long way to hear Joss speak.[20] And he made an unforgettable impact – a towering six foot two and resplendent in full Highland dress. On either side of him were the two most important guests, Governor Sir Joseph Byrne and Lord Francis Scott, Leader of the Elected Members of Legislative Council and member for the Rift Valley constituency. Byrne had a nickname, Butty Byrne, a sobriquet arising from his habit of prefacing his every response with the words, 'Yes, but . . .'[21] Joss was one of the few people cheeky enough to call him 'Butty' to his face. After dinner he presented Byrne with 'a handsome silver quaich', and there was a toast to 'The land we live in'. Everyone was relaxed, replete with a good meal, settling comfortably into cigars and brandy, intending no doubt to pay only half an ear's attention to Joss's response to the proposers of the toast. However, he was about to make everyone sit up and listen.

It was tradition for the Chieftain to make reference to the important topical events – as Joss remarked humorously, 'every Scot [is], of course, a politician at heart'. He had chosen to speak of 'contrasting attitudes to present-day problems' – a mild title for what was to be a fairly savage speech. He delivered his message caustically, not only taking the assembled Scots by surprise, but reinforcing his collision course with the Colonial Office for his criticism of the Government's financial policy. He apologised for not providing the Governor with a copy of the speech, but pre-empted any comment on the oversight with the excuse that 'events moved so rapidly that to make the speech at all topical meant leaving the preparation of it to the last moment'.[22] Then he launched into his invective, tearing to shreds the most recent Government budget policy, keeping just within the boundaries of politeness:

At the outset, I want to state that what I have to say has nothing whatever to do with His Excellency personally. We all realise that the Budget speech was written for him by his advisers. There is one basic fact, however, that we must face at once and that is in spite of an apparently balanced Budget, and in spite of the fact that our tyrannical dictator, Sir Philip Cunliffe-Lister, in his usual presumptuous manner had the impertinence to inform the House of Commons a short time ago that this Colony was in a happy financial position, we are nevertheless bankrupt. If the Secretary of State for the Colonies believes that bankruptcy is a happy financial position for any Colony, then it is no wonder to me, that the Colonial Empire is staggering to the brink of destruction.[23]

Joss accused the Government of sheltering 'behind that [Expenditure Advisory] Committee without heeding the warning clearly given by it'. He scoffed at 'the entirely fictitious value placed on the revenue estimates', for it was 'quite obvious that the various Heads of Departments sat down and put any revenue figures they thought fit as their estimates, so long as the total added up to balance the expenditure' – 'in one breath His Excellency had said the alternative taxes had failed and in the next, that he intended to re-impose them next year'. Joss observed that to reimpose a failure seemed to him a paradox, 'but might only be an Irishism which my peculiar Scottish sense of humour failed to appreciate'. His audience were laughing but Joss did not let up, pointing out that the true reason that the alternative taxes failed was 'because the taxable capacity of the country was reached years ago'. 'It is no earthly good Government trying to draw the red herring of income-tax across the trail,' he admonished. 'This is not the time to discuss whether income tax is a good or a bad tax or whether the fiscal structure of this colony should be altered, and we are not to be taken in by the political ruse to split us on this point. The basic fact remains that we cannot afford any additional taxation whatsoever, whether it is income tax, graduated in-native poll tax or any other kind of tax. The only way left to balance the budget is by economy,' he concluded.

Joss again criticised Cunliffe-Lister for having told the colony 'in a high-falutin way that we must not lose our integrity'. He turned the tables and accused Cunliffe-Lister of hypocrisy for producing 'a Budget which made the subscribers to the Colony's loans believe that the financial position was much better than actually was the case'. In Joss's opinion: 'The only honest way is for us to lay our cards frankly on the table and inform the subscribers and the Government that although we have done our best we are unable to continue paying interest at the average the Colonial Secretary had suggested of 5.1 per cent on these loans and that if we do, we shall be inevitably forced to default'; but 'if they will accept the ordinary world rate of interest, we can carry on and they will get a decent return instead of nothing'.

Joss exhorted the Government 'to realise that this Colony is not only a playground for bureaucrats but a workshop for the primary producer, whether black or white . . . We are in such a state that we must cut out whole departments.' He went on to cite several 'glaring examples of extravagance'. Things would not improve by themselves, he warned: 'Improvements require help in the way of hard work and sacrifice.' The idea that things would be better next year was not only stupid but a gamble on 'something less tangible than gold – the weather'. Bringing his attack to a close, he besought the Government . . . demanded, 'as a right, that the policy of draft be abandoned'. He believed that the situation, hard though it was, would prove a blessing by making everyone pull together more, in order to build on solid foundations a structure that in future they could afford. 'Everyone who came to Kenya is determined to stay here and see the Colony through its crisis and on its feet again.' He then sat down to applause.

Sir Joseph Byrne, if not quite rendered speechless, hardly knew how to reply, admitting that he wondered whether the Caledonian Society was wise in asking the Governor to respond to the toast. 'At one time I understand that there was a reason for the unfortunate man was invariably expected to make what was called a political pronouncement . . . as seems to be the case this year', but not having had the chance to read the Chieftain's address beforehand and having 'delivered to Legislative Council, so recently, a long and sometimes none too popular speech', Byrne asked to 'be allowed on this night to cast care to the winds and to have the unfettered enjoyment of meeting you all and talking to you informally'.[24]

The establishment afterwards questioned the suitability of Joss's speech for the occasion. While it was usual for the *East African Standard* to publish extensive coverage of such annual dinners, never before had it justified such a sensational headline: EARL OF ERROLL'S OUTSPOKEN CRITICISM.[25] The Caledonian Society in Mombasa was so outraged that, at its first general meeting after the gathering, disapproval of Joss's speech was minuted and they sent Byrne 'a letter of apology for the way in which His Excellency had been treated'.[26]

Before the old year was out, Joss had started his campaign to explain fascism to his fellow settlers in various districts of the Rift Valley. Elspeth Huxley's mother Nellie Grant was present at the first of these meetings, when Joss addressed Njoro. Nellie recounted the events to her daughter:

> Last Wednesday was Joss Erroll's meeting at the Club – which took place on a Wednesday night – to explain British Fascism. There were 198 people there, no less, and a very good-tempered meeting, as everyone cheered to the echo what anyone said. British Fascism simply means super-loyalty to the Crown, no dictatorship, complete religious and social freedom, an 'insulated Empire' to trade with the dirty foreigner, higher wages, lower costs of living ... Whenever Joss said, British Fascism stands for complete freedom, you could hear Mary Countess at the other end of the room saying that within five years, Joss will be dictator of Kenya.[27]

Early in January 1935 Joss attended a general meeting of the Rongai Valley Association to address the same subject. 'Lord Erroll tried to show how British Fascism would benefit the Empire and particularly the Colonies.' Joss assured his audience that 'a Fascist Government at home would investigate every possible means of getting the crippling burden of interest rates on the Colonial loans reduced'. He elaborated: 'The British Fascist movement is entirely unlike the Nazi movement in Germany, which latter could not possibly be applied to England.' Outlining the aims of the movement, he thought that 'the

British capital which is invested in foreign countries could be very much better employed if it was invested in the Empire'. The corporate state was also a British fascist ideal, which Joss now summed up as 'Loyalty to King and Empire. National interests to have precedence. A self-contained Empire. Exclusion of foreign imports except of necessities'.[28] After he had answered a number of questions, a 'hearty vote of thanks was carried with acclamation'.

At the end of April 1935 a gathering of settlers for the Convention of Associations took place, where Joss, representing the Naivasha Farmers' Association, put up a motion 'on the importance of keeping the Convention alive'. Discussions for the reorganisation of the Convention followed, and Lord Francis Scott expressed agreement with Joss on the importance of keeping it in existence.[29]

By July tensions in Abyssinia were increasing. Italy announced that month that it wanted a railway to run through Abyssinia to link Eritrea with Somaliland. Addis Ababa refused permission. Mussolini called up many more troops.[30] A week later Abyssinia was on the verge of war. Ras Tefari, Emperor of Ethiopia, made a 'stirring appeal' to his people.[31]

September was a busy month for Joss that year, and it did not start well. Joss and Mary had a narrow escape on Friday the 6th when their car overturned along the Njoro road which had become slippery after the recent rain. Fortunately, no one was hurt in the accident.[32]

At thirty-four Joss had become a personality to be reckoned with. By this stage he was commodore of the Yacht Club, chairman of the Naivasha District Council and Secretary of the executive of the Convention of Associations. Latent in him for years had been a talent for politics and an instinct for leadership that emerged in full force now. He was elected by a large majority to the chair of the Convention of Associations at its session in September 1935, 'succeeding Mr C. Kenneth Archer as President and Chairman'. Archer 'paid tribute to the Earl of Erroll . . . for the enormous amount of work he had accomplished'.[33]

That month's session of the Convention was explosive – in the vehement debate on taxation on Wednesday the 11th, Captain the

Rt Hon. F. E. Guest MP 'suggested that greater control over their own finances might be achieved for the unofficial community if the European Elected Members resigned their seats en bloc'.[34] Also debated at the session that day was the question of closer union with Tanganyika. Several months earlier, in March, a conference had been held on the subject of closer union in Arusha in Tanganyika at which a memorandum advocating the uniting of the colony and territory had been drawn up and sent to the Secretary of State for the Colonies. By an almost unanimous vote, the Convention supported the memorandum. It was Joss who had proposed the motion at the outset of the debate. Unity with Tanganyika was seen as essential, were the colony to achieve self-government, as the latter would be 'of little use if neighbouring territories fell into the hands of foreign nations', and 'at the back of everyone's mind is the thought that we do not want Tanganyika to go back to Germany'.[35] Union with Tanganyika had been a long-held dream of the late Lord Delamere.

Also in September, Joss headed a debate which trenchantly criticised the delay in implementing the Morris Carter Land Commission* recommendations that the 'White Highlands of Kenya should be defined and safeguarded by Order-in-Council for the exclusive occupation of Europeans outside the boundaries of existing townships'. Joss spoke scathingly and with force: 'Nothing has been done in connection with these recommendations which vitally affect the interests of the European settlers. One of the reasons for this is interference on the part of the Indian Government in Kenya's private affairs. While the Indian constitutional issue is on the *tapis* the Home Government is terrified of doing anything which might embarrass the negotiations in that regard. The result is that Kenya is being used as a pawn in the greater scheme of things.' Several other speakers, including Lord Francis Scott, agreed with Joss on the Government's fear of causing unrest in India.

---

*When the report of the Morris Carter Land Commission, which sought to settle once and for all the prolonged controversy over the extent of the security of the native lands and the white highlands of Kenya, was published in 1933, Joss and many other settlers were not pleased by its findings. Joss was to fight hard on behalf of settlers' rights.

That September 1935 meeting of the Convention marked the formation of a new Colonists' Vigilance Committee, born of disillusionment with Legislative Council Elected Members' dealings with the home government: 'It was felt that the existing organisations such as the Elected Members Organisation and the Convention were not sufficient in themselves. Somehow something new was required, if only because of the psychological value that it would have and because it would show that the settlers were determined to go further than they had done in the past.'[36] Lord Francis Scott explained to a meeting at Rongai held on 30 September that the Committee's aims were 'first and foremost to concentrate on the present unsatisfactory economic position; secondly to make Government recognise the unsatisfactory economic position of individuals as opposed to the country as a whole and thirdly to produce schemes for Government to help the individual and the country and to bring pressure to bear to make it implement them'.[37]

Also among the new Committee's aims were 'the establishment of connections with other colonies and dependencies with similar problems' and 'measures to preserve the security of the White Highlands'. The Committee was very much in favour of uniting Tanganyika and Kenya. Joss volunteered to undertake the duties of Secretary and to act as liaison officer between the Convention and the newly formed Colonists' Vigilance Committee.[38]

Margery Perham, the Rhodes House scholar who visited Kenya in the thirties, was impressed by Joss's persuasive oratorical skills at the Convention of Associations: 'at first there were a number of delegates . . . who had ideas of their own but under the discipline of their Chairman and other political leaders they all toed the line and voted very extreme anti-government resolutions'.[39]

Mussolini's grand strategy for his vision of a new Roman Empire began with the seizure of Abyssinia in October 1935. Ironically, his moves generated a temporary burst of prosperity in Kenya, owing to the demand of provisions for the Italian troops. Nellie Grant observed, 'People on the plains are coining money through baling veldt hay for the Italians.' Joss never missed an opportunity to make jokes over the fact that 'Gilgil was making Hay for the Italians'.[40]

However, by 1936 the Kenya administration realised that the Italians were not good neighbours. They had provided rifles to the Mandera and Moyale tribes who had regarded them as liberators of the Amhara tyranny, and these tribesmen used the arms to raid the British side of the border.* 'The tribesmen thought the arms had come straight from heaven.'[41] Relations between the Northern Frontier District officers and their neighbours in Italian Somaliland turned sour. Once the camps had advanced so far that they could be seen just across the border, the British administration was forbidden to communicate. Vincent Glenday, the DO, was outraged: 'The Italians are behaving like complete shits. They have closed their wells to our tribes, as a reprisal for us harbouring Abyssinian refugees. Typical macaroni.'[42] All communications and correspondence between the borders and Nairobi were now marked 'secret'.

Not only was the presence of Mussolini's troops threatening the colony to the north. From home Oswald Mosley's fascists were calling for a return of Germany's former colonies, including Tanganyika territory to the south of Kenya – something that Joss would never stand for. Thus fascism, already increasingly anti-Semitic and Hitlerite, now represented an evil menace to Joss's beloved adopted home. He withdrew his support entirely.

Over the course of 1936, Mary's health degenerated; she was now taking three grains of diamorphine per day.[43] Joss rented a bungalow in Muthaiga so that they had a Nairobi base of their own. Mary's continuing ill health and the necessity of having access to a decent hospital and doctors played a part in their reasoning for renting this pied-à-terre, which offered more privacy and permanence than the facilities at Muthaiga Club. Preferring that she be cared for in the comfort of their home, Joss had the compassion not to commit Mary to a mental hospital for her drug addiction. Not only was Joss anticipating Mary's needs but he had ambitions to stand for election

*The Amhara was the ruling tribe of Abyssinia at the time of Mussolini's invasion.

to Legislative Council and, if his campaign was successful, he would need to be in Nairobi himself more frequently.

In contrast to Oserian, the bungalow was not suited to entertaining beyond modest meals and the occasional sundowner. For entertainment on a larger scale, the Errolls continued to use Muthaiga Club. The bungalow was set back from the road not far from the club, surrounded by lawns and flowering shrubs – scarlet poinsettia and white frangipani bushes lined the driveway which swept past the front door in the shape of a horseshoe. Under the square-paned windows, nearest to the house, were low borders of Christ-thorn, with flowers as scarlet as droplets of blood. The gabled wings were joined in front by the usual veranda – which was riddled with white ants. A few steps led to the front door and hallway. To the left were the drawing-room and Joss's and Mary's bedroom. A second bedroom at the front was directly to the right of the front door. There was nothing elaborate about this dwelling. Joss moved several pieces of his ancestral furniture up from Oserian, such as the Carolingian refectory table he had known all his life, and eight dining chairs that had belonged to the 14th Countess Mary ('the very intriguing and wily lady as is any in Britain') and that bore 'not the present Hay crest but possibly an even older one'. Joss also owned an 'Armada table' – a relic of the days of smuggling at Slains – complete with rings which had once enabled it to be bolted to the ship's deck.[44]

Assuming that the crowning of King Edward VIII would take place towards the end of 1936, Joss had successfully claimed his privilege of attending the coronation as Lord High Constable for Scotland. Plans to travel to London had already been put in hand when, in December, the abdication crisis came to a head. Joss's circle, conscious that he would be taking his place for the coronation of Edward's brother, King George VI, instead, went out of their way to entertain him and Mary in early 1937. They were invited to stay with Glady Delamere at Loresho – during race week[45] – and it was while they were all there that the League of Nations recognised the Italian conquest of Abyssinia, and Mussolini 'reviewed some thousands of troops in a triumphant reception as is Roman custom'.[46]

Governor Byrne was actually in London having an audience with the new king at the time.[47]

The coronation was set for 12 May at Westminster Abbey. On 1 March, a week after the setting of this date, Joss and Mary were on their way to England by flying-boat with the intention of remaining there until October. The whole of London was waiting excitedly for the coronation. Joss had much to sort out concerning regalia before taking his place among the high officials and great officers of state in the annexe of the Abbey; they were all subject to numerous rehearsals. Joss also wanted to oversee Mary's dress fittings at Norman Hartnell. They opted for a white and silver gown, over which Mary would wear her crimson mantle, with 'three rows of miniver, to depict her rank'. Joss would be 'privileged to be attended by a page'. Details of their preparations for the coronation were recorded faithfully and somewhat breathlessly in the *East African Standard*.[48]

As if preparations for the coronation were not enough to keep him occupied, Joss also used this stay in England as an opportunity to do business on behalf of Kenya's Legislative Council. Described in the colony's press as the 'whip' of the Elected Members of Legco, Joss was acting as Secretary of the Elected Members' Organisation. On 24 March he urged the East African section of the London Chamber of Commerce to advise the Government on a delay in passing the Income Tax Bill, 'not for the purpose of stultifying the Bill, but for the purpose of improving it'. Joss was keen to show the Chamber of Commerce that the settlers were accepting the compromise over the Income Tax Bill for the sake of political peace in Kenya. He was warmly received by the chairman, Major Sir E. Humphrey Leggett, who said that 'these direct personal contacts with the leaders on the other side are exactly what the section found most helpful'.[49]

After seemingly endless rehearsals Joss found himself at last in the vestibule for the coronation procession on 12 May. He was carrying his baton, which weighed twelve ounces and was tipped with gold, bearing the King's arms at one end and his own at the other. He stood immediately behind the Lord Great Chamberlain and next to the Lord High Steward of Ireland. Nearby was the Marquess of Crewe.

On 9 June 1937 Joss made his maiden speech in the House of Lords. 'TRUST MAN ON THE SPOT' SAYS LORD ERROLL, trumpeted the proud headline in the *East African Standard*. 'A plea for the greater use of the "personal touch" of colonists and administrators living in the various territories, as opposed to increased control from White-hall, was made by the Earl . . . in a debate dealing with Empire Native policy.'[50] That afternoon, the peers discovered a persuasive, amusing, knowledgeable speaker, a young man who spoke with passion and who commanded attention. The Earl of Erroll, having appeared unexpectedly in the House, proved rather promising, not content to be just another wastrel aristocrat from Kenya.

Joss had waited for the appropriate moment to make his presence felt. Lord Noel-Buxton rose and spoke, moving the resolve:

> That this House, in view of the divergencies in native policy now developing in different parts of His Majesty's Dominions and Dependencies, believes that the time has arrived for the Imperial Conference to formulate such a policy in broad out-line, with a view to protecting the rights and promoting the advancement of the Empire, whatever may be their religion and colour, and that such a policy should be based upon the principle of trusteeship.[51]

Lord Noel-Buxton then outlined the problems that occurred 'where advanced persons lived cheek by jowl with backward peoples'.

In his response Joss stated that he did not 'intend to go into any detailed criticisms of [Lord Noel-Buxton's] remarks, but to confine myself rather to general principles from the Colonial point of view as against, perhaps, that larger aspect of the Dominions'. He empha-sised: 'I should like to make one thing quite clear . . . and that is that any one of our race who goes and makes his home in the Colonies does so with the full realisation of the very grave responsi-bility which he automatically assumes towards the native races, by his very presence there. He fully appreciates and realises that by his good example and by the teaching of his traditional experience he can, to a very large extent, mould native opinion and native life in the right and correct way.'[52]

Next, he stressed what he thought Lord Noel-Buxton was 'trying to infer about the relations between the black and white'. In East Africa 'at any rate', Joss pointed out, 'those relations are marked with very great bonds of affection', a situation which he wanted to make quite clear, 'because for some time past now, many misrepresentations and mis-statements have been made, not so much in your Lordships' House as in another place, of the value of white settlement in relation to native races'. Joss assured the House that 'the very vast majority of white colonists have far greater ideals of Empire than mere exploitation of a few unfortunate natives'. While he agreed that 'we must all be in sympathy with the underlying motive' of the motion, 'which is increased welfare and development of the native races', he was none the less concerned because he could not believe that 'any policy can yet be formulated which could meet the needs of all the divergent races, with their divergent habits, all over the Empire', reminding his listeners that there were between fifty and sixty territories under the Colonial Office alone – 'Dependencies or Colonies, whatever you might like to call them, each with its own local problems, religions and tribal customs'. Experience had served him well; never were four tribes so utterly different as the Luo, the Kikuyu, the Somali and the Maasai peoples in Kenya.

Joss illustrated how little his audience, with no direct experience of the colonies, understood the African mentality by relating an anecdote about Lord Noel-Buxton. Joss had lost none of his taste for making people squirm, and as usual the sting of his attack was cloaked in jocularity. 'I cannot vouch for the truth of the story but it will illustrate what I mean,' he promised. Apparently Noel-Buxton had approached a 'native' and asked him if he would like an increase in wages. 'Your Lordships can well imagine that the answer was in the affirmative,' Joss went on. 'When asked what he would do with that increase, the native said that he would buy some more goats; when pressed to state why he wanted more goats, he replied that it was in order to buy more wives. Further questioned as to why he

wanted to buy more wives, the answer was not quite perhaps what
your Lordships might think, but that he wanted more work done
on his plot of land.'[53] There were a great many titters. Lord Noel-
Buxton could not contain himself: 'I am sorry to interrupt the Noble
Earl, but I regret to say that I have not been in Kenya.' Joss smiled.
'I did not say Kenya, but East Africa. That is the normal logic of
the African natives.'

Joss was convinced that each territory should be left to work out
its own salvation, and in Kenya's case 'to solve its own problems
along the lines which have proved, from experience, to be the best'.
A general coordination of policy, he feared, would 'necessarily tend
to increase centralisation of the control of local native affairs in
Whitehall'.[54] What Kenya needed was quite the opposite: 'I believe
that already the local Governors are all too often the loudspeakers of
Whitehall.' Joss felt, as Delamere had felt before him, that the Governors needed more autonomy and that more could be done for the
natives by the individual effort of those who had made their homes
and lived their lives out in the Colonies than by 'piecemeal litigation'.[55]

Lord Snell, the Labour leader from the Opposition bench, con-
gratulated Joss on his speech and supported his views, hoping that
'so long as he is in England, and not in Kenya, we shall have the
advantage of hearing him again'. Lord Snell then spoke of developments north of Kenya. 'How great an influence events in Abyssinia
must have had upon the native mind,' he stressed, 'and then there
is the anxiety about certain tendencies in African administration in
regard to political and social conditions. We have to remember that
today there is a new Africa. The influence upon the mind of the
African natives of films and of the radio and the influence also of
the minority of educated natives [have] been profound, and we have
an entirely new outlook arising . . . that the natives are unwilling to
accept the allocation of a position of inferiority which has been given
to them.' Lord Snell and Joss thought that the natives were absolutely
right. As the former pointed out, 'Who among us shall put a limit
to any other person's intelligence? The only person whose limits I
know is myself.'[56]

Lord Lloyd acknowledged Joss's maiden speech with enthusiasm

— 'a speech finely phrased but illuminated by practical experience and common sense'. He hoped that he would hear Joss speak often on affairs in East Africa and on African matters generally. As one who had something to do with native administration in Africa, Lord Lloyd entirely agreed with Joss's view that 'close knowledge of and daily converse with the native is the best school for building up good relations between farmers and natives in most parts of our Crown Colonies and especially Kenya'.[57] He had not intended to make a considered speech that afternoon, but had done so on account of Joss's newly aired convictions that he thought were significant enough to stress the fact that 'the whole problem of native policy in Africa is very much at issue today and', he went on, '. . . we ought to be very careful before we encourage any elements in the Empire to think that the transference of the Protectorates to any other rule but our own, is likely to be feasible in the near future'. Joss's view had effectively carried the day.

Reaction in Kenya to his maiden speech was favourable. He was praised to the detriment of D's son Tom Delamere, whose two speeches in the Lords had been judged disappointing. The *East African Standard* welcomed Joss's increasing participation in public affairs: 'when he has outgrown a rather too impulsive tendency he should prove a valuable asset'.[58]

On 21 July, Joss spoke again in the Upper House on international trade, another subject on which he felt strongly.[59]

Joss and Mary returned to Kenya as planned, in October. Mary's health was beginning to show signs of a serious decline. Disappointed at not providing Joss with any offspring, she had become more and more dependent on alcohol and drugs, encouraged in both these habits by Kiki Preston. Mary's behaviour was erratic and at times she was outrageously outspoken. Joss did not try to stop her vicious drug habit, for which he was later criticised. But those who observed him with her at the time could see that there was nothing anyone could do for her.

Before the couple returned to the colony, Governor Byrne was replaced in April 1937 by Air Vice-Marshal Sir Henry Robert

Brooke-Popham, the son of a country gentleman, of Wetheringsett Manor, Suffolk.[60] His cautious, reserved, 'somewhat dreamy though cold personality, made him an intellectual rather than an inspirational leader', but this did not throw Joss in the least and indeed Brookham – as he was always known – and he became staunch friends. During Brookham's governorship, Joss was a habitué of Government House, enjoying an equally good relationship with Brookham's wife Opal. The Brookhams had been married for ten years and brought with them to Kenya their son and daughter and four Dalmatian dogs which shadowed Opal's every movement. Joss would help the Brookhams to raise funds for charity, setting up bridge evenings at Government House for the favourite charity of all Governors' wives, the Lady Grigg Nursing Home in Mombasa which Sir Edward Grigg's wife Joanie had founded in the twenties.[61]

On those occasions when Joss was behind the organising, everyone pitched in, even the Brookhams' daughter Diana, 'a charmingly eager little waitress'. Joss was so good at getting everything right that Opal would let him take over the preparation for these 'delightful' evenings. Flight Lieutenant Emslie, Brookham's ADC, and Joss were usually at the hub of a very noisy party, always sending up shouts of approval amid 'a laughing throng'. On one occasion about six months after Brookham's arrival in the colony, there were eight table-football games in progress at once, with players furiously waggling cardboard figures to stop the ball entering the goal. Joss was, of course, the most vociferous player.[62] These high jinks suggest that it was only in public that Brookham's manner was dour, for Joss and he shared 'a ferocious energy and industry'. Joss appreciated perhaps best of all Brookham's lack of hesitation in taking short cuts and unorthodox steps to achieve his ends.[63]

In mid-November 1937, the East African Standard published the news that 'Joss had been invited to stand for Kiambu constituency in the 1938 General Election: 'a group from the Kiambu, Ruiru and Limuru areas have extended an invitation to the Earl of Erroll to contest the constituency and he has accepted. At a subsequent meeting at which electors from Kabete and Kikuyu areas were also present, a joint committee was set up to further Lord Erroll's candidature.'[64]

Legislative Council consisted of eleven Elected Members at this time, and each of their constituencies was large. Lord Francis Scott's Rift Valley constituency stretched from Londiani to Nanyuki – over a hundred miles. Joss was in high spirits as the date for the election drew near. As part of his manifesto, which he published with that of Lord Francis Scott, he reminded voters: 'I can claim to have taken an active interest in public affairs in the past in that I have been Chairman of a District Council for three years [1935–8], and still am Chairman of the Convention of Associations and I have for some time acted as Secretary to the Elected Members Organisation.'[65] On the subject of Tanganyika he stressed: 'Every effort should be made to prevent the return of Tanganyika to Germany, as any such action would place Kenya in an untenable position strategically.'[66]

By March, Joss was introducing a new note into his campaign, calling for the revision of the Congo Basin Treaties, which imposed restrictions on preferential trade tariffs.[67]★ 'The time has come,' he said at a meeting at the Ruiru Hotel in Thika at which an estimated 60 per cent of the district's electorate were present, when 'something has to be done about when negotiations with foreign Powers are the order of the day, and it is a fair proposition that the interests of British East African Territories should be considered in such negotiations; they should be considered as part and parcel of the United Kingdom'. Captain W. Kirton, who presided at the meeting as a member of Joss's committee, stressed that 'Lord Erroll, behind the scenes, had done a tremendous lot of good public work'. Joss himself

★The Congo Basin Treaties (1885) were not solely concerned with the regulation of territorial rights, and the area to which they applied included not only the Congo Basin proper but an eastern extension to the Indian Ocean, embracing Uganda, East Africa, Tanganyika, Nyasaland and a small corner of Northern Rhodesia. The whole of the Belgian Congo, a large part of French Equatorial Africa and parts of Portuguese East and West Africa also fell within the Treaties' limits. Within that vast expanse, the slave trade was to be abolished; there was to be no form of preferential tariff; there were clauses providing for neutrality, in the event of war; free navigation of the Niger and the Congo was assured; and the Treaties established the principle of equality, as between the signatory nations, in the exploration of Central Africa's resources either by settlement or by industrial development (Mervyn Hill, *The Permanent Way*, p. 9).

held back from extolling his own virtues. 'You know all about me,' he said simply, merely reiterating that he was 'really out to do all he could for Kenya'.[68] His campaign was aimed at the farmer and planter community. He wanted to see greater attention to the organisation of industry – 'so that we can meet crises when they arise'. 'Temporary assistance to the industry is welcome,' he added, 'but if we really consider it, it is patchwork. The relief given by the railway does not reach the producer. If I have a son, I shall make him a middle man,' he concluded sardonically, amid laughter.[69]

Joss's campaign was successful. It was a three-cornered contest against the incumbent member for Kiambu, Ruiru and Limuru, Major Riddell, and the other new candidate Arnold Bradley.[70] At 11 a.m. on Friday 8 April 1938 he attended the swearing-in ceremony of the first session of the sixth Legislative Council since 1920, at the Memorial Hall in Delamere Avenue before His Excellency Robert Brooke-Popham. Joss took the oath, followed by Nyanza's newly elected Lady Sidney Farrar. She was the first woman to be elected to Kenya's Legislative Council.[71]★ This session would run from 14 April until 6 June and Governor Brookham would attend each meeting. At the first, the Governor welcomed the Earl of Erroll and Lady Sidney Farrar as newly elected members, reminding them of their responsibilities: 'We are all striving towards the same objective – the prosperity and happiness of the peoples committed to our charge. It is this we must always keep in view, use as our test and guide of our own words and actions and also as the means of judging those of other people.'[72]

★The eleven European Elected Members were Sir Ferdinand Cavendish-Bentinck, for Nairobi North; Mr S. V. Cooke, for the coast; the Rt Hon. Earl of Erroll, for Kiambu; Lady Sidney Farrar, for Nyanza; Col. Stanley Ghersie, for Uasin Gishu; Lt.-Col. Kirkwood CMG, DSO, for Trans Nzoia; M. Maxwell Esq., for Nairobi South; W. G. D. H. Nicol Esq., for Mombasa; E. H. Wright Esq., for Aberdare; Major F. H. de Vere Joyce MC (Acting), for Ukamba; E. C. Long Esq., for Rift Valley (Acting). There were four Indian Elected Members. The Arabs were represented by Sir Ali Bin Salim KBE, CMG. Two nominated unofficial members represented the interests of the African community, H. R. Montgomery Esq. CMG, and Dr C. J. Wilson MC.

In general, Joss's part in debates at Legco would be leavened by laughter, whether he was emphasising some aspect of the Electric Power Bill or discussing immigration restriction. Giving some indication of how committed he was, Legislative Council records show that, from his election to his death in 1941, Joss participated in all but two of the debates.

At the opening debate of the first session, the prospect of war dominated Brookham's speech: 'Our duty is to provide for our own internal security, for protection against frontier raids and a means of defence sufficient in the event of external aggression to hold on until we can be reinforced.'[73] The commander for the Northern Brigade was principal adviser to the Governor on military matters and was also responsible for drawing up the actual plans of operation. They had already made preparations for air-raids. A supply board had been formed, of which Joss was to become a member, and plans were made to expand it and increase its efficiency if war came.

Joss spoke for the first time since his election at a debate held on Thursday 28 April, seconding Cavendish-Bentinck on the subject of the Kenya Land Bill. He spoke forcefully and eloquently on what he regarded as one of the most fundamental issues to be faced for many years. 'We have for a long time lived in the hopes that security would be granted us.' He pointed out that everyone's hopes had been crushed not only by the recommendations of the Kenya Land Commission Report⋆ and the acceptance of it by the governments concerned, 'but also by what I can now only describe as a long series of broken promises by successive Secretaries of State. The elected representatives of the white settlers have done their utmost since the publication of the Report to assist this Government in every way to come to a conclusion and to help in the delineation of the boundaries. But we are, I think, far worse off today than we were on 7 July 1933, when the report was published.'[74] Joss thought that, thanks to Brookham's administrative abilities and to the present heads of departments of the Government in Kenya, there was 'no likelihood of our worst fears being realised. But', he continued, 'I submit that

⋆i.e. the Morris Carter Land Commission.

we should look ahead and visualise another regime out here and another at home, and I cannot allow myself to put my successors in the position of accepting a gamble which I have taken on their behalf, [a gamble] with the only tangible asset in this country, our land.'[75] He wanted to draw attention to something that had been mentioned many times before but had so far failed 'to get any "for'arder"': the question of Githaka – native squatters' – rights in the Limuru area.[76]

The issue of squatters' rights of usage and rights of ownership had been raging since 1919. Joss felt strongly that the former did not imply the latter and that Kikuyu claims on the land were often fraudulent. 'I have seen with my own eyes, the damage done . . . in particular to nine farms . . . in the area with forty-five claimant families resident on them today.' Some of the farms were only 60 to 180 acres in extent yet, in one claimant family, 'there were forty-five members, and . . . two families on one particular farm are occupying 150 acres of land'. The land was being put under too much pressure, and precious resources such as wood and water were being depleted, leaving the environment devastated.

The majority of settlers felt that the enormous sacrifices and hard work they had put into developing their farms in Kenya, as well as their Imperial rights, more than justified their proprietorship over and responsibility for the land. Joss concluded at the debate: 'I have always been an upholder of Native rights, but have we settlers no rights? The Carter report has clearly shown us how to deal with these two problems. Let us bring in the necessary legislation, not in six months' time, but now. The present unhappy position can only do harm to both communities and should be settled once and for all.'[77] He sat down to resounding applause.

In response to the threat of war, in mid-1938 the Legion of Frontiersmen in Nairobi was resurrected for the first time since the First World War, when Major John Boyes had set up the movement. Joss was directly responsible for its revitalisation, calling for volunteers and becoming the moving force and main office-holder, from chairman of its finance committee to designer, down to the last detail, of their new uniforms; he also, for the first time, incorporated a rifle club.[78] He chose the Queen's Hotel in Nairobi for the Legion's headquarters. A massive room was provided within the cellars – the first and only cellars in Nairobi at this time. Meetings could be held there without drawing outside attention: the cellars could be accessed via the cloakroom stairs, bypassing the public rooms of the ground floor. This raised the erroneous suspicion that Joss was holding clandestine meetings.[79]

It was also Joss who arranged that the *East African Standard* publish the 'Orders' for the Legion every Friday – Major Boyes was responsible for posting them each week. Another who responded to Joss's call for volunteers was John Warren-Gash: 'Before the War started, Joss was showing such promise, and was already a useful member of Legislative Council. I met him frequently at our local club in Kiambu, he was obviously heading to become a strong leader of the settler community and he turned to me to get the 2nd Battalion of Pioneers [the Legion of Frontiersmen] in order . . . They were completely out of hand and needed those of us with experience of handling Africans to take over. He was easily approachable, and always ready to discuss our local problems and I came to greatly value his judgement.'[80]

Notwithstanding his commitments to the Legion, Joss attended every Legco debate in the second session, which began on 6 August 1938 and ended on the 18th.[81] He spoke on agricultural policy and on the Native Lands Trust Bill.

On the first weekend in September, the Legion of Frontiersmen's ball was held at Torr's Hotel, Nairobi's grandest building in the thirties.[82] Joss had wanted to show off to Mary the dress uniforms, which were being donned for the first time, in their proper setting. Mary's health was so erratic by now and Joss treated each party they attended as if it was her last, ensuring she enjoyed herself as much as possible. On this occasion, he had paid his usual attention to detail, from the cabaret down to the last gold chain on the epaulettes of some of the officers' uniforms. Mary wore 'a very distinguished black gown, dark and shadowy as night, with a huge spread of skirt'. At their table, they hosted a large party, which included Lady Delamere,

Lord Stratheden, the Cavendish-Bentincks, the Chief Justice Sir Joseph and Lady Sheridan and the head of the Kenya Police and his wife, the Cavendishes. Mary danced the night away just as Joss did, even if 'those spurs did prove a little awkward on the dance floor! After all some people do put women second to horses', as the *East African Standard*'s social correspondent observed.[83] The evening proved a 'delightful occasion ... The effect was strangely stirring ... men, standing in little groups, in their smart slim uniforms with great style ... one expected them to go dashing off to war at any minute, pulling on their white kid gloves in the Waterloo tradition. The women too added to this illusion, for many wore bouffante Winterhalter dresses in white and soft pastel colours.'[84]

As September drew to a close, it brought with it Chamberlain's settlement of the Munich crisis. When peace had seemed almost too much to hope for, his announcement in the House of Commons was received with 'delirious joy'. With the rest of the Empire, Kenya sighed with relief and looked forward to a Christmas with plenty to celebrate.

By the autumn of 1938, Joss was on first-name terms with every important person in the colony, from the Governor down. He knew every member of Legco, the head of every association, every top businessman and entrepreneur, every club secretary as well as every Elected Member's secretary. And he knew their wives as well. Nor was he above chatting to Nairobi's tramp, a character called Willy Lavendar 'who always wore a straw hat and who had no teeth', and who hovered about the vicinity of Schouten's, where Joss would exchange pleasantries in the street before keeping his weekly appointment with his barber.[85]

Joss's relations with the Asian community in Naivasha were excellent, and absolutely without racial bias. The postmaster, the stationmaster, the schoolmaster – all were on hobnobbing terms. Joss never underestimated the value of contacts.

Living so close to Muthaiga Club, Joss made friends of all ages there. Molly Stoyle, eighteen at the time, and the daughters of Walter and Madge Harragin, Kath and Anna, who arrived in the colony with their mother in late 1938, soon got to know him. Their recollection of him contradicts the gossip that was spread after his death.[86] In the eyes of eighteen-year-old ingénues, Joss was 'too old for our set; he seemed fat, florid and old'. He made no attempt to make a pass at either of the Harragin girls, who found it impossible to imagine how he could possibly be the 'demon lover' everybody warned them about. They only saw him at Muthaiga, when he always greeted them courteously and was kind. Far more inhibiting was the company Joss kept. He was accustomed to mingling with the most sophisticated members of the club – usually women – from whom the Harragin girls shied: 'They were terrifyingly blasé and cosmopolitan.'[87]

October 1938 saw the formation of a principally Kenya-based organisation called the Tanganyika League, whose ranks swelled very rapidly over the coming weeks: 'The proposal made by Major Cavendish-Bentinck [on 4 October] that, in view of the imminent German demands for the return of their colonies there should be formed at once a Tanganyika League whose members would be pledged to oppose the handing back to Germany of Tanganyika, has met with a widespread response,' the *East African Standard* recorded in its following Friday issue.[88] That same issue also ran an article by Lord Francis Scott headed STEADY GROWTH OF TANGANYIKA LEAGUE, which ensured that everyone knew he too had played a role in the creation of this popular movement:

I have just read ... the appeal of Major Cavendish-Bentinck on behalf of the Tanganyika League and hasten to write and support his appeal whole-heartedly. In 1936, at the request of my colleagues, I flew to London on this very subject, among others, to try to stir up opinion there, while Major Cavendish-Bentinck organised the Tanganyika League throughout British Africa.

I think we can claim that we both had a considerable measure of success at the time, but the situation today is far more critical than it was then, and I appeal to everyone of all races in East Africa to band themselves together in adamant opposition to any suggestion of ceding Tanganyika to Herr Hitler ... Mr Chamberlain ... has never been willing to commit himself definitely on the subject.[89]

The paper's editor also spoke warmly on the subject of the League: 'We hope and believe that the League will receive such an access of membership during the next few days as to leave no possible doubt of the extent of public feeling in these territories against any suggestion of transferring the Mandate Territory to Germany.'[90]

The subject of the League must have been on everyone's lips at the Jockey Club ball held at the Royal Nairobi Golf Club on the evening of the next day, 8 October. Joss was there with Lord Francis Scott and the Duke and Duchess of Gloucester. Joss would tease Scott: the fact that his niece Alice had become the Duchess of Gloucester 'did not necessarily make Lord Francis Scott royalty'.[91]

Also in October, the Convention of Associations held its first meeting for two years. Joss's position was peculiar, for he had been elected to Legco since the last session of the Convention and could not continue as its chairman – typically, one was not a member of both organisations. When he stood up to make his final speech in preparation for tendering his formal resignation he spoke passionately against home government: 'All our enthusiasms and all the hopes of the Kenya settler were inevitably rendered void by that arrogant autocracy in Downing Street.'[92] He repeated his belief that the basis of the Convention required reform. Joss wanted to see an entirely 'reconstituted Convention to better serve the Colony's agricultural and commercial economy'. He felt that the organisation had been used on far too many occasions as a political weapon in times of crisis: 'I believe that in the future any reconstituted Convention should be as far divorced from political controversy as possible.' Nor would he fight shy of tackling rumours of the likelihood of Tanganyika being returned to Germany – indeed, he would strongly oppose such a step.[93] He stressed:

I have on many occasions both publicly and privately expressed the view that any return of Tanganyika to Germany must prove disastrous to Kenya. There are those who say, 'Give Tanganyika to Germany and the Imperial Government will be forced to fill up Kenya's empty spaces.' But they would be filled with soldiers and not farmers. Kenya would in effect become an African Czechoslovakia with Italy on the northern boundary and Germany on her southern. Nor do I believe that a return of Tanganyika to Germany would prevent a European conflagration should the totalitarian states decide that the moment had come to initiate one. Should Tanganyika be returned to Germany it would spell Kenya's doom, as it would mean that Kenya would either become a playground for a few who could afford to live here without farming or it would become, if the trusteeship of the native means anything, an armed camp which would prove to be a greater irritation to Germany than Tanganyika's non-return.[94]

By a unanimous vote Joss was persuaded to continue as chairman during the current session. On behalf of the Convention, tributes were paid to his work.[95]

Only a week after the first flurry of reports in the press about the Tanganyika League, there was another editorial in the *East African Standard*, reporting on its progress: 'The Tanganyika League has become firmly established with a growing membership . . . Its creation and main objects have been fully reported in the world's Press . . . the Executive Council of the Joint East African Board has lent its support . . . and will take the initiative in forming a representative body whose main purpose . . . will be to keep a watch on developments in London and at the same time to conduct propaganda direct against the German claims.'[96] At a meeting that the JEAB held on Wednesday 12 October they had expressed 'determination to resist cession of Tanganyika to Germany as the result of any Anglo-German negotiations [and] to ensure a continuance of the present British administration of the territory'.[97] That day, it was decided that Lord Francis Scott and a Britain-based representative, Sir William Lead, over from Europe that week to discuss the League, were to be its joint presidents. Major Cavendish-Bentinck was to be chairman and organiser-in-chief.[98]

On the evening of Tuesday 25 October Cavendish-Bentinck chaired a meeting in Mombasa, described as 'one of the most dramatic and spontaneous demonstrations which has ever taken place in the history of Kenya', to explain the purposes of the Tanganyika League.[99] Nearly the entire European population of the area turned up to hear him. League meetings were also held in Dar es Salaam and Tanga in the November.[100]

Cavendish-Bentinck organised a mass meeting for the League in Arusha on 5 November. Joss went with him. The journalist Edward Rodwell – Roddy – was also there: 'The Arusha meeting promised to be something to remember.' Rodwell and three colleagues drove two days by road to reach the venue, the New Arusha Hotel. People were expecting to contribute financially to the cause. It was a 'very outspoken gathering', Rodwell recalled. 'Harsh things were said . . . No gift to Hitler, we were united to a man in a resolve to prevent Tanganyika being handed back to Germany. The country was in an uproar, and we people of Kenya rallied round our Tanganyika brethren to stop the evil. The new Arusha Hotel was full of Englishmen, friendly foreigners, and newspaper men. We of the Fourth Estate gathered together for a number one beano . . . a resolution was passed leaving no doubt whatsoever . . . that Kenya and Tanganyika would resist in no mean manner' if Chamberlain gave Tanganyika away. 'There was no jiggerypokery then. The common people of these territories spoke in one voice . . . At the New Arusha that evening the Caledonian Society held its annual dinner dance. We were all made honorary Scotsmen for the occasion.' Joss would have been in his element, reeling with the best of them.[101]

The third session of Legislative Council began on 28 October and lasted until just before Christmas. The London *Evening Standard* noted how busy Joss was at this time. 'Lord Erroll has added his contribution to the views of the Kenya settlers on the German colonial question. As president of the settlers' parliament he has expressed himself vigorously against the return of Tanganyika to Germany . . . An office stool in Nairobi, where he acts as Lieutenant to Lieutenant-Colonel [*sic*] Ferdinand Cavendish-Bentinck now sees more of him than the wide open spaces of his farm.'[102]

Despite the widespread support it garnered around the colony and indeed within Legco itself, the Tanganyika League was given unaccountably short shrift in Legco, according to a report in the *East African Standard* on 11 November: 'Although it was made apparent yesterday that every member of Legislative Council sympathised with the terms of a motion expressing concern at the harmful repercussions of a return of Tanganyika to Germany the motion was withdrawn after His Excellency the Governor had intervened in the debate.' Even the Governor had to admit this was an unusual step, but he did not further explain his action. By now the League was attracting nearly five hundred new members a week.[103]

On Tuesday 8 November, Joss debated the draft estimates for 1939 concerning the Kenya and Uganda Railway. His acerbic wit was on top form, as he confessed that he found it very difficult to address the council on the subject of the budget. 'I am rather hampered by the feeling that I am playing the part of the Greek Chorus, which only comments on events after they have taken place and without having any serious effect on them. If, indeed, this were my only function, I should be inclined to address my Hon. friend the Financial Secretary in the words of the Euripidean Chorus, "*Omoi omoi O pai*".'* Once the laughter had died down, Joss admitted to still nurturing a faint hope that what he had to say that Tuesday morning, and the warning that he was about to give, might 'still have some effect on the Standing Financial Committee when these Estimates are before them'.[104] Joss continued his dry commentary: 'Last year for example we were told that it was a "Consolidation Budget" and for that reason Members had been asked not to press for any great relief on taxation. This year, not in the Council, but in other places, we are told that this is a "Defence Budget" and because we only have an estimated surplus of £509 we cannot expect any relief in taxation, nor can we expect any increase in expenditure on any of our own pet foibles.'[105] He wondered what 'adjectival qualification' would apply to the next budget. If there was to be one he hoped that it would be a 'Development'

*'Alas, alas, O Youth.'

or an 'Agricultural' budget, which could only be of interest to them all.[106]

On Thursday 17 November, Brooke-Popham reminded members that certain questions had been raised 'at home' in the House of Commons regarding the future of Tanganyika and other territories formerly ruled by Germany. The Prime Minister had been asked whether His Majesty's Government were contemplating the transfer of these territories on any terms. Mr Chamberlain's reply was 'No, Sir'.[107] Secretary of State for the Colonies Malcolm MacDonald was to make a statement on the matter in the Commons on 7 December. 'We are not discussing the matter. We are not considering it. It is not now an issue in practical politics,' he had said.[108] The *East African Standard* headlined its coverage of the debate with the words, ALL OPPOSED TO RETURNING LANDS TO GERMANY – BUT NO PLEDGE FOR THE FUTURE.

After the minutes of 16 November were confirmed, Joss led with the harrying question: 'In view of the statement made by the Commissioner for Lands & Settlement in this Legislature on November 14, will Government state the date on which the Native Lands Trust Bill and the Crown Lands (Amendment) Bill as passed, together with the covering despatch, were sent to the Colonial Office? This is quite a simple question to answer, I am only asking the date on which they were sent. I have had no answer, and it is obvious that I cannot get an answer until we reassemble . . . on December 7.'[109]

Walter Harragin, the newly appointed Attorney-General, attempted to placate Joss: 'Every effort will be made to supply an answer during the adjournment.'

Joss insisted: 'That is not the point: I wanted a verbal answer today.'

'I mean the usual adjournment of today.'

'I beg your pardon, I thought you meant at the end of the session.'[110]

The railway estimates debate was revived that day too.[111] In Joss's view too large sums had been extracted from the pockets of the taxpayers of Kenya and to a lesser extent of Uganda. One of his dairy farmer neighbours at Naivasha, Jack Bunyan, never forgot his cutting words that day.[112] Joss was in a particularly sarcastic mood, as his opening address conveys: 'I would like to follow what is becoming almost a tradition in congratulating the hon. and gallant mover for the manner in which he presents his estimates year after year. It is always a matter of great admiration to me how he is ever able to get away with these estimates with only an occasional and gentle kick from Council, which he can, of course, and does, in fact, almost entirely disregard.' Joss wanted money to be spent on improving the efficiency of export procedures for farming produce. 'Before building new stations and all those wonderful things that are in contemplation, we should really ask that refrigeration plants should be provided.' He believed that through such modernisation it would be possible to make the Uganda Railway the cheapest in the world for primary producers, ensuring that it returned in some form or other a large proportion of the moneys to the taxpayers which 'at present are being used for beautifying★ the railways'. The railway should be allowed to serve the public, not to master it, he stressed.[113]

After lunch, as promised, Walter Harragin informed Joss that the Lands and Settlement papers had been dispatched on 7 October. Joss countered with another question: 'Arising out of that answer, and in view of the fact that the Ordinances were passed on 18 August, can Government account for the delay in sending these home?'

Walter Harragin replied: 'The answer is in the affirmative.'

Lord Francis Scott rebuked him for flippancy: 'Will Government please answer as to why the delay took place?' Walter Harragin found himself reeling off a series of excuses.[114]

At home, Joss had to face battles of an altogether different order. Mary's intake of drugs was now such that she had become a liability, becoming less discreet in public, even during events held at Government House where guests usually behaved with decorum.[115] One of her neighbours from Naivasha remembers dancing with her there:

★An inordinate number of societies had burgeoned in Kenya, on almost any pretext, for some time. Joss was having a harmless laugh at the expense of the 'Nairobi Roads and Gardens Beautifying Association'.

'[She] may have been a bit drugged; drugs stimulated her, turning her into a real chatterbox. She was a malicious gossip and began saying amusing but outrageous things, followed by a series of poisonous remarks, at the top of her voice.' Soon enough rumours started circulating that Mary was suffering from either tuberculosis or cancer.[116] This was not true, but still, few realised except for Joss's closest friends, mainly bridge players, that by now for the greater part of the time she was drugged and if not drugged, then drunk. Therefore, since Mary was clearly not going to improve, they were not at all surprised about his need to find an alternative love-life.

Some time in 1938 Joss began an affair with Phyllis Filmer, wife of Percy Filmer, managing director of the Shell Company of East Africa. Gradually but with increasing frequency he and Mary, Percy and Phyllis would appear under the same roof, though among different groups. Joss took every opportunity to dance with Phyllis once he had fulfilled his obligations at his own table. She and Joss had already been meeting clandestinely for months before Mary started including the Filmers in her dinner invitations. Phyllis was also in England when Joss had come to London for the coronation in May.

However, friends of Joss's were 'bemused by Erroll's infatuation' with Mrs Filmer.[117] 'A small blonde, with page-boy hair', she typified the 1930s fashion for petiteness and her conversation was amusing enough, but she was plain compared to Joss's standard sexual targets.[118] In particular, Hubert and Anne Buxton were more than baffled as to why he suddenly chose Pheely Weely (their nickname for her) as a bedmate.[119] The Filmers had arrived in Nairobi in 1935 from South Africa. They lived in 'the Shell house' – the company residence, standing in Tchui Road around the corner from Muthaiga Club. Phyllis Filmer's background was colonial. Her parents, like Joss's, had been in the diplomatic corps.[120]

As 1938 drew to a close, Mary avoided coming into the Naivasha Club house if Joss was there at weekends. According to Yusuf Khan, she seemed angry.[121] She would sit outside in the car on an inflated rubber ring, so as to lessen whatever physical discomfort had begun to plague her. Joss, unfailing in his courteousness towards her, carried her drinks out to her himself. Each curve and bone of her body was stretched taut with resentment – at times almost as if over Joss's popularity. Mary became bad-tempered and bitter.

8

Josh Posh on the Warpath

'Lechery, lechery; still, wars and lechery: nothing else holds fashion.'

Troilus and Cressida, Shakespeare

The greater part of 1939 was an anxious time for Joss. Another world war seemed inevitable and Mary's addictions could no longer remain hidden from the general public. Joss's patience and kindness in the face of her increasing crankiness were regarded as something of a wonder. People watched helplessly as this state of affairs worsened. Joss's friends describe his handling of the situation as 'loving and intelligent, and really kind'.[1]

Hoping for the best and acting as if all was perfectly normal, in the New Year Joss took Mary to the Kenya Derby with the Brookhams, going on to the Jockey Club ball at Torr's among the Governor's party that night. According to someone who saw her at Muthaiga, Mary 'looks frightful these days. Brandy has practically closed up one eye completely, and the rest of her is covered with spots. She's as round as the Albert Hall too.'[2] The spots were the beginnings of heroin sores, which would eventually cover her body. For the next few months she would sit about Muthaiga Club, amusing herself by telling people's fortunes with cards.[3]

In early January 1939 questions were again raised in the House of Commons about Tanganyika. Mr Malcolm MacDonald, the Colonial Secretary, failed to give a reply when he was asked whether he regarded the territory as integral to the Commonwealth.[4] A dinner was held at the New Stanley Hotel in Nairobi on 20 January at which fifty League delegates gathered. They concluded that the

Tanganyika League needed to be ready for any eventuality.[5] Whenever the issue was raised again in the Commons, MacDonald stood
by his statement of 7 December.

At the end of January, the South African newspapers republished
Joss's vociferous criticism of the Colonial Office made at the Memorial Hall at the opening session of the Convention of Association
in October the previous year. The *East African Standard* had carefully
chosen extracts putting Joss in a bad light: 'What the noble Earl did
not say about the dictators in Downing Street is not worth repeating
and much of what he did say was too ferocious to print here.'[6] Not
a word is there of any of the sensible and far-sighted ideas that Joss
had aired in October.

It was as if the press was hardening against both Joss and the
Tanganyika League as they strengthened their resolve. For the next
two months there was a rash of anti-Kenya opinion in the press in
Europe and South Africa; a tone of acrimony presided. After Opal
Brookham had paid a visit to MacDonald, there was another unwel-
come profile on 'The Kenya Settler', an attack which incensed those
in the colony.[7] South Africa's *Daily Express* ran a piece, later syndi-
cated to the *East African Standard*, under the headline, KENYA'S NEW
DEMOCRACY. One sneering paragraph seemed to be having a dig at
Joss, echoing some words of his Convention speech:

> Kenya has always been a country of aristocratic landlords. If on
> the East African escarpments you see a man with long tangled
> locks wearing torn shorts and a bush fire shirt, don't attempt a
> superiority complex with him. He is probably, at least, an Earl
> . . . And in a new world of ours wherein the aristocrats have
> become demoncrats [*sic*], these Colonial Barons call Downing
> Street an arrogant autocracy, whereas in England, Mr Chamber-
> lain and his lieutenants are hailed as the saints of the plebeians.[8]

Not only were there concerns over who should govern Tanganyika; it would appear that the territory was already infested with
Nazism. In 1939, an in-depth inquiry began into the scale of Nazi
penetration of the German expatriate community in Tanganyika,
which outnumbered the British non-official element by the time of

the outbreak of hostilities in September. As Tanganyika was a former German colony, certain elements in the African population remained pro-German too.[9] The threat of pre-war Nazi penetration of East Africa was very real. The late Michael J. Macoun, who was transferred to Tanganyika in the September, had been marked out on account of his fluent German as a useful recruit to the 'embryonic security intelligence organisation' there and, before long, Nazi Party lists and other documents had came into his hands. As had been suspected, a comprehensive organisation was already functioning, with a *Landesgruppenleiter* (territorial leader), *Kreisleiter* and *Gauleiter* (district and provincial leaders).[10] The pro-Hitler attitude in Tanganyika gave rise to a spate of rumours about espionage and subversion. Kenya was after all in a precarious position, and paranoia was rife. Now that Lord Baden-Powell was living at Paxtu in the grounds of his friend Eric Walker's Outspan Hotel in Nyeri, Walker had been so concerned at one point over the proximity of the Italians that he had kept his car loaded with petrol, oil, blankets and food hidden behind Paxtu, ready to whisk the old man to safety at a moment's notice.[11]

Joss took on another responsibility when he was made deputy director of the Central Manpower Committee in February 1939, working for the Attorney-General Walter Harragin, who was the Manpower director. Joss and Walter Harragin got along well. They both enjoyed bridge and, according to his daughter, Walter 'loved naughty jokes or stories. He called Joss a rogue but liked him very much as a person, he was funny, charming, a tease and always pleasant to be with.'[12] The Hon. Isher Dass, Indian member for Legco, was appointed to handle Asian manpower concurrently.

Initially, Joss's work at Manpower involved helping Kenya prepare for a hypothetical emergency. Manpower secretly assigned to buildings a wartime use as hospitals, first-aid posts, decontamination centres and rallying points – not to mention internment centres. The chief aim of the Manpower Committee, though, was to meet military requirements in personnel, while at the same time maintaining levels of production with as little disruption to essential services as possible. It was not an easy job to please both the military and civilians, as

Joss would soon discover. For a start, coordination between military and civil authorities was a minefield but, for all his ruffling of feathers in Legco, here Joss seemed able to tread a careful path between the two authorities, ironing out worries and calming any brewing storms. As he pointed out in a speech he made to anxious settlers, 'If every available European in this country was used at once, the ordinary business of the country would cease, congestion and confusion would arise and there would be inevitable waste of man-power for a later stage.'[13] Thanks to his and others' strenuous efforts, by the time war was declared Kenya's registration system directing individuals into the services or into non-military jobs was fully operational.

Joss's duties on the Central Manpower Committee kept him labouring over ten hours a day, either in his office at the Secretariat on the Hill in Nairobi or, later in the year, touring the colony from end to end with his secretary Arthur Clark. Clark had been a protégé of the Provincial Commissioner of Nyanza, Sidney Fazan, who had been a friend of Joss's since mid-1937.[14] Whenever Joss visited Kisumu, he based himself at the Fazans'. The Fazan children remembered how Joss would go out by car with their father by day, covering miles of Nyanza Province, to return each evening to bath, change into black tie for dinner, and play bridge.

Joss and Arthur Clark first met at the Fazans', where Joss spotted his potential immediately. Clark's sudden appearance in Joss's office at the Secretariat in February 1939 seems to have been the result of a plan hatched between Joss and Fazan.[15]

Also in February, Joss received a request from a young man called Mervyn Cowie to back him in the cause of getting a proper game policy established in Kenya. Joss, seeing that game could be an asset for tourism, promised his full support.[16] His promise proved to be the breakthrough that Cowie had needed. He called for a public meeting to be held at the Playhouse on 7 March at which the Earl of Erroll would speak in favour of a national game park proposal. The Earl's presence encouraged further support. When the day came, visitors from Australia, New Zealand and Rhodesia, as well as the local populace, crammed into the Playhouse. There were even shouts of support from the many people who were standing outside round the entrance – there was not a seat left in the house, which had a capacity of three hundred. 'Erroll spoke forcefully and convincingly,' according to Roy Kinnear, editor of the *East African Standard*, who accorded the occasion huge headlines on the front page next day.[17] Joss also raised the subject of game policy in Legco. While his efforts to get a policy established in Kenya were interrupted by the war, Mervyn Cowie was eventually successful in his cause. By the time of his death in 1996 he had become internationally regarded as the champion of African wildlife. Joss had helped him at a crucial time when there had been no official mandate or authority to wage a battle with the Kenya Government.[18]

When he was sworn in for the first session of Legislative Council for 1939 in early April Joss had been a member of the Council for one year. He was appalled by the lack of progress in those twelve months and said so in inimitable terms, chastising Government with his habitual verve.[19] Kenya was continually stymied by the Colonial Office, he complained.

> I am afraid that the lemon is wearing rather short of sugar at the moment . . . Looking back it appals me to see how little has been achieved . . . our roads are worse today than a year ago; there is no attempt to tackle the question of agricultural indebtedness which, to my mind, is the most vital question this country has to face; there is no money for implementing the Settlement Committee Report; there is no money for the Land Bank or other developmental schemes, in spite of the millions of pounds in the banks, the railway and other places which are aching to be used – although the Hon. General Manager of the Railway may not think so. We are merely told that we are not credit-worthy, in spite of the fact that, for the last three years at any rate, our excess of revenue over expenditure has exceeded that of the United States.[20]

Joss criticised the Colonial Office for tarrying in responding to Council's questions: 'I consider this is an insult, not only to Your Excellency, but to all of us, that when you send despatches they do not even have the courtesy to acknowledge them.' He impertinently suggested to the Governor Brookham that, if he did not receive a reply to any proper despatch within six weeks or two months, he should get on the telephone to the Secretary of State and ask why not. 'I believe this modern means of communication would have a very salutary effect on that gentleman, more especially as the telephone is only open between the hours of 3 p.m. and 5 p.m. local time, which is lunch time at home.'[21]

Joss felt so strongly about the appalling conditions of the colony's roads that at the end of April he presided at a meeting in Nairobi where it was voted unanimously to set up a Kenya Road League. Attending this meeting was part of Joss's campaign to encourage tourism, since 'hundreds of thousands of pounds of tourist business annually is lost to the colony owing to the state of roads', as one local hotelier complained to those assembled.[22]

Amid debates at Legco, campaigning on local issues and making preparations for war, Joss did not entirely neglect his social life. In May he and Mary attended Kenya's first 'Caledonian Highland Gathering'. Joss had arranged that, providing Mary was up to it, she should present the prizes. Elspeth Huxley's father, Major Grant, had initiated the first Caledonian Ball in 1938, when Joss was Chieftain of the Caledonian Society's Nakuru branch. 'I don't think my father cared for him much,' Elspeth Huxley observed. Major Grant's chief objection to Joss seems to have been to do with his own discomfort over Joss's abstinence – he did not share Major Grant's relish for whisky.[23] Proceeds raised that afternoon were destined for Scottish charity.

The Countess of Erroll was indeed well enough to appear. She presented prizes for tossing the caber, for throwing the javelin and for the polo and golf tournaments. And was seen again on Joss's arm in the evening. Under the Scottish standard 'showing bold red and yellow against the wall', four hundred people filled the double ball-room at the Stag's Head Hotel in Nakuru.

Lord Erroll in full dress tartan took a hand at conducting the band during the dancing. Lou Green and his orchestra were supplemented by Mr Sutherland, Mr Black and Mr Petrie (the pipers) and kept the music going throughout the night. Five set Eightsome Reels were formed and danced with verve and spirit – a sight to quicken the heart of any home-sick Scot . . . the Dashing White Sargeant [*sic*], danced with great skill to bagpipe accompaniment, was followed by a very enthusiastic if exhausting performance of the Highland Schottische.[24]

In July 1939 the streets of Nairobi were 'brightened and cheered by the reassuring sight of the uniform of the British Navy', claimed the *East African Standard*.[25] 'The growing strategic importance of the excellent harbour facilities at Mombasa is much in evidence.'

As deputy director of Manpower, not the least of Joss's tasks that July was to reassure some two thousand European settlers in the regions for which he was responsible, all of whom were 'jittery' about the possibility of war and desperate for information. Joss and Arthur Clark toured the Highlands of Kenya throughout the month.[26] Joss addressed large gatherings in every district, allaying fears and explaining the functions of Manpower. He outlined the responsibilities and duties that people could expect to fulfil in the event of war. European manpower in Kenya amounted to 8,998. Before long, over 3,500 men would be serving in the armed forces. Three thousand would be retained to occupy jobs essential to the colony, and the majority of the residue, a thousand farmers, were either elderly or of a low medical category. In addition, eight hundred European women 'nobly reinforced the effort', of which 650 aged between sixteen and sixty provided essential services.

On Wednesday 5 July Joss and Arthur Clark went up north, staying overnight with Captain H. B. Sharpe after addressing the Thomson's Falls community.[27] 'Sharpie' was an old friend of Joss's. He was a horticulturist and a homosexual who had gone on safari with him and Idina in the twenties.

Answering every question put to him, Joss would begin by stressing that the organisation which had so far been carried out was for the day of mobilisation only, warning that once the extent of the emergency was known, the Manpower organisation would certainly have to be revised and adjusted. Obviously, it was 'impossible for the Central Manpower Committee sitting in Nairobi to allocate persons to define jobs without a more intimate knowledge of the local personnel than it possessed and for this reason the Manpower Committee had appointed Sub-Committees in every district'. During the Committee's work many other questions had arisen, dealing chiefly with the financing of farms, the organising of group farm managers, pay and dependency allowances.[28]

On the Friday, 7 July, Joss and Arthur went through a similar process at the Kitale Hotel, where well over a hundred people attended.[29] Emphasising that steps would be taken to introduce legislation to prevent foreclosures on mortgages on farms or property in wartime – Joss realised, he told the Kitale farmers, that 'dissatisfaction had been expressed in some districts, where certain individuals had not been ear-marked for special duties', and he assured them that they were being held in reserve. He urged those who had heard nothing to remain at their normal peacetime occupations if war broke out. Joss and Arthur earmarked between them 'many scores of men and women for special service . . . there were those who were detailed to ARP duties, the Red Cross, supplies and auxiliary fire-fighting services, farm management, the protection of women and children on outlying farms, guard of key points, radio experts, linguists [for the rounding up of enemy aliens]; the staffing of camps and concentration centres and all the obvious requirements of a country under war conditions'.[30]

As the two men raced from venue to venue, swarms of locusts preceded them, forming brown clouds that darkened the sky, a sinister image of menace and ravaging waste that must have haunted all those waiting for news from Europe. A swarm 'about a mile long and very dense' reached Kitale while Joss and Arthur were there. Another swarm, estimated to be 'three miles long and very dense' and comprising 'young locusts' was also heading for the Trans Nzoia. Fears over growing crops that had already suffered some damage increased, especially as Kenya was expected to be the breadbasket for the Middle East. Reports of locusts caused concern for production for the remainder of the year.[31]

Joss was inundated with questions about the plagues. At Kitale his remarks followed the pattern of those made at Thomson's Falls. The chief concern of farmers in Kitale was the disposal of farm commodities such as maize. When asked whether people would be able to leave the colony if no duty had been found for them locally, Joss warned: 'Before the outbreak of War anyone is at liberty to do as he pleases. On occurrence of a state of emergency, it is unlikely that anyone who has not received instructions, recalling them to a unit, would be allowed to leave, at least until the nature of the emergency became apparent.' On the question of the evacuation of women and children, he was reassuring; under the local security schemes, plans were already in existence for their concentration rallying points, and these 'could be readily adapted to meet the events of external aggression involving invasion'.[32]

By the end of July, Lord Erroll and Mr Clark had satisfied the districts that 'much had been done in the preliminary organisation, so that should an emergency arise, the resulting uncertainty in the minds of many people is less likely to develop into a dangerous chaotic state than would certainly have been the case but for the work done in the past ten months'.[33]

The next few weeks were used by the Kenya Government to consolidate the colony's position in the north. The Kenya Regiment remained at Kampala until the end of 1939, and it was during this period that the formation of the 1st East African Light Battery was authorised. It was a difficult time for settlers. It was impossible to obtain any training stores, clothing or equipment. Recruits began pouring in, but they often had to work in civilian clothes for weeks. In all over 3,500 members of the Regiment joined the East African forces. Of these, more than 1,500 were commissioned as officers in the battalions of the King's African Rifles from Kenya, Uganda, Tanganyika and Nyasaland, and in the Northern Rhodesia Regiment.[34]

Major-General D. P. Dickinson was appointed Inspector-General of the KAR on 22 August. Nine days later, the War Office appointed him General Officer Commanding the troops in East Africa. He established HQ at Kenton College – then at Kilileshwa – while at the European Primary School the boy's boarding block was put at the disposal of the Kenya Regiment as a mobilisation barracks.

Dickinson announced, following an inspection tour of the Northern Frontier District, that he would take over the Kenya Police in the province if Italy entered the war. Mobilisation lists were brought up to date. Joss's good groundwork came into its own, but even so Dickinson had but a meagre force under his command in 1939, numbering only seven thousand.[35] During the second nerve-stricken fortnight of August it was assumed that, when war came, Italy would side with Germany and invade Kenya. The prospect of holding an Italian invasion in the Northern Frontier District seemed so precarious that arrangements were made for the evacuation of civilians and livestock from the northern parts of the Highlands of Kenya.

It was Joss's role to allocate the best man for each role. As fast as they came in they were mustered into parties and sent off as junior officers to various battalions of the KAR.[36] In addition to the KAR, settlers with special qualifications, hand-picked almost entirely by Joss, now formed into the East African Reconnaissance Regiment, the Kenya Independent Squadron, the East African Artillery Engineers, Signals, Electrical and Mechanical Engineers (EME), Ordnance Corps, Supply and Transport, Pioneer Battalions and Medical Units. Others, with even more special qualifications, led guerrilla bands behind the enemy lines. Zeal and knowledge of the country were as invaluable now as in those who had volunteered for war in 1914. Few of them had experience of modern weapons or tactics or of the training of troops.[37]

Those who could not find a niche in any of these active units – and being in one's fifties was no bar to that – joined garrison battalions. Before he was superseded by General Cunningham the following year, Dickinson was holding a front of over eight hundred miles which ran roughly from the lava rocks of Lokitaung, across the bitter alkaline waters of Lake Rudolf to the salt shores of the Indian Ocean. It was not a continuous front but he managed to hold the strategic points, after the triumphant entry into Moyale by the Italians, by using the Northern Frontier District as a barrier, and by checking the advance of the Italians at point after point and forcing them to fight for every mile. With each week the situation grew less tenuous.[38]

Phyllis Filmer's involvement with Joss was out in the open and widely acknowledged by this stage. The affair would last until she was eclipsed just before Christmas in 1940.[39] So long as Pheely Weely did not encroach on Mary's territory, she continued to be tolerated. Mrs Filmer, however, seemed not to comprehend the loyalty of friends towards Mary Erroll once the latter, in late summer, was too ill to venture from her bungalow. Pheely Weely was made to feel uncomfortable if she turned up at Muthaiga with Joss. According to friends, 'She was not pleased to have been excluded by the Pérignys for example, at a large house-party at Kongoni, to which Joss was invited without her. She gate-crashed the Pérignys. This was considered awfully bad form' – 'a heinous crime socially'.[40]

By the summer Mary was consuming vast amounts of alcohol and drugs to fend off pain. Once she learned about the death of her friend Kiki Preston, who had taken a fatal heroin overdose in her suite at Claridge's, there was no turning back. By August she was 'going downhill fast'.[41] Now that the Errolls were spending so much time in Nairobi, Dr Henry Hemsted, their Naivasha doctor, handed the case over to the McCalden practice and Mary was looked after for the rest of her life by their young Irish GP, Dr Joseph Gregory.[42]

Whenever Joss happened upon friends from up country at Muthaiga Club, he would urge them to go across the road to see Mary so as to break the monotony of her housebound existence.[43] Mary had always loved to surround herself with young people. Invited by Joss, Molly Stoyle and the Harragin girls would sometimes drop in on her after a squash game at Muthaiga. With uncanny foresight she would frequently proclaim, apropos of nothing, 'There will never be another Countess of Erroll when I die. At least not in Joss's lifetime.' She had always had more than an inkling of what was going on between Pheely Weely and Joss, understanding more clearly than Mrs Filmer that Joss would never marry her. Acting as if nothing was abnormal, Joss would courteously offer round his Balkan Sobranies – the one thing that still gave poor Mary pleasure was smoking. She had cigarette burns on her chest and arms caused by falling asleep while smoking. Her tipple now was brandy – the days of sipping Black Velvet at the bar at Oserian were gone.[44] Anna and Kath Harragin, and Marc Lawrence's daughter Joan, another visitor to the bungalow, all thought 'Joss was wonderful with his ailing wife'.[45]

Once Dr Gregory advised him that Mary's prognosis was hopeless, Joss instructed Sabweru and Waweru to let her have whatever she wanted to drink. Joss was compassionate enough to accept that she was dying and needed the 'booze to deaden the senses'.[46] According to Dr Gregory, 'Mary's body was covered with abscesses ... She had been ill and lonely for a long time.'[47] On what proved to be his final visit to her bedside, her last request struck the young Irish GP as pathetic: ' "You will promise to come to my funeral, even if you are the only one?" I said of course I would. She died that afternoon.' The cause of her death was given as renal failure and the consequential uraemia.[48]

Mary was buried next day, 13 October, at St Paul's Church, Kiambu.[49] Contrary to her drug-induced anxieties, her funeral was well attended: 'Despite the short notice which must so often attend funerals in Kenya there was a large attendance of mourners from every walk of life, many of them in military uniform.' Lord Francis Scott, Major Cavendish-Bentinck, Glady Delamere, Lady MacMillan and Major Ewart Grogan had all come to pay their respects. Fabian Wallis was one of the pall-bearers along with Mary's old favourite, Sabweru. There were 'beautiful floral tributes piled high on the graveside'.[50] *The Times* in London gave Mary's death a brief paragraph. When probate of her will was granted in Nairobi to the Earl of Erroll (and sealed in London on 26 August 1940) the value of her effects in England was declared at only £7,862, 14 shillings and four pence.[51] Her fortune had dwindled during her marriage to Joss.

Joss's Indian friends the Khans, having observed the pair at close quarters, were struck by his grief at Mary's death. Joss also confided his sorrow to Dorothy Blin, whom he had known for six years – Dorothy's parties had often included Idina and her current husband or flame, sometimes both, although she drew the line at including

Pheely Weely Filmer. Joss regarded this woman as an older sister and kept nothing from her.

When war broke out on 3 September, just as their predecessors had in 1914 the settlers now 'volunteered to a man to offer their services to the Government and in particular to His Majesty's Forces'. Calling-up telegrams were sent up country to those on mobilisation lists. In the towns, orders to report for duty were given by telephone or by orderly.[52] Joss went into the Kenya Regiment on a temporary commission as a second lieutenant.[53] GOCHQ was a mile up the road from Muthaiga Country Club. The sentries took their place at the gates of this brand-new house of Moorish design. In requisitioning the building the Army had turfed out Mario Rocco, its tenant for the previous year (today it is the residence of the American Ambassador). One of its large, light rooms was Joss's military office.[54]

On 5 September Joss attended Legislative Council's Extraordinary Session. Brookham opened the session with 'the first real war news from Britain' – the steamship SS *Athenia* carrying fourteen hundred souls had been torpedoed off the Hebrides. Joss listened quietly, almost automatically applauding Francis Scott when it came to matters arising from the Compulsory Service Bill, which had been in force since 1937 but was now being passed as legislation.[55] The settlers had responded magnificently, Scott pointed out: 'All I can say is that there is no need for compulsory powers to make them do whatever they can do for the State at this time of crisis. They are one and all united and determined to do everything in their power to assist in whatever way they can at the present.'[56] Another member spoke up for the Africans, 'Some of us are remembering at this moment August 1914 ... The tragic memory of the sacrifices that our natives had to be called upon to bear during that war will remain. But our Africans did not fail us then, and will not now. Many of them understand quite clearly what we are fighting for ... they realise that our cause is their cause.'[57]

Eight days later, in the early hours of Tuesday 12 September, the Kenya Secretariat on the Hill burnt down, destroying a large portion of the colony's thirty years of paperwork, 'the most valuable records, dating back to the earliest days of East Africa'. Joss's entire accumulation of Manpower records went up in the blaze – the fire, it transpired later, had actually started in his office, which was next to the Manpower room. The old wood and iron buildings where Joss carried out his Manpower duties were some of the earliest in the town, having been erected at the beginning of the century. His office was one of six in line in an annexe, all connected by a veranda.[58]

By the time that the fire brigade reached the scene this annexe was one mass of flames, and there was no hope of saving much. Other departments badly affected included the offices and records of the Chief Secretary, Assistant Chief Secretary, the Financial Secretary and Supply Board, the Standing Board of Economic Development, Executive Council and Legislative Council Records, the Establishment section and others. Only the Military section and the departments of the Chief Native Commissioner and Native Affairs escaped the fire.[59] The fire came as quite a shock to Charlie Mortimer, the head of the Lands Department – leases of great value, dating back to 1899, had all gone.[60]

Next day, the Secretariat was evacuated to the Law Courts, formerly occupied by the Agriculture and Education departments. Within hours of daylight, theories abounded as to how the fire had started. Some placed the blame on Acting Deputy Financial Secretary Jack Troughton. He had been working late and might have left switched on the electric kettle in the room next to Joss's office after making a hot drink. The kettle could have fused and caused the fire. Another theory was that an overtired worker had accidentally dropped a lit cigarette into the waste-paper basket, another that 'someone' wanted to destroy evidence. The official conclusion was that no one was to blame. Troughton, who had not left the building the night before until 10.30, claimed that he noticed nothing abnormal in any part of the Manpower building.[61] The kettle, he insisted, had been switched off. Close alongside it was another switch controlling a lamp socket, however. The caretaker claimed that both switches were off when he left for the day, but if Mr Troughton had entered the room and switched the light back on later that night, the electric current to the kettle would have been used, if only for a few minutes. The magistrate concluded that such an amount of current could have caused the blaze. There was nothing to suggest that the fire was anything but accidental.[62]

Derek Erskine remembers Walter Harragin's peculiar reaction: 'Harragin was the only one to enjoy the blaze. "The best thing that could have happened," he kept saying. He loved all that paper going up in smoke, declaring, "None of it was worth anything and we can well do without it." The whole of Nairobi rushed up to the hill by car to find Harragin conducting operations; after all, his own house stood nearby . . . [We were all] ferrying buckets of water to kill the blaze but to no avail. The fire was enormous.' Erskine never believed the outcome of the official inquiry. 'It was an interesting coincidence that the mobilisation files were destroyed . . . One match and a bottle of petrol would have set that building alight like a tinder box.'[63]

Only during the inquiry did it emerge that the fire had started in Joss's office. Neither he nor any of his staff had been working there that night. Joss's death and the fire were later to be linked in people's minds as unsolved mysteries. Next day, Joss toured the scene of devastation with Brookham in what was their last shared official duty; others present included unofficial members of the Central Manpower Committee, and all 'saw before them many weeks of hard work literally reduced to ashes'.[64]

Significantly, the destruction of the Manpower lists had come about when these were subject to crucial daily scrutiny. At Command HQ, Wilfrid Havelock was detailed by Lord Francis Scott to help Joss rebuild the complete list of man- and womanpower of the European population. Joss's photographic memory really came into its own: 'Even [his] enemies came to his defence as he rebuilt the Manpower records from memory. They could not help but acknowledge that he had a brilliant mind.'[65] Havelock described the process of rebuilding the records:

His memory was unbelievably exact. He would begin work thus, 'Oh yes. James Brown. His farm is next to Sam Smith at

Endebess. Brown has a second wife whom I have met, and seven children by two marriages.' On and on he would go like that in a constant stream. His helpers would be hard put to get everything down as Joss moved on to the next feat of memory. Working with him seemed like trying to keep ahead of an express train. Because Joss never wrote anything down, it was hell for anyone who was expected to take over from him.[66]

This feat of recollection marked a turning point in people's attitudes to Joss. Suddenly they realised his true worth. Beforehand, they had not appreciated how he took in the tiniest details and made of them mnemonics imperceptible to others: the click of his dog's claws on the parquet flooring of his bungalow, the scraping of a chair as it was pulled up to a desk, the start of a girth gall on one of his polo ponies, the new servant, the latest rose to open, the new face at the club. The latest sexual challenge. He knew whether a woman wore mascara, or if she neglected her nails, what scent she wore. No detail was overlooked, and he kept the information like a trump card. Oddly enough, now that the colony was at war his barber Schouten's was especially valuable to him for gathering information. Here, through gossip, he could keep track of people and developments.

Not long after the Secretariat fire, the locusts reached Nairobi. As the brown clouds descended it was nauseating to watch the 'hoppers' moving across the land, devouring every vegetable in their path. The strong easterly wind drove the 'millions and millions' of locusts in the direction of Muthaiga, to feed on patches of its faded lawn.[67]

Soon after Britain declared war on Germany, Joss found himself working on the wartime Agricultural Production and Settlement Board, assisting Major Ferdinand Cavendish-Bentinck.[68] The Board's head office was conveniently close at hand for Joss, in Memorial Hall in Delamere Avenue, where Legislative Council also sat.[69]

Joss's secretaries were devoted to him, though he worked them hard. He had the support of two or three efficient girls whom he shared at Legco with Cavendish-Bentinck, member for Nairobi

North. Joss and Francis Scott both used Miss Somen for their office work.[70] The former secretary to the Girl Guides, poor Miss Somen was not blessed with great beauty, but Joss nevertheless won her devotion by giving her an undiluted measure of attention. Wilfrid Havelock observed his behaviour: 'He would treat her as if she were some beauty . . . touching and stroking her as he dictated. Of course she was completely charmed and would uncomplainingly work all hours for Joss.' Such behaviour today would have cost Joss his job – a case of *autres temps, autres moeurs*. And his familiar manner was affectionate rather than sexual: instead of horrifying the girls it instilled loyalty. Miss Somen never spared herself, and never let Joss down.[71]

One young army officer, Captain Edward Searle, who spent a week working for Joss in the Manpower office, saw no inkling of the playboy or of the caddish nature so frequently attributed to Joss after his death. Instead, Searle discovered an amicable and extremely hard-working man, who took his responsibilities seriously. Joss was a hard taskmaster, expecting no less a performance than his own from any of his staff. There were certain moments, this officer noticed, when he seemed exhausted. After all, the calls on his time were extraordinary. Even when he had some social engagement, he would often return to work after dinner. Yet he remained his usual good-humoured self throughout, always able to raise a laugh among colleagues – which helped to dispel the rising tensions of war. Joss's popularity only increased in those early gloomy days of war – people liked his manner, his reliability, his energy, his sense of fun and his charm.[72]

His chief task in Manpower after war had broken out was to advise the drafts of local officers and NCOs including personnel from overseas. Joss took trouble to choose appropriate posts for the men who came before him and to respect whenever possible each volunteer's preferences for postings. Jack Bunyan, his neighbour and polo-playing friend, had been turned down twice for active service because his hearing was impaired. When Jack applied to Manpower for a posting, he remembered that Joss was in a playful mood: '[He] sat at a desk in a big room, with Major Gossage, who hailed from

a property called Drinmore. Joss liked to turn things into a bit of
an act, to make people laugh. He turned to Gossage and said, "Saus-
age, drink more." ' For all his frivolity, however, Joss saw to it that
Jack was sent to help Sir Philip Mitchell, at the East African Governors' Conference in Nairobi, a small secretariat dealing with sensitive developments common to the East African territories, which
during the war also filled the role of political branch of the East
African Force HQ.[73]

John Millard was another who appreciated Joss's way of handling
his posting. Millard had left the Tanganyika administration, driving
over the border so as to join up in Kenya, and was not sure what
to expect. Suddenly he found himself in front of the Earl of Erroll.
Millard was unprepared for Joss's sincerity and consideration, finding
him 'quite charming . . . we got on well'. Millard muttered that he
fancied himself as an officer in an armoured reconnaissance unit.
'No vacancies,' Joss replied but, noting from his file that Millard had
been with the Cambridge Battery, he suggested this branch of warfare. Millard's knowledge of it was limited, he had to admit. Was
there was any possibility of a posting to a gunner unit? '[Joss]
mumbled something about the 22nd Mountain Battery fairly recently
arrived from Quetta, adding, "Smashing show, very pukka sahibs,
professionals, screw guns, Kipling and all that sort of thing, you
know." '[74] Joss's handyman, 'Roman' Khan, had been desperate to
join this same Indian division in the Kedong. While Joss could have
arranged the posting with a flick of his finger, it was typical that he
could not bear the thought that he might be responsible for exposing
such an exceptional young man to danger and death; instead he
recommended the brilliant mechanic for a posting where he could
look after motor-vehicles at East African Command First Line of
Communication – or L of C, as he called it.[75]

Joss's old friend from Sabukia, the coffee farmer and cattle rancher
Michael Blundell, had been 'rather too old for military intakes'
initially so had been ordered to continue farming and to manage
several other farms in the district whose owners had been taken into
the Army. In fact, owing to his knowledge of tribal languages, Blundell had been held back specifically in order to form the African

Pioneer Reserve. Joss realised how useful his languages would be in training the many different kinds of African. For his secrecy in this matter, Blundell was bombarded with white feathers by angry young wives who did not know why he was still there when their husbands were not.[76]

However, once Joss became Assistant Military Secretary the following year and urgently needed to fill a senior military post, he picked Michael Blundell for the job. In the fifties, Sir Michael Blundell became a prominent figure in local politics himself, as a member of Legislative Council. He never lost the opportunity then to express regret over Joss's death. When his memoir was published, he made the point that Joss had become a valuable and responsible representative member

> [who] would have made a considerable contribution to the life of Kenya, had he been allowed to live. Though the records had recently been burnt . . . when the appointment of a new commanding officer for the battalion was discussed, he is reported to have said, 'There's a fellow called Blundell up at Solai near Nakuru who speaks their language, he'll probably be able to settle them.' He had an amazing memory. [. . .] No one could have entered the Army in more unusual circumstances. I owed this extraordinary and drastic translation from civilian life as a farmer to battalion commander in literally forty-eight hours to Joss Erroll. I was sitting on my veranda, when I heard the noise of a motor-bike and as I looked up a despatch rider in khaki uniform rode up and delivered an urgent message.[77]

To Blundell's amazement, this ordered him to report immediately to the GOCHQ in Nairobi. He packed a bag with a few clothes and was there the same afternoon. The next day, Joss informed him that a battalion had mutinied in the Northern Frontier District and, as it was still very unsettled, Blundell was to command it. Joss arranged for him to serve for four weeks with the 1st Battalion of King's African Rifles before actually taking over the mutinied battalion. Thus Joss had sealed Blundell's fate: 'Very self-consciously and unsure of myself, I went into the 1st KAR with the rank of

Major.' Blundell's former impression of Joss leading 'an easy, rather aimless life' was dispelled.[78]

By the end of September 1939 it was clear in Kenya that the short rains had failed, heralding further disaster for production.[79] Meanwhile, recruits were being enlisted daily and training was in full swing. By this time, over four hundred men had been sent to active units, as well as a few to Supply and Transport.

Making life even more uncertain for the settlers, towards the end of September the Governor Sir Robert Brooke-Popham resigned suddenly, to go to found an air armada in Canada. There was genuine regret over his departure. Regarded by the settlers as one of the more successful governors in living memory, he had pushed for white settlement and extended the tea quota. Despite his natural reserve, he had endeared himself to the settlers: the *Kenya Weekly News* grumbled that the colony was losing 'by miles the best Governor we have had since the war and who, when things needed to be done, gained more attention from the Colonial Office than the normal run of Governors'.[80] Attorney-General Walter Harragin, of late Acting Colonial Secretary, was to be put over the heads of the Chief Justice and Chief Secretary, as Acting Governor. Chief Secretary Sir Armigel de Wade was on leave. This move was described as 'breaking every known precedent'. The Harragins and their two daughters moved into Government House.[81] Walter Harragin's replacement as Acting Colonial Secretary was Mr Gilbert McCall Rennie, who subsequently became Chief Secretary. 'These arrangements are somewhat abnormal and have been made to ensure the least possible dislocation of the work of the Governor ... [but] I think it is a good appointment,' the editor of the *Kenya Weekly News* commented. 'In fact,' he joked sarcastically, 'it was almost worthwhile burning all the precedents in the Secretariat in order to do it.'[82] Harragin had a real first-hand knowledge of the colony, the piece went on; he was a man 'in whom the country has confidence and there never was a time when the Governor was more badly needed'.

Walter Harragin was regarded by the loftier set of the settler community as 'the first really acceptable civil servant, socially, that

Nairobi had ever known'.[83] As one member of the committee of Muthaiga Country Club observed, 'Walter Harragin was the first Government servant to be truly accepted at Muthaiga . . . doubtless made acceptable by his Acting Governorship.'[84] The division between the administration and the aristocratic settlers was well defined; civil servants were usually members of Nairobi Club, not Muthaiga. Joss and Walter Harragin saw one another daily at this stage – in the course of their work, as well as for games of bridge in the evenings at Muthaiga when time permitted.

Joss had discussed with Brookham the possibility of a job with the Foreign Office in London, before the latter left Nairobi at the end of September. After he left he wrote twice to Joss, once from London in October and once from Canada. No copy of the first letter survives, only a reference to it in Brookham's second.

> My dear Joss,
>   I wrote to you from London to say that I had been in touch with a man in the Foreign Office about a job for you and I just got a letter from him to say that his inquiries have so far led to no result. I can only go back to what I said in my letter to you from England and suggest that you should join the fighting forces in some capacity.[85]

Brookham's departure did nothing for morale. Kenya was facing 'the worst drought since European occupation of Kenya had begun, the locust menace attaining a proportion which put any previous infestation in the shade'.[86] Furthermore, 'Production is sinking like a stone. Importation may be necessary to feed "the swarms of militaires" and not a whisper of any plan to keep production at all, let alone increase it. Truly a strange, strange war,' Nellie Grant lamented from Njoro. The Government, 'in their laudable efforts to prevent profiteering,' she continued sarcastically, 'have in many cases fixed the price of raw products so low that the farmer can barely get back his production cost. Maize at Kitale for example, which had been fixed at 6 shillings per bag, will now only be paid a quarter of crops, the locusts having eaten the remainder.' Because of fixed prices farmers were threatening to give up production, 'let the land go back' and 'either live on their separate allowances or else leave their farms'.[87] If the locust infestation increased, Kenya would be faced with having to import foodstuffs, or go without.[88]

The Government was working under difficult conditions: 'The whole machinery of Government is complicated by the necessity of steering a middle course between satisfying military needs and continuing the normal business of the country.'[89] The military were taking all available men for war. There were two thousand farmers in the colony. By now, every man of the right age in those farming families had been, or was waiting to be, called up. Wives were being left to carry on alone on isolated farms, with little experience of running them and, because of petrol rationing, no means by which to visit neighbours, so their isolation was increased. Some managed to retain a sense of humour in these trying circumstances: 'One settler's young wife who was running her husband's dairy farm informed her supervisor that she had had the bull put down because it had chased her. The supervisor reasoned, "But what are the cows to do if they have no bull?" "They will have to do like the rest of us and go without," replied the wife.'[90]

Marc Lawrence's daughter Joan married young Stephen Hemsted soon after war broke out. She went to live in Londiani – alone: 'I had to put all my time into farming and the farms were ten miles apart, I used to ride from one to the other on my horse, and managed 300 acres of pyrethrum, with masses of labour. Many were totos who did the picking. I only had a horse, a gun and a dog – no wireless and no telephone.'[91] Hundreds of Kenya wives could have told a similar story during the Second World War.

Unfortunately, government action was concentrating all war preparations – including the working male populace – around Nairobi, thereby ruining the up-country towns, which could no longer produce meat, eggs and other produce. Such centres as Nakuru, Eldoret and Kitale were fast emptying, and unless the flow of workers was checked they would have to face the closure of many business firms, and institutions like clubs and hospitals. As in peacetime, the settlers felt their plight was overlooked: 'Now in a war such as our nation is waging at the moment, the ruin and bankrupting of a small Colony like Kenya may sound comparatively unimportant.'

Colonial jitters were exacerbated as October drew on and the identity of the new Governor had still not been announced. The suggestion that Henry Moore, Colonial Secretary in Kenya in 1934, was a likely candidate, brought a faint sense of optimism to an otherwise bleak picture. The settlers liked and trusted 'Monkey' Moore, regarding him as 'one of the best Colonial Secretaries we ever had, with a charming wife and who knew the country backwards'. As Deputy Under-secretary of State for the Colonies in succession to Sir John Shuckburgh, he had barely settled into his Whitehall post when three months later it was announced that he was to succeed Air Chief-Marshal Sir Robert Brooke-Popham as Governor and Commander-in-Chief of the Colony and Protectorate of Kenya.[92] He would take up his post in the New Year of 1940.

Life in the colony was dominated by the war. At this time Glady Delamere was working tirelessly to ensure comforts for the troops, particularly of the ranks. She was always the driving force behind productions at the Theatre Royal, in Delamere Avenue. Joss, as a friend and working so nearby, automatically supported her productions, usually attending first nights.

Her latest show, Agatha Christie's *A Murder Has Been Arranged*, opened on the evening of 3 November, the day that Joss's latest appointment was published: he was now 'the newest member of the Standing Committee for rural areas under local Government (District Councils) Ordinance'.[93] Joss often attended this sort of occasion with Walter Harragin; they were frequently 'surrounded by a posse of Governors, Sir Philip Mitchell representing Uganda, Tanganyika, Zanzibar [and] Nyasaland and the new GOC, Lieutenant General Sir Alan Cunningham, and Members of Staff'.

Glady also ran the canteen for South African troops, in Hardinge Street more or less opposite Torr's Hotel (renamed 'Tart's Hotel' by settlers and troops alike), which was off limits to non-European personnel.[94] She adopted the custom of inviting warrant-officers and NCOs to lunch, turning a blind eye to rank, although commissioned officers were generally invited to dinner'.[95] Glady 'brought wonderful hampers of food to the men. She was the kindest person'; she had been one of the first people to give up her house – already Loresho had been turned into a convalescent home for South African soldiers, while she occupied her own guest cottage nearby.[96]

With the influx of the Army and the Air Force, Muthaiga Country Club opened itself to 'Military Members'. To accommodate them, a new wing was hastily added – still referred to today as the 'military wing'. The flush of young subalterns saw Idina in her element once more. Since her divorce from Joss she had married and divorced Donald Haldeman, an American. She was still living at Clouds, the home she bought after her marriage to Joss ended, where her fifth husband, Flight Lieutenant Vincent Williams Soltau, would join her on leave from war duties. One early arrival from London asked his adjutant if he knew Lady Idina. 'Well,' the adjutant replied, 'everyone knows *of* her. She has a dreadful reputation and it wouldn't be wise for you to be seen about with her.' Shortly after this cautioning, the adjutant spotted the subaltern dancing 'most amorously' with her. 'Look here,' he castigated the subaltern next day, 'I have warned you about Lady Idina . . . she's old enough to be your mother.'

'She *is* my mother' was the reply.[97] This young man, his brother and their father were all soon to be killed in action.

Dances held at Torr's were confined to ranks – officers were barred admission. These were supplemented by 'Scotch hops' at the St Andrew's Church Hall every Friday, instigated by the Moderator of the Church of Scotland, Reverend Steel, the father of the British politician Sir David Steel. The Scotch hops became so popular with the troops that by the middle of 1940 these events were held twice a week, yet no alcohol was ever served, refreshments consisting of sandwiches, rolls and cakes and soft drinks.

The first two months of the war had taken their toll on Joss's energies. Normally enjoying the best of health, by November he was suffering from the strain of overworking. Though intending to 'expatiate at some length' on the Divorce Bill at Legco, he prefaced his abbreviated comments wittily: 'Hon. Members will be relieved to hear that I have a very sore throat and shall be unable to do so here.'[98]

Michael Biggs, a young captain in the KAR in Nairobi, was in a better position than most to understand how important Joss's work had become to Walter Harragin. Living in the Harragin household when Harragin had been made Acting Governor, he said that Harragin spoke warmly of Joss's vital contribution.[99] With the likelihood of being posted at any time, there was a run of Nairobi weddings towards the end of 1939. In what would have been regarded as indecent haste before the war, Harragin's daughter Kath became publicly engaged to Michael on 22 December. Joss threw an engagement party for the couple at Muthaiga Club, and after Christmas plans were well advanced for their wedding day, 20 January 1940.[100]

The Harragin sisters were writing out wedding invitations when Anna noticed that the Rocco family were not on the list. They began to discuss how the omission had occurred. Their mother, Madge, said nothing. When their father entered, he saw at once that his daughters were puzzled. The Roccos were *personae non gratae*, he explained. The new Governor, Sir Henry Moore, and his wife had lent the Harragin family Government House for the wedding. Protocol dictated that inviting the Roccos there would be 'impossible'. 'Mario is already prepared to take over my job,' Harragin stated gravely.★ Kath and Anna were stunned by what their father told them. Faced with his explanation, there was nothing for it but to promise never to mention the subject again.[101]

The matter had been dropped in the Harragin household but it was not quite the end of the saga *chez* Rocco, at Dominion di Doriano. When Giselle Rocco discovered that she and Mario had not been invited to the wedding, she went berserk and, taking a

---

★Walter Harragin, a rampant anti-fascist, suspected Mario Rocco of supporting Mussolini. Rocco's son Dorian's unpublished letter to the *Sunday Times* on 4.2.99 states, 'My father . . . was no fascist. Having been put across the frontier into exile by Mussolini in 1926 he did not return to the country for more than a decade and had nothing to do with politics thereafter. He went to Italy in 1939 to see his eighty-year-old father. With the clouds of war approaching, he was convinced it would be for the last time.'

hammer, smashed the bust of Anna she had been sculpting.* Mario
Rocco had in fact tried to leave for Italy before the war began, but
was stopped at Eastleigh airport – 'without explanation or justifica-
tion', his daughter Mirella wrote in her memoir, *African Saga*. Once
Italy entered the war in June, Mario Rocco was interned.

During the period regarded as the phoney war, much preparatory
activity was taking place in the colony. At this point the town of
Nairobi was only partially blacked out in anticipation of air attacks.
Not until the end of March 1940 had the British Government
decided that East Africa must be brought into line with Britain and
other parts of the Empire, in making the weather a secret. Public
buildings were sandbagged; their windows were taped against blast.
But when Mussolini declared war on Britain, Kenya was threatened
with invasion by land. It was hard to believe that the enemy would
forgo the chance of bombing Kilindini and the railway workshops
in Nairobi.

Joss's friend Herbert Blin Stoyle, an authority on the whole of
the East Africa network of communications, ran the railway workshops. Blin Stoyle was hard put to meet the wear and tear on locomo-
tives or the difficulties caused by the lack of spare parts in Kenya.
'The mechanical department kept the wheels turning to the great
credit of Mr Blin Stoyle and of R. I. Kirkland, the locomotive
Superintendent, while the European, Asian and African staff knew
no rest throughout the war.' Also, the production of tanks known
as Suzies was carried out under the expert eye of another of Joss's
friends, Jack Soames.[102] Soames had helped to design tanks for the
Russians before the war.[103]

Joss deposited the Buick with Herbert Blin Stoyle at the railway
workshops one day at about this time, with a shattered windscreen.
He had turned up at Fernside & Reliance beforehand, to fill up with
petrol. Robert Creighton, the mechanic, noticing that the windscreen was shattered, asked what had happened. Jules the chimpanzee, Joss had joked, had been a better shot than he realised. Creighton

---

*Anna was so beautiful that Giselle had sought Madge's permission to make a
clay head of her.

thought no more about the matter. But Joss asked the railway work-shops for replacement bullet-proof glass to be fitted. Weeks later when he was driving his friend Ginger Birkbeck over to Oserian she gazed out of her open window, admiring the dramatic sky over the water as one of the afternoon storms blew up. Joss halted abruptly. He got out and walked round to the passenger door, opened it, and wound the window shut. 'What are you doing, Joss?' Ginger protested. 'Now I can't see properly. What's wrong with this glass?' Joss told her that a few weeks before, while passing the Somali settlement, shots had been fired at him. He believed this had actually been an attempt to kill him – hence the bullet-proof glass.[104]

By 1940 Mussolini had amassed two huge armies on the African continent, halting desert expeditions and posing further problems in this huge, silent corner of the earth with its shifting sands. Because of a woeful lack of water, in Libya the progress of some three hundred thousand soldiers had been impeded, although they remained poised to invade Egypt. Cairo was to become the heart of the Libyan desert's theatre of war. Joss's future would also be mapped out from there.

When the new Governor Sir Henry Moore and his wife Daphne arrived in January 1940, he spoke warmly of how well the settlers had responded to the call for men to enlist in the face of trying conditions.[105] Kenya was still feeling the effects of the drought of the previous months. Although 'good rain' was now beginning to fall in many districts, the prospect of thrips could not be avoided – expert forecasts for coffee planters were poor.[106] The Saturday morning before Katherine Harragin's wedding, Joss attended a public meeting 'the best attended ever', at the Blue Posts Hotel in Thika, organised by the Thika Farmers' Association to discuss the crisis that had arisen from the famine conditions following the drought in the settled areas and adjacent reserves. Ewart Grogan was there too, as were the Kenya Farmers' Association chairman Mr Whitmore and general manager Colonel Griffiths. Joss was able to announce the comforting news that, following discussion of the matter in Executive Council, the Government 'was willing to bear a certain amount of the burden' and would help maize growers by subsidising their railway freight costs. His words were greeted with warm applause.

Two days before Mussolini joined forces with Hitler on 10 June 1940, Joss was made a Staff Captain East Africa Force HQ. On 18 July he was appointed Assistant Military Secretary at East Africa Command Headquarters, still with the rank of captain.[107]

By now even Alice de Janzé had donned the uniform of the St John's Ambulance volunteers and was working at the Maia Carberry Nursing Home in Girouard Road. With all the troops flooding in, Nairobi soon became so short of accommodation that people took a bed where it was given and without complaint – 'a woman who could not get a room in a hotel . . . slept at the Maia Carberry Nursing Home in her sick child's room'.[108] One of Joss's friends found herself sleeping in the bath in one of the suites at the Norfolk Hotel.

The privations of the European settlers in Kenya were not always recognised by the Government at home. Indeed, echoing round the corridors of Whitehall was the complaint that Kenya was engaging troops who would be more usefully deployed elsewhere. On 12 August, after a meeting of the War Cabinet, Churchill sent a message to General Wavell (GOC Middle East) reflecting the concern he had expressed to Lord Lloyd, the Colonial Secretary, in Whitehall: 'Let me have a return of the white settlers of military age in Kenya. Are we to believe they have not formed any local units for the defence of their own province? If not, the sooner they are made to realise their position the better. No troops ought to be in Kenya at the present time other than the settlers and the KAR.' Churchill's message caused great offence in Kenya. As W. E. Crosskill put it in *The Two Thousand Mile War*, 'his minute [12 August 1940] is badly recorded in his history of the Second World War without comment or clarification and is therefore, by implication, a slur on the British people of East Africa. His doubts should have been withdrawn as publicly as they were uttered as they were utterly unfounded.'[109]

Captain John Gouldbourn had been a subaltern with the Royal Leicestershire Regiment, at the time when troops were desperately needed for Kenya and recruitment notices went up in army messes all over England. He had applied because not only was pay tax-free there, but triple the amount soldiers were being offered in Britain.[110]

Gouldbourn arrived in Mombasa in November 1940 on the SS *New Amsterdam*, a Netherland Lloyd Line refrigeration ship: 'The fact is that the KAR consisted of only six hundred raw recruits, farmers, lawyers, DCs and DOs and the Kenya Police themselves were given quick training on Eldoret Race Course. It was Erroll who advised on drafts of officers and NCOs who came out from home like myself. I suppose it was his action which sent me to Eldoret and the Kenya Regiment Territorial Army.' After six weeks in Nairobi, Captain Gouldbourn had applied to GOC for a posting to Ethiopia, which was when his only encounter with Joss occurred. 'I never forgot this, perhaps because Erroll was killed so soon after-wards: I had to apply through Francis Scott, who was occupying an inner office. As I approached the door, Erroll came out of Scott's office, asked what I wanted, and having listened took charge, "You needn't see Francis Scott, I'll deal with it."' Gouldbourn had the distinct feeling that Erroll was 'keeping tabs on everything, monitor-ing what was going on. Anyway, I got to Ethiopia so I cannot complain.'[111]

Another officer who arrived on the same ship was the Hon. Frederick Fermor-Hesketh, of the Scots Guards. According to Gouldbourn, 'Fermor-Hesketh was part of "the club" – all Old Etonians – as was Lizzie Lezard' – a friend of Joss's. Lezard was in the KAR and had arrived in the colony in 1940. Fermor-Hesketh was in Intelligence and 'went into the Adjutant's Office, the nerve centre of Operations'.[112]

Since accommodation now became so difficult in Nairobi, Lizzie Lezard often shared Joss's bungalow. Lizzie was particularly witty, perhaps the most amusing of all Joss's male friends. The bungalow's accommodation was frugal compared to Oserian, but Joss's hospital-ity was no less generous in Nairobi than in the splendour of his Naivasha home. Fabian Wallis, another old schoolfriend, stayed in Joss's spare room while waiting for the RAF to post him.

In August 1940 Mrs Filmer left her husband and went to reside alone at Muthaiga Club. Her exit from 'the Shell house' in Tchui

Road had been prompted by a row with her husband over her involvement with Joss. Joss saw her occasionally during his luncheon break at Muthaiga, when they would retire to the privacy of her room. He seemed to avoid those times when her children might appear. In fact Pheely's twelve-year-old son, Peter, met Joss only twice. Both encounters left the enduring impression that Joss was 'distant, not the least avuncular and had no interest in children at all' – and yet such an impression is so strongly at odds with Joss's response to children in general that it could simply have been that he had already met Diana Delves Broughton by the time he met Peter and that his feelings for Pheely Weely were ebbing, leaving him no need to cultivate her son. If Joss was putting up his guard against complicating the relationship further by befriending her son, he continued to be kind to Mrs Filmer. Her son Peter recalled, 'I left Kenton a few days before the end of term, early in December. I was fetched by my mother in Joss's Buick with his driver. I suppose my father had been called away, up-country with his driver.'[113] Apart from that all thought of a future with Mrs Filmer had already been put behind him.[114] Joss knew that her departure was imminent (Peter was due to enter Hilton College in Natal in January 1941), but with passages so difficult to obtain, none of them knew exactly when she would leave. There was little doubt that she expected to become the next Countess of Erroll,[115] but, much as she may have wanted to become his wife, their relationship was entering its third year and, whatever had been the motive for Joss's closeness to her originally, their affair seemed to have run its course.

In the closing months of 1940 Joss again became extremely agitated about his personal safety – concerned enough to drive the long journey to Kisumu, when he had scant free time, to seek 'the indefatigable Fazan's' advice.[116] He did not seek advice or opinions readily, but Fazan was one whose opinion Joss respected, and whose discretion he could count upon utterly. As liaison officer for the East Africa Force, Fazan inspired great confidence. 'When Fazan arrives, everything will be all right,' people used to say.[117]

Fazan never spoke directly about what Joss had confided to him. The matter of his visit only came up because a newspaper article about him had caused Fazan to remark to his daughter Eleanor that Joss was not as 'black as he was painted'. Her father told her that Joss had been in some sort of trouble, and that he had advised Joss to apply for active service as soon as possible. Whatever reason lay behind Joss's impromptu drive to Kisumu from Nairobi, his fear was palpable.[118]

Between 6 and 14 August, Joss missed two debates in Legco, the first time since his election to Council that he had been absent.[119] Quite out of character for one so punctilious, he sent no apologies. Furthermore, it is easy to document all his movements in those months in some form or other, except for that particular week when none can be accounted for.[120] The delicacy of the military situation made everyone wary, and Joss too started to move with much more discretion.

9

The Infernal Triangle

On about 12 November 1941 Sir Jock Delves Broughton and his new bride Diana arrived in Nairobi.[1] Ostensibly Broughton had come over to Kenya to farm land he had been awarded in the 1919 Soldier Settlement Scheme. He himself claimed that the colony offered him the opportunity to obtain some 'proper war work', since there was nothing in England for someone over forty to do.[2] Broughton would restrict his comments on his work to generalisations. Often he would hint mysteriously at having come to Kenya 'to undertake certain things connected with the War', implying that he was 'contributing to feeding the mass of troops' gathering in Nairobi.[3] But it was known that he was keen to redeem his own poor army record from the First World War, which continued to give rise to rumours of cowardice. An Old Etonian, Broughton had held a commission with the Irish Guards for seventeen years, but he had never reached France at the start of the war.[4] Having caught sunstroke while 'rushing hither and thither' at Wellington Barracks, London, he continued to work for a day or two, but succumbed to sickness when sailing with his regiment on 9 August 1914. He was sent back to England in a tender before reaching the shores of France.[5] To Broughton's eternal shame, this episode was mentioned in print by Rudyard Kipling.[6] In 1915 he had a car accident, which fractured his right wrist. In 1916 'he had sufficiently recovered to be sent again to France to a School of Instruction, to attend a course which fitted him to become Brigade Major in Dover'.[7]

Not only did he have a poor war record to make up for. Ever since 1938, when his daughter Rosamund had married the head of the Fraser Clan, Lord Lovat, Broughton had longed to impress his son-in-law, the well regarded scion of the Frasers, one of the Catholic Highlander families. On the outbreak of war, Lovat joined Lovat's Scouts, the yeomanry regiment founded by his father. During the phoney-war period he became involved with various irregular forces out of which the commandos grew. His war record was brilliant; he was awarded a Military Cross and a Distinguished Service Order.[8]

Sir Jock Delves Broughton, at fifty-seven, was generally accepted to be an irascible, cold, remote and vain individual. According to Peggy Pitt, Walter Harragin's secretary, he was 'well preserved, with sleek, dark hair without a trace of grey, an upright slim frame, always impeccably tailored, with something of distinction in his bearing and apparently perfectly fit'. 'I never met anyone who truly liked Jock,' one of his distant cousins observed, recognising his forty-year struggle for popularity and his craving for friendship and adulation.[9] Broughton was also a compulsive letter writer, possibly to combat loneliness. The lavish way in which he entertained at his beautiful eighteenth-century family seat designed by Samuel Wyatt, Doddington Park in Cheshire, was his way of overcoming the antipathy of those around him. In public view, Broughton did things in style – for instance, hiring the banqueting hall at the Adelphi Hotel in Liverpool so as to host a luncheon party before the Grand National at Aintree every year. The food for this annual jamboree in the Broughton calendar was always cooked and prepared at Doddington, and transported to Liverpool along with his private staff who waited upon his hundred or more guests at the Adelphi.[10]

Broughton had first met Diana Caldwell in 1935. She soon became his mistress – he referred to her as 'my blonde' – and he installed her (unbeknown to his wife Vera) in the Garden House, which she occupied with her mother and sister at Doddington. Broughton was old enough to be her father. Indeed, by a quirky coincidence, as a young man he had met Diana's mother when she was pregnant with Diana.[11]

Diana had worked in a cocktail bar, the Blue Goose, in Bruton Mews, off Berkeley Square, and earlier as a model in a London fashion house before becoming intimate with Broughton. She too liked to attract attention, to be 'caught' by society journalists and be photographed with 'the right people' for the pages of the *Tatler* or the *Sketch*. She and her sister Daphne used the Blue Goose to meet the 'right sort' – men with a private income and a title.[12]

Diana got on better with men than with women. Her need to shine in her father's eyes and outdo her older and far prettier sister had set her from an early age on a course of beguilement. Lacking confidence as a child, having inherited her mother's heavy jaw and developed a lumpish figure in adolescence, once she reached adulthood Diana transformed her straight, mousy hair with a perm and peroxide, and made the most of her looks with stylish clothes and make-up. Also, '[s]he was a fantastic sportswoman, a woman of action living up to her name "huntress" . . . good at squash, fishing, deep-sea and fly-fishing . . . always applying herself, like an actress learning a role, taking on whatever the interest was of her current lover, in order to share his world'.[13]

As a company director of the Ashanti Quartzite Gold Mining, British Maikop Oil Company and Whim Well Copper Mines,[14] Diana's father had taught her the value of precious metals. Her obsession with gems and gold had been stimulated by her early awareness of their raw values. In 1937 she married Vernon Motion – a union which lasted less than a year. According to a friend, each had wedded in the belief that the other was rich. It had taken a fortnight to discover that neither had a penny.[15]

The date of Broughton's decision to undertake the journey to Kenya is not known. Because he and Diana were unmarried when they embarked for South Africa en route to Nairobi on one of the few Union Castle Line boats that was destined for Cape Town, she purported to be travelling as his secretary.[16] His decree absolute would occur just as they docked in South Africa. Despite wartime restrictions and difficulty in obtaining passages for civilians, the couple apparently had no problem getting berths. In her seventies, Diana would confide to a close friend how she and Broughton had never intended to marry – and she also admitted later that she had slept with at least two other men on the voyage.[17]

Broughton's first application to Immigration for entry into Kenya for himself, Diana and her maid Miss Dorothy Wilks was refused because of the women's single status, thanks to a law passed on 4 September 1939 forbidding any unmarried white woman entry into the colony. 'The administration was frightened that all the South African whores would come up in droves to start business here.'[18]

Before marrying Diana, therefore, Broughton made a pact with her which he legalised in Cape Town on 21 September 1940, before the notary public Otto Kemna Dose and witnesses. By this pact he promised to make over to 'Diana Caldwell, Spinster of 4 Duke Street, Manchester Square, London' the sum of £5,000 a year. To quote from this unusual document:

> The Appearer of the One Part [Delves] do cede to, make over, give to and settle upon the Appearer of the Other Part [Diana] as and for her own sole free and absolute property use and benefit, as and by way of marriage settlement the sum of £5,000.00 Sterling per annum, for the period of seven years . . . on condition . . . that should the Appearer of the Other Part [Diana] predecease him the Appearer of the one Part [Delves] during the said period of seven years, or should the said marriage be dissolved for any other reason during the said period . . . then the said income shall revert to him the Appearer of the One Part [Delves] to be his sole and absolute property as if these presents had never been made.[19]

With the pact secured, on 5 November 1940 at a register office in Durban, 'Miss Diana Caldwell, Spinster' – as Mrs Diana Motion saw fit to call herself – married Sir Henry John Delves Broughton, divorcee.[20] Afterwards Broughton took her to stay at the Gleneagles Hotel outside Durban, where the aviation pioneer J. C. Carberry happened also to be staying. Straight after the wedding Broughton applied for a second time to the authorities in Kenya for permission for himself, his bride and Diana's Wilks to enter the colony.[21] (Diana had persuaded this young Englishwoman to abandon her job at the Marine Hotel in Durban, where she and Broughton had first stayed that October, and to work for her instead.)[22] However, Miss Wilks was still in the 'disallowed' category. Unusually for a civilian application, Broughton's second request for permission to enter the colony arrived on the Governor Sir Henry Moore's desk. Unaccountably overriding the embargo on spinsters, he wrote in the official red ink, 'Let them all come.'[23] Once the Broughtons had received clearance, they arranged for Wilky, as they called her, to sail up to Mombasa. They themselves came in to Mombasa by flying-boat. June Carberry was there to meet her husband J. C. off the same plane; the four travelled up country together on the train, forging a close friendship that was to have a great effect on the last few weeks of Joss's life. The Broughtons reached Muthaiga in mid-November. Miss Wilks arrived a week later.[24]

Another untoward aspect of the couple's presence in Kenya was Broughton's excessive consumption of petrol – well beyond what he would normally have been rationed – which raised a few eyebrows. Coupons were impossible to come by, no matter how wealthy one was, yet Broughton somehow obtained them. As Lord Erroll's son-in-law later pointed out, when it came to parcelling out the coupons, the onus lay with the issuing authorities.[25] It was also noted that there was 'no sign extant of Broughton and his wife seeking opportunities to join any of the numerous projects to help' with the war effort.[26]

Also landing in Kenya around the time of the Broughtons' arrival was Lieutenant Hugh Thompson Dickinson, who had already got himself posted to Nairobi where he was eagerly awaiting the arrival of Diana. An intimate friend and intermittent lover of Diana's since 1934, Dickinson had often filled for her the role of escort. Her pet name for him was Hughsie Daisy. Dickinson was waiting at Nairobi Station on the platform when the Broughtons stepped down from the train on 12 November.[27] There and then Diana passed him something that even the closest of lovers would not normally be given – an envelope containing the papers that the notary public had drawn up formalising her curious marriage pact with Broughton.[28]

The Broughtons started house-hunting immediately. Broughton, who already knew of Oserian, had heard that Joss was now occupying a bungalow virtually opposite Muthaiga and asked whether he could rent Oserian from him. He had already been introduced to Joss fleetingly over a decade before, in 1927, at Muthaiga Club. Joss politely declined to let Oserian to him, but the friendship between the Broughtons and Joss grew from this point. Instead of Naivasha, the couple's accommodation was to be a house in Marula Lane, in Karen, which belonged to a Dr Gielinger. He was absent, so his daughter handled the letting of the house with his lawyer Lazarus Kaplan, who acted for Broughton as well.[29] Broughton was to rent the house in Marula Lane for £15 per month for six months. It was fully furnished, and as part of the property there was a guest house which Diana would offer to Hughsie Daisy. Dickinson would come and go as he pleased from here, back and forth from the coast. Among themselves, Diana, Broughton and Hughsie Daisy referred to the guest house as the 'rest house'. It edged on to Tree Lane, a murram track used by a few neighbouring residents and bordering the rest of the property.[30]

Broughton was told that he could move in around 15 December, and meanwhile he and Diana stayed at Muthaiga making brief sorties so that he could introduce her to old friends.[31] One such visit was to Jack Soames' farm, Burgaret Hall, in November, where they spent a few days under the snow-capped Mount Kenya in Nanyuki, indulging among other things in leisurely revolver practice. For this exercise Broughton used one of two Colts that he had failed to declare upon entering Kenya, although he had declared his other weaponry.[32]

The first entertaining that Broughton did in Kenya was to hold a party at Muthaiga for forty-four guests including Glady Delamere, Jack Soames and the Carberrys.[33]

Everyone who had been at Muthaiga when the newly married couple arrived remembered how, from mid-November, Lady Broughton began to show a keen interest in Joss. Female members were disapproving of the way in which she appeared during the daytime, on her honeymoon, bespangled and glittering with diamonds. Furthermore, when Broughton suggested that Diana go and unpack, her loud protest – for all to hear – 'Darling, you know I can't unpack without my lady's maid', had then done the rounds among the members' wives. They were appalled by the vulgarity of this newcomer.[34] But Diana's disregard for 'good form' had not fazed Joss in the slightest; typically, he was drawn to such brazen behaviour.

Before long, several friends noticed also that Joss had abandoned his habit of lunching at home; he had previously opted for solitude at the bungalow, taking two hours off to take stock after a busy morning at GCHQ, and Waweru had prepared his meal. He now spent the break in the company of the Broughtons. Initially he had hesitated over Broughton's invitations to join himself and Diana at 1 p.m. for lunch. Broughton, however, had been insistent, pressing Joss with the argument that he needed to eat somewhere so he might as well join them at the club. Accordingly, Joss, Diana and Broughton were lunching together every day.[35]

Next, this odd trio started taking early-morning rides out towards Dagoretti from Derek Erskine's Riverside Stables. 'The Broughtons were both very keen on horses and used to hire ours to go riding.' Erskine, on compassionate leave, was getting to know the couple well: 'I found her to be extremely charming. He was obviously a conceited man . . . After a while they brought Joss Erroll up to ride. Joss's horses were at livery at Chiromo, in the same area [at Lady MacMillan's stables] so Joss would bring his own horses. I would take them for long rides in the Kikuyu Reserve. Soon Broughton started to feel his bad leg which had been wounded in the First World War and would not go out at all, and Joss and Diana would come out alone. After a while they told me that they knew their way about. I was no longer required as Cicerone.'[36]

Joss's circle was struck by the physical resemblance between Diana and Phyllis Filmer. Both were 'blondish, with bobbed hair, in the fashion of the day'. Yet these rivals for Joss's affection were in a different class, as Molly Stoyle remarked: 'Pheely Weely was pathetic compared to Diana – of the same type – but plain and small.'[37] Even before Joss and Diana found the opportunity to go to bed together, Joss was instantly and wildly attracted to her; and there was now a subtle shift in his relationship with Pheely, friends noted, besides a muting in his reactions to her when Diana was in the same room. When Pheely's husband secured berths on the SS *City of New York* which was due to sail south on either 3 or 4 December, and Pheely accompanied her son Peter to his new school in South Africa, she had no choice but to conduct her affair with Joss by correspondence.[38]

Once Pheely had disappeared, Joss's attraction to Diana gained momentum, provoking much comment: 'Diana and Joss's relationship was quite different from Joss's relationship with Pheely. It had a glow.'[39] 'When Joss fell in love with Diana, we smelled danger,' observed Patsy Chilton, the then nineteen-year-old wife of Dr Roger Bowles.[40] Young and inexperienced as she was, Patsy (Bowles) could see for herself that it was not Joss but Diana who was making the running: 'Joss was a Restoration cuckold so when Diana first made advances to him at Muthaiga Club for all to see, it was a joke among us. Plenty of women threw themselves at Joss, they always had done. He could take or leave them. But with Diana, suddenly it was serious.'[41]

Between 18 and 22 December, somewhat oddly, Broughton spent three or four days at Joss's bungalow. The fact emerged at Broughton's trial; the question of where Diana was at this time was not raised there.[42]

By Christmas, Joss and the Broughtons seemed inseparable. As Derek Erskine remarked, 'It was very obvious that something was brewing, because Diana and Joss were always together and Jock would sit brooding and he didn't dance . . . it seemed to us that a climax was approaching.'[43] Diana was exactly Joss's kind and Joss sensed that he had met his match in her. The love they experienced appeared to be a physical, practical love, devoid of emotional agonising. No one could help but notice them as a couple whenever they took to the dance floor. Joss had requested 'Let's Fall in Love' so many times for Diana that not only the band at Torr's, but the quartet at the Blue Room and at the Four Hundred Club too, would automatically play their theme song for them. The quaint Swahili translation of the club's name, *Eenie hapana iko hapana iko* – 'Four, is not there, is not there' – appealed to the lovers so much that it became a key phrase that they would often repeat to each other with a smile, part of that private code that springs up in all intimate relationships.[44]

Whereas, before, Joss had discarded women when he pleased, now he was confiding to Dorothy Blin and Glady Delamere about his emotional bond with Diana, making the point that she was the first girl younger than himself – at twenty-seven she was twelve years his junior – whom he felt he could truly love.[45]

From the beginning of the New Year 1941, Joss and Diana were caught up in a vortex of gaiety, taking every opportunity to spend as much time together as Joss's duties allowed. On 3 January – the first Friday in the New Year – they escaped from everyone, even Broughton, to be alone together for the weekend. Joss's chauffeur Noor Mohammed drove them to the Carberrys' coffee estate, Sere-mai, near Nyeri about a hundred miles from Nairobi. Joss's intention was to spend forty-eight hours there.[46] As soon as they reached Seremai Noor Mohammed retreated to the servants' quarters until his services were required again. Joss asked him to report back for duty on the Sunday. At last no longer confined by protocol or opinion, the pair could enjoy themselves for two whole days. Both were consummate lovers, normally restive in relationships but now their opportunist natures seemed to be overruled as their passions fed each other.

Diana was so smitten that she believed she had eclipsed all other women in Joss's eyes. He began to make plans for their future, seeking outside approval for them, which in itself was unprecedented. On the way back from Seremai on Sunday 5 January he instructed his driver to go to Eastleigh racecourse. It was the big January meeting – the annual East African Derby. Taking the Blin Stoyles by surprise, he arrived with Diana and walked straight up to them in the members' enclosure. When Diana slipped away to powder her nose, Joss took the opportunity to ask Dorothy what she thought of her. She had always been straight with Joss, as she was now –

'Beautiful but hard.' Joss replied defensively without preamble, 'I love her. And I will marry her.'[47]

That night and for the two following, Diana remained with Joss at his bungalow, making no attempt to return to her house on Marula Lane until Wednesday 8 January.[48] Broughton never questioned Diana's trip to Seremai with Joss, seemingly assuming that the Carberrys had been in situ. Nor did Broughton ever raise any objection to Diana's absences, whether he thought she was with Joss or not – but for one occasion, an exception that was to prove extremely significant.

Often after dining together, Joss, Diana and Broughton drove the five and a half miles from Muthaiga to Kiambu along the murram track through coffee plantations to the Clairmont, a small hotel. The owner Jane Westbrook ran the place like a private house and produced very good food. Since the beginning of the war the Clairmont had become a favourite watering-hole for officers and Female Auxiliary Nursing Yeomanry nurses – FANYs – with only a twenty-four-hour leave pass. Not only was Jane Westbrook congenial, she also turned a blind eye to unmarried couples booking a room for the night. There was gramophone music to dance to, pools in the river in which to bathe; horses could be hired for rides in the forest at dawn, with breakfast waiting when the riders returned, and more dancing – even at that hour. The walls and ceiling of the Clairmont's large hall, the main room, were now permanently draped in blackout fabric which Jane Westbrook had decorated imaginatively with suns and moons, creating a romantic and 'lovely atmosphere in which to dance', turning day into night around the clock.[49]

Harragin's daughter Kath and her husband Michael Biggs witnessed several unforgettable moments between Joss and Diana at the Clairmont. Cheek to cheek, their heads as close as could be, their bodies pressed indecently against one another, this couple moved expertly around the floor 'as if glued together'.[50] In those days, even the younger generation regarded such open displays of intimacy as 'somewhat startling behaviour'. Joss and Diana became more and more uninhibited in public.

On 9 January Joss attended the funeral of Lord Baden-Powell in

Nyeri. He had known and admired the Chief Scout. More often than not, Joss's driver was behind the wheel during the daytime but he almost always drove himself after dark. Returning from the funeral that evening while en route for Nairobi, he had a slight accident on account of some minor mechanical failure. Luckily he had been able to drive himself back to Muthaiga, though the mishap forced him to put his own vehicle in for repair.[51]

Joss took the Buick routinely into 'L of C', where by now all vehicles were conscripted for war purposes. Roman Khan happened to be on duty and took in Joss's car himself. He hailed Roman as cheerfully as usual.[52] Whenever Joss's own Buick was in for service or repair, he habitually took an identical Buick that was owned by Gibbs Auto Tours. Joss requested this car now. Viscount Gerald Portman, a 2nd lieutenant at GOCHQ who had been a contemporary of Joss's at Eton, had just returned the very same vehicle to the L of C pool.[53]

On 10 January Broughton paid a visit to Bunson's travel agency in Nairobi to cancel a provisional booking he had made a few days earlier for two passages to Ceylon. Diana had strongly objected to going away. That same Friday Joss and an old-time settler friend of his, 'Long Lew' Llewellyn, dropped in on Lorna Swinburne-Ward (Joss's frequent partner at bridge) and spent the night at Gilston, Njoro. Lorna and her daughter Anne Buxton had witnessed Joss in love before, and decided that his love for Diana was different. Lorna asked him, 'And how is the lovely Diana?' Joss replied, 'I am not sure that I can keep her in the way to which she is accustomed.' For all these playful misgivings, Joss emanated happiness.[54]

On Saturday 11 January, Joss attended a Red Cross fête in Karen at the home of Mr and Mrs Parker. Their large garden bordered the Broughton property; their house stood not far from the guest house which Hughsie Daisy occupied from time to time. Parker was a retired bank manager from Mombasa; he and his wife Marion had been among the first to offer their home up for convalescent officers. The Fazans happened to be up in Nairobi from Kisumu and their daughters were out in force that day, doing their bit. Anthea Fazan was selling sweets wrapped in small cellophane packets laid out on a tray. Joss, in uniform, approached and asked if he might buy the entire collection of bonbons. Anthea was delighted, especially when he refused to take any for himself: 'Off you go and sell all of them to the other guests,' he said, promising her that she would 'make twice as much as anyone else'. He had been right, and it made her very happy. That encounter was to be her lasting image of him.[55]

The next day, Sunday, Joss was invited to a dinner party at the Broughtons' house in Marula Lane and to spend the night in the 'rest house' rather than drive all the way back to Muthaiga afterwards. Seven sat down to dine: the Broughtons, Joss and Glady, Dickie Pembroke, Gerald Portman and a Miss Lampson, a tall broad-shouldered blonde with a seductive voice. Diana was oblivious to the fact that the latter had been one of Joss's fleeting conquests; Betty Lampson appears to have partnered Gerry Portman that night. Gerry was 'fat, a great womaniser and singularly unattractive'. Glady arrived looking as chic ever, eyelashes laden with mascara, the usual gardenia pinned to her gown, floating in a cloud of Chanel No. 5 – like Diana. Few could ignore Glady's theatrical presence; some found her intimidating. Leichner stage make-up emphasised the effect: 'Not only did she apply liquid white to her face but also to her matronly bosom.'[56] Glady was unpredictable but could be counted upon to be provocative. Even those who loved her dearly regarded her sometimes as a mischief-maker.[57]

Early that evening Glady picked a fight with Gerald Portman. They were discussing the relative contributions of Britain and the colonies to the war effort. If he felt as he did, Glady shouted shrilly, 'why the hell had he come out here?' The shouting match had been unstoppable. At one point a glass candlestick was broken by someone hammering on the table. According to Broughton the evening was 'very unpleasant . . . Gerry and Glady abused each other like pick-pockets, which is always embarrassing for a host.'[58] And when they left the dining-room to go and dance, the row began all over again – which effectively cleared the dance floor although the gramophone was still playing.[59] By now, all the women but Betty Lampson had disappeared. Glady and Diana had retreated upstairs to Diana's bed-room where they remained for half an hour. Broughton and his male guests 'were very bored with no one to dance with'. When she reappeared, Joss managed to take Glady aside to Broughton's small study downstairs, where he admitted how fond he was of Lady Broughton. 'Very fond,' he stressed, adding that he would do anything for her; that he had never been so happy. He asked Glady's advice. She told him to make a clean breast of his love for Diana to Broughton. Having listened carefully, Joss brought the conversation to an end: 'You are often right. I will think about it and let you know' – his stock reply when he needed to mull things over.[60] Almost immediately afterwards Glady found Diana back in the drawing-room and confronted her.

'Do you know Joss is very much in love with you?'

'Yes,' Diana replied.

'What are you going to do about it?' – one of Glady's favourite challenges – 'Does he want to marry you?'

Diana said that he did. Glady appeared enthusiastic at the idea; wanting to see Joss happy. Diana's response had been to express fondness for Broughton: she did not want to hurt him. Glady had argued the point: 'But he is an old man and has had his life. Take your happiness where you can find it. There is a war on.' Finally, Glady gave Diana the same advice she had given to Joss – to make a clean breast: 'He will never give you up. It's the best thing you can do.' Joss had already tried to persuade Diana that the marriage pact should now be invoked – Broughton had given his word after all. Diana had nevertheless wavered: she had felt that she could not go through with it.[61] At the end of the evening Joss and Dickie Pembroke retired to the guest house, sharing it for the night.

Early on the Monday morning the Broughtons went hacking out in the plains below the Ngong Hills, accompanied by Joss who was mounted on one of their horses.[62] After breakfast, Joss left Marula Lane for GCHQ in Muthaiga.

At 4 p.m. Diana caught the train for Mombasa, and Waweru, Joss's major-domo, also boarded at Nairobi. Joss, however, drove to Athi River, the next station along the line, where he too caught the train. On Joss's instructions Waweru had already prepared refreshments for the couple so that they had no need to expose their presence to other passengers using the dining car. That night Joss joined Diana in her sleeping compartment. Broughton had taken himself off to stay with his friend Jack Soames at Burgaret Hall in Nanyuki for that week.

Upon reaching Mombasa, Diana was met by June Carberry, and they headed off for Malindi by road to the Eden Roc, J. C.'s hotel, named after June's favourite hotel in Cap Ferrat. Joss, meanwhile, went off to work at Kilindini – there was an Intelligence HQ near the deep-water harbour – telling Waweru to meet him at 3 p.m. at Mombasa Club. By teatime he was heading off to join Diana at the Eden Roc. A crowd of young officers including Hughsie Daisy enlivened the atmosphere at the Eden Roc that evening. Hughsie Daisy had come in from a 'working party' stationed in the bush on the Malindi–Mombasa road.[63] A full moon, shining high above the vast beach below the hotel and highlighting the breakers, created a stunning and romantic setting. Joss and Diana decided to swim naked in the sea – stripping off at the bottom of some two dozen very steep steps leading from the terrace of the hotel to the sand, they left their clothes on the bottom step. While they frolicked in the Indian Ocean, J. C. retrieved and hid their clothes. Appearing naked before strangers seemed not to trouble Diana in the least.[64]

On the Wednesday Joss and Diana, accompanied by Hughsie Daisy and Waweru, began their return journey to Nairobi. Hughsie Daisy took their photo on the 'singing' ferry* at Kilifi – the only known photograph of the smitten couple. They looked like honeymooners. That afternoon they took the up-country train to Nairobi.

On Thursday 16 January Waweru and Diana were deposited at Joss's bungalow, where Diana spent the rest of the week – Broughton being still at Burgaret. June reappeared at the bungalow on Friday morning, spending the night there, so that when Broughton returned on Saturday the quartet lunched at Muthaiga as usual. Though it was Saturday, Joss went back to work in the afternoon. The Brough-

*So called because the Africans who pulled the chain-ferry across the creek would sing to their passengers, making up lines about individuals on board.

tons drove back to Karen, meanwhile. On that drive Diana and her husband appear to have done some serious talking, for later that afternoon Broughton telephoned Joss to arrange 'an interview'.[65] By 5 p.m. he was at Joss's bungalow, only to find that he was still at his office. Joss arrived an hour later, and for half an hour the men talked until they were interrupted by Diana's appearance at 6.30 p.m.

At seven Joss drove Broughton across to Muthaiga Club, returning home to host a dinner party to which Broughton had been invited, but he did not turn up. Before the other guests arrived Joss gave Diana the Erroll family pearls, taking them from his own neck to place them round hers with the usual declaration, 'Pearls must be worn.'[66] Diana had never handled pearls as exquisite before – only envied such heirlooms worn by others. She had by now accumulated quite a wardrobe of clothes at Joss's and had left them there as if on the brink of moving in with him permanently.[67]

After the dinner party, at 3.30 a.m. on the Sunday morning, Diana returned to Marula Lane with June because she was expecting guests for luncheon.

Derek and Elizabeth Erskine hacked over for the occasion from Riverside via Dagoretti with their two young children Francis and Petal, to attend what Erskine would describe as a 'big lunch party' although there were only ten guests. The usual clique – Glady, June, Joss and Dickie Pembroke – was there plus two strangers, newcomers to the colony, a Major and Mrs Lyons.[68] After the meal, everyone except Broughton went for a swim in the pool. Diana was wearing the Erroll pearls with her bathing costume.[69] Derek Erskine recalled, 'Everything seemed to go nicely, and things seemed to have calmed down' – meaning that there had been no hint that day of the brewing scandal though it was obvious that Joss was 'very fond' of Diana. Young Petal Erskine, who adored Joss, noticed 'a little episode in the swimming bath' and was surprised at the couple's intimacy.[70] To Petal, Joss was 'the first truly elegant man I ever saw . . . a merry personality who loved children' and who possessed 'an innate enjoyment of life. He would crack vulgar jokes.' Joss's conversations, with their endless double entendres, tended to rouse the curiosity of the younger generation.[71] Thus her father found himself having to explain that Joss's and Diana's intimacy was 'quite normal in modern times'.

Francis Erskine remembers that Sunday when, looking up towards the house from the pool, he caught sight of Broughton 'brooding and sinister, watching the frolicking by the pool, from an upstairs window'.[72]

Typically, Joss left the party promptly at 3 p.m. At about five in the evening Broughton remarked to Diana and June, 'You'd better be leaving as you are going to Nyeri [the town nearest Seremai].' June would later state that this was the first she had heard of Diana going with her.[73] Diana, of course, had no intention of going to Nyeri – she had just given a public excuse to cover up an assignation she had made with Joss that afternoon as they were parting in the driveway. She intended to join him at his bungalow. Once she and June turned up, Joss requested that June remain so as not to compromise Diana – there was only one spare bedroom besides his own. June stayed until Wednesday 22 January. Joss had tried to get himself accommodation at the club, leaving the two women to sleep in the house, but the club was bursting at the seams with army personnel, with no spare bed available, let alone a room.[74]

Joss and Broughton each consulted his lawyer about divorce on Monday 20 January.[75] At about lunchtime that same morning Broughton took his two Colt revolvers (the same weapons he had used during the shooting practice at Soames' farm in November) from his bedroom, where they had hitherto been kept unloaded together with the ammunition, and brought them downstairs to his study prior to locking them up in his gun cabinet.[76] For the time being he placed these weapons on the mantelpiece in the study, along with a box of ammunition, placing a five-shilling note under one of the revolvers.[77] By Tuesday morning, both revolvers, the ammunition and the five-shilling note had disappeared along with, allegedly, a silver cigarette-case. No one had ever seen the case because Broughton never used it, claiming it had been a gift from an old friend.[78] At his trial, Broughton became confused over the denomination and number of notes he had put under the gun. One witness said it was a ten-shilling note. Another suggested there were two English £1 notes; yet another claimed that there had been seven £1 notes.

Broughton left Marula Lane specifically to report the 'theft' to the police that morning. Inspector Clarence Fentum, the officer in charge of Kilimani police station on the outskirts of Nairobi town, went to investigate. Fentum found nothing to indicate a break-in except that a rambler rose had come away from the wall. Broughton said that probably the veranda door had been left open or unlocked the night before, and that the thief had come in that way. According to Fentum's testimony in court at Broughton's trial, Broughton had mentioned to him during this exchange that he wanted to do more in connection with war work. Fentum suggested he join the Special Police, whose duties involved patrolling the municipal area and Karen district in the evening and at night. He advised Broughton to contact Mr Armstrong, the senior police officer, with a view to enlisting. Broughton said he would follow it up. That same day he wrote to Jack Soames describing what had taken place and telling him, 'I have taken your advice and spoken to Erroll and Diana. They say they are in love with each other and mean to get married. It is a hopeless position and I am going to cut my losses. There is nothing in Kenya for me to live for.'[79]

Broughton made sure that a lot of people knew about the theft. But the majority were convinced, including Walter Harragin's secretary Peggy Pitt, who attended the whole trial, that 'Broughton staged a burglary of his own revolvers which was extremely bogus'.[80] Peggy Pitt was also intrigued by the impossible speed with which Broughton's letter reached Soames. It arrived in Nanyuki in absolutely record time: 'It had never been understood how it arrived there to be collected by Soames on the Wednesday morning. It surely could not have been written before Tuesday morning because the burglary had not [yet] taken place. Somehow the letter reached Nairobi early enough that morning to catch the train to Nanyuki and for delivery to the post office there and collection. The journey took about 7 hours. Later, in court, Soames claimed that he had burnt the letter. The mystery will never be solved.'[81] Also on the Tuesday the last of three anonymous letters arrived in Broughton's pigeon-hole at

Muthaiga, reading: 'There's no fool like an old fool. What are you going to do about it?'[82] The first, which Broughton received in early January, had said, 'You were like a cat on hot bricks last night. What about the eternal triangle? What are you going to do about it?' The second letter had been received two or three days beforehand and challenged: 'Do you know your wife and Lord Erroll have been staying at Carberry's house at Nyeri together?'[83]

Some time mid-week, Derek Erskine, alone at Riverside Stables, received a visit from Broughton who had come to hire The Pantaloon, 'a skewbald, a remarkably good-looking animal' which had once belonged to Brookham and subsequently became a favourite with General Dickinson, the Commander-in-Chief. The Pantaloon was renowned for its vigour, stamina and beauty. 'He was the sort of horse that elderly men fancied themselves on because he set one off very well.' To Erskine's surprise, Broughton arranged to hire The Pantaloon from the coming Friday until Sunday, telling Erskine that he intended 'to get himself fit and do a lot of riding over this weekend'.[84] Erskine was struck by the oddness of Broughton's request when, after all, he had three horses of his own, but nevertheless he arranged for a syce to deliver the horse to Marula Lane on the Friday.[85]

On Wednesday 22 January Joss had a telephone conversation with Hugh Hamilton, the managing director of the major trading company, Mitchell Cotts. For some weeks he had been assisting Hamilton with information on how best to work up trade relations as the British forces moved on towards their goals in Ethiopia – the farmers of Kenya stood to benefit from the larger export market. Hamilton's junior secretary, Shirley Brown, clearly recalls putting Joss's call through to Hamilton – apparently during his phone call Joss had touched on 'Madagascar, Abyssinia, Eritrea among other things'.[86] In his impulsive enthusiasm to further the colony's trading activities he was perhaps not being particularly circumspect in discussing the commercial opportunities offered by a military campaign then still under wraps.

That evening Joss took Diana to dance at Torr's in its romantic round ballroom beneath the hanging balcony, and once more she spent the night with him in the bungalow alone. Generally, however, their brief affair followed the decorum of the day and the lovers did not spend nights together without a chaperone. June had returned to Seremai following Wednesday's lunch, but she was back at the bungalow at 12.45 on Thursday ready to go to lunch at Muthaiga as usual with Joss, Diana and Broughton as though she had acted as Diana's chaperone throughout. (Broughton later claimed to have believed that both Diana and June were in Nyeri from the Sunday to the Wednesday.) During Diana's absence Broughton had spent each afternoon at Muthaiga with Phyllis Barkas, another club member and the smartly turned out wife of Colonel 'Sweetie' Barkas, commander-in-chief at Eldoret racecourse. To outward appearances Broughton spent each day in customary recreational pastimes, playing golf-croquet, bridge and backgammon with Phyllis Barkas.[87]

After their lunch Joss left for work on foot at 2 p.m. Borrowing his car, June went to Theo Schouten's to have her hair done with Diana in town. At Diana's request Broughton drove back to Marula Lane to fetch a particular gown for her, but by 5 p.m. he was back at the club so as to play backgammon with Mrs Barkas. Over lunch the foursome had made plans to meet at Muthaiga Club for drinks in the peristyle at 8.30. When the idea cropped up of their spending the whole evening together, Broughton had insisted that Joss bring her back to Marula Lane – sixteen miles away from Muthaiga in Karen – before 3 a.m., pointing out that she was tired.[88] This was the only time throughout Joss's and Diana's six-week relationship that Broughton intervened in the lovers' arrangements. When Joss went back to the bungalow to change for dinner he repeated what he clearly thought was an odd request to Lizzie Lezard, who was staying with him at the time: 'I don't know why the old boy wants her, but he insists that I must get her home by 3 o'clock. It suits me, I'm tired too and I have to be at work early in the morning.'[89] On Friday, his schedule was tight with a long way to drive by midday – to Eldoret, after which he was planning to return to Nairobi to spend the weekend with Diana, to take her to Oserian, his home on Lake Naivasha, with the intention of introducing her as his future wife to Gilbert Colvile.[90]

*   *   *

Patsy (Bowles) Chilton remembers coming across Diana, Joss and June at sundown at Muthaiga. The lovers, 'entwined on a large sofa in the peristyle', asked her to join them for a drink. Diana and Joss were talking about going on to the Clairmont after dinner, suggesting to June that instead of joining them, as they had often done, she should take Broughton off to Torr's Hotel to dance, leaving them to their own devices. As Broughton arrived, Joss turned to June and said, 'Take the old boy off for a game of backgammon', not caring that Broughton overheard. This June dutifully did.[91]

Joss and Diana invited Patsy to join them for dinner but she declined, leaving the two of them 'lounging on a sofa together, making no attempt to hide that they were in love, flaunting it openly', according to Kath Biggs who also passed by.[92]

Diana and Joss, June and Broughton went in to dinner. The evening then 'partook of the nature of an engagement party or celebration'.[93] Unprompted, Broughton raised his champagne glass, 'To Diana and Joss. I want to wish them every happiness in the future and may their union be blessed with an heir. To Diana and Joss.'[94] Such a gesture might have gone unnoticed by the other diners, but Broughton had spoken loudly enough to be heard across the far side of the room. Implausible though this seemed, he appeared to be publicly 'performing an act of renunciation' – handing over his twenty-seven-year-old bride to Joss. For a moment those at the Broughton table sat uncomfortably still, then, led by June, Diana and Joss lifted their glasses and smilingly pledged the toast.[95] In all the confusion following Joss's death people never forgot how, during the Earl's last supper, Broughton had seemed wholly resigned that his wife had settled on her future with his thirty-nine-year-old rival. In court, Harragin would make the point for the prosecution: 'There was a great change in his attitude after he toasted his wife and Erroll at the Muthaiga Club.'

At around 10.15 p.m. Joss took Diana off to the Clairmont to dance. They left the hotel earlier than usual.[96] Jane Westbrook remembered that Joss had asked for his bill just before midnight – it was the last time they spoke. The couple went back to Joss's bungalow to make love before Joss delivered Diana back to the Broughton home in Marula Lane as promised.

Broughton and June, meanwhile, had remained at Muthaiga. When Dickie Pembroke passed Broughton at about 10.30 p.m. Broughton inquired when he would come and play bezique again. Pembroke had made some polite response. Thereafter for about an hour Broughton sat with June 'alone, unobserved',[97] but then, according to June, he became 'suddenly rather cross and peevish', raising his voice and drawing attention to himself. On the witness stand June related how he had announced, 'I'm not going to give her £5,000 a year or the Karen house' (Broughton denied this in court, pointing out that the house was not his to give)[98] 'and . . . she could bloody well go and live with Joss – they had only been married for two months and look how it was for him.' June ostensibly tried to quieten Broughton, with little success. Phyllis Barkas later claimed in court that she had overheard Broughton saying, 'To think that a woman would treat me like this after being married two months.' Another witness put it differently again: 'Juney, it's all very well, but we've only been married two months, and she does this.'[99]

That night, Phyllis Barkas, Gerald Portman and two other long-time settler friends of Joss's, Captain 'Long Lew' Llewellyn and Jacko Heath, were having a late supper of bacon and eggs at Muthaiga. They invited June and Broughton to join them. Broughton refused. Jacko Heath remembered later how 'edgy' Broughton had looked at his suggestion that he and June join them for a nightcap instead of supper. The alternative, too, had been refused. Yet Jacko had not failed to observe that June and Broughton remained at Muthaiga Club, and he regarded this hanging about as odd. He was puzzled enough to think that perhaps Broughton was supposed to be somewhere else with June, and that Broughton somehow feared that if they had joined Jacko's group this could make them late.[100] Broughton's version in court was different, saying that he had stayed on at Muthaiga *with that crowd* – giving them as the reason why he had not reached home until 2 a.m.

On the witness stand at his trial Broughton claimed to have been so drunk that he could not recall which car, nor which chauffeur, had driven himself and June back to Karen. The Broughton chauffeur, presumably, was not drunk and would have known the time, but this character was never seen again, much less called as a witness.[101] June did remember, however. She told the court that it was his driver and his car that took them back to Marula Lane that night.[102]

Joss and Diana reached the house in Marula Lane around 2.30 a.m. Wilks opened the door to bring in the luggage, having heard the Buick arrive. According to Wilks, Diana came in with 'a face like thunder'. She assumed they had had a row. The maid then pointed to a tray of bottles, suggesting that Lord Erroll have a whisky. 'Why, Wilky,' Joss said, 'don't you know that I never touch whisky?'[103] Joss's friends always thought Wilks's suggestion had been most odd. Everyone who knew Joss knew of his abhorrence for the stuff.

According to Diana, her parting words to Joss were cautionary: 'Darling, please drive carefully.' And Joss responded, she said, with characteristic verve, 'Carefully, darling, but not slowly.'[104] Joss got back into his car and drove out of Broughton's driveway but, taking the short cut home, turned in the opposite direction from the route by which he had come, choosing a less travelled track to reach the main Ngong–Nairobi road.[105]

Meanwhile, a few hundred miles away a mass of troops had begun marching towards Eritrea in a highly secret military exercise, which would count as one of the great battles of the war on account of Wavell's brilliant strategy to reclaim Addis Ababa from the Italians. The trade opportunities Joss discussed with Hugh Hamilton would now be realisable thanks to this military success, but Joss would play no part in setting their ideas in motion.

18. Alice de Janzé and Joss. Their on-off affair was happily tolerated by their respective spouses.

19. Idina and Alice de Janzé set a trend in velvet trousers. They both fell for Joss in Paris in the early 1920s. Far from causing a rift of jealousy between them, their joint passion for Joss cemented their friendship.

20. Raymund de Trafford and Alice de Janzé, enraptured by one another, Christmas 1926. Their tempestuous love affair ruptured the easy going bonhomie between the de Janzés and the Hays.

21. Muthaiga Country Club, Nairobi. Parties held here during race week did much to heighten the decadent reputation of the Happy Valley set.

22. Joss's daughter Diana Denyse Hay with her mother Idina.

23. Idina with the Mosleys and friends at Savehay, the Mosleys' country house. From left: Idina, Tom Mosley, Nicholas Mosley, Cecil Beaton, Ivan Hay, Dick Wyndham, William Walton, Georgia Sitwell, Cimmie Mosley, Vivian Mosley, Sacheverell Sitwell.

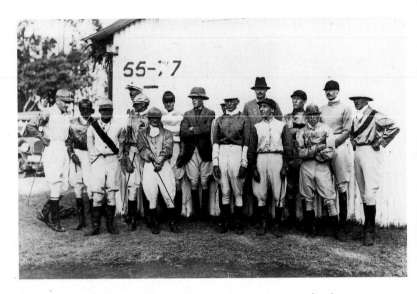

24. The first royal tour in Kenya: HRH Edward Prince of Wales, centre, and Prince Henry, Duke of Gloucester, back row, 4th from right, at Nairobi racecourse, Eastleigh, with professional and gentlemen jockeys of the day.

25. Joss presenting trophies with Princess Alice, Duchess of Gloucester, 1938. The Duke of Gloucester and Mary Erroll are on the far left.

26. At the races, Nairobi, 1938 (l to r): Captain Mario Rocco, the Begum Aga Khan and Joss. Rocco was interned once Italy entered the war in June 1940, under suspicion of supporting Mussolini.

27. Joss on deck of the SS *Modasa*, sailing back to Kenya shortly after his marriage in London to his second wife, Mary Ramsay-Hill, in February 1930. Edward Prince of Wales was also on board.

28. Mary Countess of Erroll by Dorothy Wilding. Wilding's portraits were published frequently in the press in 1937 when Joss and Mary returned to London for the coronation.

29. Oserian, dubbed the 'Djinn Palace' by Joss, overlooking Lake Naivasha. Mary managed to extract this palatial dwelling from Cyril Ramsay-Hill in her divorce settlement.

30. The first Erroll Cup Race started beneath the Oserian gazebo from Joss's and Mary's jetty. Joss spent a fortune on improvements at Oserian, with Mary's blessing.

31. A weekend house party at Oserian. Sundowners were enjoyed here at Oserian's bar by visitors from near and far. Sir Edward Buck from India, whom Joss enlisted to help him promote tourism in Kenya, is sitting on Joss's left.

32. Joss with his pet chimp, Jules, who alarmed visitors by hurling stones at their cars as they drove up Oserian's drive. 'Don't worry, he's a pretty rotten shot,' Joss would reassure his guests. He spoke to Jules in French, addressing him as '*mon ami*'.

33. Joss and Mary with guests at Oserian on the shores of Lake Naivasha. Hippo Point, around which yachts would sail in the Erroll Cup race, is in the distance.

34. Yusuf and Rehman Khan in the courtyard at Oserian. The Khan brothers worked for Joss for many years, and adored him.

10

The Investigation

'See how love and murder will out.'
The Double Dealer, Epistle Dedicatory,
William Congreve

Around 3.30 a.m. on Friday 24 January, two African dairy workers set out on their pre-dawn milk round from Grange Park Dairy, and noticed a stationary Buick on the grass verge of the road to Nairobi. They stopped to investigate what looked like an accident. The Buick had come to a halt at an angle over the edge of the first of a series of shallow pits from which murram had been dug. The car's headlights still glowed through the slits of their wartime blackout device. All they could make out about the body inside the front of the car was that it was a white male, in uniform. Without touching anything, they sought help at once, driving back to the nearest police post at Karen. Accordingly, two African constables went to the scene.

The police report would confirm that the Buick – a right-hand drive car – had come to a halt over a shallow murram pit, on the right-hand side of the Ngong road 150 yards from the junction into the Karen road and 17 yards on to the verge.[1] The ignition was switched off, the key still in the slot, and the hand-brake was off too.

While the African constables scrutinised the exterior of the black saloon, Leslie Condon, manager of Grange Park Dairy, was flagged down by one of them on his way to Nairobi. Condon got out of his car and peered through the open window of the Buick. He at once noticed a wound behind the ear of the dead man and, right away, suspected that this was from a bullet.[2] Condon claimed in court that he drove straight to Kilimani police station in Nairobi to report what he had seen, and that he had found Assistant Inspector Frederick Smith on duty. When questioned in court as to whether he had told Smith about the gunshot wound, Condon replied yes. Having done his duty, he drove on into town to the Grange Park shop in Jeevanjee Market.[3]

Smith told the court that he 'had received a telephone message from Mr Condon to the effect that there was a car with the body of a European in uniform'. Smith was not asked whether he was told of a gunshot wound.[4] He said he then telephoned various personnel, including Inspector Anstis Bewes and Inspector Clarence Fentum, the officer in charge of Kilimani police station. Both lived within a mile of where the Buick was found.[5] Bewes was sent for because he was on night call for any incidents in the Karen area.[6] Smith and Fentum reached the Buick at 6.09, according to Smith's testimony. Inspector May and Assistant Inspector Bewes were already there, with several native constables. Bewes had thought that the cause of the man's death was a road accident. As he opened the door and stuck his head into the interior of the Buick to investigate further, a powerful scent assailed his nostrils.[7]

By now people had begun to make their daily journey to Nairobi, where the offices opened at 8 a.m. One happened to be a government pathologist, Dr Geoffrey Timms, who, when he was flagged down by a policeman, imagined that he was needed to deliver first aid.[8] One glance at the body showed that it was too late for that. Rigor mortis was setting in. Arms and legs were tucked beneath his body, his head was in his hands, and he appeared to have expired while in the act of praying. Noticing the congealed blood by the ear, Dr Timms thought initially that the body must have somehow been thrown forward and sideways, and that this graze had been caused by a quarter-inch spike on the dashboard where the light-switch knob should have been.[9] Yet at the same time, it was impossible to understand how this hefty figure could have ended up with his knees folded neatly beneath his torso in this 'praying' position in the passenger well. His body must have been pushed on to the floorboard and deliberately positioned in this manner – perhaps to make room for someone else to get into the driver's seat so as to move the Buick?

Both the Buick's front windows were fully open. The windscreen was flecked with blood. The rear windows were closed but the carpet in the back was crumpled up on the near side. On the rear seat itself, there were white scuffs from pipeclay – the type of cleaner used to clean tennis shoes and military puttees.[10]

More police arrived to assess the situation: Assistant Superintendent Desmond Swayne and Chief Inspector Herbert Lanham. However, not one policeman had brought along any fingerprint powder and not a single fingerprint impression was taken. More damaging still to forensic evidence, the Buick itself had been washed as soon as it was returned to the garage from which it had been hired.[11] Another unusual departure from standard procedure was that no one had bothered to rope off the area where the vehicle had been found, even though there had been a second set of wide tyre tracks leading from it in the direction of Nairobi. Rain had fallen in the night, and as eleven pairs of feet were constantly trampling the sodden grass during the investigation, the turf around the saloon car began disintegrating into red mud and this second set of wide tyre tracks was all but obliterated. These tracks were never to be accounted for, but the police shrugged this off with the excuse that it was hardly the investigating team's fault that the ground was wet.[12]

Chief Inspector Lanham, however, did take photographs of the site of the 'accident' as well as of the peculiar position of the body and the head. His photographs showed the angle at which the Buick had come to rest.[13]

At about 8.15 a.m. an ambulance arrived at the scene and it was suggested that the body be lifted on to a stretcher, so that Timms could have a better look. Only now was the corpse recognised as that of the Earl of Erroll.[14] According to Fentum's statement under oath at Broughton's trial, he had objected to the removal of the body[15] which, he claimed, had been removed on Timms' instructions. Timms claimed that it was on Fentum's orders that it was taken from the car. He still feels strongly about Fentum's blaming him; after all, crucial evidence – which it was the duty of the police to protect – was disturbed by this careless action.

Before towing the Buick to Nairobi, J. E. Butcher, a mechanic from Motor Mart and Exchange, considered the damage to the vehicle. This was so slight that he concluded that the Buick had reached its position at no more than 8 m.p.h., and might even have been rolled into that position. Butcher was struck by the position of the gear lever, which, as he explained in court at Broughton's trial, was 'almost in top gear . . . It was rather a peculiar place to find the gear [lever] and I assumed that the gear lever had been moved possibly from a gear other than top by someone endeavouring to place it in top gear.'[16] Butcher found a bloodstained cigarette-end and a bloodstained hairpin in the front of the car, and in the back he found another hairpin. For some reason both of the roof-mounted arm slings had become detached and were lying in the back of the car as well.[17]

Joss's corpse reached the laboratory shortly after 9 a.m. by which time Dr Vint, the senior government pathologist, had been forewarned by his young assistant about the identity of the body. Once it was on the slab, Dr Vint instructed his assistant to remove the dried blood from behind the left ear. He watched as the young man delicately cleaned up the congealed blood with a tiny sponge – and within seconds he exclaimed, 'Christ! The bugger's been shot! We'd better call the police.'[18] Vint telephoned Assistant Inspector Poppy.[19]

Dr Vint discovered:

The wound passed inwards through the soft tissues of the neck, and passed between the first vertebra and the base of the skull, through the medulla of the brain from left to right and then passed out of the spinal canal between the base of the skull and the first vertebra on the other side . . . The bullet [was] in two parts in the ligament attaching the vertebra to the base of the skull, lying in a mass of blood clot underneath the skin on the right side of the neck almost opposite the point of entry. The track of the bullet showed that the bones had been slightly chipped by the bullet in passing.

Death would have been instantaneous.[20] As the Earl had been right-handed, Vint immediately ruled out suicide.[21]

That Friday afternoon while Vint was examining the corpse, Fentum was guarding the car, alternating with Smith, and discovered a piece of metal under the accelerator pedal which appeared to be a spent bullet.[22] Forensic concluded that somehow this .32 bullet must have passed over Joss's head: 'Erroll must have ducked sharply and struck his forehead on the steering wheel. He must have been slightly stunned when the second shot, which killed him instantly, was fired.' The muzzle of the revolver, it was also concluded, had been held between three and nine inches from his left ear.[23] As the post-mortem continued the assistant government analyst Mr Nefdt removed the stomach intact; it contained about a cupful of digested food.[24] Evidence could narrow down the time of Joss's shooting to somewhere between 2.30 a.m. and a few minutes to 3 a.m.[25] Vint stated: '[A]fter his death Lord Erroll's body had been dragged from the seat of the car in which it was found and placed on the floor boards and it would appear that someone else then drove the car to where it was found by the police. It was unlikely that one person would have been able to drag the Earl's body into the position in which it was found.'[26]

Assistant Inspector Arthur James Poppy, ex-Metropolitan Police, was appointed to head the murder inquiry. Deep-voiced, an imposing and friendly man with a meticulous attention to detail, Poppy was a good investigator; he was regarded as 'extremely level headed, an experienced officer who inspired confidence in his colleagues and his judgement was good too'; indeed, he was 'an excellent judge of character'.[27] In April 1933 he had been a sergeant under Superintendent Batley, well known as a fingerprint expert in police circles of the day. Under Batley's guidance, Poppy learned the craft and extended the field, where he was much praised for his innovation in footprint detection. He was so successful that someone went to the length of composing a bit of doggerel about him:

> A. J. Poppy, Chief Inspector,
> Is a first class crime detector,
> He could even count the ridges,
> Of the fingerprints of midges.[28]

When he took charge of the investigation into Joss's murder, Poppy had been in Kenya for six years.[29] His first duty was to ensure that news of the cause of death was kept quiet for a while; after all, Erroll had been Kenya's Assistant Military Secretary. 'Clearly Lord Erroll had been murdered but this discovery was kept a close secret.'[30]

After visiting the mortuary on the morning of 24 January Poppy went to Government House to inform the governor, Sir Henry Moore, that the Earl of Erroll had been shot, requesting that the facts be kept quiet for twenty-four hours.[31] After lunch that same day Poppy called the press together. Just after 2 p.m. he informed Reuters that Kenya's Assistant Military Secretary had died in a road accident. Next day the *Glasgow Herald* carried a full-scale obituary, whereas *The Times* devoted only a two-inch single column to the late Earl of Erroll.[32] One South African evening paper caught the event in time for publication that same Friday. The world read the news of this 'accident' as Joss was being buried in his constituency Kiambu with full military honours.

Mourners foregathered at the small grey stone church, St Paul's, where Joss was to be buried next to Mary. The firing party lined the entrance to the cemetery as the hearse approached, draped with a Union Jack. The firing party then reversed arms and stood with bowed heads as the cortège entered the gates, preceded by the officiating clergy and followed by his Excellency, Sir Henry Moore, and the GOC Lieutenant-General A. G. Cunningham.[33] The service was conducted by the Church of Scotland minister and Chaplain to the Forces, Reverend R. A. Howieson. As the simple but impressive service came to an end, the firing party loaded and three volleys were fired. Then the bugler sounded the Last Post, followed by the Reveille. In addition to the Governor and the GOC many other senior officers were present, as well as military representatives of the various branches of force headquarters, the Royal Air Force and senior officers of the Union Defence Force. Most of the principal heads of government departments, including the Commissioner of Police, were there. Members of Executive and Legislative Councils, including European and Indian Elected Members, attended, as well as representatives of many public bodies, societies and clubs and a considerable number of personal friends of Joss's. Practically every section of Kenya life was represented at the funeral; Joss had been much respected. His mother the Dowager Countess of Erroll, his daughter Dinan and other members of the family sent wreaths – nearly a hundred accumulated in all.[34]

Broughton arrived late at the funeral, carrying an envelope which his wife had asked him to drop into the grave – Diana had gone to Seremai with June, being too overwrought to attend. At some point in their affair, when together but unable to speak openly, Diana had written to Joss on a scrap of paper, 'I love you desperately', to which Joss's reply on the reverse was 'And I love you for ever'.[35] Afterwards, once Poppy had eventually decided to scrutinise the contents of the envelope, Harragin was difficult about exhuming Joss's body on the grounds that it would involve 'immense problems of red tape'. So Poppy ventured, 'Nothing, I suppose, to prevent me planting a rose tree?'

'No,' replied the Attorney-General.

'Even if I dig rather deep?'

He had undertaken this at midnight, returning to Kiambu with six convicts from Nairobi gaol; he successfully retrieved the billet-doux which had slipped down to one side of the coffin.[36]

A private memorial service was held in Scotland on 6 February, attended by Joss's mother and the rest of his family. His mother must have been devastated; her dearest son had died before reaching forty. In exchange for the life of her favourite child, she later received the following citation, which she framed:

By the King's Order the name of Second-Lieutenant (Acting Captain) the Earl of Erroll, The Kenya Regiment, was published in the London Gazette on 1 April, 1941, as mentioned in a Despatch for distinguished service. I am charged to record His Majesty's high appreciation.

[signed] David Margesson. Secretary of State for War.[37]

At Spye Park, Idina's sister Avie and her husband Uncle Frank did not tell Dinan immediately of her father's death, but she had read it for herself at the local newsagent's.* In March, she noticed that chunks were being cut out of the daily newspapers. Guessing correctly that the censoring was for her benefit, Dinan took to creeping out to read the newspapers before her foster parents came downstairs, and in this way she followed the trial, and all the speculative details, as the evidence emerged. But she never let on at the time that she knew anything. In fact, according to her son, Dinan would never mention her father again.[38] She did tell her husband Sir Iain Moncreiffe – the only time she ever referred to the matter – how the headmistress of the school she was attending at the time of her father's death requested she leave her establishment because of the opprobrium associated with the murder.[39]

Phyllis Filmer read about Joss's death in the *Natal Mercury*, while staying in a hotel waiting for the start of term when she could deposit her two boys at Hilton College. Her younger son Peter happened to be with her on the morning of 25 January, when she bought the newspaper.[40] He witnessed her reaction as she noticed the item at the bottom of page 20: 'THE EARL OF ERROLL . . . has been killed in a motor accident, reports SAPA-Reuter.' Phyllis had been incapable of disguising her grief, and it was only now that her son gleaned any idea of the intensity of her feelings for Joss. Unable to contain herself, she broke down, blurting out that she had been hoping to marry him.[41] Once Hilton College opened, Pheely Weely returned to Kenya, but meanwhile she summoned all her generosity and kindness, writing a note of commiseration to Diana.[42] It would be to Idina that Phyllis turned for solace; they supported one another like grieving widows. Phyllis went to live at Clouds for about three years.[43]

People were generally not surprised to learn that Joss had perished in a road accident. As a director of Kenya's *East African Standard* wrote in his journal, having heard Cable and Wireless announce Joss's death on the 7 p.m. news on Friday, 'Errol [*sic*] killed himself

---

*In 1931 Dinan had gone to live on a more or less permanent basis with Avie and her second husband Captain Frank Fane Spicer at their Wiltshire home, Spye Park.

in a car smash last night. He always was a reckless driver.'[44] Sidney and Sylvia Fazan heard the radio bulletin too. They were appalled to have lost a beloved friend but had to admit that Joss had always driven far too fast.[45]

It was Gerald Portman who had broken the news of Joss's death to the Broughtons. Portman had been driving into Nairobi on the Friday morning when he was flagged down by a policeman accompanied by 'Tiny' Gibbs, owner of Gibbs Auto Tours. The policeman asked Portman what car Lord Erroll had been driving, and he reeled the details off pat: Joss was driving a black Buick, registration number T7331. Portman explained that he had hired the same vehicle himself just before Joss had. He was now informed by the policeman that Lord Erroll was dead. There had been a car smash and he had broken his neck. Portman pointed out in court certain idiosyncrasies in the Buick, such as how the light-switch on the instrument panel had broken while he was using it. At 9 o'clock, shortly after his encounter with the policeman, Gerald Portman rang Marula Lane and broke the dreadful news to Diana.

Broughton had been up for at least two hours, so he can hardly have had any sleep. According to his sworn statement at about 7 a.m. he had gone out for his usual short walk, then returned to his bedroom before summoning his houseboy Alfred to ask for early-morning tea. Broughton then went back to bed, clad in pyjamas. His evening clothes were still in his bedroom, which Alfred now collected in order to press and clean them before returning them to the wardrobe. There was no unfamiliar mark on them; this was pure routine. When Broughton dressed for a second time, going downstairs for breakfast he became aware of 'a considerable amount of movement upstairs' – doors opening and shutting and the sound of the women's voices. The stir was created by Diana who, having taken Gerald Portman's telephone call, had rushed into June's room crying, 'He's dead. He's dead. Joss is dead. He has broken his neck in a motor smash.' Diana was 'beside herself with grief, distraught, hysterical'.[46]

Broughton had gone upstairs to investigate, bursting into June's room and demanding to know what the trouble was about. June answered, 'Joss has killed himself in a motor accident.'

'Good God!' Broughton exclaimed, then sat down on the bed.[47]

Diana, in floods of tears, repeatedly expressed disbelief. 'Do go and see, Jock,' she beseeched. 'See if it's really him.' As if to pacify her, Broughton asked whether she would like him to put 'anything belonging to her, something personal', on the body. Her handkerchief, she said.

The sound of car wheels in the drive below now prompted Broughton to hasten down to the hall to see who had arrived, and he was confronted by Inspector Fentum and Assistant Superintendent Swayne.[48] Unable to contain himself, he asked, 'Is he all right? Is he all right?'

'Is who all right?' Fentum responded.

'Lord Erroll.'

The policemen expressed surprise that Broughton knew there was anything wrong with Lord Erroll. He told them about Gerald Portman's call. Fentum and Swayne then informed Broughton that the only reason that they had called by was because they knew that Lord Erroll had been a close friend of his and of his wife. Then they asked several more questions: Had Erroll been to the house in Marula Lane the night before? Was he under the influence of alcohol? Had he been unduly tired?

Broughton answered 'nervously . . . very much upset by the news . . . but without reluctance'. He talked about the dinner party the night before at Muthaiga. Everything that Broughton told Fentum, he wrote down. After reading it over, he gave Broughton the statement to sign.[49]

Fentum had glimpsed Diana at one of the upstairs windows as they entered the house. He now asked to see her. Broughton refused, saying that her ladyship was in no fit state to be interviewed by anybody. Fentum and Swayne then departed. As distraught as Diana was, she had already asked June whether she would drive her back to Joss's bungalow, to which June had agreed. Diana wanted to retrieve her love letters to Joss. While they had been in bed together the night before, she had asked him to burn all her letters to him. He kept these in a notecase. Joss had refused. When they got up

Diana had hidden the notecase in a box of tissues, by way of a prank.[50]

June now drove Diana to the bungalow but like a chauffeur remained in the car, parked in the driveway, while Diana went indoors. Just as she was retrieving the box of tissues from its hiding place in the drawing-room Lizzie Lezard took her by surprise, noticing that she had already gathered together photographs and other mementoes, such as Joss's forage cap. (Poppy was to be outraged when he learned how Diana 'had sneaked back'. But what shocked him more than anything, he said, was how she had stolen Joss's pyjamas from under his pillow.)[51] Later Lizzie would claim in court that, not long after midnight, he had crept into the bungalow very late and had overheard the unmistakable groans of pleasure coming from Joss's bedroom. In Cairo months afterwards, Lizzie would describe to Lady Ranfurly, his stepdaughter-in-law, how he had come across Diana in the drawing-room when he emerged from the spare bedroom next morning, 'collecting things, saying to herself, "He would have wanted me to have this. And that . . .".' Lizzie claimed that he had had no idea that the reason for Diana's desperation was that Joss was dead.[52] Before leaving the bungalow, Diana loaded Joss's three dogs into June's car so as to care for them herself at Karen. One of the dogs in fact belonged to Fabian Wallis. While awaiting his posting by the RAF Fabian had been staying at Joss's bungalow, and Joss had looked after his dog when he left for Abyssinia. However, Fabian sent Diana a message soon afterwards, 'forbidding her to keep the dog and ordering her to deliver it to a friend of his'.[53]

Later that morning, Lizzie went to see Alice de Trafford at Portulacca Cottage, her Nairobi pied-à-terre next to GOCHQ, and accompanied her to the mortuary to view Joss's body. Then he went by motorcycle to take news of Joss's death to the officers' mess in Eldoret.[54]

At 9.30 a.m. Glady Delamere rang the house in Marula Lane. This time Broughton picked up the phone. 'Is this terrible news true?' she inquired, and Broughton explained how Gerald Portman had broken the news to Diana by telephone; that the police had just been to the house and had confirmed that Joss was dead. Broughton commented, 'It is too tragic; we were all dining together last night. Such a cheerful party. He must have killed himself through driving too fast.'[55]

Broughton then went off to carry out his bizarre errand for Diana. He asked at Nairobi police station for directions to where the body was being held. Assistant Superintendent Swayne and Inspector May who were there found him shaky and nervous. He explained that he wanted to place the handkerchief 'on the dead man's breast on behalf of his wife, as she had been very much in love with the Earl of Erroll'. Inspector May led the way by car to the mortuary, but Broughton was not allowed inside to see the corpse. Someone else would carry out the errand for him.

He next made for Bunson's travel agency to rebook his and Diana's passages on a ship leaving on 31 January for Ceylon.[56] Then he drove back to Marula Lane in Karen by the same route that Joss had taken the night before with Diana, past the spot where the Buick had been found, near the road junction to the road across the vlei. The Buick had gone, although several people were still standing about as he inspected the verge for extra tyre marks or 'any other signs of an accident'. He found none.

By the time Broughton returned to Marula Lane Diana was also back from Joss's bungalow. He explained what had happened at the mortuary.[57]

That same Friday June Carberry and her fifteen-year-old step-daughter, Juanita, who had been driven from Seremai with her governess Isabel Rutt that morning, had lunch with the Broughtons. Whether this arrangement had been made before Joss's death or because of it, Juanita could not remember.[58] Before sitting down to that meal Broughton had been determined to light a bonfire, claiming in court that this had been on his mind before leaving for the mortuary:

for some time past I had been talking to Wilks, my wife's maid, with regard to burning up rubbish in the garden. Mwangi, my chauffeur, had told me that my dhobi had wanted some aviation spirit. I had bought him some prior to 25 January. I told Abdullah, my head boy, that I intended to burn rubbish and instructed him to bring me the bottle of aviation spirit. Either on Friday 24th or Saturday 25th . . . it was before the funeral at any rate and I am almost certain that it was after the car crash and it was in the middle of the day, about 11 a.m. or noon I should think.[59]

Setting alight a pile of garden rubbish could quite easily have been left to one of Broughton's *shamba* boys, but he loved bonfires and igniting them was a procedure he had enjoyed from boyhood.[60] However, he seemed deliberately to be drawing attention to the bonfire, alerting the household needlessly.[61]

Earlier, Broughton had placed in the hallway outside his bedroom upstairs an old gin bottle containing aviation fuel. He could perfectly well have carried this bottle downstairs himself. Instead, he summoned his house servant Abdullah, making a great point of handing him the old gin bottle, and they proceeded together to the rubbish pit. Broughton had then taken the bottle of fuel from Abdullah, emptying half the contents over the refuse. Wary of the amount of spirit being used, the servant moved well out of the way, cautioning, 'Bwana. You'll burn yourself.'[62] Broughton seemed to need to make an issue out of what would normally be undertaken between himself and a *shamba* boy. No gardener from the Broughton household was cross-examined at the trial.

Once the bonfire was properly alight Broughton went back indoors and joined his three guests for lunch. Diana remained out of sight. She and June left for Seremai that afternoon. Juanita was the one person who could have given evidence about that bonfire, but actually she saw no sign of one. On the day when she was due to go on to the stand at Broughton's trial, Assistant Inspector Poppy denounced her as an unreliable witness.[63] She still has in her possession the blue witness slip as proof of having been summoned. When Broughton was asked at the trial why the child had not gone with him to light the bonfire, his excuse under oath was that he did not know that she was there. Juanita is still nonplussed by his extraordinary claim: 'He suggested after lunch that I [might] like to accompany him to the stables to see the horses. It is nonsense to claim he was not aware that I was there, I was sitting at the same lunch table!'[64]

Why did Broughton deny that Juanita had been present at the lunch on the Friday after his visit to the mortuary? June's tomboyish stepdaughter could hardly be described, even at that age, as a forgettable personality. Broughton's actions between then and his departure for Ceylon render it unlikely that confusion had caused him genuinely to overlook Juanita's presence that day. His manner of handling any detail connected to his evidence seemed either deliberately erratic or exaggerated, but he always appeared to be in control. His fuss over the bonfire was but one of many baffling aspects of his behaviour in the hours preceding and the days following Joss's murder.

At around midday on the Saturday morning, Kath Biggs, having done some shopping in town, burst in on her father the Attorney-General Walter Harragin at home to ask about the news. She had heard that Joss had crashed the Buick. Could it be true that he was no longer alive? She never forgot her father's reply: 'Joss didn't die in a motor accident. He's been murdered.'[65]

On the Sunday, Broughton had The Pantaloon saddled up, riding away from Marula Lane on this, the showiest mount from Riverside Stables, at 9 a.m. He headed off across country. Around teatime he returned The Pantaloon to the Erskines, who were astounded at the state of this sturdy cob which had obviously been ridden too hard. It was muddy, blowing and herring-gutted from exhaustion. Broughton was in a pretty poor way, too. When he said he had not eaten since breakfast the Erskines offered him tea, but he indicated that he would prefer something stronger. So they invited him to help himself: he poured a tumblerful of gin and downed it in one.[66] While Broughton had been on his mysterious ride, the police had driven to Seremai to take statements from Diana and June.[67]

On Monday, the day of the inquest, locally the 'accident' story was maintained:

The East African Standard regrets to announce the death of the
Earl of Erroll, which occurred in the early hours of Friday
morning. The car, in which he had been driving alone, was
found in a damaged condition in a murram pit, a short distance
off the main Ngong–Nairobi road. Lord Erroll was dead when
the car was discovered. The cause of the accident is being
investigated by the police.[68]

Once reports of the inquest came out later that day from Reuters,
it was revealed that a dramatic development had taken place: while
'it had been assumed that death was due to a motor car accident
and . . . the police report to the Press referred to it as an "accident"
. . . the Earl of Erroll was probably murdered'.[69]

Broughton, for some reason best known to himself, had instructed
Mr Lazarus Kaplan his solicitor to attend the inquest on his behalf.
When it was over, Mr Kaplan – known in Nairobi as Kappy –
telephoned his client and informed him that the verdict was murder.
As soon as he heard the news, Broughton was galvanised into action.
Taking a car that June Carberry had hired and had left at Karen, he
drove at once to his solicitor's office in Nairobi. Immediately he
ordered another car and driver to be sent round to Mr Kaplan's
office and then to drive him to Nyeri. After a brief talk with Kaplan
he set forth. 'There was no time to lose,' Peggy Pitt claimed. 'He
was anxious to see June and Diana before they started making statements to the police.'[70] He was too late for that.

According to Juanita, Broughton had arrived while June and Diana
were out at Nanyuki, and but for the servants she was alone at
Seremai. 'He seemed uneasy that nobody else was there. So I offered
to take him to the stables to see my pony, as a way of entertaining
him. It was on the way to the stables that he mentioned to me that
he was being followed by the police.'[71] She should not be alarmed
if the police came, he said. 'I asked him why and he told me that
they probably thought that he had killed Joss.' Being a direct child,
she asked whether he had. His reply had been 'In a way you could
say that I did.' Broughton had then laughed, Juanita continued, and
said, '"They even watched from their car when I stopped by the

bridge over the river, close to the Blue Posts at Thika, and walked to the edge of the Chania Falls, where I just dropped the gun over, but they didn't notice or see what I was doing!" He saw it as a joke.'[72]* The Chania Falls were a local beauty spot, so spectacular that it was indeed not uncommon for travellers to break their journey at the Blue Posts Hotel to take in the view opposite.

Back at the house, Juanita ordered tea for Broughton, and asked him to sign her autograph book and contribute to her questionnaire: What were his favourite animals? Against this he wrote 'horses and bears'. (He had had a menagerie at his Cheshire home, Doddington, among which was a tame bear.) His pastime and sport? Hunting. His favourite subject? Roman history. His favourite country was England, his favourite book, *Mr Pickwick* [*sic*] and his favourite film was *Ben Hur*. The thing that he feared most was 'Loneliness'. Juanita noticed that the shaking of his hand distorted the L. Broughton then wrote on the facing page:

> Here's to myself and one other,
> And may that one other be she,
> Who drinks to herself and one other,
> And may that one other be me.[73]

One of Joss's former mistresses Priscilla Ussher was also staying at Seremai, and arrived back from Nanyuki with June and the distraught Diana. Mementoes that she had collected from Joss's bungalow on Friday were lying about; Juanita remembered that the room Diana was occupying was filled with photographs of Joss. His forage cap and his tunic were lying on the bed.[74] When Diana saw Broughton had arrived, there was a major scene. She accused him 'hysterically and loudly' of the murder, an outburst that had a great emotional impact on Juanita. 'I felt very protective towards him after that.' Priscilla Ussher stayed with Diana once she returned to Marula Lane,

*Juanita, flattered to be trusted by Broughton, told no one of this conversation until 1977 when I was interviewing her for *The Kenya Pioneers*. In someone who was accustomed to being abused verbally and addressed as the 'little sod' or 'brat' her reticence is not as surprising as it might otherwise appear (Juanita Carberry correspondence, 17/9/98).

in the hope that the two women could be of solace to each other in their joint misery.[75] Broughton asked June a lot of anxious questions about what she and Diana had told the police when they'd been interviewed by them the preceding day.

Also on the Monday of the inquest Joss's brother, Captain Gilbert Hay, anxious for any further news, contacted the Colonial Office – as confirmed by a minute sheet dated 27 January, requesting 'any information in connection with the death of my brother'.[76]★

When it came to missing paperwork, those who had to take over from Joss at GOCHQ were astonished that 'there were no files, no other papers to indicate what Erroll was doing'. Joss's replacement as Assistant Military Secretary had to start from scratch, 'with no knowledge of the work that Erroll had been engaged upon'.[77]

The investigation of Joss's murder presented great difficulties for the Kenya Government. At that time the CID department of the Kenya Police was small. There was no properly equipped firearms forensic department for the expert examination of firearms or other murder weapons such as pangas, knives and so on, from crime scenes.

Perhaps the problems the Kenya Police experienced were indeed partly due to lack of resources, but it stretches belief to accept that this was the sole cause of the catalogue of astonishing oversights in the investigation. Just a summary look at the handling of the primary evidence at the scene of Joss's death shows a level of incompetence which strongly suggests deliberate sabotage.

1. No fingerprints were taken from the Buick until after it had been washed by the garage attendants.

2. The police did not stop the removal of the corpse from the car even though no measurements had been taken of the position in which it had been found.

3. The question of the scent in the Buick was made much of, when it was probably no mystery at all. Joss reeked of the Truefitt & Hill scent CAR, as all his close friends knew. No

★The reply from GOC to that request has been 'weeded' from the file in the Public Records Office at Kew.

one suggested that the smell was emanating from the corpse itself.

4. The second set of tyre marks in the murram by the Buick was trampled to oblivion by the police themselves.

5. The police did nothing to stop the Public Works Department excavating more soil, which meant that Lanham's photographs of the pit no longer represented evidence of any sort.

6. The Buick was towed back to Nairobi and taken directly to be examined by the insurers for the hire company, Royal Exchange. Trevor Cole, the manager of Royal Exchange, assessed the damage to the Buick, then telephoned his wife, Leone, about the accident as soon as he returned to his office. She was a notorious gossip and the news of the Earl of Erroll's death by car accident spread rapidly. Hence, curious citizens flocked down to town to have a look at the Buick for themselves. Before long a sizeable crowd had gathered. One of the spectators, Nancy Miller, watched everyone milling around it. 'I didn't get into the car myself, but a lot of spectators did climb into the Straight Eight . . . Suddenly the police arrived and it was removed.'[78] Then the car was washed.

7. The mystery of the two detached arm-slings, which according to Juanita Carberry had been in place on either side of the Buick's back seat the day before, was never solved. An expert on vintage Buicks was emphatic that the slings could not have come out on impact because their manufacture was of such high quality; they could only have been unscrewed.[79] Yet the police did not pursue the matter and this part of the evidence was skated over in court. Similarly, the pipeclay marks on the back seat were remarked upon but not investigated.

8. The typewriter on which the anonymous letters received by Broughton were written was never traced.

9. As soon as Joss's secretary had learned of Joss's accident, before the police investigated anything in his desk she had cleared his filing cabinet and desk drawers of all his personal correspondence.[80] Poppy failed to get hold of any of Phyllis Filmer's letters although she had written very often to Joss from Natal since December.

10. The police did not attempt to find Broughton's missing chauffeur, who was never seen again after the night of 23 January.

11. The accounts concerning the discovery of the body given at the trial by the dairy manager Condon and Assistant Inspector Smith did not corroborate one another.[81]

Thus the scant proof that might have served the case for the prosecution was obliterated.

Percy Filmer was investigated in a perfunctory way by one of Poppy's team, but 'was not the sort of person who was ever really suspect'. In fact Filmer's own secretary, 'Mugs' Muggeridge, had simply vouched for her employer's whereabouts, and that was that.[82] Filmer was not even called as a witness at the trial. Apparently, he was not the type to have sought revenge.[83]

Instead, suspicion fell on the cuckolded husband Sir Jock Delves Broughton. *Le tout* Nairobi knew that Lord Erroll had been conducting an affair with Broughton's new young wife. The assumption in every quarter – the administration, the police, the judiciary, the military and the gossip-mongers – was that Broughton had taken his revenge. Kenya by now was seething with excitement over Joss's death. It was the main topic of conversation in every mess, in every home and in every club.[84]

In the intervening weeks before Broughton's arrest, Assistant Inspector Poppy and Diana developed a rapport. She nicknamed him 'Popski'. Whenever he needed to ask her questions, she would murmur flirtatiously, 'Popski darling, I am not going to answer any questions until you've given me a double brandy.'[85]

On account of the shooting practice Broughton and Diana had done at Burgaret in November Chief Inspector Elliott and Inspector Wink visited Soames' farm on 2 February. They found four spent .32 calibre bullets near where the shooting practice had taken place. Mr Maurice Fox, the government chemist, and Assistant Superintendent Alfred Harwich spent weeks comparing those bullets with the two crime bullets.[86] After a discussion with J. C. Carberry on 5 February at Marula Lane, Broughton asked to see Soames at the

Avenue Hotel for a drink. J. C. had told him there was a 'wonderful new machine' for establishing whether bullets came from a certain weapon or not, and J. C. had said they had one of these machines in Johannesburg. The following day Broughton asked Poppy whether or not this was true, and told the jury at his trial that he had also asked Poppy, ' "What chance have the police to find revolvers if they were buried somewhere in Africa?" ' 'I meant how very difficult would it be for the police to find revolvers if they were not found at or near the car?' Broughton explained. 'I was interested as if they found the revolver they might be able to find the culprit.'[87]

On 12 February the Broughtons took themselves off on safari to southern Maasailand with Hughsie Daisy. For eight days this was how this curious trio avoided public speculation and harassment from the police.[88]

Broughton was arrested on 10 March. Armed with a warrant from the resident magistrate, Poppy, accompanied by Chief Inspector Elliott, Chief Inspector Lanham and Inspector Wink, reached Marula Lane at 5.55 p.m., but Broughton was not at home. They waited for his return in the garden. The Broughtons had gone out for a hack, but during the ride there had been a tiff over jewellery, and Broughton rode back to Marula Lane alone. After he dismounted, Poppy approached, touching him on the shoulder and charging him with murder in front of the other policemen. Broughton said, 'I'm sorry. You've made a big mistake.' Diana now rode up to find her husband surrounded by policemen. Before anything else, she apologised to him for the quarrel. Broughton then asked Poppy, 'Do you mind if I have a whisky?' By 7 p.m., he was in a cell at Nairobi police station.[89]

Broughton's solicitor Kaplan had warned his client for some time that he should expect to be arrested. Even so, Broughton was taken by surprise. Kappy suggested that Diana spend the night at his house with Louise, his wife, and their three children. Kappy had not wanted Diana to remain alone at Marula Lane 'with all that jewellery'.[90] Kappy was a neat, small, precise-looking man, with a conscience. He liked Diana, finding her both generous and beautiful. She broke down that night in front of the Kaplans, expressing her love for Joss, explaining how he had been the only man she had actually ever loved.[91] Kappy advised her to engage the most gifted barrister he could recommend, an influential South African called Israel Aaron Maisels who was serving with the South African Air Force in Kenya, carrying out Intelligence duties up at Wilson Airfield at the time.

Maisels was eager to accept the brief, but had to get permission from the Air Force to do so. In the interim, Diana invited Kappy and Maisels to dinner at Marula Lane. Maisels noticed that the set she moved in was 'pretty hard drinking. I saw more champagne bottles in the yard of the house than I have ever seen in my life.' Diana offered them vodka – it was fashionable at the time to serve vodka and caviar, 'but Lady Broughton omitted the caviar, and then [she] conducted them on a tour of the house, at pains to point out the drain-pipe down which – at some stage – it seemed to have been suggested Broughton had climbed in order to get out of his house and get to the spot where he was alleged to have shot and killed Erroll'. By the time they were called to the dinner table at 10.30 p.m. (they had expected to sit down at 7.30) the lawyers were thoroughly inebriated. Not long after that evening, Maisels received a reply from South Africa forbidding him to accept the brief: 'I was in Nairobi not to defend murderers, but to fight a war.' Yet, Maisels wrote, 'we ended up at an airfield in Nairobi with absolutely nothing to do'.[92]

Kaplan was then obliged to seek another counsel and, Maisels wrote in his memoir, was 'fortunate indeed in obtaining the service of "Harry" Morris instead of me . . . Morris's knowledge of firearms was of tremendous – if not vital – importance to the trial.' A man with a taste for difficult cases and who had several famous acquittals behind him, Henry Harris Morris KC was reputed to be the only counsel outside England to be a ballistics expert.[93] In fact Morris had been instructed by SIS to defend Broughton. Diana flew to South Africa to meet him, where she also bought herself an entire new wardrobe to wear during the trial.

The day following his arrest Broughton had appeared in the resident magistrate's court at Nairobi to be charged formally.[94] The charge sheet alleged that on the night of 23–24 January, Sir Delves Broughton murdered the Earl of Erroll. Assistant Inspector Poppy was called and asked for a remand until 19 March, which was granted. The preliminary inquiry began on that date. The Crown was represented by Crown Counsel H. E. Stacey, a most able South African. During the inquiry forty-three witnesses for the prosecution were called. The day the inquiry began, court no. 3, Nairobi central court, was crammed; 'On this occasion, the regulation under which all court galleries were closed as an air-raid precaution was waived and the gallery was filled.'[95] Benches were brought into the courtroom for further accommodation. This administrative measure ensured maximum word-of-mouth coverage of the inquiry and was guaranteed to set the gossip-mongers' tongues wagging.

Joss's reputation suffered immediately as a result. In the April session of Legco following his death, reference to him was made in the briefest way possible. 'We welcome Mrs Watkins, the late Lord Erroll's successor to the Kiambu Constituency, whose death we all deplore.'[96] In contrast, a lengthy eulogy had been read out at Memorial Hall in 1938 for Joss's predecessor as member for Kiambu, the late Marcus Maxwell, and two minutes' silence had been observed. Joss's diligence in Legislative Council seemed all but forgotten and the cursory mention almost a slight – the only association people were now making with Lord Erroll was that of a philanderer who broke up marriages.

It was during the preliminary inquiry that the public gallery began to take note of Diana's wardrobe, which she had chosen with such care in South Africa and upon which she had spent a small fortune: 'Lady Broughton was again in court wearing a dress of polka-dotted cocoa brown crêpe, with a small white collar and short sleeves. Her tiny brown felt sailor hat was tied at the back with wings of veiling.'[97] Like the star at a command performance, Diana appeared in a new outfit each day.

Mr Rudd the magistrate ruled on 15 April that in his opinion the Crown had disclosed a prima facie case of murder, and committed Broughton to trial by supreme court on that charge. Broughton was held in custody in Kilimani gaol from that day until his acquittal in July. The veteran settler Ewart Grogan, horrified that a European could be imprisoned at Kilimani, instructed his agent, Percy

Wheelock, that a suite of furniture be sent up to wherever Broughton was under arrest. Food and cigars were also delivered each day from Torr's, as well as a menu.[98] While incarcerated, Broughton 'sent a cable to Lord Moyne [his first wife's lover and Secretary of State to the Colonies] asking him if he could help him in the predicament in which he found himself. The reply . . . was to the effect that his Lordship could not interfere with the processes of the law.'[99]

During the weeks of Broughton's imprisonment, everywhere in the colony tension surrounding the forthcoming trial began to mount. Who knew what might happen next? Surely they would never hang a white man? In Nairobi, the argument ran that if Broughton was found guilty of murder, the verdict would set a precedent. Nevertheless, since he so obviously had the strongest motive, he *could* be the first white man to hang . . . Everyone in the capital was impatiently awaiting the trial, where 'startling statements and titillating details were expected'. As Walter Harragin's secretary Peggy Pitt observed, 'Each man and woman being slightly ashamed of their exclusive interest in the case at such a time tried to excuse himself. "After all," they said, "it isn't every day of the week that an eleventh baronet is on trial for murdering a twenty-second earl, who had stolen his wife when they were still practically on their honeymoon." '[100]

Shortly after the preliminary inquiry Gerry Portman, who was one of the Crown witnesses, was found naked and unconscious 'lying at the bottom of a staircase, in his own house'.[101] Portman claimed that 'he had fallen down his own stairs after being clubbed on the head, by the irate husband of his African maid, whom he had tried to seduce'. By now there was so much rumour flying about Nairobi that it was said that Broughton was killing off all the Crown witnesses.[102] At any rate, it was widely suspected that someone was attempting to silence Portman – his close association with Joss went back to 1924.[103]

The truth was rather different from Portman's claim under oath in court. Dr Roger Bowles had been summoned by Portman that morning. After his visit, Dr Bowles confided in his wife what had happened. Apparently, Portman had been near his front door that morning when the doorbell rang and he himself opened the door, instead of one of his African staff. Somebody – the assailant was unknown to Portman, but he was European – had thrust a broken bottle into his face, inflicting considerable damage. Despite such a vicious attack, Portman seemed to want to keep it quiet. His friend Bowles could offer both medical help and confidentiality, so he summoned him. Dr Bowles drove straight from Kabete to Muthaiga, and at Portman's house found blood everywhere from his facial injuries. Since Dr Bowles specialised in tropical diseases rather than head injuries, after examining the wounds he had summoned a neighbouring doctor, Dr Boyle, for a second opinion. Dr Boyle was sworn to secrecy over the matter at Portman's house in Naivasha Avenue that morning. Each doctor now felt reassured, having a reliable witness should there be further complications, and kept the matter secret. Dr Boyle dressed Portman's facial wounds that morning and continued to treat him until they had healed.[104]

Neither the true circumstances of the attack on Portman, nor the real reason behind it, ever emerged at the trial.

The court case, which began on 26 May, became the longest trial ever held in Central Africa at the time, ending on 1 July. With the Earl of Erroll's death plastered over newspapers worldwide, it was conceivable that the case could become the crowning achievement in the defence counsel Morris's not undistinguished career. He had sensed that there was more to the facts than he had been told. His biographer would write that Morris had noticed how hesitant the police had seemed to be to arrest Broughton on a murder charge, despite their belief that he had a strong motive of jealousy.[105] Although he was happy to defend Broughton he was suspicious of his report of the theft of the Colts, which might well have been part of a predetermined murder plan, he thought.

The Chief Justice Sir Joseph Sheridan presided. Sheridan and the Attorney-General Mr Walter Harragin KC, who led for the Crown, had of course both known Joss well for over five years. During the course of twenty-six days a jury of twelve farmers and businessmen sat under Nairobi central court's domed glass ceiling and listened as

Walter Harragin prosecuted for the Crown and Morris defended the accused. Broughton was the focus of an audience made up of local socialites, some titled, and a rota of British soldiers – those who happened to have a few days' leave – who would drop in to join the eager spectators, many of whom stood, since every seat in the courtroom was taken. Broughton, who had always craved attention, must have enjoyed this aspect of the trial, at least.

On the opening day, 'Lord Erroll's ear, in a small glass jar, was handed by the police to the Judge and Jury for examination. Diana turned pale. She whispered to the person sitting next to her, "I really can't take this, poor Joss,"' and left the court hurriedly. She returned ten minutes later, 'perfectly composed and [she] never flinched after that'.[106]

Hughsie Daisy during the trial would claim that he had been in hospital in Mombasa recovering from a septic toe at the time of Joss's murder.[107] In fact he had been posted to Nairobi from the coast, on the pretext that he needed to recuperate up country. He was staying at Mr and Mrs Parkers', next door to the Broughtons' guest house in Marula Lane, where Joss had attended the Red Cross fête just days before his death. Patsy (Bowles) Chilton, with whom June Carberry stayed at Muthaiga during the trial, remembered that Dickinson had been in Nairobi on ten days' leave from the desert when Joss was murdered.[108] The court was never made aware of the inconsistency.

The day before Juanita had been supposed to testify, June had drilled her stepdaughter: 'Be careful what you say to Poppy. Remember that what you say could be responsible for Jock's swinging.'[109] According to Patsy Bowles, too, quite a lot of 'drilling' had taken place in that household – Patsy witnessed June 'in front of a mirror like an actress learning her role', rehearsing what she was to say next day in the witness-box.[110]

Diana's maid Wilks had also used the same expression, 'drilled', in connection with the trial. Like Juanita, she never testified. A policeman on Poppy's team had claimed that Wilks had left Diana Broughton the day after Joss's murder and gone to stay with a neighbour, a Mrs Napier, as she was ill at ease with 'Lady B. drilling it into her again and again what she must tell the police'.[111] But in an interview given in South Africa in 1988, Wilks denied this. 'Nobody drilled me. It's all talk, talk, talk.' She had known how frequently Hugh Dickinson had occupied 'the rondavel in the garden' (the Marula Lane guest house). 'He was in the army but he was back every weekend. He and Diana were very close. I had sharp ears.' She described that friendship as platonic. She had allegedly told Diana that if she was called as a witness she would tell the truth. Wilks had visited Broughton in gaol, at his request, after she had been scheduled as a defence witness. His advice to her at the prison was 'Say yes and no, Wilky, nothing else. Make no sentences or you'll get me sentenced.' Soon after this, Wilks was walking the Napier dogs when Dickinson himself drove up and gave her a piece of paper – 'a warning. I'd get the same if I wasn't careful. I had to get away. One night I took a dog and just walked through the night. Somebody's servant found me and took me to his boss. They took me in. I never went back. The police came looking for me but this lady said, "She's ill. You can't see her." So I never gave evidence.'[112]

Broughton's trial depended heavily on ballistics – proof of his guilt or innocence hung on the identity of guns and bullets. The Crown case against him was that the bullets that killed Joss had been fired from one of Broughton's revolvers lost in the 'burglary' the Tuesday before Joss died. The fact that Broughton had failed to declare these weapons at customs on entering Kenya, although he had declared his other weaponry, came up in court. On the witness stand he claimed that because the Colts had happened to be in his briefcase, rather than with his other guns, he had simply 'overlooked' the formality. Luckily for him, the two firearms certificates that had been issued to him in August 1940 by the Cheshire Constabulary – one for a Colt .32 revolver, the other for a Colt .45 – were proof of the weapons' calibre and design, proof that would eventually let him off the hook. Jack Soames was the only person other than Diana to have seen these guns – Broughton had fired them during his shooting practice at Burgaret. Soames' witness was therefore rather key. At a crucial point during the trial, Morris's hand pressed on

Broughton's shoulder while Jack Soames gave evidence for the defence. 'And if Sir Delves tells his Lordship and the jury that the gun was not a gun that broke [non-Colt] but one in which the cylinder fell out [Colt] you would not dispute that?' Morris asked. He released his grip as Jack Soames replied, 'I would believe him.'[113]

It was evident in court that both Morris and Poppy were familiar with Sir Gerald Burrard's classic study *The Identification of Firearms and Forensic Ballistics*. Since publication in 1934 Burrard's was accepted as the standard reference book, used by police everywhere. The book showed a way of matching bullets scientifically to the weapons from which they were fired, by the marks on the bullets.[114] Morris examined every scratch, every mark, every groove on every photograph of each bullet at the scene of the crime tests and succeeded in confusing everybody, with the result that the ballistics evidence numbed all who tried to focus upon it.[115] At one point Morris teased Kaplan for falling asleep during the ballistics evidence. Morris had pleaded with Chief Justice Sheridan, saying he was making the defence's case all alone, to which the Judge had replied, 'But you have Mr Kaplan.' Morris objected, 'And he is asleep.' The Judge, who did not much like Morris,[116] thought him very rude in court. 'Your Lordship, what should we do now? Should we wait till my junior, Mr Kaplan, has woken up or do we go on with this while he sleeps?'[117] In fact Kappy's eyes were merely closed while he was concentrating; he was not amused.

Perhaps Morris's jocularity was a front. He later claimed that he had been too afraid to admit even to himself that it was 'too easy, too straightforward, too incredible that others had failed to spot an obvious flaw in the Crown case. He kept the bombshell even from his junior until it was time to toss it at the prosecution.' 'Both Alfred Harwich and Maurice Fox [expert witnesses for the prosecution] agreed that the bullet which killed Erroll and the others used at Nanyuki were fired from a weapon with five right-hand rifling grooves', and the markings showed this clearly. 'It stands to reason', Morris would say in court with slow precision, 'that you cannot get a five-grooved bullet out of a six-grooved gun. And the missing

Colts were both six-grooved, were they not?'[118] As Broughton put it in a letter he wrote after his acquittal:

> The crown case depended entirely on the fact that their two ballistics experts said the bullets Erroll was shot with came out of one of my revolvers. I had two revolvers which were stolen from me about four days before the crime. I had had a revolver practice up at Nanyuki. Luckily Morris, my counsel from Johannesburg, had a wonderful knowledge of ballistics himself, one of the few counsels in the world who have, and produced a ballistics expert who denied the bullets were all fired from the same gun i.e. the bullet which killed him, and the bullets which I had fired up at Nanyuki. He showed three marks on the bullet which killed Erroll which you could see with the naked eye, and which were not to be seen on the bullets found up at Nanyuki ... Also luckily, I had my English firearms certificate, which showed the make and numbers of both of my revolvers and that they were both Colts which were six-grooved revolvers, and it was proved that he was shot with a five-grooved revolver.[119]

As one of Kappy's daughters remembers, 'telegrams were flying back and forth from the USA about the guns. It was a very dramatic moment when the results of one of the telegrams came back in favour of the defence.' The most up-to-date forensic expertise was in the States.[120]

When the time came for Judge Sheridan to sum up he would draw the jury's attention to the ballistics evidence specifically, calling it the 'pivot evidence in the case': '[I]f the Jury were to be dissatisfied with the bullets evidence, or found themselves in a position that they could not say with legal certainty that the Nanyuki bullets were fired from the same weapon as the crime bullets, it would be a case of their giving the accused the benefit of the doubt.'[121]

Broughton was finally acquitted of Joss's murder on 1 July. The jury considered the verdict for three hours and twenty-seven minutes, Broughton boasted in the above-quoted letter.

Later in July Broughton and Diana made a trip to Ceylon and

India on the SS *Union Star*, and Broughton wrote many letters while anchored off Colombo.[122] Diana told James Fox, 'I was so upset and so unhappy that nothing mattered to me, if you know what I mean, I felt I had to set him up on his feet again. I don't know whether he *was* set up.'[123] Broughton wrote to his former mistress Marie Woodhouse defiantly, 'I always had the sympathy of the general public as [Joss] was a professional breaker-up of homes with lots of enemies, and the popular saying in Kenya was, "whoever had done it deserved a medal".'[124] He communicated regularly with Marie Woodhouse until he died. Before the trial he had written, 'Wish me luck darling, I think wistfully of Madeira now!'[125] He explained his resentment at having to pay out of his own pocket for Morris to get him off, telling Marie after his acquittal, 'Well, all's well that ends well. But the fact remains that I was in jail for nearly four months which was a severe jolt to my well-organised and happy life. It shows just how easy it is to get into trouble through no fault of your own.'[126]

However, despite his protestations, the Broughtons were ostracised; Broughton was confronted with his worst nightmare – obscurity and loneliness. In March 1942, he rented Oserian for Diana and himself – a striking response to their predicament, but apparently it pleased Diana. She claimed that she found it comforting to be surrounded by memories of Joss. 'If it was anything to do with Joss, I wanted to do it,' she told James Fox in 1981.[127]

Broughton now began to drink more heavily than ever. One night in 1942 at the house of Percy Wheelock, Ewart Grogan's agent, he fell down the stairs after a visit to the lavatory and injured his back badly.[128] The plaster of Paris used to treat the injury had to be explained, so Broughton lied about how he had hurt himself so badly, glamorising the humiliating truth.

By the autumn of that year the Broughtons' relationship had fallen apart. Broughton took a passage to Liverpool in the October. On the voyage back to England, he cabled Gilbert Colvile – he and Diana had formed an unlikely friendship – referring to his relationship with Diana and Joss's beloved home, Oserian: 'You've got the bitch. Now buy her the kennel.' Diana then received a letter from Broughton, written in Mombasa before his departure. He was livid: 'I am determined to punish you for ruining my life in the way you have done,' he wrote, blackmailing her with the promise that if she did not rejoin him in England he would tell the police about a box lodged in her name containing a necklace which had been part of a bogus insurance claim early in 1939. Diana took this letter to Walter Harragin, who advised her to ignore it.[129] Broughton died from a morphine overdose in the Adelphi Hotel in Liverpool on 5 December 1942.[130]

In 1943 Diana married Gilbert Colvile. Despite apparent incompatibilities, the marriage lasted twelve years. Colvile and Diana had a baby girl who died when only ten days old, appearing to fulfil a curse Waweru had laid upon Diana – he blamed her for Joss's death – that she should never have children.[131] They divorced so that Diana could marry Lord Delamere's son, Tom, a friend of Colvile's and the only man apart from Joss that Diana had ever really loved, she claimed. Her amicable divorce from Colvile was handled by Lee Harragin, Walter Harragin's son.

11

The Sallyport Papers

'Never believe governments, not any of them, not a word
they say. Keep an untrusting eye on all they do.'

Martha Gellhorn

'Had it not been for the war,' Walter Harragin's secretary Peggy
Pitt wrote, 'this would have been one of the most famous trials in
history, when the 11th Baronet of Doddington was tried for the
murder of the 22nd Earl of Erroll, Chief of the Hays and Lord High
Constable, whose family goes back into the mists of Scottish history.'[1]
However, long after the Second World War ended, the subject of
who killed Lord Erroll continues to fascinate – not only because
of the glamorous aristocratic personalities involved but because the
murder was never solved.

Some of the many theories that various people came up with as
to who pulled the trigger have been outlined in the first chapter of
this book. There were hints that the affair with Diana had been a
red herring all along. One particularly recurrent theme was that Joss
had been murdered by a woman. Alice de Trafford (formerly de
Janzé), Glady Delamere and Diana all came under suspicion in various
circles. All three women usually reeked of Chanel No. 5 and the
scent in the hired Buick was cited as evidence.

Joss's close circle of friends never doubted, initially, that his death
had been a political assassination, especially the younger group who
socialised with him at Muthaiga Club while he was Assistant Military
Secretary.[2] But these friends were shouted down, ridiculed even, by
those in authority, for the conclusions they had reached.[3] According
to Rupert Allason, who writes under the pseudonym Nigel West,
'There is no doubt, that if Erroll expressed support for the Fascists,

he would have come to MI5's attention.'[4] In an arresting turn of phrase Anthony Cave Brown, the biographer of Stewart Menzies, head of the British Secret Service, wrote: 'the Earl of Erroll was murdered . . . *execution style*', implicitly acknowledging the hallmark of a Secret Services hit.

Colin Imray, the former Kenya Police superintendent who befriended Arthur Poppy back in England, claimed there had always been a 'rumour of British Intelligence participation' in Joss's death. His view was: 'I know well that between the Wars there was a very strong Fascist/Nazi cell in Tanganyika and probably in Kenya as well. I know this through my friend the late Michael Macoun . . . He was a German speaker and was reporting constantly on the East African Germans, Italians etc. I can very well believe that Joss Erroll may have been prominent in all this. That his elimination would therefore have been desirable, particularly in view of his position in 1940 . . . in Nairobi.'

However, a former agent who had been deeply involved in spy-catching between 1939 and 1940, specialising in German espionage in Europe, claimed: 'I never heard a whiff about Erroll. I thought that his private life was terrible but that his public life was impeccable.'[5] It began to seem improbable that Joss had been a double agent. He would never have been given his job as Assistant Military Secretary had there been the slightest suspicion in the Secret Services of his being a traitor.

Among the army officers at Eldoret, the suggestion that Joss's murder had been a crime of passion never gained credence. 'Talk about his death did not last long. Regarded as just one of those casualties of war – there was work to do and the Abyssinian Campaign now took priority.'[6] Hectic top-secret negotiations were under way to get the Emperor of Ethiopia back to his country. Jack Bunyan, on the Governor's executive working out of Shell House, known as Rhodes House until 1940, on Delamere Avenue, remembered that there had been talk of Joss being on the brink of becoming Assistant Adjutant GOC, which would have amounted to double promotion to lieutenant-colonel, had he not been killed. When a brother officer told him that the Secret Services had been behind the killing, he had simply not wanted to believe Joss's fate.[7]

*   *   *

It was with the Sallyport papers, compiled by former Intelligence officer Tony Trafford, that the whole picture of the political assassination emerged. The Sallyport Papers are so named after the Sallyport Inn in Portsmouth, where Tony Trafford first offered the account of Joss's death.

Tony Trafford was educated at Downside. He had known B. A. Young, Colonel 'Sweetie' Barkas's intelligence officer, and had worked with Bertie's twin, Hugh, in Intelligence in the 9th Tanganyika King's African Rifles in the early months of the war.[8] Having returned to England after Kenya's independence, Tony met a retired naval commander, now deceased, whom he referred to simply as Edmund, keeping the man's identity secret because his widow is still alive. Tony and Edmund had met socially when Tony was an employee of Commodore Shipping in Portsmouth. They had Kenya in common and became friends. Edmund regularly invited Tony to meet him at the Royal Naval and Royal Albert Yacht Club once the latter retired.[9] Edmund introduced Tony to four other men who had partial knowledge of Joss's assassination: the Sallyport Papers represent a compilation of their accounts.

Like Tony, Edmund had grown up in Kenya, attending public school in England, then coming back to Kenya just before the war when he joined the Royal Navy in Mombasa. He was later recruited by Naval Intelligence. Edmund had served in the Army also, in Signals and Engineering branches of the Royal Engineers during the war. Much later he had served under Sir James Somerville in 'H' Force, at the Naval HQ Mediterranean Fleet, and the British Eastern Fleet in Alexandria.[10] Edmund and Trafford would exchange news about friends in Kenya when they met at the club. Out of their shared views and common interests a great trust grew up between them. Gradually their mutual disgust with all the distorting rumours spread about Lord Erroll began to emerge.

In the late 1980s Edmund was told by his doctor that he was terminally ill. Prompted by this news, and distressed by the misinformation spread about Erroll's death by the book and then the film *White Mischief*, he determined to place on record his personal knowledge of exactly how the 22nd Earl had died, and he chose Tony Trafford as the repository for this knowledge.[11] Possibly Edmund's conscience was pricked into a confession of this nature because he had in fact known Erroll. Now that he was retired, he had no objection to his knowledge being published, he told Tony, as long as his identity was kept secret. Edmund's dying hope was that Joss's 'detractors' would make an appropriate note of his 'outstanding qualities [because] there has been precious little so far . . . and there could only have been an extraordinary reason for carrying out the operation'.[12]

The story that Edmund told Tony was so incredible that he wrote down Edmund's account specifically to try to verify as much as possible. He queried all that Edmund told him, through inquiries with friends of his who were serving members of the Royal Navy, and satisfied himself that Edmund was genuine. He found out after Edmund died that the latter had served in Intelligence from 1940 to 1944. It was then that Tony realised that, although he and his father H. H. Trafford had not known of Edmund's existence in 1941, all three of them had played different parts in the circumstances surrounding Lord Erroll's murder. As described earlier, H. H. Trafford had been taken out of retirement during the war to carry out certain Intelligence duties, among which was a secret interrogation of Broughton. Tony himself had been recruited as an eighteen year old in 1940 as a sleeper. His role was to 'keep his ear to the ground' and report on Joss's social activities, which he was able to do inconspicuously because of the social standing of his parents in Kenya. He reported his observations to the South African Military Police.

The notion of 'coming clean' is not tolerated by the Security Services, yet most men wish to go to their graves with a clear conscience. Tony, a staunch Catholic, also began to question whom he was protecting, when it came to secrecy, over what he now knew of Lord Erroll's death. He handed over the twenty-five-thousand-word document that he had written setting out how and by whom Erroll had been shot – the Sallyport papers – in the knowledge that it would be made public.

What follows is an abridgement of the Sallyport papers, lightly paraphrased for the most part except where the passages are set in quotation marks. Trafford's style was pedantic and idiosyncratic. He was in his late seventies and suffering from severe angina when he wrote the document. It had obviously been a mammoth task for him to assimilate and put down on paper all that his friend Edmund had told him, not forgetting that Edmund had gathered together his information from disparate sources. Trafford was prone to repetition and the continuity of the narrative was often disrupted while he digressed or laboured a point. He described the information that Edmund had passed to him as being 'of such a fantastic nature as to be incredible, though not if one bears in mind the history of the British government in its dealings with the European community in Kenya from 1900 to 1964'.[13]

The real reason for the murder of the 22nd Earl of Erroll was not adultery . . . It was a politically motivated murder: 'Erroll was murdered by person, agency, or organisation, aided and abetted by the British Government.'

At the time of the Erroll murder and for some time previously MI5 and MI6 had agents in the colony whose function included surveillance of both those expressing extreme right-wing sentiment and those thought to be 'leftist'. It was known that Joss Erroll had views sympathetic to the fascists and had been a member of Oswald Mosley's British Union of Fascists. Unlike some of his friends, he was to moderate these views on becoming elected the member for Kiambu for Kenya Legislative Council. MI5 and MI6 agents were required to report back to their UKHQ, who in turn would advise the War Cabinet.

It is necessary to point out that the Foreign Office has its own Intelligence services accountable only to a specified director and the Foreign Secretary. In the case of the operation under discussion here it appears that the rules of guidance were changed, and it is possible that only two specified officers would have known something, but not all, of the details of the operation.*

---

*Trafford explained to me during one of our meetings that many of those working within the framework of an Intelligence operation will often have no idea what a colleague is working on because agents function within a triangular cell of 'A', 'B' and 'C'. A was the contact point between B and C, but B and C never even knew of the other's involvement. This ensured that few operatives really understood what their ultimate goal was or who was working on the same case, a method that almost guarantees watertight security. (Interview with Tony Trafford, 4/10/97)

The operation to assassinate Lord Erroll was implemented, executed and financed by SOE, finance being obtained from special sources and unspecified funds.

Between July and September 1940, a group of highly placed persons in Scotland held three meetings in the Scottish Highlands to discuss the issue of the Earl of Erroll. Among those present was said to be the Duke of Hamilton (very right-wing). At the third meeting, held on 7 September, it was discussed whether it would be possible to get the Earl of Erroll killed in front-line action, but this solution was dismissed because of the Earl's lack of military training; it would be blatantly implausible to send him to the front line – C-in-C Middle East would not allow it. His military work was behind a desk. Further discussion followed. One man suggested that the whole matter might profitably be handed over to a new special unit called the Special Operations Executive. One of its commanders, a Captain Buckmaster, a skilled Intelligence operative as well as a military operative, had contacts in MI5 and MI6 and specialist Foreign Office Intelligence departments.

The matter was formally handed over to SOE at 2300 hours on 12 September 1940.

A friend of the Duke of Hamilton who lived in Kenya was able to obtain from friends in government administration, in the ADC's office in Government House, Nairobi, and from other sources a very full report on Josslyn Hay over the years.

SOE decided to hand over the responsibility of the operation to their newly formed office in Cairo, Egypt, Middle East.

According to Edmund, SOE had a headquarters in Nairobi. The Controller there had formerly been employed in the Intelligence branch of the Foreign Office. He was rich and very well connected, and had made many business contacts – for example, seniors in Mitchell Cotts (East Africa), Gellatly Hankey and the Gezira Cotton Board (Sudan). SOE's Nairobi HQ had contacts with the Deputy Director of Military Intelligence East Africa Force, DDMI mobile field force, Union Defence Forces (SA) now in Nairobi, Office of the Chief Secretary* to the Government of Kenya, and the Commissioner of Police, Kenya.

SOE had two offices in the Union of South Africa – one in Church Street, Pretoria (the HQ) and one in Cape Town. Very probably there was a sub-office in Durban, but Edmund was unsure here. He stated that the South Africa SOE controller was a very senior police officer (an Afrikaner), a 'Smuts man' called Colonel Adriaan Van Rooyen – one suspects not his real name. Later Van Rooyen would nominate a deputy to be employed with the South African forces in Kenya.

When the SOE office in Cairo was opened in August 1940 the Controller Middle East received a signal from SOE HQ London saying that 'a very senior officer' would be posted from London for the purpose of a special operation to be executed in the Crown Colony of Kenya. This operation would be entirely separate from any military or other operation already being undertaken against the Italian or other Axis forces in Ethiopia, Eritrea or Italian Somaliland. The Controller ME would be advised of the details of this separate operation in Kenya in due course. The Special Officer from London would be directly responsible in the final analysis to SOE HQ London, though of course he would work with SOE Cairo as necessary. SOE Cairo would provide all assistance to the Special Officer.

The Special Officer had many friends in Egypt, particularly in financial circles (Bank of Egypt) and the cotton industry. At the time of his posting to Cairo he apparently held the rank of a British army colonel. The Special Officer from London wasted no time, and requested a meeting with Controller Cairo and two other officers some time in late September to give them details of the special operation to be mounted in Kenya under instructions given to him by SOE London.

The Special Officer introduced himself at the meeting saying his name was Alistair MacDonald, and told those present that he would use the cover name Grampian in telegrams. He then

*Gilbert McCall Rennie was Chief Secretary to Kenya, 1939–47.

advised the meeting that the purpose of the operation would be the elimination of Josslyn Victor Hay and would be of the utmost secrecy to all involved. The operation was known only to very few in the UK, including a certain source in the War Cabinet. It was certainly not known to the C-in-C Middle East Force, GOC East Africa Force, the Governors of the three East African territories, the British resident of Zanzibar, or the civil administrations. The operation would be made known to the Governor of Kenya, Sir Henry Moore, only *after* it had been completed.

Weekly meetings were held by the Special Officer from this point. At the second meeting it was decided:

1) The exercise would be called Operation Highland Clearance.

2) A hit team would be recruited, composed of two persons, one female and one male. These would have to be of the highest calibre, well connected and financially viable – i.e., not reliant on a military or other salary – and able to mix socially. Languages would be an asset. In addition the female member of the team would have to be sexually attractive. The intention was that she was to become involved intimately with Joss Erroll. It was well known by Intelligence that Erroll always had one other besides his current mistress.

3) The routing of the agents to East Africa would have to be so arranged that the minimum use of military transport was involved, difficult as this would be.

4) Salary and expenses for the two agents would be handled through the national bank of Egypt by means of two personal accounts, which the Bank of Egypt would arrange to be opened with the National Bank of India in Nairobi, the official bank of the Government of Kenya. The SOE Controller in Kenya would be advised of all details.

5) Personal documentation for the agents would be provided by SOE Cairo and London, which included appropriate military documentation (Army and RAF) plus civil documents such as passports.

Another meeting was held in early October. Changes in military command in the Middle East war theatre were discussed, including details of forthcoming operations in Italian East Africa. At the conclusion of the meeting, Grampian announced that Highland Clearance must commence not later than 1 December 1940 and conclude by 15 February 1941 at the latest.

The recruitment of the agents – especially the female – presented many difficulties to SOE Cairo. Grampian now made approaches to many of his contacts within the Army, Navy and RAF, the Intelligence branch of the Egyptian Army and commercial circles in Cairo and Alexandria also, besides the SOE agents and informants in Cairo.

The British female civilian personnel and evacuees and military wives were considered to be a rich hunting ground. A somewhat delicate contact was made with Betty Lampson, niece of the Ambassador Sir Miles Lampson, later Lord Killearn, of the British Embassy, Cairo. Betty, who had recently arrived from Kenya, was asked specific questions about Erroll by SOE at one stage.

The recruitment of the female agent took a dramatic step forward when Cairo received a special report from the Controller Pretoria that he had been in touch with a Lady Ranfurly. This lady had been evacuated to South Africa from Egypt in August 1940 under the scheme for the evacuation of military wives ordered by C-in-C Middle East. After intensive interrogation by the SOE Controller Pretoria (an authority from SOE London), she had been recruited as an agent for SOE. Up to the time of the report she had not been allocated any specific duty or task.

Knowing that Lady Ranfurly wanted to return to Cairo to be with her husband, Controller Pretoria offered her services to SOE Cairo. Immediately SOE Cairo advised Pretoria that Lady Ranfurly could be of the greatest assistance to them, particularly if she could find a suitable woman to carry out and execute an operation of an extremely confidential nature.* In due course Pretoria would be advised of the exact details of this operation. Pretoria was then given specifications of the type of agent required.

SOE Cairo had not long to wait before Controller Pretoria was able to send a report to Cairo that the agent Lady Ranfurly had found 'a lady likely to be of considerable interest and to meet advised requirements'. Pretoria was instructed to send the necessary details of the agent forthwith, but the final decision of employing her would rest with SOE Cairo. The following details concerning the agent were despatched to Cairo by Pretoria:

FEMALE AGENT

(1) Personal details

a) Name: said to be Susan Melanie Van Der Pleyden (née Laurenz) (probably false)

b) Age: 30–35 years old. Place of birth: UK

c) Race: white. Hair colour: light brunette

d) Skin: light to fair

e) Nationality: British (British passport holder)

f) Resident: Union of South Africa. Lived in suburb of Rosedale, Johannesburg

g) Occupation: employed as a confidential secretary/social secretary to a highly placed executive in Consolidated Goldfields Pty and Eckstein & Co, an old private finance company in Johannesburg.

(2) Family background

a) Father (deceased) was of high social standing and financial status. He had held high commercial positions in the Middle East (Lebanon, Egypt and Sudan). In Lebanon he had been a 'privileged shareholder' and executive at the Lebanese national bank, in Beirut. He had been a shareholder in the

---

*At no time did Trafford suggest that Lady Ranfurly was aware of the purpose for which this woman was being recruited.

Bank of Egypt, in the Cotton Board of Egypt, and in several prominent cotton plantation corporations in Sudan. He had been on the Gezira Cotton Board and had connections at an old and well established firm, Gellatly Hankey.

b) Mother (also deceased) was an American citizen who held both a US and a British passport, no doubt obtained by her husband. She was related to the well known Boston family, the Cabots. Again, of high social and financial status.

(3) Education

a) Educated privately in the US. Moved with parents to Lebanon where she attended the American University in Beirut. Moved to UK at age twenty-two and attended Girton College, Cambridge, for an unspecified period.

b) Adept at languages. Spoke French, Italian, Spanish and Arabic with fair fluency.

c) Played hockey, lacrosse and enjoyed watersports and tennis.

d) Indoor activities: good bridge player, played chess and mahjong. First-class cook.

e) Of particular interest to both Pretoria and Cairo was that SM [Susan Melanie] was a first-class shot. She was proficient with a rifle, namely calibres of 22, 275, 300/303, 375/450 (heaviest), and also proficient in the use of handguns, namely calibre pt 22, pt 25, pt 32, pt 35, pt 45 (heaviest) [among many others]. She held firearms proficiency certificates from a US school of musketry/firearms and a well known rifle club in England.

f) SM had knowledge of first aid, a great deal of which she had learned in an African context.

g) On leaving university in the UK, she spent a year travelling. She then obtained employment in a City finance office in London.

h) SM had many friends, and because of her social background was able to mix at all social levels. She had stayed at many well known houses and estates in England.

i) SOE in London had discovered that she had had contact with British Intelligence Services at some point in her career.

j) SM arrived in South Africa in late 1937 and was provided with a residents' permit without the usual waiting period.

k) SM had had many love affairs. She was extremely attractive and sexually highly aware. She had married a Captain Christiaan Van Der Pleyden in the summer of 1939. The marriage was brought to the attention of the security branch Pretoria – Christiaan was in the South African police force. His choice of career was not regarded favourably by his well-to-do family. He was killed in a traffic accident in January 1940.

Having received the Pretoria report, Cairo dispatched Alistair MacDonald to interview Susan Melanie. The interview took place on 3 November 1940 at 10 a.m. in a 'safe house', thirty miles north of Pretoria off Great North Road. MacDonald arrived at the military airfield now known as Waterkloof. At the safe house he met the SOE controller Van Rooyen. Susan Melanie had been instructed by letter to report at 1400 hours on 2 November to Defence HQ Pretoria at the office of General Staff Officer 1, where she would be required to undertake 'military duties'. She was to bring with her an overnight bag for two days' stay. Susan Melanie's employers Eckstein & Co were notified that she was being called up for military service from 1 November 1940. When she reported to Defence HQ she was enlisted into the newly formed South African Army Auxiliary Women's Service. After an overnight stay in a hotel in Pretoria she was taken to the safe house. On enlistment, on 2 November, she had been given the cover name Susanna Meintjies and the rank of private, army clerical grade 1.

The interview began on the afternoon of 3 November and concluded on the morning of the 4th. Present were SOE Controller Pretoria Van Rooyen and MacDonald. The interviews were searching. Susan Melanie was given a detailed firearms examination which included standard and advanced army tests for soldiers and war training. She was also given a driving test and a first-aid examination; both exams were to an advanced level. In the last two hours of the interview on 4 November, Susan Melanie was briefed as to why she had been selected as an agent for Military Intelligence. She was told she had been recruited jointly by Military Intelligence UK and SA, and SOE. She was warned there would be specific tasks, not pleasant, for her to undertake in Kenya. For this she would be assisted by a male agent being recruited in the Middle East. The male agent and she would travel together to East Africa.

In the meantime, she returned on 5 November to Defence HQ Pretoria to report for duties of a normal nature. Her next orders were to proceed to Cairo on 12 November as part of an advance party to set up a South African Army HQ team to be attached to GHQ Cairo Middle East Force. She was promoted to the rank of A/Sergeant, effective from 10 November. The advance party consisted of about fifteen people. On 12 November they flew by special military aircraft from Pretoria to Cairo. Susan Melanie arrived at Cairo Almaza Airport – a civil airport under the control of the RAF – at 1800 hours on 16 November.

Some time during November* SOE Cairo received a report from MI6 concerning an involvement that Josslyn Victor Hay had with the British Union of Fascists, noting that he had been friends with Sir Oswald Mosley, leader of the BUF. This was not merely a political and social contact, said the report – through Mosley Lord Erroll was put into contact with an extremely powerful cabal of British Government officials in the Civil Service and Foreign Office and of senior officers of the Royal Navy, Army, RAF and police, as well as senior members of the Church of England and Roman Catholic Church. These people were extremely right-wing. The cabal was involved in negotiations directly (until the outbreak of the Second World

*SOE Cairo were told only at the last minute, to minimise the risk of leaks.

War) with Germany and with von Ribbentrop, German Ambassador to the UK, 1936–8. These negotiations, in summary, were that:

(1) England would form a new alliance with Germany and certain Scandinavian countries (Sweden in principle), which would be called the Nordic Alliance.

(2) The purpose of the Nordic Alliance was to carry out war with the Soviet Union – in fact, an earlier version of Operation Barbarossa of 22 June 1941. There would be the usual economic and political advantages attached.

(3) The UK and the Dominions would not engage in hostilities against Germany and other partners in the Rome–Berlin Axis.

On the outbreak of war, all direct negotiations ceased between the combatant powers. However, negotiations continued between the cabal and certain diplomatic officers of the Foreign Office and Germany, through the Swedish Government and the German Ambassador in Stockholm.

Joss had a considerable knowledge of the negotiations and contacts mentioned above. Before his election to Legco he had joined a movement led by Lord Francis Scott to prevent Tanganyika territory from being returned to Germany, as this territory was among Britain's contribution to the proposed Nordic Alliance.

The main reason why Operation Highland Clearance was so secret and complicated was that highly placed persons in the British Government believed that the extremely delicate information in Josslyn Hay's possession could, if it became known outside certain circles, cause extreme embarrassment to, and very possibly the resignation of, the Government. Joss was known to have been indiscreet concerning the information in his possession and concerning his involvement with the cabal's and the Chamberlain government's negotiations with Germany for the cessation of hostilities between the two countries. If the information was leaked, it could also lead to an embarrassing situation between three friendly countries – namely Sweden, the United States of America and Great Britain.

Notwithstanding Joss's assurances to both the British and the Kenya Governments, through the Governor of Kenya, that he had ceased his association with the BUF and the cabal, it was known from certain sources (certainly MI6, possibly MI5 and possibly the Special Branch of the Metropolitan Police) that Joss was still in contact with the cabal, and the BUF and their friends.

The report from London to Cairo was the final authorisation for Operation Highland Clearance.

Edmund was able to give some details on the male agent, though not as thorough as the report on Susan Melanie.

It appears that a male agent was recruited by a captain of the Royal Signals Corps stationed in the office of the Director of Signals GHQ Middle East Force. The agent was a regular army officer and had been stationed in the Middle East since May 1939. He was extremely well educated and had attended Oxford University, gaining a high-class BSc degree. He was socially very acceptable, with a good family background, and was financially independent. He had two uncles who had served in the Sudan political service. One uncle had joined the Gezira Cotton Board, and the other Gellatly Hankey, serving in their merchandising department, cotton sales. He was said to be called James Gregory Hewitt (no doubt a cover name).

Agent James Gregory duly reported to SOE Cairo as requested, and he was briefed to be a number two, or 'minder', to the female agent whom he would meet in due course. After these interviews, he returned to his normal post at Directorate Signals GHQ Middle East Force to await further orders.

On 30 November James Gregory was contacted by SOE and told to report to a Major Hemming.

The final briefing of the two agents took place somewhere in Cairo at the end of November. It was conducted by Alistair MacDonald and two other members of section A committee

SOE Cairo. Both agents were again briefed as to the nature of the operation they were to undertake. It was impressed upon them that in the event of any compromise due to neglect on their part they would be 'disowned, forgotten'.

At their briefing the two agents were told to proceed by rail from Cairo to Aswan, then to pick up the Nile river steamer from Sudd el Ali Port to Wadi Halfa in the Sudan. From there they would travel by the mail train on the military railway to Khartoum. On arrival at Khartoum Station, as was customary for all military persons travelling from Egypt, they were to report to the railway transport officer for the usual checks and to receive instructions for any onward journeys in the Sudan involving rail travel, as well as any official documents, including letters, relative to their stay in the Sudan and their posting to their units for military employment. They would travel in uniform – James Gregory as an officer, going to an infantry battalion at Kassala, Advance HQ for the Force, to be engaged in the operation against the Italian forces in Eritrea; Susan Melanie as a lieutenant (nursing sister) in the Queen Alexandra Imperial Military Nursing Service, for employment initially in the military hospital at Khartoum. All movement documents etc. were issued to James Gregory in the name of Arthur Mesham and to Susan Melanie in the name of Elizabeth Potter. Thus the briefing concluded.

The two agents undertook the first stage of their journey as instructed, leaving some time between 1 and 3 December; they suffered one or two delays along the way, arriving at Wadi Halfa three days later. They then took the mail train from Wadi Halfa four hours after arriving there and arrived at Khartoum at 1745 hours the following day. There they reported as instructed to the railway transport officer, a captain in the Royal Engineers (movement control). The RTO gave them two sealed envelopes which he had received that morning from Q (Mvts) Army HQ in Khartoum. The agents were then informed that owing to shortage of accommodation they would stay for three days at the Grand Hotel in Khartoum.

Once they were settled into their hotel rooms the agents opened their sealed envelopes, in which they found onward briefings for their movement from Khartoum and an instruction to ring a specified telephone number there. They were told to use a code word, 'Metemma', when making the call. When they called the number they were advised that they would be met in the Grand by a Captain Frobisher at 8 p.m. that night. At the appointed time he arrived, and the three went into a private anteroom where Frobisher briefed the agents as follows:

(1) Captain Frobisher said he was employed in G Branch (G.INT&OPS).

(2) Instructions had been received from SOE Cairo and SOE Nairobi regarding their onward journey to Kenya.

(3) The movement instructions were that they would travel from Khartoum to Kosti by the Elobeid mail train, departing on Thursday afternoon, the day after tomorrow, at 1500 hours, and arriving at 0700 hours next morning.

(4) From Kosti the agents would travel south to Malakal, whence they would take the Nile river steamer to Juba, a slow journey taking four days. There they would disembark and report to the Political Officer, who would arrange overnight accommodation in the railway rest house. From Juba they would take the Sudan Railways bus to Nimule on the Sudan–Uganda border. Travel would then be down the Nile to Butiaba Port (Uganda) on Lake Albert, by Kenya and Uganda Railways & Harbour Administration river steamer. They would then travel by KUR&H bus service from Butiaba to Masindi Port (Lake Kyoga), by KUR&H lake steamer to Namsagali, and there they would board a train that would eventually join the main KUR&H rail line from Kampala via Jinja, Tororo, Eldoret, Nakuru and Gilgil to Nairobi.

(5) Susan Melanie would henceforward travel under the name Miss Mary Shaw, a personal assistant to the cotton broker (cotton and merchandise department) of Gellatly Hankey in Khartoum, and James Gregory would travel as Mr Richard

Murrey, an executive on the Gezira Cotton Board, Khartoum office. These names had been allocated by SOE Cairo and received by SOE Khartoum some thirty days before the arrival of the two agents. The cover story – of which SOE Nairobi were also aware – was that they were sent by the Governor-General's office (HQ Agricultural Cotton Department) to attend a forthcoming conference concerning a cotton-growing and production scheme to be started at the termination of hostilities. The conference was under the direction of the Kenya Government Department of Agriculture, and the Governor Sir Henry Moore would be in attendance. The conference would start on 2 or 3 January and last ten to fourteen days.* The agents would be issued with the necessary documents and further briefed on their function at the conference in Nairobi.

(6) Frobisher now issued them with the necessary documents – tickets, passports, transit passes etc., all in their new names of Mary Shaw and Richard Murrey.

During their journey down the Nile from Khartoum, the agents studied the documents that Frobisher had given them.

The Sallyport papers provide further minute details of the orders contained in these documents, including instructions to communicate by telegram once they reached Nakuru Station with the code word 'Metemma'.

The agents eventually arrived at Nairobi Station at 1530 hours on 11 December, where they were met by George Wheeler, an SOE informant. Wheeler took them to a safe house arranged for them by SOE Nairobi, in the Parklands area of Nairobi. The safe house was fully furnished down to the last teaspoon; it had a larder stocked with a month's supplies, and it was fully staffed by a Seychellois housekeeper, four domestics, a kitchen boy and a Kipsigis nightwatchman.

*The Sallyport papers explained that the conference was eventually 'downgraded to a meeting of 3 or 4 days', with only Melanie, Gregory and two other delegates.

The Controller SOE Nairobi visited the agents and together they went over the details of the operation to be executed. Also, they were given a full background on Josslyn Victor Hay, right down to his current mistress and other intimate details. The Controller also told the agents that there would be a daily course of instruction given by a member of his staff about cotton, cotton-growing and cotton products which they would need for the Department of Agriculture conference to be held in January. They would be given the agenda for the conference (which Controller SOE Nairobi had obtained from one of his sources closely connected with the Department of Agriculture).

The agents were also told that they would meet a Miss Priscilla Barlow, who was one of the two senior personal assistants to the Chief Secretary to the Kenya Government at the Secretariat. This was simply a courtesy gesture that would be made by any person attending a government conference, though Miss Barlow was an informant for SOE Nairobi and MI6. The agents were to continue to use the cover names Mary Shaw and Richard Murrey in all aspects of their lives in Nairobi.

SOE Cairo was informed by SOE Nairobi of the safe arrival of their agents and of all the detail of their briefings. Operation Highland Clearance was now ready to proceed.

While Susan Melanie and James Gregory were making their journey to Nairobi, SOE Nairobi had sent a report to SOE Cairo covering the backgrounds of Joss, Broughton and Diana. According to this report, Diana was 'known to both MI5 and MI6 and the Spec. Int. Sec. Foreign Office'. The report also relayed – via two informants at Muthaiga Club, one a member and one a long-serving and reliable African servant – the developing intimacy between Joss and the Broughtons, the frequency of their shared lunches at Muthaiga, and in particular that 'as early as 20 November Diana had already made the first moves to an intimate relationship with Joss'. Reports were coming in through other sources too – namely, Broughton's friends and 'Jock himself' – that the affair between Joss Erroll and Diana was gathering momentum.

During this same stage of the agents' journey, SOE Nairobi had received a visit from a Major Lawson of the South African Corps of the Military Police, attached to the office of the Deputy Assistant Provost-Marshal East African Corps of the Military Police, Nairobi area HQ. The SOE Pretoria Controller knew all about Major Lawson. A wealthy, well-born South African, part of the Johannesburg 'High Society set', he was their rep in East Africa Force. SOE London had sanctioned his appointment. Lawson was allocated the code name Elaandsvlei ('Eland Valley') and was to assist in Operation Highland Clearance, as well as being responsible for overall liaison with SOE Nairobi, issuing fortnightly reports to Pretoria. Copies of Lawson's reports would in turn be sent to Cairo.

At this point in the narrative, the Sallyport papers go into some detail about the 'military situation in EAF (Kenya) Oct. 40–1 Feb. 41', covering the positioning of troops and the secondment of forces into the KAR and the Kenya Regiment. Then the narrative picks up the thread of Operation Highland Clearance, when Edmund introduces the final part of the operations before the actual 'hit'. He relates that SOE Cairo had made a mistake in sending the agents down to Nairobi as late as December – 'October would have been the ideal month' – as they had hardly enough time to inveigle themselves into Nairobi society before the hit, which 'had to be completed' by the end of January or early February 1941.

So the agents lost no time in getting to work, Susan Melanie taking the more active role. Her first contact was a well known settler of many years' standing, Ewart S. Grogan. Susan Melanie went to meet him at Torr's Hotel in Nairobi, where every day Grogan held court over coffee between 11 a.m. and 2 p.m., holding forth to all who would listen about his former escapades as a young man. He had an eye for attractive women, and Susan Melanie certainly fell into this category. His agent Percy Wheelock would always be with him at these informal gatherings, and having attended several meetings, Susan Melanie got herself invited by Grogan to a private dinner party. This happened to be a dinner party hosted by Joss, who knew Grogan well. Diana did not attend. There were other friends at the dinner, including a businessman from Mitchell Cotts. After the dinner, Joss asked Susan Melanie if she would have lunch with him, telling her his weekly routine so that she would know where to reach him each day in case she needed to contact him before their tête-à-tête. Susan Melanie relayed all this information back to Controller Nairobi.

For his part, James Gregory decided to obtain information by attending places of entertainment and recreation for commissioned officers and other ranks in Nairobi. He did not until very late enter Muthaiga Country Club as he considered that this might pose security risks.* He attended Torr's Hotel and the canteen for NCOs, officers and other ranks in Hardinge Street, where he met Glady Delamere on a number of occasions. She invited him to a private lunch party and later to a dinner party at which Joss had been present. (Apparently Controller Nairobi was well aware that Glady had a soft spot for good-looking young men.) Glady proved a useful source of information on Joss for James Gregory. In his recces for information, James Gregory also attended the weekly dances for other ranks (known as 'Scotch hops') at St Andrew's Church Hall in Nairobi. At these dances European partners were provided for unaccompanied males by dance-committee ladies. These females were culled from the local businesses – Dalgety & Co, Mitchell Cotts, the railways and government offices, and a well known hairdressing establishment, Theo Schouten's. A large secretarial establishment, Remington Business, Typewriting and Shorthand School, was also a good source of these 'unattached young ladies'. Susan Melanie herself sometimes went dancing here. She and James Gregory had been instructed never to make contact, should they happen to spot one another.

Meanwhile Susan Melanie was getting more intimate with Joss, taking great care that Diana did not find out. One report

*Muthaiga was a hotbed of Intelligence employees.

by a club servant to SOE Nairobi <u>and MI6</u> [Trafford's underlining] was that Susan Melanie and Joss met at Muthaiga, after which he took her back to his bungalow. One of Joss's house servants had volunteered to a Muthaiga Club employee – if not an actual informant, then a gossip who could be counted upon to spill the beans – that they had gone to bed together. Susan Melanie's duty was to report activities and progress to the Controller. This was how even the most mundane and casual chit-chat between African staff maintained a useful back-up to SOE – in this case, proof that Susan Melanie was telling the truth.

At yet another party, given by a Major Pembroke and at which Joss Erroll was a guest, Susan Melanie actually met Diana. The two were polite to one another, 'though Diana was reported to have said of Susan Melanie "not quite but all right I suppose" [*sic*]'.* According to Edmund, it was known from other reports at the Kenya Government (Chief Secretary's office), Government House and ultimately to both SOE and MI6 and the Foreign Office, that Diana also had 'lovers on the side' like Joss.

Interrupting the chronology of the account, the Sallyport papers next cover a report from SOE Controller Nairobi to SOE Cairo describing in detail a 'violent' quarrel that took place between Joss and Diana in the early hours of 24 January, after they'd arrived back at the Broughtons' Karen house.

Both accused each other of various matters – love on the side, meetings with other women and 'old flames'. Joss said he could now no longer contemplate marriage and accused Diana of wanting to marry him only for spurious reasons: his money and social status. Diana was brutally blunt with him, calling him disgusting and accusing him of deceiving his friends and herself, in particular as to his financial position. Joss believed Susan

---

*There is no evidence that Diana ever found out that Joss had slept with Susan Melanie.

Melanie would be waiting for him back at the bungalow, after he had dropped Diana off at Marula Lane.

The Sallyport papers next come to what Trafford described as the 'hardest part of this report, namely "the hit" and the events leading to it'.

The Controller Nairobi knew the location of the Broughtons' house at Karen. His agents had obtained photos of the house and the grounds, the access roads etc. These details were obtained from the Lands Department, Nairobi, and from agents working for both SOE and MI6 Nairobi.

SOE Controller Nairobi had now to consider the best means of killing Joss. He applied to Major Lawson for help in working out a plan. The two men spent a day and a night discussing the matter at the Brackenhurst Hotel in Limuru. SOE Controller Nairobi asked Lawson to visit the Broughtons in Karen and survey the house, the gardens and the adjoining lands thoroughly. He asked him to pay particular attention to any veranda, patio or back door, and also to the 'rest house' occupied by a Lieutenant Hugh Dickinson. The Controller said he would send an SOE agent along with Lawson to carry out the recce, though he did not say who this would be.

Controller Nairobi also asked Lawson to take responsibility for any transport or other equipment that would be needed for carrying out the hit.

At the meeting in Limuru Lawson also told Controller Nairobi that he knew friends of Joss's including Glady, J. C. and June Carberry, and the Broughtons. He had been to dinner with the latter so his presence there if he turned up unannounced would not raise eyebrows.

As the meeting concluded Controller Nairobi told Lawson that he would call another meeting within the next seven to ten days.

Two days after the Limuru meeting, Lawson went to the Broughtons' house with a team he had selected himself, plus an SOE agent sent by Controller Nairobi who introduced himself as Ray Morgan (Morgan was in fact James Gregory, unbeknown to Lawson). As they made their detailed reconnaissance of the place, the whole team came to the conclusion that it would not be possible to 'make a kill' in the house itself. The getaway of any sniper unobserved would be too difficult. The fact that the house had a phone was also an obvious disadvantage. Furthermore, police officer Anstis Bewes lived nearby and could be on the scene in no time. The possibility of planting a bomb in the house was also ruled out because none of the Broughtons' regular visitors – were they to have been deployed in the operation – had the expertise to plant and arm the device.

Lawson reported his findings back to SOE Controller Nairobi, and so did Ray Morgan, the two reports independently satisfying the Controller that both participants were telling the truth.

SOE Controller Nairobi then called another meeting with Lawson, at the White Rhino Hotel in Nyeri, to work out a final solution for taking out Joss Erroll. The White Rhino Hotel was preferred both by SOE and Lawson to the Outspan Hotel for 'security reasons'. Two days after the recce at the Broughtons', here SOE Controller Nairobi and Lawson thrashed out some ideas and came up with the following plan. The hit would have to take the form of an ambush – i.e., stopping Erroll's car and then shooting him. They fixed a date for the hit – some time between 1800 hours on 23 January and 0400 hours on 24 January 1941: 'Agents Susan Melanie and James Gregory would carry out the necessary action. Susan Melanie was to be disguised as a not unattractive early-middle-aged lady. Her hairstyle altered to platinum blonde. A Morris 10 saloon car 4-door 38/39 model would be made available to the agents for conveying them to the designated hit area at Karen to execute the hit. James Gregory was to drive. After the hit both the agents would return to a designated house in the Girouard Road area (near the Maia Carberry Nursing Home) to report to Controller. SOE Nairobi to make the necessary reports and debriefings.'

At another meeting 'thought to have taken place 20 January 1941 at Brackenhurst Hotel, Limuru', SOE Controller Nairobi told the agents that the Morris 10 had been supplied by an Asian dealer in the second-hand and car-hire business who had considerable dealings with military personnel in Nairobi. The Morris 10 was now parked behind the Controller's house.

Lawson knew a Captain Koos Odendaal in the office of the Deputy Assistant Provost-Marshal, who was also the officer commanding the special investigation branch of the South African Corps of Military Police. Lawson asked Captain Odendaal to carry out surveillance when Joss Erroll attended parties at the Clairmont Club [hotel]. Odendaal had several informers amongst non-commissioned ranks. He would call on these to assist him especially, as they attended the Clairmont to carry out surveillance and gather information on South African military personnel. This was now particularly important in view of the forthcoming operation to be mounted against Italian forces in Ethiopia and Somalia. Odendaal and his 'spook team' should be in the Clairmont on the of nights 21, 22, 23 and 24 January. He would supply a regulation South African Army staff car or station-wagon, which would also have a radio wireless transceiver. From another source – 'through "good offices" of a contact in the United States consulate office in Nairobi' – a small US Hallicrafter transceiver would be supplied, to be carried in the Morris 10 conveying the agents to the hit site. Both radio sets were fitted with scrambler devices in case transmissions were picked up by signals sections of the various forces stationed in the area.

A further meeting was called by SOE Controller Nairobi for 21 January 1941 at the safe house in Girouard Road, and began at about 0900 hours. Present were SOE Controller Nairobi, Major Lawson and Captain Koos Odendaal. The Controller confirmed that all requisite transport was assembled. Necessary wavelengths were chosen and the sets were 'netted in' accordingly. Details of Joss's car were then supplied – a Buick 8 saloon, reg. no. T7331. The Buick would be followed by Odendaal, driving the station-wagon. A radio operator would operate the radio set and render any other assistance required. The Morris 10 would proceed to the Karen hit area on receipt of a transmitted signal from the station-wagon. As a double precaution against interception, Joss Erroll would be referred to as Roger and Karen as Kay.

Lawson informed those at the meeting that he had learned that there would be a party in the Clairmont Club on the night of 23 January after drinks at Muthaiga Club. Sir Jock and Lady Diana Broughton would be present.

SOE Controller Nairobi finally confirmed that he had himself obtained a radio transmitter/receiver – it was a type known as a No.11 set, used by both the British and the South African armies. Furthermore, he had obtained the services of an exceptionally good radio operator – a Corporal Munyao Nzai of the 3rd King's African Rifles. The radio transmitter was netted in to the same wavelength as the other two. Code names were given out for use in transmission procedure – these would also be used as a call sign:

Odendaal team = Bontebok [Afrikaans for 'buck']
Hit team/Morris 10 = Nyoka [Swahili for 'snake']
SOE Controller Nairobi = Control or Pamba [Swahili for 'cotton']

The meeting ended at 1800 hours. SOE Controller Nairobi confirmed that there would be a final briefing at the safe house on Girouard Road at 1000 hours on 22 January.

Lawson, Odendaal and agents Susan Melanie and James Gregory attended this meeting. Final and specific orders were given as follows:

To Captain Odendaal's team
Odendaal and his spook team would assemble at the Clairmont by 2000 hours on 23 January. SOE Controller Nairobi had been informed that the Broughtons, Joss, Dickie Pembroke and others would be at Muthaiga Club from about 1800 hours until

1930 hours, when they would go to the Clairmont to have their party. The party would go on probably until about midnight or 0115 hours at the latest. As on previous occasions, Joss Erroll would leave the Clairmont with Diana and drive her to his bungalow in Muthaiga. They would spend some time at the bungalow; then Joss would drive Diana back to her house at Karen where again he might spend some time before returning to his bungalow.

The station-wagon with the rest of the team would remain in the Clairmont area until definite information was to hand. The surveillance team had a Harley-Davidson motorbike and side-car (SA Army standard issue equipped with a wireless transceiver No. 11 set). The Harley-Davidson was recognised from its distinctive engine sound by Stephen Carnelly, chief magistrate for Nairobi. The motorbike team were to follow Joss and Diana from the Clairmont to Joss's bungalow, and send signals to Odendaal in the station-wagon using the wavelength and form of message given to them by Odendaal.

As soon as they received a message from the motorbike surveillance team that Joss was leaving with Diana from his bungalow for Karen, the team in the station-wagon would go on five minutes' standby. A second message from the motorbike surveillance team would be sent to the station-wagon indicating the route Joss was taking. If Joss's car was moving towards Nairobi, the motorbike team would follow until the station-wagon could catch up and pass them. The motorbike team would then slow down and the station-wagon would take over the tailing.

The Erroll car would then be followed to its final destination. SOE Controller Nairobi would be advised by radio signal when this had been accomplished. The communication would include any message from Nyoka [Susan Melanie and James Gregory] for onward transmission to Pamba [SOE Controller Nairobi]. If a signal was received from the two agents that they had successfully executed their mission, the team would proceed to the designated area, meet with the agents, give any assistance required and then return to base.

To Susan Melanie and James Gregory

On receipt of the signal from the motorbike team that Joss and Diana were leaving the bungalow, SOE Controller Nairobi would advise the agents to proceed to the designated hit area in fifteen minutes' time. Odendaal's station-wagon team would signal SOE Controller Nairobi that the agents had left for the designated area. The agents would advise the station-wagon team of their arrival at the designated area, and they in turn would advise the SOE Controller. This was because the station-wagon team's radio equipment was more powerful than that of the agents.

Once the agents had carried out their mission, they would advise the Controller via Odendaal's team. Then they were to await the arrival of Odendaal's team.

To SOE Controller Nairobi

SOE London controlled the whole operation. If any part of the plan were to go wrong, SOE London reserved the right to abort. The consequences of this would be very severe for all concerned. 'In making this observation it appears that SOE Nairobi, Pretoria and Cairo were quite aware of SOE London's capabilities, determination and ruthlessness.'

Teams and equipment and personnel were to be in place at 1000 hours on 23 January. Controller Nairobi was to advise all of the designated area of operation on 23 January and provide all with a sketch-map of the designated op area.

The next day, 23 January, from 0600 hours, the form-up of the operational teams began. This involved Controller Nairobi, Major Lawson, Captain Odendaal and his team. The agents Susan Melanie and James Gregory assembled at 0815 hours, having spent the previous night at the Girouard Road safe house.

During 22 January, after her briefing by the Controller, Susan Melanie had been made up to look like an attractive middle-aged lady by an assistant from Schouten's and a make-up artist from Nairobi Amateur Dramatic Club. These two were obtained by SOE Nairobi – 'one assumes they were also SOE informers'. All necessary clothing for Susan Melanie had been obtained from Ahmed Bros Outfitters in Hardinge Street.

It was not until the morning of 23 January that SOE Controller Nairobi informed Odendaal and the agents of the area in Karen designated for the hit. Sketch-maps were issued. SOE Controller Nairobi then briefed separately both Susan Melanie and James Gregory about the details of their tasks, including the necessary positioning of the body after the hit was completed. The transmission of the signal '*Ich hatt' einen Kameraden*'* was to be followed by the date and time.

That evening Odendaal and his team went to the Clairmont at 1930 hours. Joss's party arrived there at 2230 hours.† A South African officer, apparently a friend, joined the party, which lasted until just after midnight. Joss and Diana left the Clairmont at about 0015 for his Muthaiga bungalow. June Carberry remained behind with Broughton, who by now was drunk and ill. She herself was not too well. Broughton complained continually of being ill. They were finally driven home to Broughton's house at 0100, arriving shortly before 0200 hours.

Odendaal was furious over the information regarding the timing of events. The Broughtons' party had dined at Muthaiga Club instead [of the Clairmont], before proceeding to the Clairmont. It appears that SOE was given unsound information by the club servant at Muthaiga. This mistake caused problems.

---

*Translated into English this means, 'I had a comrade'. It is the opening line of a German hymn by Ludwig Uhland (1787–1862) called '*Der gute Kamerad*' quoted in full at the end of the book.

†Edmund seemed to be under the impression (from *his* informant?) that Dickie Pembroke went on to the Clairmont with Joss and Diana after dinner at Muthaiga. This is not borne out by the trial evidence.

Odendaal's Harley-Davidson surveillance team followed Joss and Diana to his Muthaiga bungalow. On arrival, the team advised Odendaal by radio of Joss's arrival. Odendaal in turn advised the Controller Nairobi.

Again at 0115, when Joss and Diana left the bungalow, Odendaal was advised by radio that the motorbike team was tailing them. After continual messages on the radio, the motorbike team was caught up with finally in Whitehouse Road (outside the Railway Club) by Odendaal's station-wagon, which had left Muthaiga Club on receiving the 0115 signal.

The station-wagon proceeded along Whitehouse Road up to its junction with the Ngong road by the entrance to the Nairobi Club. Odendaal caught up with Joss's car at this point, following it to the Broughtons' house. They arrived at 0200 hours. Odendaal sent one of his team up to the house to keep watch and he himself kept the station-wagon concealed some distance away, in Marula Lane. The surveillance operator signalled to Odendaal by torch the moment that Joss came back to his car, which was at about 0225. As soon as Joss had driven down Tree Lane to join the Ngong road and turned right towards town, Odendaal started to tail him again. Both SOE Controller Nairobi and the two agents were advised by radio that Joss was on his way back to Nairobi. Odendaal followed him along the Ngong road stopping at some distance from the Karen road junction and awaited further reports from the two agents. This was some time around 0250 hours.

As soon as the two agents had received the signal from both SOE Controller Nairobi and Odendaal that Erroll was being tailed [back to the Broughtons'], they left the safe house in Girouard Road and joined the Ngong road. Turning right, they proceeded along the Ngong road to its junction with the Karen road. They noticed off to the left, near the road, that there was a large open murram pit. There the agents waited until they received the signal from Odendaal that Joss Erroll was on his way back to Nairobi from the Broughtons'. At about 0225 the agents moved to a point approximately 150–200 yards beyond the junction towards Ngong, and stopped their car. They both got out. James Gregory opened up the bonnet and bent over the engine bay to look as if he was trying to repair the engine. Susan Melanie walked out into the road. They soon noticed a car speeding towards them from the direction of Ngong. Susan Melanie shone her torch (army issue) at the oncoming car, which pulled up sharply. Joss stepped out of the car. Susan Melanie asked him for a lift to the New Stanley Hotel as their car had broken down, indicating that her friend was endeavouring to repair it. James Gregory looked up from the engine and repeated the request to take Susan into Nairobi, as he would continue to try to get the car started again. Joss complied, of course.

Susan Melanie got into the front passenger seat of the Buick and Joss drove off. Just as he passed the parked Morris 10, a blinding light from James Gregory's torch hit the windscreen. Susan Melanie then shone her torch right into Joss's eyes. She then drew her revolver and shot him just behind his left ear. (Edmund's informant said that the Colt PT 32 revolver was a Colt PT 32 Special, and was Susan Melanie's own, *not* the weapon issued to her by SOE Controller Nairobi.)

Joss's dying movements caused the car to swerve off the road into the murram pit. As the car came to a halt, James Gregory drove up in the Morris 10 and radioed Odendaal that the agents had completed their task, signalling as arranged, '*Ich hatt' einen Kameraden* 24 0255.' Odendaal relayed the message to SOE Controller Nairobi and, next, drove down to the Karen road junction, pulling up beside where the Buick had halted. Now Susan Melanie, James Gregory, Odendaal and his assistant all helped to shift the body into the foot-well. Susan Melanie was instructed by Odendaal to fire a second shot, from outside the car. This was intended to throw the police investigators. Indeed, these tactics would lead them to believe that both shots had been fired from outside the car on the passenger's side.

A signal was sent by SOE Controller Nairobi to both Odendaal and the agents to return to base, as Operation Highland Clearance was now complete. The two agents returned to their

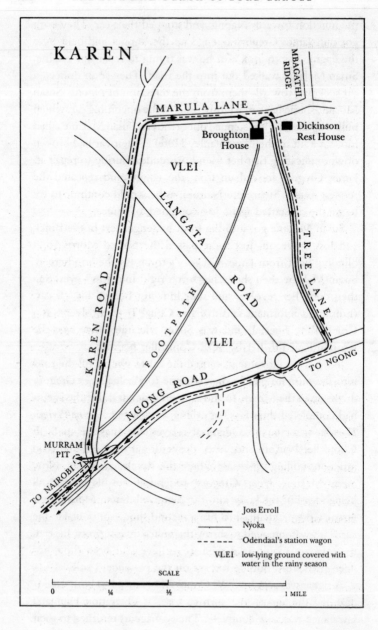

KAREN

MBAGATHI RIDGE

MARULA LANE

Broughton House

Dickinson Rest House

VLEI

LANGATA ROAD

KAREN ROAD

FOOTPATH

TREE LANE

VLEI

TO NGONG

NGONG ROAD

MURRAM PIT

TO NAIROBI

Joss Erroll

Nyoka

Odendaal's station wagon

VLEI   low-lying ground covered with water in the rainy season

SCALE

0   ¼   ½   1 MILE

Girouard Road safe house and Odendaal to his house in the Parklands area, while his various surveillance team members dispersed to their military quarters.

The Sallyport papers then proceed to cover the aftermath of the killing. Edmund's informant told him that there were various discrepancies regarding the accounts of discovering Joss's body. The narrative then returns to the fate of the agents:

At the debriefing of the agents the Controller reminded them now in 'no uncertain terms' that if either was guilty of indiscretion they would be 'exposed to their own neglect'. Not only would they be disowned, steps would be taken to show how they had been in the colony as 'unauthorised persons'. The civil authorities would treat them as agents of an unfriendly power, but the military would denounce them more specifically, as acting for Italy or Germany. Interrogation and trial by court martial would follow, which meant that as 'discredited agents' they would end up in a cell in HM prison and in due course would come face to face with 'Mr Marshall'. 'Hoppy' Marshall, so called on account of his wooden leg, was Kenya's Executioner Judicial, and he would be ordered to carry out this 'distasteful but necessary function'.

Debriefing took until 0415 hours, when Susan Melanie and James Gregory retired at last to sleep. When they emerged later that day from the driveway opposite the Maia Carberry Nursing Home, Miss Mary Shaw, a secretary in the merchandising department of Gellatly Hankey, and Mr Richard Murrey of Sudan's Gizera Cotton Board, proceeded into Nairobi, now freed from all their mission obligations to enjoy forty-eight hours of time to themselves and for 'shopping', should they wish. On the morning of 26 January they were flown back by military air transport firstly to Khartoum, still under the names Mary Shaw and Richard Murrey. They spent the night at the Grand Hotel in Khartoum – arranged by SOE Cairo with SOE Khartoum – and on the morning of 27 January they flew back to Almaza Airport in Cairo. They travelled this last stage in military uniform under different names again. On arrival in Cairo the agents were met by a field security officer of the Field Security Unit Cairo and taken to a hotel in Cairo. Next morning the agents reported to Colonel MacDonald. They were retained for duty with SOE Cairo. SA Military Mission and the Director of Signals GHQ Cairo were advised accordingly. James Gregory returned to his duties as a Signals officer. After some eight months in that position he was posted to a Royal Signals formation and remained with this unit until June 1942. He was killed at Bir Hachim during the advance by Rommel and the subsequent retreat of the British 8th Army.

Susan Melanie was employed in Cairo for some four to five months and thereafter, thanks to her language skills, she was posted to London. She took part in several air drops and SOE operations in conjunction with French Resistance movements. Then SOE London received reports about her being a double agent for German intelligence. The reports came from various sources – MI6 Nairobi, a Major Sampson and Field Security Company in Cairo, Cairo Police Special Branch and finally the British Embassy in Ankara. She had also been indiscreet about the operation while working in London.

In October 1942 Susan Melanie was dropped with a group of agents to join a French Resistance cell in Limoges in France. The group was compromised by an Abwehr double agent in SOE HQ London. The group literally fell into the hands of the German security forces in Limoges. While some members of the group were captured and interrogated, Susan Melanie was shot to death. 'A classic case of the operation (by both British and German Intelligence forces) of double agents' [Trafford's wry comment].

In August 1942 a 'theft' was reported from the office of Colonel Douglas Fabin*, Deputy Director of Military Intelligence at

*Colonel Douglas Fabin was the boss of my source Neil Tyfield who had been in Military Intelligence at Force HQ in Nairobi and had a 'team of young ladies' working for him.

GOCHQ in Muthaiga. In fact, Tony Trafford witnessed a South African staff sergeant weeding the files. The papers he removed were headed 'Operation Highland Clearance'. The name meant nothing to Trafford until he met Edmund in the Sallyport Inn more than forty years later. One of the files from the DDMI was said to contain: information relating to both SOE and MI6; certain information passed to the DDMI by the Commissioners of Police, Kenya and Tanganyika; letters from the GOC East Africa to the Governor of Kenya Sir Henry Moore, the Chief Secretary and the Attorney-General's department. A court of inquiry was conducted but the results were never disclosed. Nor were the files ever recovered.

Colonel Douglas Fabin, according to S.P.J. O'Mara used the name Alistair MacDonald, the same name used by the Special Officer who recruited the agents for Operation Highland Clearance in Cairo.

Having detailed the eradication of all traces of Operation Highland Clearance, the Sallyport papers end by returning to the question of why Joss Erroll had to be murdered. It is significant that in his final point Tony Trafford emphasises how many careers would have suffered had Lord Erroll been allowed to live:

> We feel the reason must be because of certain information Joss Erroll had which would have served to ruin many careers and faces [sic] if the Op had been compromised. WE SAY NO MORE (Trafford's capitals).[14]

12

All's Fair in Love and War

'The world is governed by quite other people than the citizens imagine.'

Benjamin Disraeli

The Sallyport papers certainly provided solutions to some of the better-known discrepancies concerning the murder case – they explained how Erroll's body had been put into the foot-well, for example. The trigger had indeed been pulled by a woman, supporting the persistent rumour of a female perpetrator. It had been because Joss seemed unable to resist women that a woman had been chosen to carry out the hit, Tony Trafford said. There is no record of whether one of the hit team unscrewed the arm-slings from the back of the Buick, but such an act could easily have been carried out by either Susan Melanie or James Gregory, simply to throw the police and set them on a false trail, like the firing of the second shot. The 'white pipeclay' marks on the back seat could have been made by her shoes while she was unscrewing the straps; military puttees worn by James Gregory or one of Odendaal's team could equally well have left these scuff marks.

Since the first publication of this book a long list of the 'cogs' in operation Highland Clearance have been confirmed by S.P.J. O'Mara – see Appendix. Yet Maurice Buckmaster's★ 'guardian angel' and secretary, Vera Atkins, claimed: 'We sent trained organisers,

---

★Colonel Maurice Buckmaster was head of SOE's F Section.

radio operators, couriers and supplied arms, sabotage material etc. . . . but at no time was Kenya a field of operations for SOE.'[1]*

This flat contradiction of the Sallyport papers was countered by several sources. Neil Tyfield, who was in Military Intelligence at Force HQ in Nairobi, states that a Security Service bureau existed at Shell House, an imposing grey stone building opposite the Memorial Hall on Delamere Avenue (Kenyatta Avenue today), which contained the offices of the Shell oil company among others. Joss's neighbour Jack Bunyan had worked during the war at the East African Governors' Conference, the secretariat that dealt with sensitive developments common to the East African territories such as defence, railways and the interchange of civil servants at topmost level. It was based in Shell House, formerly Rhodes House, on Delamere Avenue. Bunyan spoke of an organisation in Nairobi called the Combined Services Security Bureau – this was 'a special organisation, under very tight security',[2] which operated out of Shell House. Michael Macoun in his book *Wrong Place, Right Time* describes it as 'a curious organisation, with MI5 and MI6 responsibility, and with a small staff comprising a security service officer in charge and supported by an ex-Inspector General of the Indian police, an Army Major from IB East Africa Command and myself. We were attached to the offices of the East African Governors' Conference . . . and acted as a clearing house for all security intelligence and counter intelligence activities in the command.'[3] Macoun does not mention any of his Combined Services Security colleagues by name. My counter-intelligence source S. P. J. O'Mara confirms that Shell House housed the Combined Services Security Bureau in 1940/1, and so does Diana Lane who worked in Civil Intelligence in Nairobi from 1941.[4] She and colleagues in her field recognised that anyone who worked out of that office in Shell House was regarded as a defence security officer. My Nairobi Controller, I concluded, would have worked there.

---

*Tony Trafford made clear that Operation Highland Clearance was a closely guarded secret even within Intelligence.

Another former agent suggested that Malcolm Muggeridge's books might prove a fruitful hunting ground, since his field in Intelligence had been Portuguese East Africa. In one of his books there was an odd reference to Secret Service chief Stewart Menzies' 'man in Nairobi', whom Muggeridge describes as 'a kindly . . . avuncular figure whose attitude towards [me] . . . was that of a bishop briefing a curate in some distant and possibly hazardous mission in the field'. The connection was tenuous at best, but Jack Bunyan had mentioned a man called 'Bish' in connection with the Combined Services Security Bureau.[5] Had Muggeridge hidden a clue to the name of the 'man in Nairobi in his choice of simile? Diana Lane had also heard the name Bishop in connection with the Shell House Combined Services Security Bureau. John Gouldbourn had mentioned someone called Alex or Alec among the names of those who, he believed, had some connection to the cabal, who had been in authority, though the man's surname escaped him.

The *Kenya Weekly News* mentions that a Colonel Bishop inspected the school of instruction at Nakuru in December 1939 accompanied by General Lewin. When asked if Bishop was in charge of Operation Highland Clearance, O'Mara responded cryptically as always, 'Yes. The Archbishop! Easy to obtain photos from newspaper archives.'[6]

Bunyan confirmed that he had actually known Bishop, reiterating that whatever went on in that bureau in Shell House was highly secret. 'He had some connection with the chaps at Rhodes House [Governors' Conference], but was not part of their organisation. His subsequent career was brilliant,' Bunyan commented in a letter.[7] Helpfully, he also enclosed an obituary and a death notice from the *Daily Telegraph* dated 17 May 1984. Major-General (retired) Sir Alec Bishop KCMG, CB, CVO, OBE (the latter awarded in 1941) had died aged eighty-six, the death notice announced. 'Alex [*sic*] Bishop had been educated at Plymouth College and Sandhurst, and had been commissioned into the Dorset Regiment, serving in the 1914–18 war in Mesopotamia and Palestine,' read the text, also stating that Bishop had served in India from 1919 to 1925.

Bishop's unpublished memoir is held in the Liddell Hart Military Archive at King's College, London. It is called 'Look Back with

Pleasure', and dedicated 'To my grandchildren, with the hope that they will enjoy their lives as much as their grandfather has done in his square circles'. Sir Alec had a distinguished military career behind him. His own memoir corroborates the Controller's qualifications given in the Sallyport papers. He had worked in the Intelligence Department and in the Dominions and Colonies Department of the War Office in the early 1930s, during which he travelled the African continent. Liaison was his speciality. Some time in 1940 – Bishop is imprecise with dates throughout his memoir – he visited South Africa for discussions with military and political authorities in that country. Interestingly, much earlier in my research O'Mara had suggested I try to find out if 'detailed records exist of arrivals in Nairobi by air from South Africa in the months (not many) before the assassination[.]' 'I believe three particular men arrived together,' he continued, 'two South African soldiers and an English official. The official had . . . easy access to wherever he wanted. He, I am told, was the "organiser" with final on-the-spot authority.'

Early in March 1940 Bishop was involved in the arrest and internment of German settlers. Also in 1940, he relates, 'secret waste – draft copies of secret papers' – was incinerated. He was in charge of requisitioning vehicles and aircraft for military purposes and he had responsibility for Kenya and Uganda Railway Workshops, which were making military equipment and so would have been in a good position to find cars for Operation Highland Clearance and exit routes for the agents involved. He describes his own job in 1940–1 as 'keeping governments of the Commonwealth in the picture'. His memoir is inconclusive about his whereabouts in January 1941.[8]

Some of the people in the Sallyport papers are easily identifiable, of course. All the background details about them in the papers are accurate. There is Lady Ranfurly, for example. Her wartime diaries *To War with Whitaker* confirm she had been employed by SOE.[9] I wrote to her asking for information about the female agent she was alleged to have helped recruit, providing her with the cover names and the following details: 'She was half-American, held an English passport, had South African connections, was aged between thirty and thirty-five and was a first-class shot. She also spoke several languages including Arabic.' While Lady Ranfurly recalled none of the agent's cover names, she appeared to recognise the description I had provided her with: 'In the hurly burly of Egypt in the War, there arrived in Cairo one young woman' whose qualifications seem to fit: 'She used many names, was completely amoral and quite nice-looking and presentable but was mad keen to sleep with VIPs. We quite liked her, provided she stayed away from our husbands.'[10]

The agents Susan Melanie and James Gregory would have been failing in their duties if either of them had stood out in the circle of Joss and his friends. There is one sighting of Joss with a mystery female, however. *East African Standard* columnist Edward Rodwell happened to spot him aboard the Likoni ferry on the south side of Mombasa island in late December 1940, just when the Sallyport papers claim that Susan Melanie was becoming intimate with Joss. Rodwell remembered it was late in the afternoon. His own vehicle was some way behind Joss's in a short queue; 'There was a woman in the passenger seat.' He could see only the silhouette of her hair and he could not tell whether she was fair or dark, but, getting the sense that discretion might be called for, had kept his distance. 'I merely hailed Joss with a wave of the hand. I liked him and thought that he was a good chap.'[11]

The companies that the Sallyport papers mention – Consolidated Goldfields Pty and Eckstein & Co. – both existed in the 1930s, as did Gellately-Hankey and Mitchell Cotts. The senior figures at the latter were friends of the Nairobi Controller, according to the Sallyport papers. Joss knew Mitchell Cotts' managing director Hugh Hamilton – he telephoned him the very morning before he died. The link with Hamilton may have been purely coincidental, but it would have been helpful to the Nairobi Controller to get feedback on Joss's activities, political, business or otherwise, and Hamilton was well placed to provide him with Joss's views.

Coincidental timings and dates provided another means of authenticating the Sallyport papers. One leapt out straight away. 'The White Rhino Hotel was preferred both by SOE and Lawson [of the SACMP] to the Outspan Hotel for "security reasons",' the Sallyport papers say. This was because Baden-Powell's funeral was taking place at the Outspan that day. The Highland Clearance team would not have wanted to be spotted together by the mourners, of whom Joss was one. Then there was the timing of Joss's car accident – given how soon before his death he had needed to hire a car, had the hiring of the Buick been intended as part of Highland Clearance and had the accident to his own car been the result of sabotage? Joss's Buick could so easily have been tampered with while he was attending Baden-Powell's funeral. It was not immediately obvious how it would necessarily benefit the operation for Joss to be driving a hired car but O'Mara explained, 'its mechanical condition could be controlled with no evidence of interference'.[12] There was also the bullet-proof glass that Joss had had fitted into his own Buick – perhaps this could have been seen as a potential obstruction to their plot to ambush Erroll, already being formulated by this stage.

As to the timing of Operation Highland Clearance itself – the eve of the Abyssinian campaign – it would appear from the Sallyport papers that the two events were connected. Exactly why is not clear – unless if it was hoped that the Abyssinian campaign would deflect attention from the Erroll murder. Or perhaps the Controllers just wanted the operation finished before it started in case the campaign could adversely affect the operation in some way, disrupting Joss's life in Nairobi to the extent that it would not have been possible to carry out the hit as planned.

What the Sallyport papers had to say about Diana's and Broughton's actions at key moments was particularly interesting where it contrasted with other accounts of their activities. For example, Diana denied to James Fox that there had been any row between herself and Joss on the night when he was killed.[13] This denial could have been out of shame for the subject-matter: few would want to admit that they had rowed with someone just hours before that person was killed.

Whether Diana ever fully understood the sensitivity of Joss's position politically in 1940 is a moot point. If she did, out of deepest affection for his memory she chose not to reveal such knowledge. Her secretary was not sure how much she knew beforehand, but was sure that she had known later what had really happened.[14]

By implication, the Sallyport papers raise the question of whether the Broughtons were involved or, at least, had any foreknowledge of Joss's fate. If extremely high-level authorities had sanctioned Operation Highland Clearance, why did they allow matters to develop into the very public trial of an innocent man? The most obvious answer would be that it was a convenient cover-up and successfully hid the truth behind the murder for half a century. But does that therefore mean that the Broughtons were innocent of all knowledge of Operation Highland Clearance, innocent pawns caught up in a highly complex game? Had it not been for Jock Broughton's extraordinary behaviour it would be tempting to think so, but the strangeness of his activities before, during and after the trial suggests forcefully that he must have played some part in the whole business. Certainly, if one believes that his arrest, trial and acquittal were all part of a premeditated plan to deflect interest away from the real killer, it makes sense of many, if not all, aspects of his behaviour at that time. The wish to deflect attention from the real killer also explains the police bungling the evidence and the efforts to ensure maximum word-of-mouth coverage of the trial by waiving the air-raid precaution at the inquiry.

A closer look at Broughton and his trial proved revealing.

One of the anonymous callers who had told Rodwell that he had got it wrong as to the identiy of Joss's killer had said that, before booking passages for Kenya, Broughton had paid a visit to the MI6 London offices in Broadway to offer his services.[15] Colin Imray, the former Kenya Police superintendent, described the procedure Broughton would have undergone

> The curious experience of being interviewed in Whitehall involves being ushered in to [the offices'] left-hand entrance off Broadway [then] escorted along corridor after corridor so that it becomes impossible to establish where one has been. A two-hour long chat follows 'with three men' when either the recruit takes up their offer or does not. Afterwards having signed or not signed the Official Secrets Act, as the case may be, the interviewee emerges out of the other side of Whitehall at an exit into the daylight with no idea of where he has been.[16]

Broughton, as a member of the exclusive London club White's, may well have initially been approached here about his willingness to undertake 'war work' in Kenya by fellow member Stewart Menzies, head of the British Secret Service, who, according to M. R. D. Foot and Menzies' biographer Cave Brown, used to do some recruiting there, picking up useful information and generally hobnobbing with the top men of his day.[17] '[He] always sat in a special chair there.' Menzies, as his former brother-in-law, would have been in a good position to discuss Joss. Broughton in the late thirties was often seen in White's hovering about, 'always immaculately dressed, slim and upright and altogether *le grand seigneur* – his vanity knew no bounds'.[18] It would have appealed to his vanity to have been approached by the head of the British Secret Service.

Broughton was apparently asked during his interview for MI6 whether he knew Lord Erroll. He had met Joss 'once at Muthaiga Country Club, during one of his earlier trips', he said. Broughton was familiar with Nairobi and knew many of its uppercrust inhabitants, not to mention Kenya ways.[19]

A desire to impress his son-in-law Lord Lovat and Broughton's inherent vanity would have been strong psychological motivations, one suspects, in his recruitment in Whitehall.[20] Lovat could in fact have served as a conduit for Broughton to Secret Service work. According to the writer Stephen Dorril, Lovat was heavily involved with SOE work in 1940. He ran one of SOE's training grounds; indeed, some SOE members were trained on his estate in Scotland.[21] Anna Miskin, Walter Harragin's daughter, was told by one of Diana's personal secretaries 'in strictest confidence later that Joss's death had to do with spying and that Broughton had come out to spy on Joss'.[22]

Tony Trafford had explained that 'Broughton was what is called a "compromise risk" in this type of exercise' – a non-professional involved in a highly organised operation.[23] Trafford's father's top-secret interrogation of Broughton in 1941 was all part of the latter's preparation for court, to make sure that he would not crack under cross-examination. The ex-DC insisted to his dying day that 'the murderer was known by the Administration ... the killer was a woman and although all the vital evidence is hidden, the Foreign Office and the Commonwealth people know [who did it]'.[24]

O'Mara was intriguing on the subject of the Broughtons. He made two points about their involvement. Firstly,

> Joss had access to normal intelligence 'input' . . . Was Joss a double agent? No. No more than any of the aristocratic appeasers portrayed in the novel *The Remains of the Day*. He was involved in matters that went far beyond local politics or subversion. Broughton and Diana's role was to find out what he might do with the knowledge. He [Joss] was willing to give it to the Foreign Office and said so via 'Brookham' – fine. But there were people who very much would have disliked the results and they decided Joss was only safe when dead.[25]

Secondly,

> Broughton's role was to be the means of destroying Erroll. Was he conscious of the end result when he accepted the mission? No. He thought 'destroy' meant socially and politically. Who were his employers? The ex-appeasers in the Establishment . . .*
> Why was Broughton necessary at all? To give a plausible reason (Diana) for Joss's death.[26]

The only proof for O'Mara's assertion of Diana's conscious involvement was that she had been the one to make a noticeable beeline for Joss, rather than the other way round, and that Broughton had never raised any objection to her absences with Joss – except, of course, to insist that she be back at Marula Lane at a specific time on the night of his murder. Further compounding the case for Diana as accessory was the claim she made that she and Broughton had not intended to marry. They had needed to marry in order to enter Kenya – the strange pact shows it was essentially a marriage of convenience – and yet Miss Wilks's entry had been allowed by the

---

*According to O'Mara these included the Duke of Hamilton, senior figures in Chamberlain's last cabinet, close friends of Edward VIII and Edward himself (O'Mara correspondence 13/8/99).

Governor Sir Henry Moore despite her single status. Was a greater authority ordering the Governor not to obstruct the couple's entry so that they could carry out their roles as informants? The Governor could easily have missed Broughton's first request as it was made to Immigration, and not directly to him. Once alerted to this obstruction, perhaps, he ensured, in person, that it was waived. The mystery of where Broughton was getting his petrol coupons also suggested the rules were being relaxed for the Broughtons for some reason.

As far as proof of Broughton's role as an Intelligence source was concerned, it seems likely he had been told to make direct contact with Joss on arrival in Kenya: his asking Joss if he could rent Oserian from him had been a pretext for establishing contact. The friendship between the Broughtons and Joss sprang from this point, and would have given Broughton ample opportunity for gleaning information about him. Also, MI6 recruitment would explain why Broughton made such a mystery of what his war work actually entailed. He was no more forthcoming in reference to his work after his acquittal than he had been before. In a letter written to his Aunt Evelyn in July 1941 while anchored off the coast of Ceylon he writes only: 'We are now on our way to Ceylon to do a job of work I have been waiting since June to do.'[27]* Furthermore, while in Bhopal later on their trip he and Diana were welcomed and lavishly entertained by the Military Secretary, perhaps in recognition of the role assigned to him by Whitehall, 'his contribution to the war effort'.

Looking at Broughton's strange behaviour in loosely chronological order, the first question raised by his actions is why he spent four nights at Joss's house in the run-up to Christmas 1940? Diana was not there. The Broughtons had in fact only just moved into their home in Marula Lane a few days previously, so apart from anything else the timing of Jock Broughton's visit seems almost inconvenient. One would think he would be settling into his new home with his new wife. However, the stay with Joss makes sense if one believes

---

*This makes sense of Broughton's repeated efforts in January 1941 to book a trip to Ceylon, despite Diana's objections.

Broughton was trying to pump him for opinions so as to pass these on to some authority.

Then on Tuesday 21 January 1941 there is the bogus burglary of Broughton's two revolvers. Was this part of Operation Highland Clearance? According to the Sallyport papers, the method by which Joss was to be eradicated had been decided some time around 12 January. It is possible that Broughton had been told soon after this by one of the SOE informers to whom he passed information on Joss to 'lose' his handguns, probably without being told why, though he may have surmised that Erroll was to be murdered and that, as Joss's and Diana's affair by this time was public knowledge, he would quickly fall under suspicion.*

Many observed how oddly nervous Broughton was in the last few days of Joss's life. Up until now, it has always been thought this was because he was planning a murder. But it could equally have been because he had guessed Erroll was to die, but not how, and was therefore naturally anxious that he would be framed – if he had been planning the murder himself he could have covered his tracks as thoroughly as he liked. Retired DC H. H. Trafford had confided in his son Tony that Broughton had commented, 'Look, I did not murder Joss. If I had wished to I would have chosen another venue for his dead body. I would have taken it out at night or very early morning and by 6.30 a.m. there would have been nothing left . . . The most suitable place would have been the Athi Plains some fifteen to twenty miles from Nairobi.'[28] If Broughton thought Joss was going to die, it makes sense of his renunciation of Diana. His letter

*At one point I wondered whether the issue of the two revolvers went back further than the 'burglary', to when Broughton failed to declare them on entering Kenya in November 1940. However, his failure to declare the handguns cannot be linked to Operation Highland Clearance, since according to the Sallyport papers the method for disposing of Joss by revolver had not been agreed until early January 1941. And yet, if his omission to declare the guns cannot be explained in the light of Operation Highland Clearance, nor does it endorse the theory that Broughton was the revenge killer – he could not have seen the need to conceal potential murder weapons on entering Kenya because he could not have foreseen that he would need to use them on a philanderer. Maybe it was an oversight as simple as Broughton professed it to be in court.

to Soames about cutting his losses, which so puzzled Peggy Pitt by the haste with which it reached its addressee, was all part of this renunciation act. Who but Broughton or one of his contacts would have ensured the letter reach Soames in record time, not just because Broughton needed to spread the news about the burglary but because he wanted to start clearing himself of a jealousy motive as soon as possible.

The most public example of his self-vindication is without doubt the famous toast – his act of renunciation – at Muthaiga on the eve of Joss's death. But then he got very drunk and his true feelings emerged – hence the crossness that June described; the mask was beginning to slip. Jacko Heath later remarked on Broughton's edginess at Muthaiga later that evening, which suggests that Broughton was aware, even if only approximately, when Joss was to be killed that night. His reluctance to spend time with Jacko's group could have been because he needed to be able to leave Muthaiga at a specific time – without any pressure from friends to stay on – in order to be home before Joss dropped Diana off. Otherwise, he risked running into and accidentally interfering with the hit. And he had been very specific with Joss – the only time he had intervened in arrangements for Diana's meetings with him – about what time Diana should be dropped off back home.

Peggy Pitt was evidently puzzled by Broughton sending his solicitor Kaplan to hear the results of the inquest – but this action is understandable in the light of his paranoia about being framed for the murder. The frantic hiring of cars on the day of the inquest shows just how nervous he was.

If the burglary was bogus, then what really did happen to Broughton's two handguns? It is most probable that both of his missing revolvers ended up at the bottom of the Chania Falls – one of them deposited during Broughton's ride on The Pantaloon – it was about twenty-five miles cross-country from Marula Lane to the Chania Falls at Thika. Such a long journey would account for the state of The Pantaloon when he was returned to the Erskines' yard, and explains the reason why Broughton had had to borrow a mount despite having three horses of his own – he needed an especially sturdy animal to cover so much ground so quickly. The other gun was disposed of during the episode he related to Juanita in which the police had been following him and not noticed him drop the gun into the water. He did not get rid of them both at the same time because, if he had been unlucky and had been spotted with two guns on him at once, it would have raised immediate suspicion.

Ironically for Broughton, his innocence could have been proved much more conclusively had the guns been available as evidence for, if the Sallyport papers are to be believed, it was not Broughton's gun that killed Joss. And indeed, the defence expert witnesses showed that the bullets that killed him could not have come from the type of revolvers that Broughton said he owned. Yet, thanks to the obscure, highly specialised nature of the evidence clearing Broughton of the murder, a question mark has hung over him ever after – a result that would, of course, have suited the purposes of Operation Highland Clearance: their informer had been acquitted so would not rat on them; the real killer had not been found. Meanwhile, enough suspicion had been cast on Broughton as a cuckolded husband to keep people for ever speculating on his guilt.

Years later Arthur Poppy, in discussion with Colin Imray, mentioned that he had realised in court that Broughton was familiar with Burrard's classic firearms book. Initially struck by Broughton's coolness in the face of the accusations levelled at him by the prosecution, Poppy was convinced that the man in the dock was 'a first rate actor, a little Napoleon who put up a magnificent performance in Court'.[29] Then Poppy realised that Broughton had studied Burrard's book because he too was aware early on in the proceedings that the whole case hung on the ballistics issue. His familiarity with the book accounted in part for his composure in court: it reassured him that he could not be found guilty on ballistics evidence.

Edward Rodwell, who attended the trial, was also struck by Broughton's mien – as 'composed as any man could be, urbane, straightforward and even humorous at times'. Roddy too wondered whether his relaxed air was an indication that Broughton had known he was on safe ground.

Considering the importance of the ballistics evidence, had Henry

Morris KC's services been secured through the manipulations of the Pretoria faction of Operation Highland Clearance? It would explain why Maisels was denied the chance to defend Broughton. The pretext that Maisels had been given – that he was in Kenya to fight a war, not to defend murderers – seems unreasonable, given that he had had so little to do at Wilson Airfield. It was essential that Broughton be acquitted as far as Operation Highland Clearance was concerned, to preclude the risk of him talking. It was clear from the outset that ballistics evidence was going to be crucial; knowing Broughton to be innocent, the organisers of Operation Highland Clearance would have been almost certain that he would not be convicted on any other kind of circumstantial evidence, so they made sure a ballistics expert was hired. Given his shock at the 'obvious flaw' in the Crown case, it seems unlikely that Morris would have been aware of these machinations.

Lazarus Kaplan, Broughton's solicitor, may have had an inkling about untoward proceedings, however. Kaplan insisted years later to Cyril Connolly that Broughton was innocent.[30] He was convinced that Broughton's motive had not been strong enough to kill Joss, that he had never left the house on the night of the killing, that murder was not in keeping with his character; that while in prison, Broughton would have given something away to his warders 'or the South African soldiers he was constantly drinking with had he been guilty'.[31] Kaplan had even warned Fox and Connolly, 'You will never get anywhere if you think that Broughton did it.'[32] Kappy had observed also that there had never been a shooting with less blood. In his opinion the murderer must have been an excellent shot. He also ventured, apparently, that the killer could have been 'a jilted girlfriend, or the husband of one, or a political assassin'.[33] He had spoken about the extreme inefficiency of the police, particularly their failure to examine the car for fingerprints, and by the time Connolly left Nairobi he believed 'like Kaplan, that Broughton was innocent'.[34] Having initially been helpful and having wanted to participate in Connolly's and Fox's investigation of the murder, Kappy later withdrew his support altogether, insisting to the journalists through intermediaries that he wanted all traces of his cooperation removed. James Fox surmised in *White Mischief*, 'Something or some-one had given Kaplan a great fright.'[35] Kaplan wrote up a paper shortly before he died, remarking to a colleague, 'If this became public knowlege, it would cause an international sensation.' No one ever saw what Kaplan wrote because the papers were destroyed.[36] His daughter also remembers how deeply troubled her father was at the time, recalling how her mother had burned her father's papers including a manuscript they were never allowed to see.[37]

There were only rather feeble clues as to whether the prosecutor Harragin was aware of Operation Highland Clearance:

1) John Gouldbourn claimed that the judiciary *was* involved in the murder; he could have meant Walter Harragin.

2) According to Harragin's son Lee, Broughton teased Harragin shortly after the acquittal with the words, 'You know that I know, that you know, that I did it.'[38]

3) In his foreword to his secretary Peggy Pitt's unpublished manuscript 'Who Killed Lord Erroll?' Harragin admits that 'by a concatenation of circumstances an *innocent man* was nearly con-victed' (although he could simply have meant innocent at law).

Peggy Pitt in her manuscript mentions 'a strange interview' sought by Broughton, between Harragin and Broughton. 'The baronet was anxious to discover from what source the Attorney-General had gleaned the intimate details on which he had cross-examined him.' Harragin did not reveal anything. He was astonished by Broughton's visit. 'This must be unprecedented, for a man recently charged with murder to seek an interview with Counsel for the Prosecution in order to discuss the trial.'[39] Harragin's daughters had heard Broughton saying to their father, 'I'm a damned good actor, aren't I?'[40] Others witnessed this defiant bragging. Even in prison with his warders, he made a point of mentioning aspects of the trial that had greatly amused him. He also paid a visit to Walter Harragin's office when it was all but unoccupied, during lunch hour a few days after his acquittal. There was an Asian clerk on duty who deferentially showed Broughton into Harragin's office, where Broughton went through the court case in front of the clerk, telling the Goan where Harragin had

35. Rehearsing for the coronation outside Westminster Abbey. Joss lifts his voluminous cape out of harm's way.

36. Joss's close friend Sidney Fazan chatting to Opal Brooke-Popham, the governor's wife. 'The fox stole, the kid gloves, the corrugated iron roof; that odd mixture of tat and grandeur that all we colonial children grew up in,' Fazan's daughter Eleanor remarked.

37. Sir Jock Delves Broughton with a Maasai girl at Nderit, Boy Long's estate, looking at cattle. Broughton was allocated land in the Soldier Settlement Scheme of 1919 and paid regular visits to the colony to inspect it from then on.

38. Outside the Blue Goose, an exclusive cocktail bar off Berkeley Square, where Diana worked before her affair with Broughton. Diana is flanked by her sister Daphne and Betty Somerset. The Blue Goose was a good hunting ground for rich, titled husbands.

39. Miss Diana Caldwell as 'Electrical Lamps' at a theme party in London to raise money for charity.

40. Diana contributing to the war effort in London, 1939. When she and Broughton arrived in Kenya in 1940, their apparent indifference to the colony's war effort did not go down well.

41. Sir Jock Delves Broughton in 1938. Aloof, irascible and intensely vain, Broughton craved attention and popularity.

42. Lenare's portrait of Diana in 1937.

43. Phyllis Filmer, Joss's mistress when Diana arrived in Kenya. Regarding Mrs Filmer as 'plain and small', friends were mystified by Joss's affair with her.

44. Joss and Diana on the Kilifi ferry. The only known photograph of the lovers together during their six-week romance, it was taken by Diana's intimate friend, Hugh Dickinson.

45. The Broughtons' house at Marula Lane.

46. June Carberry. She often acted as chaperone to Diana during her affair with Joss.

47. Dickie Pembroke. In Intelligence and in love with Diana, Pembroke was a 'nice P. G. Wodehouse guardsman' and Old Etonian chum of Joss, who was posted to Nairobi during the war.

48. Hugh Thompson Dickinson, Royal Army Service Corps, Nairobi, c. 1940. Devoted to Diana since 1934, Dickinson claimed he sought his Nairobi posting in order to be near her.

49. Joss's body in the foot-well of his hired Buick, photographed by Chief Inspector Lanham. People were asked to believe that Joss had rolled off the car seat into this position after having been shot.

50. Inspector Poppy, who headed the investigation into Joss's death, shown here in the 1950s.

51. Poppy took this photograph of Diana during his investigation of Joss's murder. An inveterate nickname-giver, she called him Popski.

52. The Chania Falls at Thika where Broughton claimed to Juanita to have disposed of the guns, as they were in 1941.

53. Walter Harragin, Prosecuting Attorney-General at Broughton's trial.

54. Dinan in her early teens, living with guardians in England. She found out about her father's death at the local newsagent's.

55. Captain John Gouldbourn in 1940. Gouldbourn set me on the trail of the real murderer of Joss Erroll.

56. The 22nd Earl of Erroll and Hereditary Lord High Constable of Scotland, in his thirties, at the start of his involvement in the colony's politics.

gone wrong in his prosecution.[41] Broughton spent that lunch hour more or less patting himself on the back for his performance.[42] The last thing he did before returning to the north of England, where he died in December 1942, was to visit the London offices of the *East African Standard*, going through a similar procedure with the press coverage of the trial in front of Winifred Paul, their stringer.[43]

David Christie-Miller, a friend of Broughton's children who was a Kenya Regiment sergeant during the war, had said at Torr's Hotel to Broughton after the trial, 'I am so glad that you were acquitted, sir.' Without so much as a thank you Broughton smugly retorted, 'I never enjoyed myself so much in my whole life.'[44]*

These words of Broughton's are hard to justify in any light other than that he was playing some kind of role about which he could not talk openly – he would have signed the Official Secrets Act when recruited for Intelligence work. Indeed, contrary to his boast to Christie-Miller, there is evidence that, in spite of having been acquitted, Broughton was not entirely happy about the outcome of events – a resentment that he would not have harboured had he been guilty and got away with murder. 'I wish I could tell you the inner history,' Broughton complains in a circular letter of which he dispatched over a hundred copies to friends after he was acquitted, 'but it would be censored so it is no use. It was always a ridiculous case and I was a victim of unfortunate circumstances.' He would hardly have complained of having to pay his counsel Morris out of his own pocket had he been guilty. (He was in essence grateful to Morris and, after the trial, sent him an autographed photograph of himself which he signed 'With deepest respect'. By bizarre coincidence, Morris had slipped the picture into a copy of *Genius for the Defence*, his biography by Benjamin Bennett, which turned up in the British Library, discovered by my researcher.)[45]

---

*Broughton's response had so puzzled Christie-Miller that years later he tackled the Minister for Defence and Home Secretary of Kenya Sir Anthony Swann on the issue, asking directly who had really killed Joss. Swann, who had served in the Abyssinian campaign as a major with the KAR, told Christie-Miller that he had 'seen through all the police papers. It was quite clear that it had been a hired assassin' (David Christie-Miller correspondence, 16/7/97, 14/8/97).

Another letter from Broughton to his aunt Evelyn dated 29 July 1941 repeats his complaint and comes nearer to the truth than Broughton had dared to express in other missives: 'I was just a victim of unfortunate circumstances; some clever person or persons took advantage of an unrivalled opportunity for getting rid of Erroll and most successfully throwing all suspicion on me.'[46]

Broughton's bitterness towards Diana at the end – his angry attempt at blackmail – was probably born of vanity. She had abandoned him, having publicly made a fool of him. In fact, one cannot help but pity him in the final analysis. It was Broughton's plan that his past lover Marie Woodhouse should be with him at the Adelphi in Liverpool in 1942 – she had even agreed, as a nurse, to ease him through his suicide. Their plans went awry, however. She never kept their assignment because her small son became ill. Broughton committed suicide, presumably, because there was no honourable way out for him. Keeping silent meant that he would never clear his name of Erroll's murder. If he told the truth, he would have been in breach of the Official Secrets Act and possibly would not have been believed anyway. His cable from gaol to Lord Moyne, Secretary of State to the Colonies, asking him to intervene on his behalf, suggests he had been hoping for support from high authorities, and Lord Moyne's stonewalling would have proved to him that he was very much on his own. Perhaps Broughton, like the agents in Operation Highland Clearance, had been threatened with horrors if he was indiscreet. On top of this his first wife Vera, who had not married her great friend Moyne as she had expected to do, would not even consider a full reconciliation with Broughton, refusing his suggestion that they return to one another.

A few issues still remained regarding Broughton's culpability, and one was June Carberry's odd rehearsing of lines before the trial and her warning to Juanita that what she said in court 'could be responsible for Jock's swinging'. Most likely she sincerely believed Broughton was guilty and, as a friend, was intent on getting him off the hook. Years later, according to Harragin's daughters, Harragin came across June in South Africa and she admitted to him then that she had lied at the trial, claiming, contrary to the evidence she gave in court, that she *had* heard

Broughton walking past her bedroom door in the middle of the night of Joss's murder.[47] Harragin had asked her why she had perjured herself. She had smiled wryly and replied, 'I couldn't let the old boy down, could I?' The fact is that June need not have perjured herself. Judge Sheridan in his summing up had told the jury virtually to ignore all evidence but the ballistics, anyway.

One final mystery connected with Broughton was the disappearance of his Somali chauffeur. Certain people believe that the hit had been done by a 'hired Somali Irregular' and that the disappearance of the driver 'was of the greatest significance'.[48] Yet in court, despite all the cross-examination involving this driver, no attempt was made by the defence or the prosecution even to establish his name, let alone get him into the witness-box.[49] Presumably, the fact that June could testify regarding the journey back to the Marula Lane house from Muthaiga on the night of Joss's murder meant that the chauffeur's testimony was not so crucial. His disappearance left a trail of suspicion that would have served to muddy the tracks – a convenient red herring laid by those behind Operation Highland Clearance? Certainly, the rumour that Broughton hired a Somali to do the killing persists to this day in Kenya.

So who *was* involved in the operation? The Sallyport papers state that there were SOE informers at Muthaiga, one a servant. Broughton's head servant's previous job had been at Muthaiga. It is something of a leap to assume he was therefore planted at Broughton's house by SOE, but the fact remains that his servant would have had friends among the Muthaiga servants; wittingly or otherwise, he could have served as a conduit for feedback from Marula Lane to SOE. The Sallyport papers mention too that Joss's servants talked to informants from Muthaiga Club – so a pipeline of information could so easily have flowed from Joss's bungalow to Muthaiga. In a similar way, in order to find out as much as he could about Broughton, Poppy planted informants in the Marula Lane household.[50] It was an acknowledged way of spying.

Oddly enough, on the night of Erroll's murder Muthaiga Club had been teeming with Intelligence people, among whom were, according to Gouldbourn, Frederick Fermor-Hesketh and B. A. Young, Sweetie Barkas's Intelligence officer.

I wondered whether Phyllis Barkas was the Muthaiga Club member that the Sallyport papers referred to as an informant. *White Mischief* describes her as 'an upright and ever vigilant member of Muthaiga Club'.[51] Broughton was very frequently in her company. She met up with him almost daily on the pretext of playing back-gammon, bridge or 'golf-croquet'. She was called as a witness during the trial as one who just happened to overhear a number of phone calls made by him to Joss, as she would testify.[52] B. A. Young claimed that Phyllis telephoned her husband with unusual frequency during the weeks leading up to Joss's murder. If Phyllis Barkas disapproved of anyone, Barkas would have been the first to know. John Gouldbourn was another who thought that she had been passing information on activities at Muthaiga back to her husband in Eldoret, informing him of who was hobnobbing with whom. In 1942 Barkas took up a post in Mombasa at the naval Intelligence base there.

Gouldbourn told me that Mrs Barkas and Lizzie Lezard were in close contact between 15 November 1940 and April 1941.[53] Gouldbourn claimed that Lezard was in Intelligence. In fact, he recalled, between the time Lizzie had returned to Nairobi following the withdrawal from Mega in November 1940, until he was posted to Cairo, he had seemed to be under no orders from anyone in particular, coming and going between Nairobi and Eldoret, where Sweetie Barkas was in com-mand.[54] Lizzie had amused everyone with his sense of humour. When General Cunningham had asked, 'Tell me what you did when the Italians strafed you at Mega?', he had replied, 'I jumped into the deepest hole that I could find and pulled the rest of the platoon over me.' Gouldbourn pointed out that he had admired Lizzie because he was the only one who dared address the C-in-C Colonel Barkas as 'Sweetie' to his face – an extremely sarcastic reference to the fact that 'he was commonly regarded as a "smiling shit"'.[55]

Lady Ranfurly, in *To War with Whitaker*, describes what Lizzie (her husband the Earl of Ranfurly's stepfather) told her about the murder: '[Lizzie] was staying with Lord Erroll on the night he was murdered and was a witness at the trial of Sir Delves Broughton in

Nairobi and regaled me with every detail of this strange and dreadful story and ended up in his cheerful way: the murderer's weapon was never found, which goes to show how large Africa really is.' In Anthony Powell's memoirs, Lizzie claimed for some obscure reason: 'I had to say I was in a black brothel at the trial.'[56] When I wrote to Lady Ranfurly asking her to expand on what Lizzie had told her, she told me that 'untypically' Lizzie would not talk about the murder.[57]

The information that the Sallyport papers claim Government House had on Joss from his BUF period could have been supplied by the governor's wife Marjorie Byrne. According to her niece, on account of Joss's involvement with the BUF she had kept a discreet eye on his activities until the end of Byrne's term in 1936.[58] Marjorie Byrne's niece always understood that, though little was known by the family as to what she did, her aunt was in touch with Britain's overseas Security Service MI6. Doubtless on account of the nature of her work, Marjorie Byrne destroyed all her papers from this period 'during one of her many moves'.[59]

Both Imray and Gouldbourn were independently convinced that Hugh Dickinson had had something to do with Joss's murder. Dickinson's family never understood why Hughsie Daisy, as a young lieutenant in the 9th Lancers, got himself posted to Kenya, accepting a posting as a 2nd lieutenant in the Royal Army Service Corps. As far as his brothers were concerned, this step was not only retrograde but 'quite out of character'. When his brothers quizzed him later Dickinson explained this anomaly with the rather baffling words, 'I thought I'd be where the action was.'[60] There was no conventional military 'action' in Kenya itself, so did Dickinson mean 'action' in the sexual sense of pursuing Diana? Or was he alluding obliquely to his involvement in Operation Highland Clearance? At Broughton's trial, Dickinson's explanation was that a Kenya posting enabled him to be near Diana.

Dickinson shared a shady past with Broughton. He had gone as far as to steal for Broughton, taking part in two separate insurance-fraud thefts. One had involved Diana's pearls on the Riviera; not long after that, Dickinson had taken part in a 'break-in' at Doddington, Broughton's ancestral home. This had been stage-managed by Broughton himself — he had given detailed instructions (down to where a step-ladder should be bought), directing the removal and destruction of four oil paintings from the house.[61] Even his family admitted that Broughton was 'fundamentally [as] dishonest as a man with insurance fraud inclinations'.[62] (What Broughton did have, however, which the Security Services could use for their own ends, was a finely tuned skill for arranging deals at a localised level so as to look like something else.)*

It was not just Patsy (Bowles) Chilton, the young doctor's wife, who knew that Dickinson was in the 'hit location' on the night of Erroll's murder despite his claim to be in Mombasa. Marion Parker, who ran the convalescent and rest home for officers on Tree Lane on the plot adjoining the Broughtons' house, claimed he was staying in her rest home at the time and did not return there until 3.30 a.m. that critical morning. 'Her servant Mohamed had remarked to her the next day that he had to scrub Dickinson's boots for hours because they were full of mud.'[63] Then there was Wilks's anecdote about Dickinson – that he had delivered a note threatening that she could expect the same fate as Erroll 'if [she] wasn't careful'.

Were Gerald Portman's facial injuries a warning from those behind Operation Highland Clearance not to talk? He too could have played a role in the operation. As the last person to have hired the Buick before Joss, he was called as a witness; and he was also valuable as a witness for having been at Muthaiga with Phyllis Barkas on the night of the murder.

Finally, what of Gouldbourn's claim that the police were involved in the cover-up? The most obvious 'proof' would be the catalogue of errors concerning the handling of the Buick when Joss's body was discovered. Assistant Inspector Poppy, the 'first-class crime dedector' who led the investigation, admitted bitterly, 'There were tyre tracks, and the police and others went across the scene like a herd of buffalo.' He felt he had never had a proper chance of solving the crime.[64] The botching would rankle ever more with him. His main resentment had been against Inspector Fentum, the man who lived just around the corner from where Joss was shot. In fact Inspec-

*E.g. the bogus burglary of his revolvers.

tor Fentum had been seconded into the police only at the time of the murder. There were conflicting claims over the crucial evidence-destroying decision to move Erroll's body from the car. Fentum would surely have had the final word; if, as he claimed in court, he had objected to the pathologist Dr Timms' alleged instructions to remove the body, then his words would have been obeyed. Fentum boasted about the part he played in the investigation, and Imray claimed that he had 'crawled' into his promotions – one cannot help wondering whether Fentum had indeed been told by some 'higher authority' (as Assistant Superintendent Swayne called it) to be as careless as possible at the scene of the crime. Perhaps that was what Fentum meant when he told my husband and me back in the 1960s that he 'had been in charge of the murder investigation'.

If one can conclude from the foregoing that Operation Highland Clearance was real, then a glaring question is raised: *what* did Joss know that would have been so sensitive as to require such an elaborate, expensive and above all top-secret plot to eradicate him? Who stood to lose so much? Why did Joan Hodgson, MI6 agent in Nairobi, insist Joss was a severe security risk, and he was shot because unlike the Oswald Mosley Nazis who could be Interned Errol's [sic] case was much more complex'.[65] O'Mara's suggestion that Joss had told Brookham he was going to talk is interesting – after all there is that conspicuously missing letter in the correspondence which took place between Joss and Brookham after the latter's departure from the colony at the outset of the war. He was insistent that the missing letter contained some reference to Joss's sensitive knowledge. O'Mara was convinced that Joss had some unpalatable information on the Duke of Windsor:

Lord Erroll was put out of the way because he knew too much, perhaps including knowledge about the Duke of Windsor's sympathies and links with the Nazis. Someone may have believed he was going to make use of his knowledge and saw his affair with Lady Broughton as a perfect cover for having him 'terminated'. At that time British determination to fight on was not nearly as rock solid as is usually claimed. There were negotiations and the likelihood is that Hess's dramatic flight to Scotland was part of them. They could have involved removing Hitler for a more acceptable figure, perhaps Hess himself. There were certainly people in high positions who would have considered this in Britain and Germany.[66]

Then in a later letter O'Mara wrote, 'Why were they determined to eliminate Joss completely? He talked too much, knew too much, wanted too much, for silence about the Duke of Windsor's doings and ambitions . . . he was almost as untouchable as the Duke of Windsor.'[67]

Tyfield, too, thought that Erroll's death had 'some link to the Duke of Windsor', but was no more specific than that.

Ultimately, when asked directly by letter, 'Who do *you* think wanted him out of the way?', O'Mara responded by returning the letter with an annotation next to the question: 'SIS★ – Lord E. had become an embarrassment.'[68] About a month later, O'Mara mentioned a 'source' whose identity he never revealed and to whom from this point on he referred, obliquely or directly, in all his correspondence – 'The best of sources have their own agenda but mine seems really willing to help. If you have any "yes" or "no" questions, I am told answers may be forthcoming.' In this suggestion lay an opportunity to test his, or rather his source's, genuineness.

I drew up a long questionnaire, compiled from the Sallyport papers, inserting various false names and traps, asking O'Mara to tick the items relevant to Lord Erroll's murder. The 'source' passed with full marks. Again my original questionnaire was returned to me, marked with answers that showed that O'Mara's source knew of Operation Highland Clearance. He recognised the cover names Susan Laurenz, Colonel Alistair MacDonald and Susan Melanie Van Der Pleyden. SIS was involved; the Duke of Hamilton was one of an inner cabal; the widespread notion that Broughton had done a public service (in eliminating Erroll) was actually clever propaganda. O'Mara's source confirmed also that the Happy Valley scenario, in all its decadence, continued to act as a decoy to cover something deeper and wider.

★The Sallyport papers claim it was SOE. SOE was of course formed from a section of SIS known as Section D (for Destruction). Perhaps this accounts for the confusion.

Hess, Moyne and Erroll shared a knowledge of some 'ugly' secret.[69] Suggestion of Moyne's knowledge of the secret lends a strong motive to his refusal to help Broughton in gaol: Moyne would not have wanted to show his hand by appearing to support Broughton's innocence. Broughton, with his partial knowledge of the business as a whole, would not have been aware that Moyne too was implicated.

Mrs Helen Pearson, a settler who had known Diana well and who as a keen historian had researched into Erroll's death, had deduced some connection between his death and that in 1944 of Lord Moyne, Secretary of State to the Colonies during 1941/2. 'Moyne had been Vera Broughton's greatest male friend. His son was married to Diana Mitford who was married secondly to Oswald Mosley, leader of the British Union of Fascists . . . Moyne was assassinated in Cairo . . . so there you have it.'[70] While no proof has emerged connecting the two deaths explicitly, if Moyne really had been a party to the same sensitive information that Erroll was, then Moyne's assassination* would have wiped the slate clean.

So what *specifically* was it that Erroll knew that could possibly have been sensitive enough – to quote the Sallyport papers – to bring about 'the resignation of the government'? O'Mara's answer was: 'What Joss knew was what the UK government was actually offering Germany – as opposed to what it was saying in public. It involved the future of Europe – as Yalta did later.'[71] O'Mara later amplified his answer:

> Joss had intelligence responsibilities but that was irrelevant. Reason for his death was what he knew from other sources, and the well-grounded fear that he was going to talk, and in doing so would cause great injury to the British Government . . . A number of people were in the same position and all of them died in or around the year of Joss's death† (some escaped

---

*Officially attributed to Jewish terrorists (M. Gilbert, *Churchill: A Life*, p. 803).
†Lord Rothermere and Sir Harry Oakes, friends of the Duke of Windsor, died under mysterious circumstances in the Bahamas while the Duke of Windsor was Governor there. Rothermere suffered a breakdown, dying on 26 November 1940. Oakes was found charred and battered to death on 8 July 1943. The mystery of his death has yet to be solved (Philip Ziegler, *King Edward VIII*, pp. 480, 481).

longer, but were dealt with eventually, even the poor 'false Hess', the final victim). The point was not that Churchill had discovered the conspiracy and was enraged but that he had been part of it, balancing advantages against disadvantages of a deal with Germany – not with Hitler, but with 'the Generals' and Hess. Churchill was a close friend of the Duke of Windsor and while he was angry over the Duke's antics at the time of the fall of France, and later in Portugal, the friendship remained along with the possibility of using the Duke. When Churchill decided that to continue the war was to the best advantage of Britain – and calculated as insufficiently encouraging the chances of Hess and the General Staff in Berlin of ousting Hitler and dealing with the SS – it became a dangerous possibility that those on the losing side of the argument would take their revenge, by letting it be known that there had been an argument, and that Churchill had been on their side of it, until he ratted on them. It will be a good many years before this becomes an acceptable subject for historians to examine [...] The simple heart of the matter is that Erroll knew about it, and what is more he let it be known that he intended to talk about it. What is forgotten now, is that he represented a point of view about war with Germany that was rational . . . reasonable and patriotic people held it just as other reasonable and patriotic people disagreed. And the anti-war faction could, ten years later, claim that their argument, if it had prevailed, would have saved Britain from enormous losses, tremendous hardships and half of Europe from Communist tyranny. Joss was not a villain – he was a brilliant man who happened to be on the losing side and threatened to talk in order to have revenge against the winners.

Erroll was . . . one member of a powerful element in British society and politics that thought Britain had made a very serious mistake in entering the war against Germany.* It would mean

*Joss had been at Eton with King Leopold III of Belgium, whose decision not to join his government in exile led to accusations of collaboration with Nazi Germany.

ruin for Britain and a Communist take-over of Europe. Up to the time of his murder it was still possible that this view would prevail and lead to a peace treaty with Hitler. That came nearer to happening than anyone today is willing to admit. The Windsors had a role in it – and of course Hess – and so did leading members of the British government. If it had happened Erroll would – he hoped – have been a very important figure. He began to be indiscreet and this persuaded <u>both</u> sides in the argument [i.e., those pro a peace with Germany and those in favour of war] that he must be silenced.[72]

It is hard not to greet with scepticism the claim that Churchill had ever balanced 'advantages against disadvantages of a deal with Germany'. Historical evidence of Churchill's having been totally in favour of war is there for all to see, whereas there is scant evidence to substantiate O'Mara's belief that Churchill had ever considered a peace deal except the (at the time) secret visit of Major Ewald von Kleist, the envoy of the anti-Nazi group the Schwarze Kapelle, to Churchill in August 1938, which shows that Churchill was indeed at one point in discussion with the 'Generals' O'Mara mentions. According to Anthony Cave Brown, in *Bodyguard of Lies*, Churchill had 'incited the Schwarze Kapelle to rebel'.[73] However, by May 1940, a few days before he became Prime Minister, Churchill was absolutely against any mention of brokering a peace deal:

In Cabinet on May 6, Halifax took an initiative when, he later noted, 'I suggested one way to gain time was to delude the Germans with peace talk'. Churchill flared up in anger, accusing Halifax of treason, whereupon Halifax passed him a note: 'You are really very unjust to my irresponsible ideas. They may be silly, are certainly dangerous, but are not high treason.' Churchill gave the note back to Halifax with an apology: 'Dear Edward, I had a spasm of fear. I am sorry if I offended. It was a very deadly thought in the present atmosphere of frustration. You could not foresee this. Forgive me, W.'[74]

The issue of negotiating a general peace – in response to an offer from Mussolini – arose again when Halifax suggested 'in the secrecy of [Churchill's] five-member War Cabinet' that Britain should take up Mussolini's offer. Churchill condemned the idea, saying that 'Britain would rather go down fighting than negotiate peace'.[75] So O'Mara's assertion that British determination to fight on was not 'rock solid' could be justified by these debates going on after Britain had declared war on Germany; but his pronouncements about Churchill's volte face are impossible to prove. Operation Highland Clearance succeeded in burying whatever truth it was that Erroll knew. Churchill too was a firm advocate of secrecy in wartime: 'In war time, truth is so precious that she should always be accompanied by a bodyguard of lies.'[76] SOE was Churchill's brainchild.[77] Despite the thirty-year rule, very few documents concerning SOE have been released, and 'as for the files of SOE Cairo, it is doubtful if any of any interest at all[;] the burning of SOE's files was authorised and carried out in 1945'.[78]

Primarily SOE had been formed 'specifically to encourage resistance movements in enemy-occupied countries'. There had been a major branch of SOE in Cairo. The author Basil Davidson observes, 'It was the source of many sorrows for the lords of SOE in London[.] Cairo was subordinate to "London" but Cairo's commanders were far away, subject to urges and intuitions of their own and liable to be sure of knowing better. A coolness came between the two, not to say a strong dislike, instituting what became an annual August purge of Cairo's senior personnel.'[79]

However, as Richard Deacon, the author of *A History of the British Secret Service*, makes only too clear, with the SOE often the left hand did not know what the right hand was doing: 'Many have tried to probe the full story of the ... suspected treacheries and chaotic relationships which typified the SOE, but few have succeeded in solving what one critic has called "a skein so tangled, a story so convoluted, attitudes of mind so Byzantine, as so far to have defied rational analysis".'[80] Anthony Cave Brown confirms that the world of Special Operations was one of '"Proustian complexity" where even the lives of agents could be used as pawns', bearing out the fate of the agent Susan Melanie and, in a sense, that of Broughton too.[81]

Furthermore, the Sallyport papers emphasise that Operation Highland Clearance was exceptionally confidential: 'The rules of guidance
were changed and it is possible that only two specified officers would
have known something but not all of the details of the operation.'
M. R. D. Foot, the authority on SOE, points out, 'The whole East
African campaign of 1940–1 awaits reassessment in the light of the
hitherto ultra-secret papers from Bletchley that transform the picture
of how the very senior staff made up their own minds. The SOE
aspect of the campaign . . . also calls for some rethinking.'[82]

In many respects, Operation Highland Clearance does bear the
markings of an SOE exercise. The exaggerations of Joss's sex life, for
example, were in keeping with SOE tactics: they spread propaganda
exaggerating the peccadilloes and sex lives of key Nazi figures to
give the impression to the German public that their leaders were
involved in non-stop orgies.[83] On the subject of female agents,
Richard Deacon, in *A History of the British Secret Service*, writes, 'of
the fifty-three women agents SOE put in the field, twelve were
executed by the Germans and twenty-nine were either arrested or
died in captivity.' This was the sort of treatment dealt out to Susan
Melanie.

There was one further story that linked Churchill and Lord Erroll
directly. It came from a German-speaking Dane by the name of
Jacobson, who had once farmed near Naro Moru, halfway between
Nyeri and Nanyuki. During the war he was a warder of German
prisoners of war, as he was too old for active service. After Joss's
death in 1941 he overheard conversations among the German prisoners about how 'the British had murdered Hay, who was one of
our men in high places, and what a blow this was'.[84] The Germans
were discussing a British battleship the *Royal Oak*, which had been
sunk by a German U-boat at so-called 'impregnable anchorage' at
Scapa Flow in October 1939.[85] Churchill had been told, the Germans
were saying, that Joss Hay had been responsible for tipping off the
German U-boat. Apparently Churchill, enraged, rather in the
manner of Henry II cursing Thomas Becket, ordered that Erroll be
dealt with, saying that as it was well known that he was a philanderer,

a perfect alibi existed for his murder to be seen as a revenge killing.[86]

According to O'Mara, most of what Jacobson had overheard was 'disinformation' spread by Intelligence, 'to turn attention from the real reasons for Churchill's agreement to "executive action" in regard to Erroll. These ran much deeper than the sinking of a ship due to Erroll's activities. And Erroll's activities have nothing to do with that sinking or any other such event.'

Apocryphal or not, this anecdote suggests a possible way in which Churchill became involved in Erroll's assassination: had Churchill put a Becket-style curse on Erroll in the presence of SOE, who then followed out his curse to the letter?

O'Mara mentions Joss's own Intelligence role. There are aspects of Joss's life that support this idea. One former agent considered the Secretariat fire as a classic case of arson, especially when she learned that this most notorious of fires in the colony's history had started in Joss's own office. O'Mara claimed that the Secretariat fire had happened in order for Joss 'to edit the archives' of the Manpower resources, presumably as part of his role in Intelligence.[87]

Then there was Joss's affair with Mrs Filmer, a relationship that his friends could not understand. Tony Trafford believed that Joss was gathering information about the Shell oil company through Mrs Filmer. Of course Shell House was home to the Combined Services Security Bureau, too, though it has not been possible to prove that the Filmers were a link to goings-on there.

Also possibly as part of his Intelligence duties, Joss paid an inexplicable visit to Geita in Tanganyika in February 1939 shortly before his appointment to the Manpower Committee. He flew to North West Tanganyika by the Wilson Airways Goldfields Service.[88] Indeed there was a goldfield at Geita, and an airfield and processing centre on the River Msoma at the southern end of Lake Victoria, but there is no evidence that Joss had mining shares or interests in gold as a raw commodity. Nevertheless he stayed overnight in Geita and returned the following day. Michael Macoun refers to an 'embryonic security intelligence organisation' set up to watch the pro-German factions of the population in the territory. Joss, with his good German, would have been able to contribute usefully to British Intelligence work there.

Then, in August 1940, when Joss missed two debates in Legco without explaining or apologising for his absence, he could, in his capacity as Assistant Military Secretary, have been accompanying General Wavell who was at that same time on a secret visit from Cairo to Wajir. General Wavell had insisted on inspecting Wajir in person because of its crucial strategic position in the Northern Frontier District – the enemy was carrying out almost daily raids on it in connection with the Moyale operation.[89]* Wavell's visit was not made public until three months after it had happened.

Joss was certainly well connected enough to have known about, or taken part in, a cabal, as claimed by both O'Mara and the Sallyport papers. He grew up with royal families both as a child in Europe and at school. His parents socialised with those in power between the wars. Joss himself had rubbed shoulders with Ribbentrop in Berlin in the early 1920s. Certainly in the first half of the 1930s he was in close touch with Mosley and the activities of the BUF; he had known Mosley since the 1920s. Documents do not survive testifying to how involved he was in the BUF, but then virtually no documentation about Joss or written by him seems to have survived the years.† Joss had contacts in all walks of life. He could even lay claim to having been related, briefly, to the head of MI6 Stewart Menzies, his former brother-in-law. Muggeridge states, as quoted above, that Menzies had a contact in Nairobi – through his connection with Menzies, Joss could have known this contact and hence had a channel to SIS and its goings-on.

---

*Troops were being mobilised in this area in connection with the advance into Abyssinia (Crosskill, *Two Thousand Mile War*, pp. 62–64).

†One possible instance of information on Joss being removed is provided by some 'strictly private and confidential' correspondence, conducted towards the end of 1937, between the Governor Brooke-Popham and Ormsby-Gore of the Colonial Office. The exchange refers to a number of 'diehards' on the income-tax issue, such as Grogan and Lord Francis Scott. Peculiarly, Joss is not mentioned, whereas there is ample evidence in the contemporary press reporting public debates that Joss was a vociferous and persuasive speaker on this matter throughout the thirties.

When it came to considering the latter part of the 1930s it struck me that, through his involvement in negotiations over Tanganyika as part of the Tanganyika League, he would have known, if the Sallyport papers are to be believed, about the cabal's intentions to include Tanganyika 'among Britain's contribution to the Nordic Alliance'.* As early as 1933, there were nervous rumours in the press that the cession of Tanganyika to fascist powers was under discussion:

> A sensational statement has been made in a Paris newspaper that during the Rome conversations the British Prime Minister and Signor Mussolini agreed on the cession to Italy of certain territory in Kenya and Tanganyika. Mr MacDonald has emphatically denied that any reference was made at Rome to Tanganyika as a possible sop to Herr Hitler.[90]

The subject was already sensitive at that stage. The article, which had appeared in the *East African Standard*, continued, while condemning the sensationalised report from Paris: 'it is not impossible that the current negotiations for the purpose of affecting revisions of the Peace Treaty may involve the future of the Colonies.' Joss, like most settlers, adamantly opposed a return of Tanganyika to the Germans from the moment Italy threatened Abyssinia. A letter from a D. Sutherland in New Zealand backing the Tanganyika League and published in the *East African Standard* in early February 1939, just after Joss's mysterious trip to Geita, gives an interesting slant on appeasement:

> What did 'appeasement', together with talk of a 're-formed' League of Nations and a manifested desire for Germany to rejoin the League, and a refusal to give any guarantee as to

*O'Mara does not mention a Nordic alliance specifically in his correspondence, but in one letter he does refer to Erroll needing to be silenced because he also knew about the Russian situation: 'What was all-important at that period was the threatened German invasion of Russia, and what the Allies would do about it. It was by no means a foregone conclusion. Suppose they made peace with Hitler to free his hands against Russia? Sacrificing de Gaulle in favour of Pétain and Vichy France' (O'Mara correspondence, 29/4/97).

Tanganyika and other British Colonies, mean? As I read the whole ambit of British policy I have concluded that 'appeasement' really meant the sacrifice of British colonies. The talk of a 're-formed' League of Nations really meant a League so 're-formed' that it would consider possibly, if not certainly, a change in the Mandate of certain British territories such as Tanganyika. Appeasement received two blows, one the formation of the Tanganyika League, the other the diabolical programme instituted by Germany against German Jews . . . even Mr Malcolm MacDonald★ has been forced to say, with some reluctance, that the matter of transfer of British Colonies to Germany is not now a political question. This in itself is proof enough that it was a political question and might even be so in the future.[91]

Suppose that O'Mara is right and that negotiations for peace were continuing, by the end of 1940 British public opposition to any such dealings would have been guaranteed and would have put a stop to the possibility of Tanganyika being returned to Germany. Joss might have threatened to be indiscreet about such negotiations in order to prevent any possibility of Tanganyika being handed back. The political consequences for those people – whoever they were – seen to be talking to the enemy at that stage in the war would have been catastrophic – and avoided at all costs. O'Mara commented, 'The idea of peace with Hitler's generals to allow Germany a free run at the Soviet Union was very widespread in upper-class England (and in the Vatican and in right-wing America) . . . The return of German Africa (i.e. Tanganyika) was considered and of course Joss knew this and much else . . . He could damage a great many reputations but even more important could cause ordinary people to doubt their leaders' trustworthiness and unity of purpose.'[92]

Whether the mystery of Joss's murder will ever be completely understood is a moot point. From the evidence that my years of research

★Ramsay MacDonald's son and one of Chamberlain's ministers.

have compiled I believe the story of the 22nd Earl of Erroll's life and death as recorded in this book is as close to the truth as we can ever get. So much documentation about Joss has simply disappeared, however, that there must always be caveats when proclaiming truths about him. Even the photographs that he took of Africa disappeared from Oserian after his death – the *East African Standard* described a collection of albums containing glorious pictures of game on the estate. It seems as though Joss's enemies wanted systematically to destroy everything that might prove that he had ever done a stroke of work or taken an interest in anything but the seduction of other men's wives.

Before the Union Jack was lowered at Kenya's Independence in 1963, a great many files were removed, destroyed or sent back to London. The Governor of Kenya Sir Philip Mitchell, who had been working in Nairobi's East Africa Governors' Conference during the early 1940s,* was responsible for seeing that papers concerning 'subjects common to the three East African Territories, on defence, railways [and] the interchange of senior civil servants' contained in the East Africa Governors' Conference office at Muthaiga between 1941 and 1942 were safely out of the way; there had been very tight security there, and Sir Philip Mitchell carried it out to the letter. He apparently promised at a dinner party to leave an 'exposition of his theory of the [Erroll] case in his Will', but never did.[93]

As Richard Thurlow wrote, 'an obsession with secrecy has characterised all British Governments during the twentieth century with reference to national security considerations . . . Often this had no relation to current problems, rather than the need to protect sources of information in intelligence-gathering activities. And, of course, primarily to cover up the often dubious methods employed in security and espionage operations. The lie that is told in the name of security is recognised for what it is nowadays – chiefly for the benefit of the liar.'[94]

---

*During 1940 Sir Philip Mitchell, on the Executive Council, had been frantically making arrangements from this office for the return of Haile Selassie to Ethiopia (Bunyan correspondence, 2/5/97; Lt.-Col. John Gouldbourn correspondence).

Epilogue

With the death of Josslyn Victor Hay, 22nd Earl of Erroll, came the end of an era. To posterity, his murder seemed to close a unique chapter in colonial history. The shot that rang out that night in January 1941 shattered the glamorous image of Happy Valley, and seemingly pointed up the darker side of exuberant living. There was a shift of mood, too, as troops based in Nairobi marched off to an uncertain fate in Ethiopia. The characters whose lives were entwined with Joss's continue to inspire writers and film-makers. Robert Young, the film director whose connections with Kenya span nearly four decades, knew Diana as the wife of Tom Delamere. She, of the many women mourning Joss's death, was the most enigmatic, not only because she carried to her grave whatever she knew about the end to Joss's life, but also because she cultivated a personal mystique as if to shield herself from the treatment she received after his murder. She became an outcast among European settlers in Kenya for more than a decade, and in fact only scaled the heights of that society again in the 1960s. This was in some measure owing to her marriage to Thomas, 4th Baron Delamere, in 1955. With Diana as the glamorous wife at his side to encourage him, this hitherto shy and reserved man blossomed.

Yet each time the story of Joss's death was dredged up Diana's reputation would suffer again. Her sister, Lady Willingdon, was so horrified at how Diana was portrayed in the film *White Mischief* that she was too ashamed ever to holiday in Kenya again. The sisters met up only in England.[1] Robert Young saw more to Diana than the role of fallen *femme fatale*, however. His fascination and respect for her inspired this powerful description:

Diana Delamere was a woman with a past that seemed to glow round her like a glittering animal that wishes to attract certain species and to repel others. One look from those steel-blue eyes could entrap and kill. And she never looked anything but immaculate. Soysambu [Delamere's farm] was miles and miles from anywhere in the middle of Maasai country. Diana would ride every morning . . . a black mare, which had been groomed to perfection, as indeed was its rider. Diana wore tight black breeches . . . black riding boots which were so polished that these acted like mirrors, reflecting the passing bush . . . a white silk shirt with ballooned sleeves and a black bolero, which was richly embroidered with a black filigree design. Her hat was a Spanish sombrero set at a raffish angle, showing off her blonde hair, and not one strand out of place. Black whip and gloves completed the picture. If ever a passing Maasai moran saw her I doubt he would ever forget this sight, just as I have never forgotten.[2]

Once the Second World War ended, Joss's medals were sent to his nineteen-year-old daughter Dinan. There was little else left for her to inherit. The Errolls were bereft even of family memories of the 22nd Earl. For, according to her husband, Dinan could not 'bear any mention of the whole affair . . . the whole thing [was] an open wound for her'. She never once mentioned her father to her son Merlin.

The next occupants of Oserian were the exiled Prince Paul of Yugoslavia and his wife Princess Olga, who moved in with their children on 28 April 1941. The Governor, Sir Henry Moore, had received very little warning of the Yugoslavs' arrival. His instructions were specific: 'The Prince was not (repeat not) to be received at Government House.'[3]

As Prince Paul entered Oserian, he observed wryly, 'So they send me to the house of a murdered man on my birthday.' Princess Olga's reaction was no more positive: 'Brown water oozed from the taps because the filter had long ceased to function; the ice-box was worse than useless and the sunken bath so cracked that it could not be filled . . . A complete nightmare. Impossible to live here. We must not lose faith and courage.' During this difficult interlude, great kindness was extended to them by Tony Trafford's parents, for which Princess Olga was ever grateful. Only when Prince Paul appeared to be on the point of a nervous breakdown did General Jan Smuts relent, allowing them to move to South Africa.[4]

The sale of Oserian – to Gilbert Colvile, who bought it for Diana in 1943 – would have raised about £12,000. Today the 'Djinn Palace' is worth millions. Oserian's present owners farm flowers – mainly roses – and Joss's former home is believed to be the biggest rose farm in the world. Five million stems daily are packed in cartons, driven to Nairobi and air-freighted to Europe, all the year round. In 1998 Kenya exported thirty thousand tons of flowers, the bulk of which were grown at Oserian.

Joss's brother Gilbert deputised as Lord High Constable for Scotland at the coronation of Queen Elizabeth in 1953. Joss's portrait in coronation robes now hangs at the Erroll family home in Bedfordshire. Merlin Erroll continues in his grandfather's tradition of lively participation in politics. He was one of the few to survive the purging of the 700-odd hereditary peers from the House of Lords in November 1999.

'There's always something more to everything'

Robert Frost

Appendix

Publication of the hardback edition has generated considerable correspondence; readers and original interviewees came forward with fresh corroborative information pertinent to the Sallyport papers. While no one has refuted the basic thrust of Tony Trafford's claims, some of the new details differ from his descriptions. For example, I had believed that no more than half a dozen people were involved in Operation Highland Clearance. However, S. P. J. O'Mara has pointed out that as many as fifty personnel actually had 'some knowledge' of the exercise. The following list, probably still incomplete, names those known to have played some part.

After this book was published I learned that Tony Trafford had been recruited as a 'sleeper' in August 1940 and he had seen a written reference to Operation Highland Clearance in 1942 at GOCHQ in Nairobi. S. P. J. O'Mara's knowledge of the hit occasionally varies from the Sallyport papers and he has been able to dispute and confirm certain details. However, he refuses to reveal the identities of the two assassins on the grounds that it would be 'furiously denied' and their families would be very distressed. O'Mara feels to name the assassins would mean that the case would move 'to full disclosure'. For reasons not explained satisfactorily to me, 'full disclosure' of events in 1940 and 1941 is still regarded as very sensitive.

Gaps in the historical record are suggestive. But what can be said confidently is that, for whatever reason, a plan of considerable complexity to murder the Earl of Erroll was hatched. The following people were among its principals:

Colonel 'Sweetie' Barkas (203, 239, 289)
Barkas was not only in charge at Eldoret but acted as a military contact for SOE. This explains why Lizzie Lezard and he were in touch so frequently.

Phyllis Barkas (203, 205, 290, 292)
Her role had been to keep Broughton under surveillance for SOE, hence those daily meetings at Muthaiga Club on the pretext of playing backgammon or golf croquet.[1] The Late Lieutenant-Colonel John Gouldbourn had hinted at the necessity of this relationship in my first interview with him five years ago.[2]

Major General Sir Alec Bishop, KCMG, CB, CVO, OBE (274)
In his review of this book in the *Spectator* Patrick Marnham, Bishop's son-in-law, concluded, '"Opa" is innocent, dammit!' At no point was there any suggestion that Bishop murdered Lord Erroll or that he was even in Nairobi in January 1941. S. P. J. O'Mara confirms that Bishop's role was as SIS Controller in London with overall authority, answerable to Churchill.[3] Bishop's 1940 visits en passant in Kenya and 'in and out of Shell House', Nairobi, were in connection with arrangements for Operation Highland Clearance.[4]

Sir Jock Delves Broughton
Although Broughton was acquitted of Lord Erroll's murder, he had been recruited by MI6. His knowledge of Erroll's fate is implicit (see p. 289). Of several duties Broughton carried out for MI6, one was to hire and pay for his so-called chauffeur, a Somali irregular who was masquerading as a driver.[5] This revelation hardly comes as a surprise; it supports the same suggestion published by a South African Journalist in 1989[6] as well as Colin Imray's conviction that the Somali could quite easily have been hiding in the back of the Buick just before Joss's death. Since Broughton's driver was never called as a witness at the trial, his disappearance fuelled a persistent rumour among the African fraternity. This rumour states that from the moment Broughton had hired him in November the Somali had posed as his chauffeur. In the early hours of 24 January, dressed in

his off-duty clothes, Broughton's driver had simply thumbed a lift from Joss near the end of the driveway of the house in Marula Lane on the pretext that Broughton had given him a day's leave. He was already in the car when Joss stopped for Susan Melanie on the road, when he got out of the passenger seat to make way for her and climbed into the back. The white scuff marks on the back seat of the Buick had come from his plimsolls. This rumour would also explain why, ever since that night, certain Africans had taken fright at the very mention of the Erroll murder; they knew through the grenadilla vine that a Somali, who was a crack shot, had been given a lift in the Buick and they were terrified lest they too could be connected to the murder. The gunman was said to have left Kenya, following the debriefing in Girouard Road.[7]

According to S. P. J O'Mara, Broughton's suicide had been 'staged'. One of the problems the Coroner faced was to establish which pharmacy had supplied one of the drugs that killed Broughton by overdose.[8] In 1988 Nairobi's Coroner, Mervyn Morgan, had written to Edward Rodwell (see pp. 5–6), 'Broughton after being rightly acquitted by the jury left a note for the Coroner in Liverpool at the inquest of his death. NB The Liverpool Coroner declined to make public Broughton's letter and wouldn't disclose the contents to anyone – he was rightly or wrongly much criticised for his acts and ommissions but a Coroner does have almost omnipotent powers.'[9] Broughton apparently knew far too much and had to be silenced once and for all, so he was taken out in a manner that looked as if he had committed suicide. S. P. J O'Mara suggested that OSS had supplied the American drug.

Richard Cavendish, Commissioner of Kenya Police (5)

Cavendish had MI6 connections. Though he had never been named during the investigation, Cavendish was kept informed about aspects of Operation Highland Clearance. The Mercedes-Benz agent in Nairobi who told Edward Rodwell in the Fifties that 'the Chief of Police was ordered to have Erroll shot, on account of his Nazi sympathies' was referring to Cavendish.[10] Ultimately he was responsible for Arthur J. Poppy, who headed the investigation at his level, and in turn Poppy selected his team from the Kenya Police Force. The two African dairy workers who 'discovered' the body in the Buick were actually police askaris.

Major Ferdinand Cavendish-Bentinck, later Duke of Portland (38, 105, 140n, 141, 144, 145, 147, 148, 165, 169–70)
Cavendish-Bentinck was recruited by MI6, probably as early as 1934 after Joss had announced his intention to act as Mosley's delegate for the BUF in Kenya. He had been in the ideal position to pass on any information to Whitehall, having known Joss since 1924 as well as his political views from the time Joss became an elected Member of Legco and Assistant Military Secretary.[11]

Lietenant Hugh Thompson Dickinson (189, 190, 195, 198, 226, 231, 232, 259, 291, pl. 44, pl. 48)
Dickinson, another 'sleeper', had been keeping Diana under surveillance and carrying out tasks required of him as matters developed. The ruse of sending Broughton, Diana and Dickinson on safari before Broughton was charged was to keep them out of sight of 'the chattering classes' before Broughton was arrested.

Colonel Douglas Fabin (271n)
Fabin a.k.a 'Grampian' for whom Neil Tyfield had worked, had been used by SOE for Operation Highland Clearance in 1940–1, acting out of the DDMI office at GOCHQ, Muthaiga. Without Alistair MacDonald's permission, Fabin had used his name as a cover. Since the real MacDonald was in London, it is unlikely that he ever learned of this deception.

Inspector Clarence Fentum (1, 8, 201, 208, 209, 216, 292–3)
Fentum would have received his instructions from SIS.[12] Colin Imray's claim that Fentum had only been seconded to the Kenya Police at about the time of Erroll's murder has its foundations in his appointment when he was put in charge of Kilimani Police Station and is linked also to Fentum's 1962 claim that he had been 'in charge' of the Erroll murder investigation.[13]

James Gregory died *genuinely* in the front line.

Lazarus Kaplan (190, 221, 226, 227, 233, 234, 283, 285–6)
Having received instructions originating from SIS, Kaplan's role was to send Diana Broughton down to secure Harry Morris for the trial.[14]

Lizzie Lezard (182, 203, 217, 290–1)
Lezard had been recruited by SOE;[15] he 'came, from Cairo, as an HQ chap and returned to Cairo'.[16] It had been a simple matter for Lezard, a fellow Old Etonian, to befriend Joss who warmed to Lezard's buffoonery. His stepson's wife, Lady Ranfurly, pointed out that he was 'rather too old to be on active service but with his usual enthusiasm and great sense of humour . . . determined to be a hero'.[17] By profession Lezard was a barrister but had not practised for some time and was better known as a tennis player, having arrived in London from South Africa with the Davis Cup team. Both well born and well off, thanks to a rich ex-wife, as mentioned in the Sallyport papers he was of independent means. Lezard took his orders from Fabin.[18] It was to Lezard that Joss confided that 'Jock couldn't have been nicer. He has agreed to go away. As a matter of fact he has been so nice it smells bad.' Joss added that Broughton had told him that he must bring Diana home by 3 a.m. after the party – a piece of evidence to which the defence had strongly objected on the grounds of inadmissibility.[19] In the jury's absence Kaplan had objected to their submission, because a sinister import might be read into 'it smells bad'.[20]

Broughton told Lezard that he was looking forward to going to the Clairmont that night, giving Lezard to understand that he would be taking June as a partner.[21] This is the information that Odendaal received about 'timing and sequence of events at Muthaiga Club', later inspiring Odendaal's fury during the hit due to 'difficulties' caused by Broughton and June, who remained at Muthaiga instead of going along to the Clairmont with Joss and Diana.

Years later, Lezard told the writer Anthony Powell that at the trial, 'I had to say I was in a black brothel' because he could not possibly reveal his whereabouts and he had been unable to come up with anything better. His friend, Alistair Forbes had also found Lizzie 'untypically evasive' on the subject of the Erroll murder.[22]

'Long Lew' Llewellyn (195, 205)
Llewellyn provided the Somali crack shot for Operation Highland Clearance and was responsible for his safe passage out of Kenya after the debriefing.

Sir Philip Mitchell (171, 176, 304)
Mitchell's ultimate responsibility had been to oversee the transfer of sensitive papers out of Kenya upon Independence, and he would have been acting upon instructions that originated from SIS.[23]

Sir Henry Moore, Governor of Kenya (10, 176, 178, 180, 189, 212, 244, 254, 271, 281)
Moore was selected to replace Brooke-Popham who was transferred out of Kenya because he had been Erroll's close friend.[24]

Henry 'Harry' Morris, KC (7, 227, 230–5, 284–5, 287)
Moore was instructed by SIS to fly to Kenya and defend Broughton.[25] There seems to be little doubt that Morris had also been primed with regard to the crucial ballistics evidence. This is surely the reason behind Morris's ebullient approach in court throughout the trial. Tactics of 'deliberate mystification' on every aspect of the guns had been maintained throughout Operation Highland Clearance.[26]

Viscount Gerald Portman (38, 195, 196, 205, 215–17, 229–30, 292)
Portman's responsibilities included the hiring of the Buick, providing evidence in court, justifying the use of pliers for the broken knob on the instrument panel of the Buick, having hired the same vehicle immediately before Joss.[27] The attack on Portman at his house in Muthaiga was a warning to him against indiscretion.

General Brian Robertson (later Sir), then South African Chief of Staff (1940–1) Robertson was working for South African Military Intelligence and it was thought that he had been somehow connected with the 'Inner Cabal' and the cover-up to kill Lord Erroll.[28] Robertson had been responsible for the South African personnel, military and police, employed behind the scenes for Operation Highland Clearance.[29]

Susan Melanie Van Der Pleyden (246–9, 251–60, 262–7, 269–70, 272, 275–6, 294, 299)
Pleyden was killed as described. MI6 were responsible for eliminating her with the approval of SIS.[30]

Notes

Abbreviations

CC   Crown Case
CO   Commonwealth Office
EAS   *East African Standard*
int., ints interview(s)
MOD   Ministry of Defence
PRO   Public Record Office
WO   War Office

Prologue

1. Int. Charles Huxley, London, 26/1/99
2. Lyn Sampson, *Style*, December/January 1989
3. Brigadier M. W. Biggs, *Daily Telegraph*, 10/3/88

1 Quest for the Truth

1. Corresp. Mervyn Morgan to Edward Rodwell, 8/1/88; corresp. Nancy Miller, 24/8/98; int. the late John Carter, Nairobi, 13/3/90
2. Int. the late Lonnie Miller, Kilifi, 9/2/95
3. Genesta Hamilton, *A Stone's Throw, Travels from Africa in Six Decades*, Hutchinson, London, 1986, p. 227
4. Corresp. the late Elspeth Huxley, 12/7/96
5. Corresp. and ints Alison Jauss, July–November 1994
6. Int. Edward Rodwell, Mtwapa Creek, 7/2/95, 14/2/95; 'That Happy Valley Murder-Mystery . . .', Coast Causerie, Edward Rodwell, *Standard* (Nairobi), 2/10/87; 'Juanita and the Cheater', 'Sunday Première: The Happy Valley', BBC1, *Radio Times*, 5–11 September 1987; *Standard* (Nairobi), 8/1/88, 18/1/88
7. Corresp. Mervyn Morgan to Edward Rodwell, 8/1/88
8. Corresp. the late Kate Challis to Edward Rodwell, 13/1/88
9. Corresp. Charles Elwell, Easter Day 1996
10. Confidential correspondence with the author, 1/8/96
11. Int. Persimmon, London, 31/1/96
12. Peterborough, Quentin Letts, *Daily Telegraph*; undated clipping from Mary Clark, received March 1995
13. *The Overseas Pensioner*, Autumn 1995, p. 57
14. Int. J. N. P. Watson, Lavinia Watson and the late Colin H. Imray, Horsham, 6/4/95
15. Ibid.

16. Int. the late Colin H. Imray, Haywards Heath, 17/6/95

17. Imray papers, 1995; corresp. the late Colin H. Imray, 21/4/95

18. Ibid.

19. Int. 24th Earl of Erroll, Bedfordshire, 7/8/95

20. Sir Iain Moncreiffe of that Ilk to Peggy Pitt, 28/7/55

21. War Office to 24th Earl of Erroll, 28/2/83

22. Corresp. 24th Earl of Erroll and Major Parsons, MOD, 28/5/88

23. Kenya Regiment Army Form B199A C/1; Hay family papers, 7/8/95

24. Corresp. A. J. Parsons, MOD, to 24th Earl of Erroll, 15/6/88; Hay family papers

25. 'UK Confidential – a Leviathan Special', BBC2, 1/1/99

26. Int. Tom Bower, London, 10/10/95; int. Persimmon, London, 31/1/96; corresp. Charles Elwell, Easter Day 1996; obit. Anne Elwell, *The Times*, 17/1/96

27. File CO 967/160

28. Murray Ritchie, 'Hundred-year Shroud on Happy Valley Mystery', *Glasgow Herald*, 22/2/88

29. Corresp. Margaret Bryan, 21/3/96; PRO, CO 533 529/12

30. PRO, Kew; CO 628/36; corresp. K. Skinner, 4/4/97; trnsf. CO 38507/41

31. Author's diaries, 21/2/95

32. Letters to the Editor, *Daily Telegraph*, 18/3/88; int. 24th Earl of Erroll, 28/7/95

33. Corresp. the late Lt.-Col. John Gouldbourn to 24th Earl of Erroll, 18/3/88, and John Gouldbourn to author, 21/9/95

34. Int. the late John Gouldbourn, Lytham St Anne's, 8/10/95

35. Corresp. S. P. J. O'Mara, 12/1/98

36. Ibid., 26/6/97

37. Corresp. Anthea Venning, 8/11/96

38. Corresp. Tony Trafford to Anthea Venning, 14/2/97

39. Sallyport papers, 15/12/97

2 Gnarled Roots

1. Photograph album of Lady Kilmarnock, 1901

2. Int. 24th Earl of Erroll, Bedfordshire, 15/1/95

3. Alan Hay, Proceedings of the Scottish Tartans Society, *Clan Hay Magazine*, Series 5

4. *Debrett's Illustrated Peerage*, p. 332

5. Isobel Crumb, 'The Hays and the Jacobite Attempt of 1708', *Clan Hay Magazine*, vol. 1, p. 11

6. 'The Hays and Turriff', *Clan Hay Magazine*, vol. 1, p. 29

7. *The Complete Peerage*; corresp. Alan Hay, 6/4/98

8. Tel. conv. Petal Allen, 30/12/94; int. Anne (Buxton) Wadley, Tilford, 22/1/96; int. Shirley Heriz-Smith, London, 7/10/97; int. the late Sylvia Richardson, Kiganjo, 3/12/86; int. Bunny Allen, Lamu, 17/2/95

9. Rupert Hart-Davis, *The Arms of Time*, Hamish Hamilton, London, 1979, p. 7

10. *The Complete Peerage*, p. 103

11. Barbara Belford, *Bram Stoker, A Biography of the Author of Dracula*, Weidenfeld & Nicolson, London, 1996, p. 234

12. Livio Negri, Warwick Hembry, 'Altitude, Alcohol and Adultery: The

British Aristocracy in Kenya Colony',
BBC1 documentary, 4/6/93
13. Extract from *Black's Guide to Scotland*, Edinburgh, 1871; *Clan Hay Magazine*, vol. 6, p. 30
14. Corresp. Alan Hay, 22/6/98; 6/4/99; tel. conv. 24th Earl of Erroll, 14/6/98; *The Complete Peerage*, p. 103
15. *The Concise Encyclopaedia of Modern Literature*, Hutchinson, London, 1963

3 Boyhood and Eton

1. Photograph albums of Lady Kilmarnock
2. *Who Was Who 1916–1930*
3. Photograph albums of Lady Kilmarnock
4. Int. the late Bettine Anderson, Aldeburgh, 12/1/96
5. Photograph albums of Lady Kilmarnock
6. Photograph albums of Lady Kilmarnock; *The Faber Book of Plays*, 1952
7. Ibid.
8. Corresp. Dr Thérèse Fürstin von Schwarzenberg, 17/4/97
9. Int. Princess Caroline Schonburg von Hartenstein, Vienna, 10/4/98
10. Photograph albums of Lady Kilmarnock
11. Tel. conv. Alan Hay, 22/6/98
12. Photograph albums of Lady Kilmarnock; int. 24th Earl of Erroll, Bedfordshire, 7/8/95
13. Int. 24th Earl of Erroll, Bedfordshire, 7/8/95
14. Int. Patsy Chilton, Golini, 15/3/97
15. Int. the late Bettine Anderson, Aldeburgh, 12/1/96

16. Ibid.
17. Corresp. Sir Wilfrid Havelock, 2/9/96
18. Photograph albums of Lady Kilmarnock; Peter Haining and Peter Beresford-Ellis, *The Un-Dead: The Castle of Dracula*, London, 1997, p. 152
19. Ibid.; int. 24th Earl of Erroll, Bedfordshire, 17/1/96
20. Ibid.
21. Corresp. Jack Bunyan, 5/10/96
22. Int. Bunny Allen, Lamu, 17/2/95; corresp. Bunny Allen, 8/1/95; *EAS*, 1934 (undated), press profile 22nd Earl of Erroll, syndicated from London
23. Photograph albums of Lady Kilmarnock
24. *EAS*, 9/9/38
25. Corresp. Dr Thérèse Fürstin von Schwarzenberg, 1/4/97; photograph albums of Lady Kilmarnock
26. Corresp. Dr Thérèse Fürstin von Schwarzenberg, 1/4/97
27. Photograph albums of Lady Kilmarnock
28. Int. and corresp. Pat Donnelly, Watamu, 29/7/95, 12/11/95
29. Photograph albums of Lady Kilmarnock; corresp. Alan Hay, 7/4/98
30. Int. the late Bettine Anderson, Aldeburgh, 15/1/96
31. *Who's Who 1926*; corresp. David Christie-Miller, 22/3/96; Eton College Records
32. Eton College Records
33. Ibid.
34. Margaret Bellars, 'Chessington: Five Noble Homes and a Zoo', *Kingston Borough News*, 31/8/73
35. Int. 24th Earl of Erroll, Bedfordshire, 7/8/95

36. *Dictionary of National Biography*;
Richard Deacon, *A History of the
British Secret Service*, Frederick Muller,
London, 1978, p. 45

37. Anthony Cave Brown, *Bodyguard
of Lies*, Harper & Row, New York,
1975, p. 14

38. Corresp. David Christie-Miller,
20/7/95, 11/11/96: Eton School
Register, 1909–19; int. 24th Earl of
Erroll, Bedfordshire, 7/8/95

39. Int. the late Bettine Anderson,
Aldeburgh, 15/1/96

40. Photograph albums of Lady
Kilmarnock

41. Osbert Sitwell, *The Scarlet Tree*,
Reprint Society, London, 1947,
p. 6

42. Eton School Register, vol. VIII;
corresp. C. Vickers, 25/9/96, Eton
College Photographic Archive

43. Tim Card, *Eton Renewed, a History
from 1860 to the Present Day*, John
Murray, London, 1994, pp. 122–3;
Eton Today, Nigel Goodman, Eton
College, Slough, p. 16

44. Int. the late Bettine Anderson,
Aldeburgh, 15/1/96

45. Corresp. David Christie-Miller,
28/10/96

46. Eton College, 28/10/96, School
list Michaelmas 1914; tel. conv. Anne
(Buxton) Wadley, 15/10/95; int.
Tilford, 22/1/96

47. Corresp. Sir Charles Markham,
17/5/96

48. Int. Anne (Buxton) Wadley,
Tilford, 22/1/96

49. Int. Eton College, 28/10/96

50. Int. Eton College, 20/7/95

51. Card, *Eton Renewed*, p. 134

52. Int. Anne (Buxton) Wadley,
Tilford, 22/1/96

53. Int. the late Bettine Anderson,
Aldeburgh, 12/1/96

54. Int. Molly Hoare, Farnham,
23/1/96

55. James Fox, *White Mischief*,
Penguin, London, 1984, p. 29

56. Int. Eton College, 28/10/96

57. *EAS*, 1934, press profile 22nd Earl
of Erroll, syndicated from London

58. Corresp. David Christie-Miller,
22/3/96

59. Int. Patsy Chilton, London,
10/5/95; int. Patsy Chilton, Golini,
14/3/97; Livio Negri and Warwick
Hembry, 'Altitude, Alcohol and
Adultery', BBC1, 4/6/93; Kenya
Regiment Army Form B199A
C/1

60. Ibid.

61. Int. the late William Pitt, Oxford,
31/5/95; int. Molly Hoare, Farnham,
23/1/96

62. Tel. conv. Anne (Buxton)
Wadley, 19/10/95

63. Alisdare Hickson, *The Poisoned
Bowl: Sex and the Public School*,
Duckworth, 1996, p. 34

64. Card, *Eton Renewed*; Hickson, *The
Poisoned Bowl*, pp. 132–3

65. Corresp. Merseyside Maritime
Museum, 3/6/97; W. D. Rubenstein
and Sir John Reeves Ellerman,
Dictionary of Business Biography,
Butterworth, 1984, pp. 248–9

66. Corresp. Alan Hay, 6/4/98

4 'To Hell with Husbands'

1. Int. the late Bettine Anderson,
Aldeburgh, 12/1/96

2. Ibid.; Kenya Regiment Army Form
B199A 1941

3. Corresp. British Embassy, Berlin office, 6/9/96; Foreign Office Lists, 1923/4, vol. 32

4. I. Kirkpatrick, *The Inner Circle*, Macmillan, London, 1959, pp. 27–9

5. Iain Moncreiffe, review of *White Mischief, Books and Bookmen*, February 1983

6. *EAS*, 3/3/28

7. Int. the late Bettine Anderson, Aldeburgh, 12/1/96

8. Michael Bloch, *Ribbentrop*, Bantam, London, 1992, pp. 11, 13, 15

9. Ibid., p. 15

10. Ibid., p. 9

11. Press profile of 22nd Earl of Erroll, syndicated from London to *EAS*, 1934

12. Frédéric de Janzé, *Vertical Land*, Duckworth, London, 1928, pp. 140, 141

13. Cecil Beaton, 'The Measure of an Artist', *Vogue*, 1/4/80, p. 158

14. Cecil Beaton, 'Spotlight on the Changing Face of the Model', *Vogue*, 15/3/67, p. 106

15. Ibid.

16. Int. Patsy Chilton, Golini, 15/3/97

17. Int. the late Bettine Anderson, Aldeburgh, 12/1/96

18. Charles Hayes, *Oserian: Place of Peace*, Rima Books, Kenya and Canada, 1997, p. 256; *Hansard*, 1937

19. Int. the late Bettine Anderson, Aldeburgh, 12/1/96

20. Daphne Fielding, *Mercury Presides*, Eyre & Spottiswoode, London, 1954, p. 93

21. Int. the late Bettine Anderson, Aldeburgh, 12/1/96

22. Int. David Fielden, Kilifi, 30/8/96

23. Corresp. the late Elspeth Huxley, 12/7/96

24. Unpub. memoir of Sir Derek Erskine, p. 50

25. Kenya Regiment Army Form B199A C/1; *EAS*, 3/3/28, p. 3

26. Frank, Knight and Rutley sale sheet for 9/5/22

27. Corresp. Merseyside Maritime Museum, 3/6/97; W. D. Rubenstein and Sir John Reeves Ellerman, *Dictionary of Business Biography*, Butterworth, 1984, pp. 248–9

28. Int. the late Robert Creighton, Kilifi, 9/7/96

29. Ibid.

30. Int. the late Bettine Anderson, Aldeburgh, 12/1/96

31. Ibid.

32. Ibid.

33. Ibid.

34. Ibid.

35. Int. Kath Biggs, Kimpton, 1/8/95

36. Int. the late Bettine Anderson, Aldeburgh, 12/1/96

37. Ibid.

38. Ibid.

39. Ibid.

40. Ibid.

41. Ibid.

42. *Tatler*, 21/3/23, p. 421

43. Ibid., 19/9/23, p. 465

44. Ibid., 19/9/23, p. 465; 3/10/23

45. Robert Skidelsky, *Oswald Mosley*, Papermac, London, 1990, p. 89

46. *Tatler*, 12/9/23

47. Marriage certificate; *Tatler*, 3/10/23, p. 3; *Sketch*, 3/10/23, p. 4

48. Sir Iain Moncreiffe of that Ilk, review of *White Mischief*, draft for *Books and Bookmen*, February 1983; corresp. Nicholas Mosley, 28/5/96

49. Int. the late Bettine Anderson, Aldeburgh, 12/1/96

50. Ibid.

51. Frankie Iceley; Livio Negri and Warwick Hembry, 'Altitude, Alcohol and Adultery', BBC1, 4/6/93

52. Corresp. Sir Iain Moncreiffe of that Ilk to Peggy Pitt, 28/7/55

53. Int. the late Bettine Anderson, Aldeburgh, 12/1/96

54. Ibid.

5 Slains

1. Sydney T. Kelson, 'Reflections on Kenya, 1923–46', unpub. Mss. Afr. S.

2. Press profile of 22nd Earl of Erroll, syndicated from London to *EAS*, 1934

3. 'The Watchman', Times Almanac, *The Times*, 10/11/55

4. Sydney T. Kelson, 'I Wore Khaki Uniform', unpub. Mss. Afr. S. 735, Rhodes House, Oxford; Peggy Frampton, *Seven Candles for My Life*, Pentland Press, 1990, p. 19

5. Int. the late Ginger Birkbeck, Mombasa, 16/5/87

6. Corresp. Patricia Goldsmith, 27/12/98; 'Some Personal Notes', Kate Challis née Beynon, in reply to 'What I Know', *Women in Kenya*, 1st issue, 1995

7. Corresp. Anthea Venning, 27/5/97

8. Frédéric de Janzé, *Vertical Land*, Duckworth, London, 1928, p. 27

9. Elsbeth Huxley, *White Man's Country*, vol. II, p. 27

10. Charles Chenevix-Trench, *The Men Who Ruled Kenya: The Kenya Administration 1892–1963*, Radcliffe Press, London, 1993, p. 72

11. Nicholas Best, *Happy Valley: The Story of the British in Kenya*, Secker & Warburg, London, 1979, p. 106

12. Elspeth Huxley, *White Man's Country*, vol. II, Chatto & Windus, London, 1935, p. 52

13. Best, *Happy Valley*, p. 102

14. Int. the late Gertrude Alexander, York, 1978; Hayes, *Oserian*, p. 236

15. *EAS*, 4/3/33, 4/11/33

16. Chenevix-Trench, *The Men Who Ruled Kenya*, p. 72

17. Frampton, *Seven Candles*, pp. 18–39

18. V. M. Carnegie, *A Kenyan Farm Diary*, Blackwood, London, 1931, p. 70

19. Pitt, 'Who Killed Lord Erroll?', p. 41

20. Ibid.

21. Maiden speech of 22nd Earl of Erroll, House of Lords, 1937

22. Int. J. D. Hopcraft by Dr Richard Waller, 26/11/73

23. Corresp. Mrs Joan Hemsted, 4/5/97

24. Int. the late Robert Creighton, Kifili, 9/7/96

25. de Janzé, *Vertical Land*, p. 53

26. Int. the late Rose Cartwright, Nairobi, 1974

27. Frampton, *Seven Candles*, p. 38

28. Extract from the diary of Lady Eileen Scott, 1919–37

29. Elspeth Huxley, *Out in the Midday Sun*, Chatto & Windus, 1985, p. 67

30. Livio Negri and Warwick Hembry, 'Altitude, Alcohol and Adultery: The British Aristocracy in Kenya Colony', BBC1 documentary, 4/6/93

31. Pitt, 'Who Killed Lord Erroll', p. 23

32. Int. Anne (Buxton) Wadley, Tilford, 22/1/96

33. Corresp. Alice Percival, 18/11/96

34. Fox, *White Mischief*, p. 37; int. the late Gertrude Alexander, York, 9/11/78

35. Frédéric de Janzé, *Tarred with the Same Brush*, Duckworth, London, 1929, p. 49

36. *The Times*, 10/11/55

37. Frampton, *Seven Candles*, p. 36

38. Int. Paul Spicer, Mombasa Club, 8/5/95

39. Peter de Polnay, *My Road – an Autobiography*, p. 78

40. Hayes, *Oserian*, p. 199

41. Ibid., p. 202; int. the late Gertrude Alexander, York, 9/11/78

42. Ibid.

43. Corresp. Mrs Joan Hemsted, 4/5/97

44. Tel. conv. Margaret McNeice, 26/3/98

45. Int. the late James Walker, Nairobi, 1978

46. de Janzé, *Tarred with the Same Brush*, p. 17

47. *EAS*, 6/11/26

48. Int. the late Robert Creighton, Kilifi, 7/7/96

49. de Janzé, *Vertical Land*, p. 38

50. Huxley, *Out in the Midday Sun*, pp. 48–9

51. Extract from the diary of Lady Eileen Scott, 1919–37

52. *EAS*, 15/4/38

53. Corresp. Anthea Venning, 26/2/97

54. Corresp. Anne (Buxton) Wadley, 20/6/96; int. Bunny Allen, Lamu, 17/2/95; Raymund de Trafford photograph album of 1926

55. Corresp. Terry Ellis, Truefitt & Hill, London, 15/10/96; corresp. Anne (Buxton) Wadley, 20/6/96

56. de Janzé, *Tarred with the Same Brush*, p. 30

57. Corresp. Anne (Buxton) Wadley, 15/8/97

58. Major-General Sir Alec Bishop, 'Look Back with Pleasure', unpub. memoir, p. 60

59. de Janzé, *Tarred with the Same Brush*, p. 109

60. de Janzé, *Vertical Land*, p. 52

61. de Janzé, *Tarred with the Same Brush*, pp. 122, 123

62. Ibid.

6 Oserian

1. de Janzé, *Tarred with the Same Brush*, p. 98; Arthur Poppy papers, 21/5/97

2. Int. the late Gertrude Alexander, York, 9/11/78

3. Keith Skinner, Boot Family Archive, 11/3/97

4. Ibid.; Hayes, *Oserian*, p. 197

5. Ibid., p. 225; int. the late Gertrude Alexander, 9/11/78

6. Int. Jack Bunyan, Norfolk, 1/11/96

7. de Janzé, *Tarred with the Same Brush*, p. 66

8. Mss. Brit. S.466, Rhodes House, Oxford

9. Corresp. Captain Gordon Fergusson, 8/2/98

10. Hayes, *Oserian*, p. 203

11. *EAS*, 28/1/28

12. *EAS*, 3/3/28

13. Corresp. Gordon Fergusson, 17/2/98

14. Arthur Poppy papers, 21/5/97

15. Pitt, 'Who Killed Lord Erroll?', pp. 23, 24

16. Int. the late Bettine Anderson, Aldeburgh, 12/1/97; Livio Negri and Warwick Hembry, 'Altitude, Alcohol and Adultery', BBC1, 4/6/93

17. Certified copy of an entry of marriage, 8/2/30; int. Patsy Chilton, Golini, 14/3/97; int. Molly Hoare, Farnham, 23/1/96; int. Yusuf Khan, Shanzu, 10/4/97

18. *Daily Express*, 19/6/28, p. 11

19. Press profile of 22nd Earl of Erroll, syndicated from London to *EAS*, 1934; corresp. Sir Iain Moncreiffe of that Ilk to Peggy Pitt, 28/7/55

20. Ibid.

21. Corresp. the late Mervyn Cowie, 12/7/96

22. *EAS*, 15/2/30

23. Certified copy of an entry of marriage, 8/2/30

24. Int. Anne (Buxton) Wadley, Tilford, 22/1/96

25. *EAS*, 15/2/30

26. *Silence Will Speak*, p. 284

27. Ibid.; Pitt, 'Who Killed Lord Erroll?'

28. Philip Ziegler, *King Edward VIII – The Official Biography*, Collins, London, 1990, p. 191

29. Best, *Happy Valley*, pp. 121–2

30. Corresp. Patricia Goldsmith, 16/7/98

31. Int. Patsy Chilton, Golini, 15/3/97

32. Int. Yusuf Khan, Shanzu, 10/4/97

33. Int. the late Gertrude Alexander, York, 9/11/78

34. Genesta Hamilton, *A Stone's Throw, Travels from Africa in Six Decades*, Hutchinson, London, 1986, p. 103

35. Sir Derek Erskine, unpub. memoir, p. 51

36. *EAS*, 16/7/32

37. Int. Pat Donnelly, Watamu, 14/5/99

38. Tel. conv. Yusuf Khan, 6/3/97

39. Hayes, *Oserian*, p. 240

40. Ibid.

41. Int. Jack Bunyan, Norfolk, 1/11/96; int. Yusuf Khan, Shanzu, 10/4/97

42. Int. the late Ginger Birkbeck, Likoni, 5/3/74

43. Hayes, *Oserian*, p. 199

44. Ibid., p. 202

45. Ibid.

46. Photograph album of the Khan family, 1934

47. Hayes, *Oserian*, p. 202

48. Mirella Ricciardi, *African Saga*, Collins, London, 1982, p. 69

49. Press profile of 22nd Earl of Erroll, syndicated from London, *EAS*, 1934

50. Tel. conv. Patsy Chilton, 10/7/95; corresp. Sir Charles Markham, 4/6/96

51. Int. Yusuf Khan, Shanzu, 10/4/97

52. Corresp. Jack Bunyan, 5/10/96

53. Hamilton, *A Stone's Throw*, pp. 134–5

54. Corresp. Margaret McNeice, 10/6/98

55. Int. the late Robert Creighton, Kilifi, 7/7/96

56. Ibid.; corresp. Margaret McNeice, 10/6/98

57. Tel. conv. Margaret McNeice, 26/3/98; corresp. Margaret McNeice, 10/6/98; int. the late Robert Creighton, Kilifi, 7/7/96

58. Corresp. Margaret McNeice, 10/6/98

59. Ibid.

60. Tel. conv. Margaret McNeice, 26/3/98

61. Ibid.

62. *EAS*, 23/5/31, p. 12; photograph album of Raymund de Trafford

63. Pitt, 'Who Killed Lord Erroll?', p. 28; *EAS*, 11/2/38, p. 8

64. Corresp. the late Eric R. Grove to 24th Earl of Erroll, 13/5/97, 6/6/97

65. Int. Patsy Chilton, Golini, 14/3/97

66. *EAS*, 10/1/31, 23/12/35

67. *EAS*, 23/12/35

68. *EAS*, 18/3/33

69. *Sunday Dispatch*, 1/7/34, p. 15

70. Corresp. Joan Hemsted, 4/5/97

71. Corresp. Joan Hemsted, 10/7/97

72. CC 56, 1941, p. 136

73. Int. Yusuf Khan, Shanzu, 10/4/97

74. Ibid.

75. Ricciardi, *African Saga*, pp. 32, 33

76. Corresp. Dorian Rocco, 22/1/97

77. Int. the late Sonny Bumpas, Watamu, 1978

78. Int. Patsy Chilton, London, 10/4/99

79. Hayes, *Oserian*, pp. 232, 233

80. Int. Yusuf Khan, Shanzu, 10/4/97

81. Corresp. Jack Bunyan, 6/12/96

82. Ibid.

83. Corresp. Anne (Buxton) Wadley, 20/6/96

84. Ibid., 10/5/96

85. Corresp. Jennifer Stutchbury, 9/8/96

86. Int. Jack Bunyan, 1/11/96

87. *EAS*, 28/6/35, p. 15

88. *EAS*, 12/4/35, p. 34

89. Michael Blundell, *A Love Affair with the Sun*, Kenway, Nairobi, 1993, p. 35

90. Int. Sir Charles Markham, Langata, 26/2/97

91. Int. Patsy Chilton, London, 5/12/96

92. Ibid.

93. *EAS*, 19/8/33, p. 24

94. Int. the late Robert Creighton, Kilifi, 9/7/96

95. Int. Alice Percival, Cambridge, 21/2/99

96. Int. Yusuf Khan, Shanzu, 10/4/97

7 Blackshirts in Kenya?

1. Hayes, *Oserian*, p. 247

2. *Tatler*, 16/5/34, p. 284

3. *Sunday Dispatch*, 29/4/34

4. Nicholas Mosley, *Rules of the Game: Beyond the Pale*, Secker & Warburg, London, 1993, p. 548

5. *Tatler*, 30/5/34; Richard Thurlow, *Fascism in Britain: A History, 1918–1985*, Blackwell, Oxford, p. 198

6. Int. 24th Earl of Erroll, 15/1/95

7. *Sunday Dispatch*, 17/6/34, p. 19

8. Thurlow, *Fascism in Britain*, p. 156; Roger Eatwell, *A History of Fascism*, Vintage, London, 1996

9. *EAS*, 14/7/34

10. Hayes, *Oserian*, p. 251

11. *EAS*, 21/7/34, p. 5; *EAS*, 7/7/34, p. 35

12. Ibid.

13. *EAS*, 1934, press profile of 22nd Earl of Erroll, syndicated from London

14. R.N. Money, Letters to the Editor, *EAS*, 25/7/34, p. 35

15. *EAS*, 11/8/34, p. 15

16. Elspeth Huxley, *Nellie: Letters from Africa*, Weidenfeld & Nicolson, London, 1980, p. 101

17. Ibid.

18. Corresp. Patricia Goldsmith, 14/6/98

19. Ibid.

20. *EAS*, 8/12/34, p. 11

21. Diaries of Daphne Monck-Mason Moore, Mss. Brit. Emp. S. 466, Rhodes House, Oxford; Huxley, *Out in the Midday Sun*, p. 52

22. *EAS*, 1/12/34

23. Ibid.

24. Ibid.

25. *EAS*, 8/12/34, p. 28

26. Caledonian Society Minute Book, 12/6/36

27. Huxley, *Nellie*, p. 105

28. *EAS*, 19/1/35

29. *EAS*, 19/4/35, p. 27

30. *EAS*, 19/7/35, p. 30

31. *EAS*, 26/7/35, p. 24

32. *EAS*, 13/9/35, p. 34

33. *EAS*, 20/9/35, p. 35

34. *EAS*, 13/9/35, p. 26

35. Ibid.

36. *EAS*, 13/9/35

37. *EAS*, 4/10/35

38. *EAS*, 20/9/35

39. Elspeth Huxley and Margery Perham, *Race and Politics in Kenya*, Faber, London, 1944, p. 125

40. Huxley, *Nellie*, pp. 112 and 32

41. Chenevix-Trench, *The Men Who Ruled Kenya*, p. 142

42. Ibid., p. 143

43. Int. Mrs Arthur Poppy, Devizes, 21/5/97; Arthur Poppy papers

44. Corresp. the Hon. Doreen Bathurst Norman, 5/12/96

45. *Illustrated London News*, 8/5/37,

p. 809; obit. Lady Erroll, *The Times*, 14/10/39, p. 10: *EAS*, 12/2/37

46. *EAS*, 12/2/37

47. Ibid., p. 37

48. *EAS*, 26/2/37, p. 7

49. *EAS*, 9/4/37

50. *EAS*, 2/7/37

51. *Hansard*, cols 425–6, 'Native Policy in the Empire', 9/6/37

52. *Hansard*, col. 440

53. *Hansard*, col. 442

54. *Hansard*, col. 443

55. Ibid.

56. Ibid.

57. *Hansard*, col. 449

58. 'Signifier', Conversation Piece, *EAS*, 2/7/37, p. 11

59. *Hansard*, 1937, cols 776–8

60. Unidentified newspaper cutting, 10/12/36

61. Unidentified newspaper cutting, 10/12/36

62. *EAS*, 5/11/37, p. 12

63. Unidentified newspaper cutting, 10/12/36

64. *EAS*, 19/11/37, p. 30

65. *EAS*, 11/2/38, p. 1

66. Ibid.

67. *EAS*, 4/3/38, p. 28

68. Ibid.

69. Ibid.

70. *EAS*, 19/11/37

71. *Kenya Legislative Council Debates*, vol. IV, 1–15

72. Ibid., HE Sir Robert Brooke-Popham, p. 3

73. Ibid., vol. IV, Defence, col. 6

74. Ibid., Kenya Land Commission recommendations, cols 110–47

75. Ibid., col. 125

76. Ibid., col. 126

77. Ibid.

78. *EAS*, 15/7/38, p. 38

79. Corresp. Helen Pearson, 5/1/96

80. Corresp. John Warren-Gash to Rt Hon. Merlin Hay, 24th Earl of Erroll, 18/3/88

81. *Kenya Legislative Council Debates*, vol. V, cols 205–9; *EAS*, 9/9/38

82. Huxley, *Out in the Midday Sun*, p. 16

83. *EAS*, 9/9/38

84. Ibid.

85. Corresp. Anthea Venning, 26/2/97

86. Corresp. Molly Hoare to Merlin Hay, 24th Earl of Erroll, 23/4/88

87. Corresp. Anna Miskin, April 1996

88. *EAS*, 7/10/38, p. 30

89. Ibid., p. 7

90. Ibid., p. 6

91. Int. Yusuf Khan, Shanzu, 10/4/97

92. *EAS*, 21/10/38, p. 27

93. *Cape Argus*, 24/1/41, p. 17

94. *EAS*, 21/10/38, p. 27

95. Ibid.

96. *EAS*, 14/10/38, p. 6

97. Ibid., p. 27

98. *EAS*, 14/10/38, p. 30

99. *EAS*, 28/10/38, p. 5

100. *EAS*, 25/11/38, p. 27

101. Int. Edward Rodwell, Mtwapa, 11/5/99

102. Ibid.; 'They Say' column, *EAS*, 4/11/38, p. 17

103. *EAS*, 11/11/38, pp. 5–6

104. *Kenya Legislative Council Debates*, vol. VI, cols 125–38, 410–23

105. Ibid.

106. Ibid.

107. *Kenya Legislative Council Debates*, vol. VI, col. 409

108. Ibid.

109. *Kenya Legislative Council Debates*, vol. VI, cols 409–11, 423, 461

110. *Kenya Legislative Council Debates*, vol. VI, col. 419

111. *Kenya Legislative Council Debates*, vol. VI, col, 461, 17/11/38

112. Ibid.; int. Jack Bunyan, Norfolk, 1/11/96

113. *Kenya Legislative Council Debates*, vol. VI, col. 461

114. Ibid.

115. Int. Mrs Arthur Poppy, Devizes, 21/5/97; Arthur Poppy papers

116. Corresp. Jack Bunyan, 20/3/97

117. *White Mischief*, p. 48

118. Tel. conv. Petal Allen, 30/12/94; int. Anne (Buxton) Wadley, Tilford, 22/1/96; Corresp. Anne (Buxton) Wadley, 10/5/96

119. Corresp. Anne (Buxton) Wadley, 10/5/96

120. Int. Peter Filmer, Sturminster Newton, 11/11/96; Sallyport papers

121. Int. Yusuf Khan, Shanzu, 10/4/97

8 Josh Posh on the Warpath

1. Tel. conv. Molly Hoare, 17/9/95

2. Mary S. Lovell, *Straight on Till Morning*, Century Hutchinson, London, 1987, p. 212

3. Int. Patsy Chilton, Golini, 14/3/97

4. *EAS*, 13/1/39, p. 30

5. *EAS*, 17/2/39, p. 7

6. *EAS*, 20/1/39, p. 15

7. *EAS*, 24/2/39, p. 27

8. Ibid.

9. Int. the late Roger Howard, London; Michael J. Macoun, *Wrong Place, Right Time: Policing the End of an Empire*, Radcliffe Press, Oxford, 1997, introduction, p. xviii

10. Ibid., Appendix B, 'Pre-war Nazi Penetration of East Africa and Its Potential Threat, 1939–1940', pp. 129, 130

11. Nicholas Best, *Happy Valley*, pp. 137, 138

12. Int. Anna Miskin, London, 31/10/96

13. Corresp. Walter Harragin to Sir Henry Monck-Mason Moore; PRO, Kew, HMM, private corresp. CO967; *Kenya Weekly News*, 20/10/39; *EAS*, 14/7/39, p. 5

14. 'This Name Makes News', unidentified newspaper cutting, S. Africa

15. *EAS*, 17/2/39, p. 27

16. Corresp. 22nd Earl of Erroll to Mervyn Cowie, 21/2/39

17. Corresp. the late Mervyn Cowie, 29/5/96

18. Ibid.

19. *Kenya Legislative Council Debates*, vol. VI, cols 38–42, 14/4/49

20. *Kenya Legislative Council Debates*, vol. VI, col. 114, 19/4/39

21. Ibid.

22. *EAS*, 5/5/39

23. *EAS*, 19/5/39, p. 13; corresp. the late Elspeth Huxley, 14/4/96

24. *EAS*, 19/5/39, p. 13

25. *EAS*, 28/7/39, p. 23

26. *EAS*, 17/7/39, 21/7/39, p. 25

27. *EAS*, 14/7/39

28. Ibid., p. 5

29. Ibid.

30. Ibid.

31. Ibid.

32. Ibid.

33. *EAS*, 28/7/39

34. Guy Campbell, *The Charging Buffalo: A History of the Kenya Regiment 1937–1963*, Leo Cooper/ Secker & Warburg, London, 1986, p. 27

35. W. W. Crosskill, *The Two Thousand Mile War*, Robert Hale, London, 1980, pp. 80, 81, 82

36. Campbell, *The Charging Buffalo* p. 27

37. Crosskill, *The Two Thousand Mile War*, p. 81

38. M. F. Hill, *The Permanent Way: The Story of the Kenya and Uganda Railway*, English Press, Nairobi, 1949, p. 539

39. Corresp. Molly Hoare, 23/9/95

40. Corresp. Anne (Buxton) Wadley, 10/5/96; conv. Patsy Chilton, London, 10/4/99

41. Int. Anna Miskin, London, 31/10/96; int. Molly Hoare, Farnham, 23/1/96; int. Kath Biggs, Kimpton, 1/8/95

42. Corresp. Joan Hemsted, 4/5/97

43. Corresp. Molly Hoare, 23/9/96; int. Kath Biggs, Kimpton, 1/8/95

44. Int. Patsy Chilton, Golini, 15/3/97

45. Corresp. Joan Hemsted, 4/5/97

46. Int. Molly Hoare, Farnham, 23/1/96

47. Fox, *White Mischief*, p. 47

48. Hayes, *Oserian*, p. 266

49. Obit., *EAS*, 20/10/39, p. 24

50. Ibid.

51. Hayes, *Oserian*, p. 266

52. Crosskill, *The Two Thousand Mile War*, p. 200

53. Corresp. Sir Iain Moncreiffe of that Ilk to Peggy Pitt, 28/7/55; WO to 24th Earl of Erroll, 28/2/83; MOD Records, 1983

54. Int. Patsy Chilton, London, 12/7/95

55. *Kenya Legislative Council Debates*, vol. VIII, 4/9/39, 5/9/39

56. Ibid.

57. Ibid.

58. *EAS*, 15/9/39

59. Ibid.

60. Sir Derek Erskine, unpublished memoir, p. 67

61. *EAS*, 27/10/39, p. 21

62. Erskine, memoir, pp. 67, 68

63. Ibid.

64. Corresp. Sir Wilfrid Havelock, 2/5/96

65. Tel. conv. M. S. Beyers, 10/2/96

66. Corresp. Sir Wilfrid Havelock, 2/5/96

67. *Kenya Weekly News*, 29/9/39, p. 28

68. John Fox, 'Fifty Years After, Lord Erroll's Death is Still a Mystery', *Sunday Nation*, 2/6/91; int. Richard Wilson, 1979

69. Corresp. Anthea Venning, 6/12/96

70. Corresp. the late Mervyn Cowie, Elected Members' Organisation, G2, 21/2/39

71. Corresp. Sir Wilfrid Havelock, 2/5/96

72. Pitt, 'Who Killed Lord Erroll?', p. 24

73. Int. Jack Bunyan, Norfolk, 1/11/96

74. Corresp. John Millard, 25/3/97; John Millard, *Never a Dull Moment: The Autobiography of John Millard, Administrator, Soldier, Farmer*, Silent Books, Cambridge, 1996, p. 82

75. Int. Yusuf Khan, Shanzu, 10/4/97

76. Frampton, *Seven Candles*, p. 80

77. Blundell, *A Love Affair with the Sun*, p. 47

78. Ibid.

79. *Kenya Weekly News*, 20/10/39, p. 8

80. Ibid.

81. Ibid., pp. 11, 22

82. Ibid.

83. Int. Sir Charles Markham, 3rd Bt, Langata, 26/2/97

84. Ibid.

85. Mss. Afr. S. 1120, III 9/20, Brooke-Popham papers, Rhodes House, Oxford

86. *Kenya Weekly News*, 29/9/39, p. 8

87. Huxley, *Nellie*, p. 135

88. *Kenya Weekly News*, 11/11/39, p. 20

89. *EAS*, 14/7/39, p.5

90. Bishop, 'Look Back with Pleasure', unpublished memoir, pp. 50, 51

91. Corresp. Joan Hemsted, 10/7/97

92. Obit., *The Times*, 28/3/64

93. *The Times*, 10/11/39, p. 4

94. Sallyport papers, 15/12/97; corresp. Sir Charles Markham, 3rd Bt, 20/3/96; int. Sir Charles Markham, Langata, 26/2/97

95. Sallyport papers, 15/12/97

96. Tel. conv. Neil Tyfield, 25/6/96

97. Corresp. Anthea Venning, 25/9/97

98. *Kenya Legislative Council Debates*, 17/11/39, Divorce Bill, cols 153–4, 181–2

99. Corresp. Brigadier Michael Biggs, 17/1/97, 28/7/98

100. Int. Kath Biggs, Kimpton, 1/8/95; int. Anna Miskin, London, 15/4/96; int. Lee Harragin, London, 23/3/95

101. Ibid.

102. Hill, *The Permanent Way*, p. 556

103. Corresp. Mervyn Carnelly, 8/2/97; *The History of the Kenya Armoured Car Regiment during the Abyssinian Campaign 1939–1941*, compiled and published by M. D. Carnelly, 1996

104. Int. the late Ginger Birkbeck, Likoni, 5/3/74; int. the late Robert Creighton, Kilifi, 9/7/96

105. Mss. Afr. S. 1120, Rhodes House, Oxford

106. *EAS*, 26/1/40

107. Army Record Office corresp., Sir Iain Moncreiffe of that Ilk, 4/2/83, MOD ref. WO 169/699. FG 18/40; A.2., PRO, C. D. Chalmers to Sir Iain Moncreiffe of that Ilk, 28/2/83

108. S. H. Powell, diary, 24/11/40; Mss. Afr. S. 1120, Rhodes House, Oxford

109. Crosskill, *The Two Thousand Mile War*, Churchill's minute, 10/8/40, p. 77

110. Int. the late Lt.-Col. John Gouldbourn, Lytham St Anne's, 8/10/95

111. Ibid.

112. Ibid.

113. Corresp. Peter Filmer, 2/8/00

114. Int. Peter Filmer, Sturminster Newton, 11/11/96

115. Sallyport papers, 15/12/97

116. Brooke-Popham personal corresp. CO967/163, Brooke-Popham papers; Mss. Afr. S. 1120, III 9/20, Rhodes House, Oxford

117. Tel. conv. Eleanor Fazan, 30/9/97

118. Ibid.

119. *Kenya Legislative Council Debates*, vol. XVI, 1940

120. *Kenya Legislative Council Debates*, second session, vol. X, 6/8/40, 14/8/40

9 The Infernal Triangle

1. Pitt, 'Who Killed Lord Erroll?', p. 87

2. 'Christmas at Karen', *Sunday Times Magazine*, 21/12/69, p. 9

3. Ibid., pp. 26, 27

4. Corresp. Captain Gordon Fergusson, 25/7/95

5. Pitt, 'Who Killed Lord Erroll?', p. 7

6. Rudyard Kipling, *The Irish Guards in the Great War: The First Battalion*, pp. 30, 31

7. Pitt, 'Who Killed Lord Erroll?', pp. 7, 8

8. Obit., *Daily Telegraph*, 17/3/95

9. Int. Edome Broughton-Adderly, London, 6/7/95

10. Int. Cyril Wingfield, Doddington, 18/7/95

11. Scrapbook of Vera Boscawen, 1912–13, 30/7/13

12. Corresp. Sir Charles Markham, 26/3/97

13. Int. Patsy Chilton, Golini, 15/3/97

14. Corresp. Keith Skinner, 30/3/96

15. Int. Patsy Chilton, London, 9/5/97

16. Int. Anna Miskin, London, 31/10/96

17. Ibid.

18. Corresp. Sir Charles Markham, 3rd Bt, 26/11/95

19. Pitt, 'Who Killed Lord Erroll?', p. 5

20. Ibid., p. 6

21. Ibid.

22. *Natal Mercury*, 2/11/40, p. 7

23. Pitt, 'Who Killed Lord Erroll?', p. 6

24. Sallyport papers, 15/12/97

25. Pitt, 'Who Killed Lord Erroll?', pp. 22, 29, 33; corresp. Sir Iain Moncreiffe of that Ilk to Peggy Pitt, 28/7/85

26. Pitt, 'Who Killed Lord Erroll?', p. 290

27. Ibid., p. 15

28. Ibid.

29. Corresp. Eve Pollecoff, 4/12/95

30. Corresp. Tony Trafford, 26/2/98

31. CC 56, p. 3

32. Int. Mervyn Fox, 4/5/97; corresp. Mervyn Fox, 12/2/97; tel. conv. Mervyn Fox, 8/5/97; CC 56, pp. 248–76; 'Who Killed Lord Erroll?', p. 21

33. CC 56, p. 300

34. Int. Patsy Chilton, London, 12/7/95

35. Pitt, 'Who Killed Lord Erroll?', p. 26

36. Sir Derek Erskine, unpublished memoir, p. 52

37. Int. Molly Hoare, Farnham, 23/1/96

38. Int. Peter Filmer, Sturminster Newton, 11/11/96

39. Corresp. Anne (Buxton) Wadley, 16/7/96

40. Int. Patsy Chilton, Golini, 15/3/97

41. Ibid., 13/5/95; Negri and Hembry, 'Altitude, Alcohol and Adultery', BBC1 documentary, 4/6/93

42. CC 56, p. 291

43. Erskine, unpublished memoir, p. 52

44. Int. Anthea Venning, Croydon, 26/11/96

45. Corresp. Molly Hoare, 23/9/95

46. CC 56, pp. 136, 138, 139, 146;

Pitt, 'Who Killed Lord Erroll?', Diary of Events January 1941, p. 17

47. Corresp. Molly Hoare, 25/9/95; int. Molly Hoare, Farnham, 23/1/96

48. Pitt, 'Who Killed Lord Erroll?', Diary of Events January 1941, p. 17

49. Int. the late Margaret Kirkland, Malindi, 4/11/94

50. Int. Kath Biggs, Kimpton, 1/8/96

51. Int. Peter Colmore, London, 6/7/95

52. Int. Yusuf Khan, Shanzu, 10/4/97

53. CC 56, pp. 220–2

54. Corresp. Anne (Buxton) Wadley, 19/10/96

55. Tel. conv. Anthea Venning, 17/5/97

56. Int. Patsy Chilton, Golini, 15/3/97

57. Pitt, 'Who Killed Lord Erroll?', p. 147

58. Ibid.

59. Fox, *White Mischief*, p. 74

60. Ibid., p. 75

61. Ibid.

62. Pitt, 'Who Killed Lord Erroll?', Diary of Events January 1941, p. 17

63. Ibid.

64. Int. Patsy Chilton, London, 10/8/95

65. Pitt, 'Who Killed Lord Erroll?', Diary of Events January 1941, p. 17

66. Int. Patsy Chilton, London, 10/8/95

67. CC 56, p. 139; Pitt, 'Who Killed Lord Erroll?', p. 29

68. Ibid., p. 297

69. Pitt, 'Who Killed Lord Erroll?', p. 47

70. Erskine, unpublished memoir, p. 53

71. Tel. conv. Petal Allen, Lamu, 30/12/94

72. Erskine, unpublished memoir, p. 53

73. CC 56, p. 220

74. Ibid., p. 221

75. Fox, *White Mischief*, p. 81

76. CC 56, p. 17

77. Ibid., p. 5

78. Ibid., p. 17

79. 'Jealousy: The Peer in the Gravel Pit', *Crimes of Passion*, Treasure Press, 1973, p. 30

80. Pitt, 'Who Killed Lord Erroll?', p. 256; CC 56, p. 220

81. Ibid.

82. *Daily Telegraph*, 20/3/41

83. Ibid.

84. Erskine, unpublished memoir, p. 54

85. Ibid., pp. 51, 52

86. Corresp. Shirley Heriz-Smith, 14/7/97

87. CC 56, p. 297

88. Pitt, 'Who Killed Lord Erroll?', p. 61

89. Ibid.

90. Int. Molly Hoare, Farnham, 23/1/96; int. Kath Biggs, Kimpton, 1/8/95; int. Lee Harragin, London 23/3/95; corresp. David Christie-Miller, 11/11/94; corresp. the late Lt.-Col. John Gouldbourn to 24th Earl of Erroll, 18/3/88

91. Int. Patsy Chilton, Golini, 15/3/97

92. Int. Kath Biggs, Kimpton, 1/8/95

93. Benjamin Bennett, *Genius for the Defence*, Howard Timmins, Cape Town, 1959

94. Pitt, 'Who Killed Lord Erroll?', p. 63

95. CC 56, p. 222

96. Int. the late Margaret Kirkland, Malindi, 4/11/94

97. Fox, *White Mischief*, p. 83

98. CC 56, p. 47

99. Ibid.

100. Int. Edward Rodwell, Mtwapa, 28/7/97

101. CC 56, p. 301

102. Ibid, p. 223

103. Connolly and Fox, 'Christmas at Karen', *Sunday Times Magazine*, 21/12/69

104. Fox, *White Mischief*, p. 275

105. Sallyport papers, 15/12/97

10 The Investigation

1. CC 56, pp. 34–6, 54, 55, 232; Pitt, 'Who Killed Lord Erroll?', pp. 67–72

2. Ibid.

3. Ibid.

4. Ibid., pp. 95, 96

5. Ibid.; int. the late John Carter, Nairobi, 13/3/90

6. Corresp. Beatrice Bewes, 3/5/96; corresp. Mervyn Morgan to Edward Rodwell, 8/1/88; corresp. Nancy Miller, 24/8/98

7. CC 56, p. 133 (from Fentum's sketch, p. 128 ibid.); Rupert Furneaux, *A Crime Documentary: The Murder of Lord Erroll*, Stevens, London, 1961, p. 4

8. Int. Dr Geoffrey Timms, Salisbury, 4/8/95; CC 56, pp. 54, 55

9. Ibid.

10. Furneaux, *The Murder of Lord Erroll*, pp. 3, 4

11. CC 56, pp. 126–36

12. Ibid., pp. 42, 45, 53

13. Ibid., pp. 126–36

14. Ibid.

15. CC 56, p. 131

16. Ibid., p. 133

17. Furneaux, *The Murder of Lord Erroll*, p. 4

18. Int. Dr Geoffrey Timms, Salisbury, 4/8/95

19. Ibid.

20. Furneaux, *The Murder of Lord Erroll*, p. 20

21. *Natal Mercury*, 28/2/41, p. 18

22. CC 56, p. 127

23. Ibid., p. 84; Pitt, 'Who Killed Lord Erroll?', p. 151

24. CC 56, p. 86

25. Pitt, 'Who Killed Lord Erroll?', p. 235

26. *The Times*, 1/3/41, p. 3; *Natal Mercury*, 28/2/41, p. 18

27. Int. the late John Carter, Nairobi, 13/3/90; int. Mrs Arthur Poppy, Devizes, 21/5/97; Tanganyika police report on Arthur James Poppy, 30/9/52

28. *Kenya Police Review*, 1939

29. CC 56, p. 24

30. Furneaux, *The Murder of Lord Erroll*, p. 4

31. Fox, *White Mischief*, p. 95

32. *Glasgow Herald*, 25/1/41; *The Times*, 25/1/41

33. *EAS*, 27/1/41

34. Ibid.

35. Fox, *White Mischief*, p. 94

36. Ibid.

37. Sir Iain Moncreiffe, review of *White Mischief*, *Books and Bookmen*, February 1983

38. Int. 24th Earl of Erroll, Bedfordshire, 7/8/95

39. Tel. conv. Christian, Lady Hesketh, 11/12/98

40. Int. Peter Filmer, Sturminster Newton, 11/11/96; *Natal Mercury*, 25/1/41, p. 20

41. Ibid.

42. Ibid.; Fox, *White Mischief*, p. 246

43. Int. Peter Filmer, Sturminster Newton, 11/11/96

44. S. H. Powell, diary, Mss. Afr. S. 1121, Rhodes House, Oxford

45. Int. Anthea Venning, Croydon, 26/11/96

46. Pitt, 'Who Killed Lord Erroll?', p. 74

47. Ibid., p. 75

48. Ibid.

49. Ibid., p. 75

50. Fox, *White Mischief*, p. 277

51. Corresp. Lady Ranfurly, 3/4/96

52. Tel. conv. Patsy Chilton, 10/7/95; Fox, *White Mischief*, p. 276

53. Corresp. the late Lt.-Col. John Gouldbourn, 21/9/95; int. Lytham St Anne's, 8/10/95

54. Pitt, 'Who Killed Lord Erroll?', p. 78

55. Pitt, 'Who Killed Lord Erroll?', pp. 29, 78

56. Ibid., p. 78

57. Tel. conv. Juanita Carberry, 23/6/98; Pitt, 'Who Killed Lord Erroll?', pp. 199, 200

58. Pitt, 'Who Killed Lord Erroll?', pp. 99, 100

59. Int. Cyril Wingfield, Doddington, 18/7/95

60. Pitt, 'Who Killed Lord Erroll?', pp. 100, 101

61. Ibid., p. 78

62. Tel. conv. Juanita Carberry, 20/6/98

63. Ibid.

64. Ibid.

65. Int. Kath Biggs, Kimpton, 1/8/95

66. Erskine, unpublished memoir,

pp. 52–4; Pitt, 'Who Killed Lord Erroll?', pp. 21, 22; CC 56, pp. 248–76

67. CC 56, p. 255

68. *EAS*, 27/1/41

69. *Natal Mercury*, 28/1/41, p. 11

70. Pitt, 'Who Killed Lord Erroll?', p. 93

71. Corresp. Juanita Carberry, 16/6/98

72. Int. Juanita Carberry, Likoni, 22/1/77; int. Molly Hoare, Farnham, 23/1/96; int. Pat Donnelly, Watamu, 11/3/96; Fox, *White Mischief*, p. 90; corresp. Juanita Carberry, 16/6/98

73. Int. Juanita Carberry, London, 4/2/96

74. Fox, *White Mischief*, p. 283

75. Pitt, 'Who Killed Lord Erroll?', p. 108

76. PRO, Kew, CO 628/36; trnsf. CO 38507/41; corresp. Keith Skinner, 4/4/97

77. Corresp. Peter Ayre, 24/8/96

78. Tel. conv. Nancy Miller, 26/4/98

79. Tel. conv. Charles Howard, 10/6/95

80. Int. the late William Pitt, Oxford, 27/6/95

81. CC 56, pp. 95, 96

82. Int. Peter Filmer, Sturminster Newton, 11/11/96

83. Int. Patsy Chilton, London, 19/5/97

84. Pitt, 'Who Killed Lord Erroll?', p. 122

85. Int. Mrs Arthur Poppy, Devizes, 21/5/97

86. Furneaux, *The Murder of Lord Erroll*, pp. 32–4

87. Pitt, 'Who Killed Lord Erroll?', pp. 177–8

88. Ibid., p. 112

89. Pitt, 'Who Killed Lord Erroll?', p. 116

90. Tel. conv. Patsy J. (Atkinson) Marra, 6/6/95

91. Ibid.

92. Aaron Maisels, *A Life at Law: The Memoirs of I. A. Maisels, QC*, Jonathan Ball, South Africa, 1998, p. 39

93. Ibid.; Connolly and Fox, 'Christmas at Karen', 21/12/69, p. 13

94. Pitt, 'Who Killed Lord Erroll?', p. 119

95. *EAS*, 28/3/41, p. 20

96. *Kenya Legislative Council Debates*, vol. XI, 16/4/41

97. *EAS*, 4/4/41

98. Int. the late Gertrude Alexander, York, 9/11/78

99. Pitt, 'Who Killed Lord Erroll?', p. 121

100. Ibid., p. 122

101. CC 56, pp. 200, 202

102. Pitt, 'Who Killed Lord Erroll?', pp. 121, 122

103. CC 56, pp. 200, 202

104. Tel. conv. Patsy Chilton, 10/7/95; ints Patsy Chilton, London, 12/7/95, 2/12/96; Golini, 15/3/97

105. Bennett, *Genius for the Defence*, p. 239

106. Pitt, 'Who Killed Lord Erroll?', p. 146

107. Ibid., p. 112

108. Int. Patsy Chilton, London, 10/8/95

109. Tel. conv. Juanita Carberry, 20/6/98

110. Int. Patsy Chilton, Golini, 15/5/97

111. Fox, *White Mischief*, p. 154

112. Sylvia Osborne, 'White Mischief: Does This Durban Woman Know Whodunnit?', *Personality*, 14/11/88

113. Bennett, *Genius for the Defence*, pp. 248–54

114. Int. the late Colin H. Imray, Haywards Heath, 17/6/95

115. Bennett, *Genius for the Defence*, p. 229

116. Corresp. Patsy (Atkinson) Marra, 11/9/98

117. Erskine, unpublished memoir, p. 56

118. Pitt, 'Who Killed Lord Erroll?', p. 246

119. Letter from Broughton to his aunt Evelyn, 29/7/41

120. Corresp. Patsy (Atkinson) Marra, 11/9/98

121. Pitt, 'Who Killed Lord Erroll?', p. 273

122. Tel. conv. Shirley Heriz-Smith, 18/8/98

123. Fox, *White Mischief*, p. 272

124. Ibid., p. 213

125. Connolly and Fox, 'Christmas at Karen', 21/12/69, p. 15

126. Ibid.

127. Fox, *White Mischief*, p. 272

128. Int. Sir Charles Markham, 3rd Bt, Langata, 26/2/98

129. Pitt, 'Who Killed Lord Erroll?', Appendix

130. Ibid., p. 296

131. Undated letter from Eric R. Grove to Sir Iain Moncreiffe of that Ilk

11 The Sallyport papers

1. Pitt, 'Who Killed Lord Erroll?', p. 287

2. Ibid.; corresp. Patsy Chilton, 12/7/95; Tel. conv. Patsy Chilton, 13/3/97

3. Int. Patsy Chilton, London, 2/12/96

4. Corresp. Rupert Allason, 16/11/95

5. Tel. conv., Persimmon, London, 18/1/96; int. Persimmon, London, 31/1/96

6. Int. B. A. Young, Cheltenham, 30/7/98

7. Corresp. Jack Bunyan, 15/11/96, p. 2

8. Int. the late Tony Trafford, London, 10/6/98

9. Corresp. Major E. H. O'Hara, 1/11/98; tel. conv. Major E. H. O'Hara, 28/3/99

10. Sallyport papers, 15/12/97

11. Int. Tony Trafford, Portsmouth, 28/5/97

12. Sallyport papers, 15/12/97

13. Ibid.

14. Ibid., pp. 211–32

12 All's Fair in Love and War

1. Corresp. Vera Atkins, 22/1/98

2. Corresp. Jack Bunyan, 2/5/97

3. Macoun, *Wrong Place, Right Time*, p. 22

4. Tel. conv. Diana Lane, 12/2/99

5. Corresp. Jack Bunyan, 20/2/99

6. Corresp. S. P. J. O'Mara, 10/2/99

7. Corresp. Jack Bunyan, 20/2/99

8. Bishop, 'Look Back with Pleasure', unpublished memoir, pp. 59–62

9. Hermione Ranfurly, *To War with Whitaker*, Heinemann, London, 1994, p.73

10. Corresp. Lady Ranfurly, 31/10/97

11. Int. Edward Rodwell, Mtwapa, 28/7/97

12. Corresp. S. P. J. O'Mara, 10/2/99

13. Fox, *White Mischief*, p. 277

14. Int. Anna Miskin, London, 31/10/96

15. Int. Ronald Duke, London, 20/5/97

16. Int. the late Colin. H. Imray, Haywards Heath, 17/6/95

17. M. R. D. Foot, *History of the Second World War, SOE in France*, HMSO, London, 1966; int. Ronald Duke, London, 20/5/97

18. Pitt, 'Who Killed Lord Erroll?', p. 295; int. Ronald Duke, London, 20/5/97

19. Int. Edward Rodwell, Mtwapa Creek, 14/2/95; Rodwell papers, 26/4/95

20. Corresp. Helen Pearson; Broughton papers, private collection, 26/4/95

21. Int. Stephen Dorril, 4/8/99

22. Int. Anna Miskin, London, 31/10/96

23. Int. the late Tony Trafford, Petersfield, 2/4/98

24. Corresp. Anthea Venning, 20/1/97, 22/1/97

25. Corresp. S. P. J. O'Mara, 21/1/99

26. Ibid.

27. Corresp. Jock Delves Broughton to his aunt Evelyn, 29/7/41

28. Int. the late Tony Trafford, Old Portsmouth, 28/5/96; corresp. Anthea Venning, 6/12/96, p. 6; Sallyport papers, 15/12/97

29. Int. the late Colin H. Imray, Haywards Heath, 17/6/95

30. Fox, *White Mischief*, p. 144

31. Ibid., p. 158

32. Ibid.

33. Ibid., p. 144

34. Ibid., p. 146

35. Ibid., p. 159

36. Tel. conv. Patsy Mara 27/4/00

37. Corresp. Dennis Leefe 8/4/00

38. Tel. conv. Lee Harragin, 23/3/95

39. Pitt, 'Who Killed Lord Erroll?', p. 285

40. Corresp. Elspeth Huxley, 16/11/94

41. Int. Kath Biggs, Kimpton, 1/8/95

42. Ibid.; Negri and Hembry, 'Altitude, Alcohol and Adultery', BBC1 documentary, 4/6/93

43. Corresp. the late Winifred Disney to Edward Rodwell, 27/2/88

44. Corresp. David Christie-Miller, 31/9/96

45. Corresp. Keith Skinner, 30/3/97

46. Corresp. Sir Jock Delves Broughton to his aunt Evelyn, 29/7/41

47. Int. Kath Biggs, Kimpton, 1/8/95; int. Anna Miskin, London, 31/10/96

48. Int. Edome Broughton-Adderly, London, 6/7/95

49. CC 56, pp. 145, 289, 293, 298, 301, 315; corresp. Helen Pearson, 5/1/96

50. Int. the late Colin H. Imray, Haywards Heath, 17/6/95

51. Fox, *White Mischief*, p. 80

52. Corresp. David Christie-Miller, 11/11/94; Sallyport papers, 15/12/97

53. Corresp. the late Lt.-Col. John Gouldbourn, 21/9/95

54. Int. the late Lt.-Col. John Gouldbourn, Lytham St Anne's, 8/10/95

55. Corresp. the late Lt.-Col. John Gouldbourn, 21/9/95; int. 8/10/95

56. Anthony Powell, *Journals 1982–1986*, Heinemann, London, 1993, p. 49

57. Corresp. Lady Ranfurly, 23/4/96

58. Int. Alice Percival, Vipingo, 21/3/96

59. Corresp. Alice Percival, 17/4/96

60. Int. David Dickinson, Grantham, 11/10/96

61. Pitt, 'Who Killed Lord Erroll?', p. 290

62. Int. Edome Broughton-Adderly, London, 6/7/95

63. Leda Farrant, *Diana, Lady Delamere, and the Murder of Lord Erroll*, Nairobi, 1997, pp. 94–5

64. Imray papers: corresp. the late Colin H. Imray to Captain Gordon Fergusson, 5/9/94

65. Corresp. Kate Challis to Edward Rodwell 13/11/88

66. Corresp. S. P. J. O'Mara, 21/9/96

67. Ibid., 20/4/99

68. Ibid., 4/8/97

69. Ibid., 25/3/98

70. Corresp. Helen Pearson, 24/1/96

71. Ibid.

72. Ibid., 22/4/99, 25/4/99

73. Cave Brown, *Bodyguard of Lies*, p. 168

74. Martin Gilbert, *Churchill, a Life*, Heinemann, London, 1991, pp. 637–8

75. Ibid., pp. 650–1

76. Cave Brown, *Bodyguard of Lies*, p. 7

77. David Stafford, *Churchill and the Secret Service*, John Murray, London, 1997, p. 186

78. Basil Davidson, *Special Operations Europe*, Gollancz, London, 1980, p. 262

79. Ibid., p. 79

80. Deacon, *A History of the British Secret Service*, p. 344

81. Cave Brown, *Bodyguard of Lies*, p. 7

82. M. R. D. Foot, *SOE, an Outline History of the Special Operations Executive 1940–46*, BBC, London, 1988, p. 76

83. Michael Evans, 'Sex: SOE's Secret Weapon', *The Times*, 23/7/98, p. 7

84. Corresp. Nick Day, 23/3/98

85. Deacon, *A History of the British Secret Service*, p. 283

86. Corresp. Nick Day, 23/3/98

87. Corresp. S. P. J. O'Mara, 10/2/99

88. *EAS*, 10/2/39

89. *Natal Mercury*, 6/11/40

90. *EAS*, 1/4/33

91. *EAS*, 3/2/39

92. Corresp. S. P. J. O'Mara, 13/8/99

93. Fox, *White Mischief*, p. 3; corresp. John Parker, 25/6/98

94. Thurlow, *Fascism in Britain*, p. 189

Epilogue

1. Int. the late Kathleen Fielden, 30/8/96

2. Corresp. Robert Young, 24/7/97

3. PRO, FO 371/30255 P. Dixon minute, 19/4/41

4. CO 533–529/12; Neil Balfour and Sallay Mackay, *Paul of Yugoslavia, Britain Maligned Friend*, Hamish Hamilton, London, 1980, pp. 266–7

Appendix

1. S. P. J. O'Mara, 6/6/00

2. Int. the late Lt.-Col. John Gouldbourn, 8/10/95

3. Corresp. S. P. J. O'Mara, 14/7/00

4. Corresp. the late Jack Bunyan, 2/5/97; corresp. S. P. J. O'Mara, 13/4/00, 13/6/00

5. Int. the late Lt.-Col. John Gouldbourn, 8/10/95; Negri and Hembry, 'Altitude, Alcohol and

Adultery', BBC1 documentary, 4/6/93 – Frankie Isley, Gerry Edwards; Mrs Pearson, confidential corresp., 5/1/96

6. Lyn Sampson, *Style*, December/January 1989

7. Corresp. S. P. J. O'Mara, 21/7/00

8. *Chesire Examiner*, 19/12/42; Liverpool Coroner's Records, Ref: 347 Cor/L/8/50 (508)

9. Corresp. Mervyn Morgan to Edward Rodwell, 8/1/88

10. Corresp. S. P. J. O'Mara, 13/4/00

11. Corresp. S. P. J. O'Mara, 14/7/00

12. Ibid.

13. Imray papers; corresp. Captain Gordon Fergusson, 5/9/94

14. Corresp. S. P. J. O'Mara, 6/6/00–13/6/00

15. Corresp. S. P. J. O'Mara, 7/4/00

16. Corresp. David Christie-Miller, 20/7/95

17. Ranfurly, *To War with Whitaker*, p. 114

18. Corresp. S. P. J. O'Mara, 17/4/00

19. Rupert Furneaux, *The Murder of Lord Errol*, p. 268

20. C. Case 56, pp. 198–9

21. Fox, *White Mischief*, p. 160

22. Ibid., p. 193

23. Corresp. S. P. J. O'Mara, 14/7/00

24. Corresp. S. P. J. O'Mara, 13/6/00–16/6/00

25. Ibid.

26. Corresp. S. P. J. O'Mara, 1/7/00

27. Corresp. S. P. J. O'Mara, 13/6/00

28. Int. the late Lt.-Col. John Gouldbourn, Lytham St Anne's, 8/10/95

29. Corresp. S. P. J. O'Mara, 14/7/00

30. Corresp. S. P. J. O'Mara, 17/4/00

Bibliography

D'Abernon, Vincent Edgar, *An Ambassador of Peace*, vols I and II, 1929–31

Belford, Barbara, *Bram Stoker, A Biography of the Author of Dracula*, Weidenfeld & Nicolson, London, 1996

Bennett, Benjamin, *Genius for the Defence*, Howard Timmins, Cape Town, 1959

Best, Nicholas, *Happy Valley: The Story of the British in Kenya*, Secker & Warburg, London, 1979

Blixen, Karen, *Out of Africa*, Cape, London, 1964

Blundell, Michael, *A Love Affair with the Sun – A Memoir of Seventy Years in Kenya*, Kenway Publications, Nairobi, 1993

Bloch, Michael, *The Secret File of the Duke of Windsor*, Bantam, London, 1988

——*Ribbentrop*, Bantam, London, 1992

Bower, Tom, *The Perfect English Spy: Sir Dick White and the Secret War 1935–90*, Heinemann, London, 1995

Burke's Peerage and Baronetage

Burrard, Major Sir Gerald, *The Identification of Firearms and Forensic Ballistics*, Herbert Jenkins, London, 1934

Campbell, Guy, *The Charging Buffalo: A History of the Kenya Regiment 1937–1963*, Leo Cooper/Secker & Warburg, London, 1986

Card, Tim, *Eton Renewed, A History from 1860 to the Present Day*, John Murray, London, 1994

Carnegie, V. M., *A Kenyan Farm Diary*, Blackwood, London, 1931

Cave Brown, Anthony, *Bodyguard of Lies*, Harper & Row, New York, 1975

——*The Secret Servant: The Life of Sir Stewart Menzies, Churchill's Spymaster*, Michael Joseph, 1985

Channon, Sir Henry, ed. Robert Rhodes James, *'Chips' – The Diaries of Sir Henry Channon*, Phoenix, London, 1993

Chenevix-Trench, Charles, *The Men Who Ruled Kenya: The Kenya Administration 1892–1963*, Radcliffe Press, London, 1993

Churchill, Winston, *History of the Second World War*, vol. II, *Their Finest Hour*; vol. III, *Grand Alliance*; vol. IV, *Hinge of Fate*, Bantam, London, 1962

The Concise Encyclopaedia of Modern Literature, Hutchinson, London, 1963

Cooper, Artemis, *Cairo in the War 1939–1945*, Penguin, London, 1995

Cowie, Mervyn, *Fly Vulture, Fly*, Harrap, London, 1961

Craddock, Harry, *The Savoy Cocktail Book*, London, 1930

Crosskill, W. W., *The Two Thousand Mile War*, Robert Hale, London, 1980

Davidson, Basil, *Special Operations Europe*, Gollancz, London, 1980

Deacon, Richard, *A History of the British Secret Service*, Frederick Muller, London, 1978

Debrett's Illustrated Peerage

Dictionary of National Biography

Dinesen, Isak, *Letters from Africa 1914–1931*. The private story behind Karen Blixen's great memoir *Out of Africa*, Weidenfeld & Nicolson, London, 1981

Domvile KBE, CB, CMG, Sir Barry, *From Admiral to Cabin Boy*, Boswell Publishing Co., London, 1947

Dower, Kenneth Gandar, *The Spotted Lion*, Little Brown, Boston, 1937

Dugan, James and Lafore, Lawrence, *Days of Emperor and Clown: The Italo–Ethiopian War 1935–1936*, Doubleday, New York, 1973

Eatwell, Roger, *A History of Fascism*, Vintage, London, 1996

The Faber Book of Espionage, ed. Nigel West, London, 1994

The Faber Book of Plays, London, 1952

Farrant, Leda, *Diana, Lady Delamere and the Murder of Lord Erroll*, privately published, Nairobi, 1997

Faulkes, Sebastian, *The Fatal Englishman*, Vintage, London, 1997

Fielding, Daphne, *Mercury Presides*, Eyre & Spottiswoode, London, 1954

Fisher, Clive, *Cyril Connolly: A Nostalgic Life*, Macmillan, London, 1995

Frampton, Peggy, *Seven Candles for My Life*, Pentland Press, Cumberland, 1990

Foot, M. R. D., *History of the Second World War, SOE in France*, HMSO, London, 1966

——Foran, Robert and Landley, J. M., *MI9 Escape and Evasion, 1939–1945*, Bodley Head, London, 1979

——*SOE, an Outline History of the Special Operations Executive 1940–46*, BBC, London, 1988

Foran, Robert, *History of the Kenya Police 1887–1960*, Robert Hale, London, 1960

Fox, James, *White Mischief*, Penguin, London, 1984

Furneaux, Rupert, *A Crime Documentary: The Murder of Lord Erroll*, Stevens, London, 1961

Gilbert, Martin, *Churchill, a Life*, Heinemann, London, 1991

Gillett, Mary, *Tribute to Pioneers*, J. M. Considine, Oxford, 1986

Goodman, Nigel, *Eton Today*, Eton College, Slough

——*Eton College*, Pitkin Pictorials, Slough, 1989

Griffiths, Richard, *Fellow Travellers of the Right: British Enthusiasts for Nazi Germany 1933–39*, Constable, London, 1980

——*Patriotism Perverted, Captain Ramsay, the Right Club and British Anti-Semitism 1939–1940*, Constable, London, 1998

Guinness, Jonathan, with Katharine Guinness, *The House of Mitford*, Hutchinson, London, 1984

Haining, Peter and Beresford-Ellis, Peter, *The Un-Dead: The Castle of Dracula*, London, 1997

Hamilton, Alastair, *The Appeal of Fascism*, Anthony Blond, London, 1971

Hamilton, Genesta, *A Stone's Throw, Travels from Africa in Six Decades*, Hutchinson, London, 1986

Harcourt, William, with Olave, Lady Baden-Powell, *The Two Lives of a Hero*, Heinemann, London, 1964

Hart-Davis, Rupert, *The Arms of Time*, Hamish Hamilton, London, 1979

Hay, Victor, Baron Kilmarnock, *Ferelith* (British Library Catalogue 012638 D21)

Hayes, Charles, *Oserian: Place of Peace*, Rima Books, Kenya and Canada, 1997

Henderson, Sir Nevile, *Failure of a Mission*, Hodder & Stoughton, London, 1940

Hickson, Alisdare, *The Poisoned Bowl: Sex and the Public School*, Duckworth, 1996

Higham, Charles, *Wallis, Secret Lives of the Duchess of Windsor*, Sidgwick & Jackson, London, 1988

Hill, M. F., *The Permanent Way: The Story of the Kenya and Uganda Railway*, English Press, Nairobi, 1949

Howell, Georgina, *In Vogue: Sixty Years of Celebrities and Fashion from British Vogue, the Reckless Twenties 1924–29*, Penguin, London, 1979

Huxley, Elspeth *White Man's Country*, vols I and II, Chatto & Windus, London, 1935

——*Forks and Hope*, Chatto & Windus, London, 1964

——*Nellie: Letters from Africa*, Weidenfeld & Nicolson, London, 1980

——*Out in the Midday Sun, My Kenya*, Chatto & Windus, London, 1985

Huxley, Elspeth and Perham, Margery, *Race and Politics in Kenya*, Faber, London, 1944

Imray, Colin, ed. H. V. Winstone, *Policeman in Palestine*, Edward Gaskell, Devon, 1995

Imray, Colin, *Policeman in Africa*, Book Guild, Lewes, 1997

de Janzé, Frédéric, *Vertical Land*, Duckworth, London, 1928

——*Tarred with the Same Brush*, Duckworth, London, 1929

Johnson, Sir Charles, *Mo and Other Originals*, Hamish Hamilton, London, 1971

Killen, John, *The Luftwaffe – A History*, Sphere, 1967

Kirkpatrick, Ivone, *The Inner Circle*, memoirs of Ivone Kirkpatrick, Macmillan, London, 1959

Knightley, Philip, *The Second Oldest Profession*, André Deutsch, London, 1986

Lamb, Richard, *The Drift to War 1922–1939*, W. H. Allen, London, 1989

Leslie-Melville, Betty, *That Nairobi Affair*, Doubleday, New York, 1975

Lewis, Jeremy, *Cyril Connolly, A Life*, Cape, London, 1997

Lewis, Roy and Fox, Yvonne, *The British in Africa*, Weidenfeld & Nicolson, London, 1971

Mack Smith, Denis, *Mussolini*, Weidenfeld & Nicolson, London, 1981

Macoun CMG, OBE, QPM, Michael J., *Wrong Place, Right Time: Policing the End of an Empire*, Radcliffe Press, Oxford, 1997

Maisels, Aaron, *A Life at Law: The Memoirs of I. A. Maisels, QC*, Jonathan Ball, South Africa, 1998

Masterman, Sir John, *The Double-Cross System in War: 1939–1945*, Pimlico, London, 1996

Millard, John, *Never a Dull Moment: The Autobiography of John Millard, Administrator, Soldier, Farmer*, Silent Books, Cambridge, 1996

Miller, Charles, *Battle for the Bundu*, Purnell, Cape Town, 1974

Mitchell, Sir Philip, *African Afterthoughts*, Hutchinson, London, 1954

Morgan, Janet, *Edwina Mountbatten: A Life of Her Own*, Fontana, London, 1993

Morris, H. H., *The First Forty Years: Being the Memoirs of H. H. Morris KC*, Juta & Co., Cape Town and Johannesburg, 1948

Mosley, Nicholas, *Rules of the Game: Beyond the Pale*, Secker & Warburg, London, 1993

Mosley, Oswald, *My Life*, Nelson, London, 1968

Nichols, Beverley, *The Sweet and Twenties*, Weidenfeld & Nicolson, London, 1958

Partridge, Francis, *A Pacifists' War*, Hogarth Press, London, 1978

Patel, Zarina, *Challenge to Colonialism: The Strugge of Alibhai Mulla Jevanjee for Equal Rights in Kenya*, privately published, Nairobi, 1997

Pollard, John, *African Zoo Man – The Life Story of Raymond Hook*, Robert Hale, London, 1975

Polnay, Peter de, *My Road – An Autobiography*

Powell, Anthony, *Journals 1982–1986*, Heinemann, London, 1993

Ranfurly, Hermione, *To War with Whitaker: The Wartime Diaries of Countess Ranfurly 1939–45*, Heinemann, London, 1994

Ricciardi, Mirella, *African Saga*, Collins, London, 1982

Roberts, Andrew, *Eminent Churchillians*, Weidenfeld & Nicolson, London, 1994

Rubenstein, W. D., and Ellermann, Sir John Reeves, *Dictionary of Business Biography*, Butterworth, 1984

Sanger, Clyde, *Malcolm MacDonald, Bringing an End to Empire*, Liverpool University Press, 1995

Scott, Pam, ed. Philip Mason, *A Nice Place to Live*, Michael Russell, Wiltshire, 1991

Sitwell, Oswald, *The Scarlet Tree*, Reprint Society, London, 1947

Skidelsky, Robert, *Oswald Mosley*, Papermac, London, 1990

Stafford, David, *Churchill and the Secret Service*, John Murray, London, 1997

Symons, Julian, *A Reasonable Doubt*, Cresset Press, 1960

Tennant, Emma, *Strangers: A Family Romance*, Cape, London, 1998

Thomas, Hugh, *The Murder of Rudolf Hess*, Hodder & Stoughton, London, 1979

Thurlow, Richard, *Fascism in Britain: A History, 1918–1985*, Blackwell, Oxford, 1987

Trzebinski, Errol, *Silence Will Speak – the Life of Denys Finch Hatton and His Relationship with Karen Blixen*, Heinemann, London, 1977
——*The Kenya Pioneers*, Heinemann, London, 1985
——*The Lives of Beryl Markham*, Heinemann, London, 1993
Vanderbilt, Gloria and Furness, Thelma, *Double Exposure*, Knopf, New York, 1987
Waugh, Evelyn, *No Abiding City 1939–1966*, Reprint Society, London, 1946
——*When the Going Was Good*, Reprint Society, London, 1948
Webb, Beatrice, *The Diary of Beatrice Webb: Volume Four April 1924–1943* 'The Wheel of Life', Virago, London, 1983
Who's Who 1926
Winstone, H. V., *The Illicit Adventure*, Cape, London, 1982
Wolfe, Gregory, *Muggeridge: A Biography*, Hodder & Stoughton, London, 1995
Ziegler, Philip, *King Edward VIII – the Official Biography*, Collins, London, 1990

Magazine and newspaper articles, television documentaries
(in chronological order)

'Happy ending to Romance', *Daily Express*, 22/2/32
Illustrated London News, coronation issue, 1937
'Native Policy in the Empire', *Hansard*, 9/6/37
'International Trade', *Hansard*, 21/7/37
Legislative Council Debates, Kenya, 1938–1941 (courtesy National Assembly of Kenya)
'Britain First', *Action*, BUF quarterly, 15/4/39
Obituary of Lady Erroll, *The Times*, 14/10/39
'Detentions', *Action*, BUF quarterly, 6/6/40
'Sequel to the Death of Lord Erroll: Preliminary Enquiry into the Murder Charge', *East African Standard*, 28/3/41
'Sequel to the Death of Lord Erroll: Mystery Witness at Murder Enquiry', *East African Standard*, 4/4/41
'Details of an Insurance Claim for "Lost" Jewellery in Cannes, 1939', *Sunday Post*, 6/7/41
'A Note of the Tradition and History of the Hays', *Clan Hay Magazine*, no. 1, January 1952; also vol. 1, nos 1, 3, 4, 6, 18, 23
'The Missing Link in the Erroll Case – Was There a Third Gun?' Letters to the Editor, *Sunday Nation*, 2/10/66
'Spotlight on the Changing Face of the Model', Cecil Beaton, *Vogue*, 15/3/67
'Christmas at Karen', Cyril Connolly and James Fox, *Sunday Times Magazine*, 21/12/69
'Chessington: Five Noble Homes and a Zoo', Margaret Bellars, *Kingston Borough News*, 31/8/73

'Jealousy: the Peer in the Gravel Pit', in *Crimes of Passion*, Treasure Press, 1973

'Murder in Happy Valley', *Cheshire Life*, 1982

'Aristocrats, Alcohol and Adultery', *Sunday Times Review*, part 1, 'Life in Happy Valley', by James Fox, 7/11/82

'Aristocrats, Alcohol and Adultery', *Sunday Times Review*, part 2, 'Diana, Love and Murder', James Fox, 14/11/82

'Aristocrats, Alcohol and Adultery', *Sunday Times Review*, part 3, 'End of the Murder Trail', James Fox, 21/11/82

'Murder Most Amusing', *White Mischief* reviewed by Auberon Waugh, 1982 (unidentified source)

'Unhappy Valley', Iain Moncreiffe, *Books and Bookmen*, February 1983

'The Ilk on the Attack', Atticus, Stephen Fry, *Sunday Times*, 16/1/83

'Who Shot Lord Erroll?', Peter Quennell, *New York Times Book Review*, 20/3/83

'Happy Valley', Patricia Blake, *Time Magazine*, 4/4/83

'A Murder of Quality', Books, Jim Miller, *Newsweek*, 2/5/83

'Diana Lady Delamere', obituary, Sir Charles Markham, *Independent*, 9/9/87

'Guilty of Murder: Victor Davis Reports from Mombasa on a Triangle of Love . . . and Death', *Mail on Sunday*, 8/3/87

'The Making of "White Mischief"', 4–11 May 1987

'Juanita and the Cheater', 'Sunday Première: The Happy Valley', BBC1, *Radio Times*, 5–11 September 1987

'Diana Home from the Sea', Striker, *Standard*, Nairobi, 5/9/87

'Millions Watch "Happy Valley"', Arnold Raphael, London *Evening Standard*, 7/9/87

'Femme Fatale Takes Kenya Murder Secret to her Grave', *Daily Telegraph*, 7/9/87

'Diana Lady Delamere', obituary, *The Times*, 8/9/87

'Truth about Killing Will Never Be Known', Sandra Maler, *Daily Nation*, 8/9/87

'A Chic Part to Play', Fashion, Liz Smith, *The Times*, 8/9/87

'Murder Secret Goes with Lady Delamere', Sandra Maler, *Standard* (Nairobi), 11/9/87

'Problems for Agony Uncles', Television, Russell Davis, 13/9/87

'Film Upsets Happy Valley Survivors', Patrick Bishop, *Sunday Telegraph International*, 22/9/87

'That Happy Valley Murder-Mystery . . .' Coast Causerie, Edward Rodwell, *Standard*, Nairobi, 2/10/87

'Salonfahig', 3/2/88 (unidentified source)

'The Last of England' *Listener*, 4/2/88

'*White Mischief*', Cinema, *The Times*, 4/2/88

'The Sordid Shades of White', Derek Malcolm, *Guardian*, 4/2/88

'On the Spoor of Scandal', Nicholas de Jongh talks to James Fox, *Guardian*, 4/2/88

'Mischief Maker', Michael Radford, director and co-writer of the film *White Mischief*, talks to Chris Peachment, *The Times*, 5/2/88

'AMREF Rejection of *White Mischief* in 'Tainted Money Hailed', *Standard* (Nairobi), 5/2/88

'Unhappy Valley', Cinema, Nigel Andrews, *Financial Times*, 5/2/88

'An Unbalanced Triangle Mars the Colonial Circle', Iain Johnstone, *Sunday Times*, 7/2/88

'Lout of Africa', Cinema, Philip French, *Observer*, 7/2/88

'Mischief in the Making,' Mick Brown, *Sunday Times*, 7/2/88

'Cads and Buffers', David Pryce-Jones, *Times Literary Supplement*, 12–18 February 1988

'Out of Africa', Dilys Powell, Cinema, *Punch*, 12/2/88

'My Thwarted Stepmother Killed the Earl', Peter Kingston, London *Evening Standard*, 16/2/88

'Hundred-year Shroud on Happy Valley Mystery', Murray Ritchie, *Glasgow Herald*, 22/2/88

'Valley Girl', Movies, David Denby, *New York*, May 1988

'Two New Movies Suggest that Shock Tactics are Best Muted into a Work of Art', About the Arts, John Gross, *New York Times*, 22/5/88

'Sex, Alcohol, Murder – Kenyan Mystery Filmed', Janine Walker, *Argus* supplement, 12/7/88

'New Turn in Murder Mystery', Farook Khan, *Daily News*, 10/9/88

'White Mischief: Does This Durban Woman Know Whodunnit?', Sylvia Osborne, *Personality*, 14/11/88

'The Happy Valley Murder', *Investigations into the Ultimate Crime*, Green-eyed Monsters, vol. 2, part 35, a Marshall Cavendish weekly publication, 1990

'Fifty Years After, Lord Erroll's Death Is Still a Mystery', John Fox, *Sunday Nation*, 2/6/91

'The Case for the Defence', Fifty Years Ago, James Oyare, *East African Standard*, 14/6/91

'Fresh Light on White Mischief', Juanita Carberry, Letters to the Editor, *Daily Telegraph*, 25/1/93

'Lose a Wing and the Rest Might Sell', Simon Courtauld, *Daily Telegraph*, 30/1/93

'Thwarted Diana Guilty of White Mischief', Sir Evelyn Delves Broughton, *Spectator*, 22/2/93

'Ill Effects of White Mischief Film', Brigadier M. W. Biggs, Letters to the Editor, *Daily Telegraph*, March 1993

'Diana Didn't Do It', James Fox, Letters to the Editor, *Daily Telegraph*, March 1993

'Who Is the Real Villain of the Piece?', Lady Colin Campbell, Letters to the Editor, *Daily Telegraph*, March 1993

'Questions About White Mischief Continue', Lord Erroll, Letters to the Editor, *Daily Telegraph*, March 1993

'More African Mischief', Brigadier M. W. Biggs, Letters to the Editor, *Daily Telegraph*, March 1993

'The Final Piece of Mischief', James Fox, *Daily Telegraph*, 31/5/93

'White Mischief Scandal Revived by "Blackmail" Letter to Cheating Wife', Tracy Harrison, *Daily Mail*, 1/6/93

'Altitude, Alcohol and Adultery: The British Aristocracy in Kenya Colony', Livio Negri and Warwick Hembry, BBC1 documentary, 4/6/93

'More Mischief from Happy Valley', Paul Redfern, *Sunday Nation*, 6/6/93

'Into Africa – Join the Club Where the Affair of a White Hunter Led to Murder', Simon Courtauld, *International Express*, 6–12 October 1993

'Tarporley Man Puts the Finger on Alice', Peterborough, Quentin Bell, *Daily Telegraph*, 16/12/93

'Innocent Alice', J. N. P. Watson, Letters to the Editor, *Daily Telegraph*, December 1993

'Lord of the Jungle', Scarth Flett, *Sunday Express Magazine*, 14/8/94

'Some Personal Notes from Kate Challis née Beynon, in Reply to "What I Know"', *Women in Kenya*, 1st issue, 1995

'Mischief, Murder and Multiple Adultery – Simon Courtauld Meets Juanita Carberry', *Spectator*, 13/2/95

'The Rich and Famous', Jan Hemsing, *Africa Life*, Nairobi, 1995

'The Last Word', *The East African*, 1–7 May 1995

'A Blackened Name in "White Mischief"', Richard Wilkinson, Letters to the Editor, *Daily Mail*, 25/7/95

The Overseas Pensioner, Autumn 1995

'The Club – Lingering Legacy', Simon Courtauld, *Spectator*, 13/4/96

Obituary of Mervyn Cowie, *New York Times*, 31/7/96

'The Lust that Led to Murder: Killing in Kenya', Caroline Cass, *Marie Claire*, August 1996

'Dear Duce . . . Yours Churchill', Nicolas Farrell, *Spectator*, 17/8/96

'Death in Happy Valley', Crime Case Study, 1997

'Dead, Buried . . . and Knocking at the Door: Grave Robbing', Paul Sieveking, *Sunday Telegraph*, 23/3/97

'Was White Mischief Mistress the Real Killer?', Fiametta Rocco, *Daily Telegraph*, 12/5/97

'Author Rejects "White Mischief" Murder Claim', Lynn Cochrane, *Scotsman*, 13/5/97

'Killing Time in the Happy Valley', Quentin Crewe, May 1997

'White Mischief Continued', Simon Courtauld, *Spectator*, 24/5/97

'The Kennedys of Kenya', Rupert White, *Spectator*, 11/4/98

'Royalty, Voodoo and Nazi Gold', Sheridan Morley, *International Herald Tribune* (undated), 1998

'High Treason in Happy Valley – Nicholas Hellen and Robin Lodge Investigate', *Sunday Times*, 31/1/99

'Clue That May Solve the White Mischief Murder', Andrew Pierce, *Sunday Express*, 21/3/99

'I Saved the White Mischief Murderer', Juanita Carberry, *Daily Mail*, 22/5/99, 24/5/99

Unpublished sources

Bishop, Major-General Sir Alec, 'Look Back with Pleasure', unpublished memoir, Liddell Hart Military Archive, King's College, London

Crown Case no. 56, 1941, courtesy 24th Earl of Erroll

Erskine, Sir Derek, unpublished memoir, courtesy Petal Allen

Oates, Titus, 'Draft History of Muthaiga Club', courtesy the late Titus Oates

Pitt, Peggy, 'Who Killed Lord Erroll?' foreword by Sir Walter Harragin, courtesy the late William Pitt

Pitt, John, 'Adui Mbele', courtesy the late John Pitt

——'Buruji 1940–42'

Trafford, Tony, 'The judicial execution of the 22nd Earl of Erroll', aka 'The Sallyport papers', 5/12/97

Acknowledgements

Many people have provided information and hospitality, generously sharing the past as much as the present, during the course of my research for this book. Firstly, I must mention the 24th Earl of Erroll, Merlin Hay, and his wife Isabelle, who have been unreservedly generous; their understanding that my only purpose in undertaking the biography has been to provide as full, as truthful and as accurate a portrait of the 22nd Earl as possible is much appreciated. None of us knew quite what I might unearth, but they have listened courteously as the twists and turns of complex matters came to light and they have never attempted to impede the process of research. Without such trust, it would have been so much more difficult to unravel misconceptions. Furthermore, they have allowed me unrestricted access to photographic archives and private correspondence. Without such leads it would have been quite impossible to discover those things that I discovered. Without exception these letters, as well as those that I received in my correspondence with the many survivors of the era, expressed views radically different about my subject from nearly everything that has been published about him. Sadly, several of those correspondents died before my book was completed. I am more than grateful that they chose to defend Josslyn Victor Hay in writing while they possessed the energy and conscience to do so.

I would like to single out in particular the late Lt.-Col. John Gouldbourn, for his courage. Thanks to his feedback as a military man, I was able to trace and meet people whose existence would otherwise have remained unknown to me. Through him I tracked down S. P. J. O'Mara, with whom I have corresponded on the subject for nearly three years. To express a simple gratitude for the key corroborative material that he provided, and for allowing me to use his cover name when I know he had misgivings initially, seems grossly inadequate in return. Yet, hopefully, at last he will realise just how valuable his help has been in solving some of the conundrums leading up to Lord Erroll's death. It is largely thanks to him, too, that it gradually dawned on me just how haphazardly the colony of Kenya became a victim of the scandal, and that, had Erroll been in Tring or Timbuktu in 1941, his fate would have been no different.

Circumstances dictate that the real identity of a number of sources must continue to be protected by anonymity. But I do so at their request. I hope that they realise how grateful I am for every scrap of information that they have provided.

I would like to place on record the generosity of the late William Pitt, in putting at my disposal his mother's unpublished manuscript, 'Who Killed Lord Erroll?'. It was his decision to provide me with all relevant correspondence pertaining to Peggy Pitt's role as secretary to Mr Walter Harragin, Kenya's Attorney-General, who led the prosecution for the Crown at the trial of Sir Delves Broughton in 1941. Peggy Pitt's observations were important because she had attended the trial daily in a working capacity, but she had also known all the witnesses and key players. She was an upright British citizen if ever there was one, not in the least flamboyant, and who had nurtured great respect for Erroll too. (By a strange twist of fate she went on to become private secretary to John Profumo, who was to generate another British scandal in the sixties.)

Special thanks go to Alan Hay, the genealogist of Clan Hay, who patiently checked the draft material several times as the manuscript developed. My old friend Edward Rodwell encouraged my quest for the truth from the outset, and for this, as well as for generously providing the contents of a confidential file, I owe him much gratitude. The information in that file gave me an inkling as to where to turn for my initial leads. Roddy's conviction that if research for a full-length biography of the 22nd Earl of Erroll might also contribute to clearing the name of Sir Delves Broughton for a murder he had not carried out, then so much the better, unquestionably provided an additional spur to my research.

I should like to thank J. N. P. Watson and his wife Lavinia, Captain Gordon Fergusson and the late Colin Imray; each made me welcome in his home, granting personal interviews as well as arranging meetings for me with other vital contacts. To begin with, Gordon Fergusson's willing excavation of published data filled many a gap left by the dearth of reference libraries in Mombasa. His guided tour of Broughton Hall and Doddington Park, where I interviewed one of Sir Jock Delves Broughton's oldest surviving retainers, was enlightening.

Possibly my greatest debt is to Anthea Venning, whose response to a small advertisement that I placed in 1996, seeking anecdotal information on my subject, put me in touch with a friend, Tony Trafford, from her youth. This lifelong contact in Kenya, whose parents and brothers she had also known, referred to himself as Mzee Kobe ('Old Tortoise'), being at that time in his seventies and a reluctant witness. At first, Anthea merely passed on my questions, diligently relaying his replies back to me by air-letter. But while I studied, probed and challenged the material she had gleaned on my behalf, it was Anthea who persuaded Tony that he must allow me to correspond directly with him. Eventually, he agreed to meet me; had we not done so, and had I not been able to regale him personally with the information I already had, supplied by Edward Rodwell, there is no doubt that Tony would never have entrusted me with the Sallyport papers.

My word-of-mouth contributors also deserve special mention: Patsy Chilton, Molly Hoare and her husband Arthur, Anne (Buxton) Wadley and Jack Bunyan for contributing greatly to my better understanding of the kind, good-natured, clever man that Joss had been; their first-hand anecdotes concerning his relationships with both of his wives and with his servants offered a wealth of insights. David Christie-Miller, as an Old Etonian himself, brought to my attention just how brief Erroll's sojourn at Eton had been, thus saving me much time and frustration. My thanks go to James Fox for his open-minded attitude and for generously allowing my publishers to use his copy of the Dorothy Wilding portrait of Erroll for the jacket of this book.

My gratitude also goes to the great team at Fourth Estate, with whom I came in contact intermittently for nearly five years while the book was in progress: to Clive Priddle, for making it a better book than it would otherwise have been; and to Victoria Barnsley, Susie Dunlop and Katie Owen for their support and for not allowing my mammoth first draft to faze them. Katie's understanding during a delay of almost four months, when my computer developed a mind of its own, was much appreciated. My thanks also go to David Palk, and to Shelly Dunsby and the team of technicians at ICL (Sorbus) Ltd for trying to rectify these technical glitches. That my 'rogue' machine defeated them was not for lack of effort on their part; and my thanks ultimately, of course, to Neil Pattie, whose solution turned out to be the best, as well as to Colin Newsome, whose expedience in setting me up with a second printer when I moved back to London was vital.

More thanks of a practical kind to Nicole Gavaghan, for tracking down a particular A–Z of Nairobi when all other attempts had failed. She can surely have had no notion that it would be this edition alone that made it possible to verify original road names in and around Nairobi and Karen in 1941.

It was to Emma Pery in 1994 that I confided my first inkling of a massive cover-up in connection with Kenya's greatest murder scandal. Neither of us imagined, on that occasion, that we should ultimately work together on this book. I like to think that she has found the experience as rewarding as I have. My thanks go to Eileen and John Rhind-Tutt for travelling many miles to look after their granddaughter so that Emma and I could work on the book.

My gratitude to my agents at Curtis Brown, Vivienne Schuster and Philip Patterson, is also inestimable; whenever I have called on Vivienne for guidance during this project, she has as usual provided psychological support and suggested wise options.

As common with married authors, whose primary debt to a spouse is illimitable, I am grateful to my husband Sbish for the exemplary way in which he has refrained from chiding me over my protracted absences. This meant spending a whole year away from home to finish the book. My thanks to him also and to Bruce our elder son for the redrawing of the hit map from Tony Trafford's original. Bruce also provided a vital link between myself and Emma Pery by allowing us, without complaint and with all necessary discretion, to use his e-mail facilities. My other children, Tonio and Gabriela, have been supportive in different but equally practical ways, and the help extended by my daughters-in-law, Pipa and Anne Trzebinski, has, as always, been much appreciated.

I would also like to thank the following for their time and, invariably, their hospitality: Ulla Ackermann; the late Ken Adcock; the late Gertrude Alexander; Rupert Allason; Bunny Allen; Jeri Allen; Petal Allen; the late Bettine Anderson; David Anderson; Peter Anderson; Vera Atkins CBE; Peter Ayre; Hazel Baldwin; Jack Barrah; Diana Barton; the Hon. Doreen Bathurst Norman; Walter Bell; Beatrice Bewes; Kath Biggs; Brigadier Michael Biggs CBE MA CEng MICE; Aldo Bigozzi; Doria Block; Billie Blunt; the Rt Hon. Robert Boscawen MC; Tom Bower; Lady Mary Bowes-Lyon; Peter Bramwell; J. D. T. Breckenridge; Tony Britchford; Edome Broughton-Adderly; Rona, the Dowager Lady Broughton; Clare Brown; Derek Brunner; Margaret Bryan; Michael Buckmaster MYPR; Yvonne Bulling; Judith Buxton; Martin P. Byers; the late Hon. Mrs Angus Campbell; Juanita Carberry; Lionel Carley; Mervyn Carnelly; the late J. L. Carter; Sir Richard Catling CMG OBE KPM; Joan Christie-Miller; Sheila Claridge; the Hon. Mrs Alan Clark; Barry Clark; Christine Clark; Dot Clark; Fenella Clark; the late Lady Margaret Clark; Mary Clark; Peter Colmore; Deborah Colvile; Artemis Cooper; Leo Cooper; George Corse, the late Mervyn Cowie; Valerie Cowie; the late Robert Creighton; Graham Crowden; Michael Curtis; Bill Cuthbert; Eileen Cuthbert; Nick Day; David Dickinson; Jan Dickinson; Rupert Dickinson; Molly Donnelly; Patrick Donnelly; Stephen Dorril; Iain Douglas-Hamilton; Saba Douglas-Hamilton; Ruth Draffan; Noel Eaton-Evans; Frances Edwards; Ken Elliot; Terry Ellis; Charles Elwell; Mary Faller; Eleanor Fazan; Nick Fazan; the late Kathleen Fielden; Peter Filmer; Judy Forbes; Charles

Fox; Mervyn Fox; Anthea Fyler; Sarah Gavaghan; Terence Gav-aghan; Jenny de Gex; Salim Ghalia; Queenie Ghersie; Nancy Gilbert; Frank Giles; Lady Katharine Giles; Brian Goode; Lucy Goode; Richard Griffiths; the late Eric R. Grove; Pat Goldsmith; A. R. Gordon-Cumming; Ted Goss; the late Sushil Guram; Jim Haggerty; James Hamilton; Sheila Hamnett; Lee Harragin; Sir Wilfrid Have-lock; Alan Hay; Sally Hay; Lorna Hayes; Anthony Hayter; Joan Hemsted; Christian, Lady Hesketh; Shirley Heriz-Smith; Derek Hodgson, Mairo Hopcraft; John Hope; Charles Howard; Jean Howard; the late Roger Howard; Rebecca Hudson; the Hon. Justice Ralph Hutchinson; Charles Huxley; the late Colin Imray; Deborah James; Alison Jauss; Martin Johnson; Mary Johnson; Count and Countess Louis Kalnoky; Tony Kennaway; Rosita Khan; Yusuf Khan; the late Margaret Kirkland; Kim Krier; Ingrid Lackajis; Diana Lane; Anne Langlands; the late Christopher Langlands; Dorothy Le Poer Trench; Dennis Leete; Valerie Letham; Gerard Loughran; H. I. Lustman; Peter Lydon; Erica Mann; Sir Charles Markham; Patsy (Atkinson) Marra; Japhet K. Masya; John McCoy; Margaret McNe-ice; M. C. Meredith; John Millard; Patricia Millbourn; Nancy Miller, Roland Minor; Anna Miskin; Peter Mitchell; Diana, Lady Mosley; Nicholas Mosley; Nicholas Myers; Noordin S. Nathoo; Kate Nefdt; Joanna Nicholas; Myra Oates; the late Titus Oates; Annie O'Carroll; Major Hamilton O'Hara; John Parker; Alice Percival; Brian Picker-ing; the late Charlie Pitt; Alice Playle; Eve Pollecoff; Frank Popely; Winifred Poppy; Dorothy Powell; Lady Prendergast; David Press-well; Paddy Purchase; Julian Putkowski; Ian Rand; Nancy Randall; Lady Ranfurly; Philip Ransley; Avice Rapley; Dylis Rhodes; Murray Ritchie; Dorian Rocco; Fiametta Rocco; Helen Salter; Philip Samoilys; Valerie Samoilys; Anthony Sattin; Richard Sattin; Miffe Schiodt; Princess Caroline Schonburg von Hartenstein; Dr Thérèse Fürstin von Schwarzenberg; the Rt Hon. Lord Selkirk of Douglas QC; Father Brocard Sewell; Lady Sheridan; Marika Sherwood; Hugh Simpson; Sylvia Simpson; Keith Skinner; Ken Smith; Paul and June Spicer; Rosamond Spicer; Jennifer Stutchbury; Rachel Taylor; Stephen Teal; Althea Tebbut; Camilla Thomas; Beryl Thompson; Esme Timms; Dr Geoffrey Timms: Sir Dermot de Trafford; Hilda

Tucker; Graham Tudor; Neil Tyfield; the Duke of Valdorano; Patricia Van Diest; Christine Vickers; Hugo Vickers; Rosemary Whiteing; Richard Wilkinson; Cyril Wingfield; B. A. Young; G. M. Young; Robert Young.

I also wish to thank the following organisations for their help: Andrew Weir Shipping; St Antony's College, Middle East Centre, Oxford; the Bodleian Library, Oxford; the British Council Library, Mombasa; the British Embassy, Berlin office; the British High Commission, Nairobi; the British Library; Caledonian Newspapers Ltd.; the Caledonian Society, Mombasa; Causeway Resources, Genealogical Research; Central Library, London; the City of Liverpool Leisure Services Directorate; the Clan Hay Society; the *Daily Telegraph* obituaries department; Eton College, School Library, College Library and Photographic Archive; the Foreign and Commonwealth Office; the General Medical Council, London; the *Glasgow Herald*; Hartley Library, Special Collections, University of Southampton; the House of Lords Record Office; the *Illustrated London News* Picture Library; *Jambo*, East African Women's League magazine; the Kenya Meteorological Department, Nairobi; Kenya National Archives; the Kenya Police; *Kingston Borough News*; Kingston Library and Archives; the Library of National Assembly, Kenya; the Liddell Hart Centre for Military Archives, King's College, London; Lincoln College, Oxford; Liverpool Libraries Information Service; the Liverpool Record Office; the London Library; Merseyside Maritime Museum, Liverpool; Metropolitan Police Archives; Ministry of Home Affairs and National Heritage; Mombasa Club Library; the National Maritime Museum reading room; Newspaper Library, Colindale; the Officers' Association; the Overseas Service Pensioners' Association; Paper Connections, Mombasa; the Pentland Press; Rhodes House Library; the Royal Borough of Kensington & Chelsea Libraries and Arts Service; the *Scotsman*; Smythson of Bond Street; the South African High Commission, London; Truefitt & Hill; University of Durham, Middle East (Documentation) Centre; *Women in Kenya*.

Emma Pery would like to thank Fergus for his intelligent, understanding support; Alix, who in the first year of her life did not begrudge her mother's focusing on Lord Erroll; and her parents for stepping into the breach on countless occasions along the way to completion of this book.

Index

I had a comrade
A better you won't find.
The drum beat called to battle,
He went by my side
In step,
In step.

A bullet came flying;
Is it meant for you or me?
It tore him away,
He lies at my feet,
As though he were a part of me.

He tries to reach his hand out to me,
Even as I load my gun.
'I can't give you my hand;
Remain in the eternal life
My good comrade!'